I0091058

Indigenous Peoples and Demography

INDIGENOUS PEOPLES AND DEMOGRAPHY

The Complex Relation between Identity and Statistics

Edited by
Per Axelsson and Peter Sköld

berghahn
NEW YORK • OXFORD
www.berghahnbooks.com

Published in 2011 by

Berghahn Books

www.berghahnbooks.com

©2011, 2014 Per Axelsson and Peter Sköld
First paperback edition published in 2014

All rights reserved. Except for the quotation of short passages
for the purposes of criticism and review, no part of this book
may be reproduced in any form or by any means, electronic or
mechanical, including photocopying, recording, or any information
storage and retrieval system now known or to be invented,
without written permission of the publisher.

Chapter 1 "Fractional Identities: The Political Arithmetic of Aboriginal Victorians"
by Len Smith, Janet McCalman, Ian Anderson, Sandra Smith, Joanne Evans,
Gavan McCarthy and Jane Beer is reprinted from *The Journal of Interdisciplinary
History*, XXXVIII (2008), 533–551, with the permisson of the editors of the *Journal
of Interdisciplinary History* and the MIT Press, Cambridge, Massachusetts. c 2008
by the Massachusetts Institute of Technology and *The Journal of Journal of
Interdisciplinary History*, Inc.

Library of Congress Cataloging-in-Publication Data

Library of Congress Cataloging-in-Publication Data

Indigenous peoples and demography : the complex relation between identity and
statistics / edited by Per Axelsson and Peter Sköld.
    p. cm.
Includes bibliographical references and index.
ISBN 978-0-85745-000-5 (hardback) – ISBN 978-0-85745-003-6 (institutional ebook)
– ISBN 978-1-78238-335-2 (paperback) – ISBN 978-1-78238-336-9 (retail ebook)
1. Indigenous peoples–Population. 2. Indigenous peoples–Ethnic identity. 3.
Indigenous peoples–Statistics. I. Axelsson, Per. II. Sköld, Peter.
GN380.I355 2011
305.8–dc22
                                                           2011006253

British Library Cataloguing in Publication Data

A catalogue record for this book is available from the British Library

ISBN: 978-1-78238-335-2 paperback
ISBN: 978-1-78238-336-9 retail ebook

Contents

List of Maps and Figures   vii
List of Tables   ix
Acknowledgements   xi

Introduction   1
  Per Axelsson and Peter Sköld

1 Fractional Identities: The Political Arithmetic of
   Aboriginal Victorians   15
   Len Smith, Janet McCalman, Ian Anderson, Sandra Smith,
   Joanne Evans, Gavan McCarthy and Jane Beer

2 Building Ethnic Boundaries in New Zealand:
   Representations of Maori Identity in the Census   33
   Tahu Kukutai

3 Counting Indians: Census Categories in Late Colonial
   and Early Republican Spanish America   55
   Steinar A. Saether

4 The Construction of Life Tables for the American Indian
   Population at the Turn of the Twentieth Century   73
   J. David Hacker and Michael R. Haines

5 The Aboriginal Population and the 1891 Census of Canada   95
   Michelle A. Hamilton and Kris Inwood

6 'In the National Registry, All People Are Equal': Sami in
   Swedish Statistical Sources   117
   Per Axelsson

7 The Registers of the 'Sami Tax' from 1600 to 1750, and Their
   Usefulness for Reconstructing Population Development
   and Settlement in Northern Nordland, Norway   135
   Lars Ivar Hansen

8 Viewing Ethnicity from the Perspective of Individuals and
   Households: Finnmark during the Late Nineteenth Century   149
   Hilde L. Jåstad

9 Finn in Flux: 'Finn' as a Category in Norwegian Population
   Censuses of the Nineteenth and Twentieth Centuries   163
   Bjørg Evjen

10 Testing and Constructing Ethnicity Variables in Late
   Nineteenth-Century Censuses   173
   Gunnar Thorvaldsen

11 Out of the Backwater? Prospects for Contemporary
   Sami Demography in Norway   185
   Torunn Pettersen

12 The Mystery of the Magnate Reindeer Herders:
   Household Structure and Economy among Lake
   Essei Iakuts, 1926/7   197
   David G. Anderson

13 Microdemographics and Indigenous Identity in the
   Central Taimyr Lowlands   219
   John P. Ziker

14 Russian Legal Concepts and the Demography of
   Indigenous Peoples   239
   Sergey V. Sokolovskiy

15 Indigenous Populations, Ethnicity and Demography
   in the Eastern Baltic Littoral in the Nineteenth and
   Twentieth Centuries   253
   Andrejs Plakans

16 Who Are the British?   273
   John MacInnes

Epilogue: From Indigenous Demographics to an
   Indigenous Demography   295
   Per Axelsson, Peter Sköld, John P. Ziker and David G. Anderson

Notes on Contributors   309

Index   315

LIST OF MAPS AND FIGURES

Maps
15.1   The Regions of Latvia c. 1920   254

Figures
1.1   Victorian Aboriginal Population, 1780–2001   17
1.2   Subgroups of Victorian Aboriginal Population   23
1.3   Evidence from KHRD of the Movement of Victoria's
      Aborigines into and out of the Census and Protection
      Board Populations   26
1.4   Changes in Aboriginal Population in Counties,
      Censuses 1861 to 1901   28
2.1   Maori Group Parameters, 2006 New Zealand
      Census of Population and Dwellings   44
4.1   Mean Percentage 'Indian Blood' by Birth Year   75
4.2   Age Distribution of the American Indian and Native-born
      White Populations of the United States in 1900   80
4.3   Duration of Current Marriage, American Indian
      and Native-Born White Women in 1900   80
4.4   Life Expectancy at Birth: Indirect Estimates from
      the 1900 and 1910 American Indian Censuses   81
6.1   Population Form from 1805   125
6.2   The Last Official Sami Census 1945   128
7.1   Number of Norwegian Tenants Registered in
      the 'Sea Finn Tax'   141
7.2   Relative Proportions of 'Sea Finns' and Former
      Nomadic Sami Dwelling on New Clearances   145
8.1   Sami Population in Eastern and Western Finnmark
      in 1855 and 1861   152
8.2   Sami Population in Eastern and Western Finnmark in
      1855 and 1861, Including Nomads from the 1855 Census   153
8.3   Extent of Sami Registration in Eastern and Western
      Finnmark in 1855, 1861 and 1865   154
8.4   Number of Ethnic Markers in Each Household
      in Finnmark 1865 and 1875   156
8.5   Mixed Marriages Categorized after Head of
      Households Ethnicity in Finnmark 1865 and 1875   157

8.6   Number of Brides and Bridegrooms Distributed
      on Ethnic Categories in Finnmark 1865 and 1875   158
9.1   Hilda and Richard visiting a photographer in Bodø
      in the 1920s.   168
10.1 Census Ethnicity Dimensions   175
12.1 The Botulu Family and Their Reindeer 2006   201
12.2 Age-Sex Pyramid for Lake Yessei 1926   202
12.3 The Chapel at Lake Essei   202
12.4 A Golomo in the Lake Essei Diaspora Region   205
12.5 The Batulu Lineage at Lake Yessei 1926–27   211
12.6 The Buatulu [Katyginskii] Lineage at Kamen' 1926–27   212
14.1 Indigenous Groups Ranked by Per Cent Urban,
      Share of Secondary and Higher Education and
      Proportion of the 'Non-Traditional' Employment
      in the 'Territories of Principal Residence'   246

List of Tables

2.1	Changes in Statistical Concepts, Definitions and Classifications of Maori	40
2.2	The Diverse Content of Maori Group Boundaries, 2006 New Zealand Census of Population and Dwellings	46
4.1	Number of American Indians in the 1900 and 1910 Indian IPUMS Samples, by Sex and General Tribal Group	78
4.2	Estimates of Child Mortality in the Late Nineteenth Century United States by Race Using the Age and Marriage Duration Estimation Methods	82
4.3	Estimates of Child Mortality in the Late Nineteenth Century and Early Twentieth Century by Race Using the Age and Marriage Duration Estimation Methods	83
4.4	American Indian Life Tables Circa 1894	84
4.5	American Indian Life Tables Circa 1904	85
4.6	Application of the Preston-Bennett Method to the American Indian Population, 1900–1910	89
7.1	Sami Clearings Assessed for Rent 1724	141
7.2	Last Time Mentioned in the Sources for Persons Registered in the 1743 Male Census	143
7.3	Estimated Sea Sami Population 1701, ca. 1740 and 1762	143
7.4	'Finns and District Lapps' on Clearings 1762	144
9.1	Definitions of 'Finn' in the Censuses from 1865 to 1970	167
9.2	Overview of the Non-Norwegian Population in Northern Nordland	171
10.1	Ethnonyms and Variable Names in the Census Questionnaires and Published Tables	177
10.2	Number of Households with Different Ethnic Groups and Average Number of Ethnic Groups in Four Municipalities in Troms Province According to the 1875 Census	180
10.3	Ethnic Groups in the Provinces by Father's and Mother's Ethnicity According to the 1875 Census. Missing and Odd Ethnicity Not Reported	181
10.4	Ethnic Groups in Three Towns and Three Rural Municipalities According to the 1875 Census. Mother's and Father's Ethnicity Combined	181

10.5	Farm or Domicile Lists with from One to Ten Persons Whose Father's Ethnicity was Sami or Finnish in the 1875 Census for Northern Norway	182
12.1	The Stratification of Essei Reindeer Herders Using the Criteria Implicit in A.P. Lekarenko's Fieldnotes	209
12.2	A Formal Model of Regional Stratification Using A.P. Lekareko's Fieldnotes	209
12.3	The Quantification of A.P. Lekarenko's Criteria of Stratification for Lake Essei and Diaspora Regions	210
14.1	Indigenous Population Groups, % Urban, (Census 2002, Vol. 13, All Ages and Regions)	244
14.2	Modernisation Scales of Indigenous Groups in Areas of Principal Residence (North, Siberia, and the Far East), Russian Population Census 2002	245
15.1	Total Population of the Territory of Latvia 1881–2000	255
15.2	Population Enumerations in the Territory of Latvia and Selected Variables of Collective Identity: 19th and 20th Centuries	256
15.3	Estimated Proportions of Select Nationalities in the Territory of Latvia 1881–2004	263
15.4	Proportion of Latvians in the Historic Regions of Latvia	265
16.1	Resident Population of England, Wales and Scotland by Date of Arrival	277
16.2	Ethnicity Question England and Wales 2001 and Scotland 2001 Censuses	279
16.3	Northern Ireland Census 2001: Ethnicity	281
16.4	Percentage Reporting British National Identity by 'Ethnic' Group LFS 2002–7	285
16.5	Percentage Claiming British National Identity by Ethnic Group and Year of Arrival in the U.K., LFS 2002–7	286
16.6	Comparison of British and Home Nation Identities, BSAS and SSAS	287
16.7	Descriptions of Britishness, Yougov Poll, July 2005	288

ACKNOWLEDGEMENTS

The production of a scientific and collaborative publication is often a complex process. Our efforts to complete the present volume have been facilitated by several institutions and researchers. We would like to thank the Swedish Council for Working Life and Social Research (FAS), and the Faculty of Arts at Umeå University for funding the international workshop, held in Umeå 29–30 September 2006. This publication also benefited from the support of the BOREAS Eurocores Program of the European Science Foundation (ESF). The Centre for Sami Research and the Centre for Population Studies at Umeå University have been key partners in the process, and have contributed valuable assistance. In addition, we would like to thank Anders Brändström and Gunnar Thorvaldsen, who together with the editors helped organise the workshop. We would also like to thank David G. Anderson, who has been of great importance in the realisation of this book. He initiated the first contacts, partly as a result of the establishment of the BOREAS project, 'Home, Hearth and Household in the Circumpolar North', and was instrumental in seeing the volume into print. To all the above mentioned, the scientific reviewers, the people at Berghahn Books, and of course to all our contributors, we would like to give our deepest gratitude.

INTRODUCTION

Per Axelsson and Peter Sköld

This volume examines the historical and contemporary construction of indigenous peoples in a number of fascinating geographical contexts around the world. Colonisation, political policies and cultural processes have often excluded or devalued representations of indigenous peoples in official statistics. Researchers are dependent on the highly variable way in which states or territories enumerate, categorise and differentiate indigenous peoples. In a long-term perspective, ethnic markers in censuses or other demographic records have shown great differences between nations, regions and parishes, and other administrative units.

In the autumn of 2006, thirty researchers gathered in Umeå in northern Sweden to attend a workshop entitled 'Indigenous Identity in Demographical Sources'. This event revealed the need for international collaboration on these issues. Generally, the situation varies substantially across countries. We need to study and understand why, for instance, Sweden does not register the indigenous population residing within its national borders, while countries such as New Zealand, Canada and Australia do. There is great significance related to the study of statistical constructions of 'indigenous people'. The scholars represented in this book highlight different aspects of indigenous demography: the creation and validity of categories for enumerating indigenous populations, the use and misuse of ethnic markers, micro-demographic investigations, demographic databases, and indigenous identities.

Anthropologists, historians, demographers and sociologists analysing historical and contemporary evidence from Canada, the U.S.A., Australia, New Zealand, Colombia, Russia, Norway, Sweden, Latvia and the U.K. are gathered together in the present volume to explore the statistical construction of 'indigenous peoples'. The approach adopted here is to a great extent historical, thereby providing the necessary long-term perspective for the understanding of the processes that have led to the present situation where statistical categorisation misses much of the cultural and indigenous perception of people and its varying representations. Moreover, there is a strong link between history and indigeneity. Indigenous peoples have used their lands for thousands of years, and their contemporary situation is to a great extent related to their ancient presence in the land.

Indigenous Peoples and Demography examines the differences between genealogical and cultural markers, groups and individuals, and subjective and objective perspectives on indigenous identity. How have different social and institutional systems defined indigenous groups in terms of inclusion and exclusion? What were the reasons for these decisions and how are they mirrored in the demographic sources? The book also discusses how a set of ethno-demographic tools can be developed to categorise how households are constructed within complex ethnic and economic environments, along with how these factors can be read into statistical data.

New Approaches to Population Studies

A complex situation is always faced when quantifications of individual behaviour are performed using traditional demographic tools. Individuals can belong to several collectives or have several identities. A person can change identity over time, but it is also possible to experience and be associated with different identities at the same time. Moreover, these identities often have varying degrees of status. These complex circumstances highlight the striking differences that can occur within groups that at first seem homogeneous. Thus, it is a problem that adequate data are often missing for factors other than imprecise definitions based on regions and nations. In order to understand demographic changes, in which social action with an impact on demographic behaviour is closely connected to such collective identities that are recognised and experienced, researchers have developed the concept of culture as an indicator (Fricke 1997; Kertzer 1997).

Population studies have long analysed changes in individual and family behaviour. Political and administrative borders have defined collectives of people. Originating from national surveys, international comparisons have provided evidence of both differences and similarities, and time trends have been observed. The general idea has been that national identities exist, and that they have an impact on demographic features. National identities have occupied demographic statistics for a long period of time. Added to the national level of investigating demography, a further macro perspective has presented more general transitional schemes in which great parts of, and sometimes entire, continents are included. They too are supposed to represent common values and aims. Based on the wholly positive acceptance of Western development, often described as the perpetual evolution of societies, a scientific demographic consensus has been shaped. Arland Thornton (2001) called this the developmental paradigm, and argued convincingly that it has largely led conclusions in the wrong directions. He suggested that demographers have reached a broader understanding of family change when they have gone beyond social and economic explanations. A key component of this extended agenda is culture. There is strong evidence that neither nations nor continents, nor

probably even regions or local societies, are the most satisfactory formations for a coherent contextualisation of cultural identity. And whatever
definition of culture we prefer, it can be stated that certain types of societies are disfavoured by the developmental paradigm.

The development of the modern state urged leaders to simplify the
reality of cultural complexity through a series of typifications (Scott 1998:
2–3, 76–81). However, an objective statistical realism is close to the pri-
mordialist notion of timeless identities, much discredited in recent social
science, particularly among anthropologists (Kertzer and Arel 2002: 19).

Demography has been criticised for its strong dependence on modernisation theories and its exclusively quantitative foundation. The lack of
social perspectives has created the need for a more reflexive science better
suited to the complexity of historical and present-day societies (Greenhalgh 1996). Robin Wright (2002), for example, states that it is particularly difficult for analysts to conceptualize indigenous societies in terms
of Western definitions of cultural identity, and that there is a tendency to
characterise them as lacking in social structure, not least regarding the
anthropological emphasis on the structure of a jural domain.

Even so, ethnographic, anthropological and other qualitative challenges to quantitative demography are dependent on the possibility of measuring and describing populations. While most of the demographic categories have developed during a long historical process, the current cultural
variables are largely the result of political and ideological constructions.
Simon Szreter, Hania Sholkamy and A. Dharmalingam underlined the
importance of reflective and critical examination (Szreter, Sholkamy and
Dharmalingam 2004: 4–8). This should preferably result in a dialogue
between demography, history and anthropology, to mention only some
of the academic disciplines involved. Hermeneutic methods with an emphasis on contextualisation and description will join a more hypothetical
deductionism aimed at the construction of categories for analysis. Szreter,
Sholkamy and Dharmalingam argued for context-based categories, un-
encumbered by any claims of universality or eternalness. This approach
offers an opportunity for historical methods, which are indifferent to cultural contexts, to be combined with anthropological perspectives.

Culture and identity are given shape from a number of disparate perspectives. We find here the outcomes of national and colonial administrative institutions, census takers' ambitions to create a logical system,
scientific experiments, different ethnic or religious ambitions of being recognised, and the ambitions of authorities connected to these collectives.
The cultural variations in and modifications of these ideological codes,
to use Kreager's terminology, are complications of the outcomes of traditional methods. Demographic thinking has shifted to considering ways in
which we can extend and redevelop the concept of culture as identifier.
Kreager argued that it is not a grand theory of culture that population
studies is seeking, but 'a more limited comparative framework that would

enable specific demographic changes to be understood as a dimension of specific cultural differentials and changing relationships between groups. More particularly, the hope has remained that such an approach would allow formalisation, in which identity could serve as a proxy for complex patterns of cultural change' (Kreager 1997: 142).

The demographic sources are often representations of processes in which individuals are turned into objects. As Melissa Nobles and others have argued, race is not an objective category; censuses help shape racial discourses, which in turn affect public policies (Nobles 2002). Ian Hacking, in an analysis drawing on Foucault, argued that what we have experienced is moral categorisation with the purpose of control (Hacking 1986: 226). One far-reaching consequence of this is that the truths emanating from this categorisation have been adopted by the subjects themselves, and have thus had a major impact on indigenous identity processes. Certainly, states have a great responsibility for this. In her chapter, Tahu Kukutai (this volume) concludes that identity categories and the groups they seek to describe are political and social constructions that often reflect prevailing race logics and state imperatives, at odds with the criteria that groups use to define themselves. Similarly, Linda Tuhiwai Smith wrote that it is difficult to speak of 'indigenous peoples' and 'research' simultaneously without acknowledging and understanding the impact of imperialism and colonialism on the creation of knowledge (Tuhiwai Smith 1999: 2). She argued that 'methodologies and methods of research, the theories that inform them, the questions which they generate and the writing styles they employ, all become significant acts which need to be considered carefully and critically before being applied. In other words, they need to be 'decolonised" (ibid.: 39).

There is a range of notions concerning indigenous peoples that include understandings of their number, of their geographical area, of their societal structure, of limitations and definitions, and of the basis of identity that do not represent the indigenous reality. The result is sometimes exclusion, and sometimes alienation from the indigenous culture. Acknowledging the negative effects that can be associated with ethnocentric perspectives, there is an overwhelming need for inside perspectives when demographic categories are discussed. This qualitative dimension represents not only the prospect of more culturally correct understandings and descriptions, but it also has the ability to bring changes into related contexts. This book scrutinises the historical and contemporary context of indigenous demographic categorisation, and it aims to improve the possibilities for comparison, revision and development.

The present volume addresses three critical challenges. One is the complicated meeting between quantitative and qualitative methods, representing widely different research traditions. Efforts on both sides have resulted in innovative and complex research design where mutual strengths are promoted and disciplinary limitations have been reduced (Bernardi and Hutter 2007). Another is the relation between the historical and the contemporary context, with geographical variation an additional complicating factor. It follows that attention must be given to all the divergences involved, but equally that favourable opportunities are acknowledged. There are excellent examples of studies that have combined comparisons of deviating contexts of time and space, investigating risk factors for measles mortality, survival of mothers and their offspring, the impact of nutrition, and social inequalities in child mortality in nineteenth-century Europe and countries in the contemporary Third World (Burström 1996; Andersson 2000; Scott and Duncan 2002; Macassa 2004).

A third challenge is the inside and outside understanding of complex indigenous societies. Externally produced censuses, surveys and administrative data are too often inaccurate when it comes to representing indigenous social structures. Nevertheless, our ambition is to foster a better use of historical sources, with our ultimate ambition being to elucidate mechanisms within demographic changes of indigenous populations that will improve the possibilities of positive developments in health. Indigenous poor health is historical, cultural and political in character. In the contemporary era, where political distinctions are frequently drawn between 'symbolic' and 'practical' reconciliation, historical records can provide a powerful contrast to this, illustrating the inextricable links between bodily health, social values and systems of colonial power (Birch 2007; Mitchell 2007; Taylor 2009). The providing of adequate indicators of health and living conditions among indigenous peoples is related to our understanding of the historical process that has led us up to where we are today (Andersen and Poppel 2002; Anderson 2007; Parkinson 2007).

Indigenous Perspectives: Definitions and Contextualisation

The definition of 'indigenous peoples' remains an open issue, and here we will not offer a definite solution to the problem of definition. Earlier works have stressed historical continuity, the experience of colonisation and self-identifications as being universal features of indigenous peoples worldwide. The time, extent and impact of colonisation varies across continents. The most used and cited definition has long been that of José Martinez Cobo – an Ecuadorian diplomat and at the time a UN special rapporteur – who coined a 'working definition' of indigenous peoples:

> Indigenous communities, peoples and nations are those which, having a historical continuity with pre-invasion and pre-colonial societies that developed on their territories, consider themselves distinct from other sectors of the societies now prevailing in those territories, or parts of them. They form at present non-dominant sectors of society and are determined to preserve, develop and transmit to future generations their ancestral

territories, and their ethnic identity, as the basis of their continued existence as peoples, in accordance with their own cultural patterns, social institutions and legal systems. (Martinez Cobo 1987).

Though a good starting point, Martinez Cobo's definition may be a too simplistic definition of 'indigeneity peoples'.

The United Nations, national governments and academic institutions have different perspectives on defining or characterising indigenous peoples. Even if indigenous groups themselves have their own concept of how they wish to be viewed and identified (Bartlett et al. 2007), self-identification has practical, and sometimes ideological, limits (Kertzer and Arel 2002: 34). Ken Coates argued that although colonial status is clearly a central element in the history of most indigenous peoples, colonising powers are not the key determinants of indigeneity (Coates 2004: 13–14). Coates presented a more extensive definition, focusing on historical processes and relationships, the aim being to remain sensitive to the circumstances of local indigenous societies. Coates exemplified this by highlighting such central characteristics as: their 'small size, attachment to the land, value system and culture rooted in the environment, commitment to a sustainable lifestyle, mobility and cultural conservatism. With the inevitable regional and historical variations, they also share several key historical circumstances: economic and political domination by outsiders, selected integration/participation with non-indigenous societies, limited or non-existent power within the nation state, emerging involvement in a local or international process of decolonisation' (ibid.: 14).

Taylor and Bell provided a series of arguments for a separate analysis of indigenous peoples. They presented arguments relating to location, social justice, social science, and context. They underlined the importance of the considerable degree of regional diversity among indigenous groups within a given country. Policy makers are committed to achieving social justice for their indigenous peoples, and to do so an understanding of demographic patterns is essential. Traditional demographic studies of fertility, mortality and migration also need to be carried out in relation to indigenous peoples. The field also needs to develop methods and measures that take into account the characteristics of indigenous cultures (Taylor and Bell 2004: 5). Historical contexts of colonisation influence the indigenous peoples of today (Snipp 1997). In many respects, the scientific and political community still lacks an understanding of how colonisation, as a demographic process, has influenced the colonised as well as the colonisers.

Censuses play a key role in the construction of social reality, especially when they employ identity categories, such as ethnicity. This has been displayed as the most basic of powers, a power to name, to categorise and thereby to create social reality. Censuses set their goal as that of objectively assessing the state of subjective identities (Kertzer and Arel 2002: 20, 36; Urla 1993: 837). Anderson has argued that statistical records are important devices employed by the colonial state to impose a totalising, classificatory grid on its territory, permitting claims of total control (Anderson 1991: 184).

Clearly one of the major problems when it comes to indigenous demography is that the sources are constructed by non-indigenous members of society. The futile attempts of colonisers to reduce ethnicity to a single criterion, such as origin or language, greatly distort complex and changing identities. Indigenous groups have been denied an existence in the records, and thus in society. However, not all groups or individuals have wished to be included and labelled. Extensive resistance towards ethnic or indigenous categorisation has been a response to the marginalisation effect of national policies, and the neglect of indigenous aims and their perceptions of identity.(Kertzer and Arel 2002: 22–30). In an Australian context, Gardner and Bourke (2000) argued that the truly fluid variable is the history of white definitions of Aboriginal identity. That is why there is a continuous need for historical approaches uncovering how, why and for what purpose data on indigenous peoples have been collected, as well as a need for studies of why colonial powers enumerated everyone but the native populations.

Organisation of the Book

When we put this volume together we were faced with several alternative ways of structuring the book. One way could have been to organise the chapters after the different administrative systems that have produced demographic definitions of indigenous peoples, while others might have been to choose analytical approaches or a chronological order. Nevertheless, we found a geographical organisation most appropriate, thereby illustrating the global perspective as well as the differences in chronology, policies and experiences. The complexity of indigenous demography and our efforts to deal with this scientifically is further developed in the epilogue, which pulls together the various findings of the chapters.

In their chapter, Smith, McCalman, Anderson, Smith, Evans, McCarthy and Beer scrutinise the early development of indigenous statistics in Australia. Established as a British colony in 1835, the state of Victoria was considered the leader in Australian indigenous administration, being the first colony to legislate for the 'protection' of Aborigines, and the first to collect statistical data on their decline and anticipated disappearance. The Victorian Aborigines Protection Act of 1886 – 'the half-caste act' – sought to accelerate the process of assimilation of the Aboriginal population. People were divided into full-bloods and 'half-castes', with the latter group consisting of people with any degree of mixed blood. Half-castes were not accepted by whites or by Aborigines until eighty years after the act was passed. A painstaking investigation combining family histories – using birth, death and marriage registries – and census and archival records provides this information. One startling finding is that the surviving Aboriginal population is descended almost entirely from those who were under the protection of the colonial state. The population reconstitution of Smith et al. resolves longstanding uncertainties about the fate of Aboriginal people in Victoria in the colonial and postcolonial era. The reconstitution confirms that the resurgence of Aboriginal Victoria during the late twentieth century resulted from the rejection of fractional identity and invisibility by the Aboriginal people themselves. They had never disappeared; they had merely been rendered invisible by legislative fiat.

Tahu Kukutai shows in her chapter how the state of New Zealand has defined and circumscribed Maori identity, and the potential consequences of this from the mid-nineteenth century onwards. The Maori were enumerated separately from the rest of the population until 1951, and a system based on blood quantum was designed. But in contrast to South Africa or the United States, the statistical deployment of blood quantum in New Zealand reflected its usage in legal definitions of Maori, but was not tied to an explicit system of discrimination. From 1916 to 1951, the term 'race alien' was used in censuses, for the purpose of enumerating those with non-European blood. This was not used to discriminate against the Maori, but rather to identify and restrict the entry of 'coloured' migrants, such as Chinese people. In modern censuses, Maori identities are more flexible and inclusive, and multiple criteria are used to define the term, including self-identification. Nevertheless, the discourse on defining the Maori is still contested, and today it represents the subjective outcomes of political consciousness and choice, the 'objective' reality of biological and cultural origin, and structural constraints that condition opportunities to access and express identity.

A global perspective is important for the advancement of indigenous studies. This book contains no contributions from Africa or Asia, and only one chapter concerns the vast region of Latin America, and thus it does not present a worldwide coverage. These continents are increasingly involved in indigenous research and there are obvious reasons for supporting this trend. The notion of indigenous peoples has been highly controversial in Africa and Asia, and a number of groups became more actively engaged in the international indigenous movement during the 1990s (Karlsson 2003; Saugestad 2008).

Steinar Saether provides an overview of the ethnic categories used during the period from 1750 to 1850 in Latin America, especially in the Caribbean provinces of Colombia, and why they changed over the years. He identifies five distinct periods from 1725 until today that have been crucial to the use and design of categories of race and ethnicity in censuses. Several changes occurred during the late colonial and early republican eras. During Spanish rule, there was a close relationship between census categories, tribute obligations and access to land. Inhabitants' resistance to being registered is also noted in some areas. In the new republics, the census categories changed mainly because the new elite constructed categories to reflect their notions of the ideal society.

David Hacker and Michael Haines use census data to investigate life expectancy and age-specific mortality among the American Indian population. They find that when life tables are created they are difficult to interpret, low in accuracy, and suffer from various types of bias. Especially when using a two-census method linking people between the 1900 and 1910 census, they find that people who were designated, for example, 'Indian' in the first census might have 'migrated' out of that category by the next. The period of investigation is also situated in the midst of a time of great change for the American Indian population, owing to coercive federal assimilation policies. The demographic evidence suggests that the indigenous population faced substantial difficulties, with higher mortality rates and lower life expectancy than the white and black populations of America.

The chapter by Michelle Hamilton and Kris Inwood considers the geographic and cultural factors that affected the enumeration of the Aboriginal population in the Canadian census of 1891. Hamilton and Inwood clearly illustrate the challenges of census taking: geography (travel of the enumerators), difficulties with language, and some of the cross-cultural differences that were manifest between Aboriginal peoples and state-employed enumerators. On top of these factors, there was sometimes a conflict concerning how to interpret the 'real' intentions of the enumerator, and the enumerators were at times met with suspicion and resistance. Hamilton and Inwood argue that during the late nineteenth century, Canadian census authorities attempted to understand Aboriginal communities better, and the Aboriginal communities learned more about the ways in which the state wanted to gather census information.

Sweden has extensive demographic registers, which in the past also included ethnic identity. Thus, Per Axelsson's chapter shows that categories intended to cover Sami ethnicity varied greatly, and that the strategies underlying classification have changed considerably between those used in 1750 and the twentieth century. The last census with information on ethnicity was carried out in 1945, after which Sweden abandoned the practice, which is currently seen as a problem. It is impossible to estimate the total Sami population, and there is no option to link ethnic information to other register data.

Norway has a national research-funding policy that guarantees a substantial amount of research on indigenous groups. From this foundation, extensive efforts have been made to address the issues of Sami identity and society. Lars Ivar Hansen's chapter on the usefulness of early modern sources for the reconstruction of population development shows that mid eighteenth-century Norwegian registers include an increasing proportion of Sami among the settled population. The records illustrate the complexity of Sami society, where large non-nomadic groups lived by the sea or on farmsteads. The settled Sami became a substantial part of the population in northern Norway, in some areas representing a third of the total settled inhabitants.

In her chapter on the Sami of Norway, Hilde L. Jåstad views ethnicity from the perspectives of the individual and households and finds that the census instructions restricted the definition of ethnicity. Nevertheless, there was some regional variation between parishes. Ancestry seems to have been the most important criterion. Some parishes had few representations of mixed households, while others had considerably more, which indicates that there was variation in the interpretation of ethnicity criteria. The increase in mixed marriages may be interpreted as a consequence of the Norweganisation process. The vast majority of Sami households included no other ethnic marker. Their marriage market was thereby rather ethnically homogeneous.

Bjørg Evjen concludes that the definition of ethnic categories had a great impact on the population structure of late nineteenth-century Norway. The instructions that were given to census takers, and how they were interpreted, need careful analysis when studying the indigenous population. What might seem to be demographic changes due to migration or fluctuating birth rates can instead largely be explained by changing official strategies of ethnic classification.

In Gunnar Thorvaldsen's chapter, three sometimes contradictory criteria of ethnicity are discussed: individual/group, ancestral/cultural (language) and subjective/objective. Individual representations were more important than those of the group, and he shows that there was not as much confusion among census takers as is sometimes argued. Thorvaldsen concludes that Sami ethnicity was an influential contextual variable.

Torunn Pettersen raises the fundamental question of who is entitled to represent the Sami people of today. The derogatory opinions of the majority population of Norway about the Sami are part of the explanation for why not all Sami actually choose to register themselves as a member of this indigenous group. This leads to shortcomings in the accuracy of contemporary indigenous demographic data, and these shortcomings have negative implications in several societal contexts. Demands for change must come from the Sami, Pettersen argues. She argues that ethnic self-identification must be the basic principle, but that the state also has a responsibility.

Using the highly informative 1926/7 polar census records, David Anderson investigates the hunting and herding Essei Iakuts living in the Evenki region of eastern Russia. By linking people's household structures to the herd structures of the reindeer supporting these households, he reconstructs novel relational patterns. The census taker lived in the region for a year and created household cards detailing age, name, occupation, income, and so on, but more surprisingly also recorded information using questionnaires concerning the formation of local reindeer-herding families. The author uncovers a complex picture of interaction between wealthy and poor families, within and outside households. The study establishes, for instance, that the Essei Iakuts had a system of social solidarity called *posobka* to help during difficult times. Anderson also offers theoretical insights into how the dual analysis of the demography of people and the demography of reindeer can strengthen our understanding of indigenous societies.

John Ziker looks at the central Taimyr lowlands region of Siberia, using both the historical polar census of 1926/7 and his own ethnographic research. He shows that the historical data together with focused observational analysis increases the possibility of studying the effects of politics and policies. Demographic data coupled with household socio-economic information provides a complex picture of land and resource use, social organisation and identity for the central Taimyr lowlands in the 1920s, where generosity was a cultural keyword. Furthermore, people of today are studied using demographic records. A striking demographic feature is the concentration of non-natural deaths in the younger age groups. The collapse of a planned economy in the 1990s affected the region, and long periods of inactivity led to vast drinking problems.

In Russia, the term 'indigenous' is not only a qualitative characteristic of certain populations or individuals as it also has a quantitative dimension, and a disputed threshold has been established according to which ethnic groups cannot amount to more than 50,000 persons. Sergey V. Sokolovskiy's chapter traces the conceptual construction of this threshold, and the influence of the legal status of identity politics. Questions of historical succession (who came first and who came later) have often served as a battleground for competing claimants. In a special decree passed during the early Soviet era, the 'small peoples of the North' were guaranteed equal rights to social advancement, and they were to be continuously enumerated. Since then, diverse statistical sources have been based on the rigid idea of primordial ethnicity and bounded and unchangeable cultural units. However, the post-Soviet era has experienced fluctuations in the numbers of indigenous peoples based on changes in state policy, legal status and identity politics, as well as changes in official linguistic and cultural classifications. Recently, urban and modernised groups have been added to the official list of indigenous small-numbered peoples of the Russian north that was previously dominated by groups with a traditional economy.

Notions of identity are untheorised in demography, and identity is often confused with identification (Gardner and Bourke 2000). Definitions should focus on what actually characterises an indigenous people, rather than on what does not. The borderline between an ethnic minority and an indigenous people has sometimes been difficult to draw. In this context, the chapters by Andrejs Plakans and John MacInnes are illustrative. Plakans's study of Latvia illustrates the relation between nationalistic motives and the concept of indigenousness. He suggests that there is a marked contrast between census categories and identities in the demographic sources of the eastern Baltic littoral during the nineteenth and twentieth centuries. Censuses have a very difficult task in that their aim is to describe the population using a number of constructed categories. The census is rarely a representation of the current situation. Changes are a necessity, and work with censuses can be characterised as Sisyphean. When constructing national and ethnic categories, there is a risk that religious, social, economic and other parameters will be either neglected or over-emphasised.

John MacInnes provides an interesting perspective when he concludes that few groups in the U.K. claim to be indigenous. One exception is the British National Party (BNP), which portrays twentieth and twenty-first-century immigration as different from its historic antecedents. He asks who the British are, and finds that identity categories are discursively constructed and do not have an external, standard referent. They are therefore much more difficult to handle using the classification systems of official censuses. The problem is that it is impossible to give them a fixed meaning. Scientists and census makers have a responsibility to be more conscious of what they are doing. MacInnes argues that despite the fact that censuses can never give a clear picture of a society in terms of nationality or ethnicity, we must be cautious not to reproduce identity categories that are irrelevant.

The present volume demonstrates strong parallels between the history and contemporary situation of indigenous peoples in different parts of the world. Furthermore, the book adds valuable knowledge to the complex relation between demographic classification, state policies, indigenous response and indigenous identity. We hope that the volume proves to be a stimulus to future research collaboration, where extended comparisons between countries and continents will play an important role.

References

Andersen, T., and B. Poppel. 2002. 'Living Conditions in the Arctic', *Social Indicators Research* 58(1–3): 191–216.

Anderson, B. 1991. *Imagined Communities: Reflections on the Origin and Spread of Nationalism*. London: Verso.

Anderson, I. 2007. 'Understanding the Process', in B. Carson, T. Dunbar, R.D. Chenhall and R. Bailie (eds), *Social Determinants of Indigenous Health*. Crows Nest: Allen and Unwin, pp. 21–40.

Andersson, T. 2000. *Survival of Mothers and Their Offspring in Nineteenth-century Sweden and Contemporary Ethiopia*. Umeå: Umeå University.

Bartlett, J.G., L. Madariaga-Vignudo, J.D. O'Neill and H. Kuhnlein. 2007. 'Identifying Indigenous Peoples for Health Research in a Global Context: A Review of Perspectives and Challenges', *International Journal of Circumpolar Health* 66(4): 287–307.

Bernardi, L., and I. Hutter. 2007. 'The Anthropological Demography of Europe', *Demographic Research* 17(18): 541–66.

Birch, T. 2007. 'The Invisible Fire: Indigenous Sovereignty, History and Responsibility', in A. Moreton-Robinson (ed.), *Sovereign Subjects: Indigenous Sovereignty Matters*. Crows Nest: Allen and Unwin, pp.105–17.

Burström, B. 1996. *Risk Factors For Measles Mortality: Studies From Kenya and Nineteenth-century Stockholm*. Stockholm: Kavolinska Institutet.

Coates, K.S. 2004. *A Global History of Indigenous Peoples: Struggle and Survival*. New York: Palgrave Macmillan.Fricke, T. 1997. 'Culture Theory and Demographic Process: Toward a Thicker Demography', in D.I. Kertzer and T. Fricke (eds), *Anthropological Demography: Toward a New Synthesis*. Chicago: University of Chicago Press, pp. 248–77.

Gardner, G., and E.A. Bourke. 2000. 'Indigenous Populations, "Mixed" Discourses and Identities', *People and Place* 8(2): 43–52.

Greenhalgh, S. 1996. 'The Social Construction of Population Science: An Intellectual, Institutional and Political History of Twentieth-century Demography', *Comparative Studies in Society and History* 38: 26–66.

Hacking, I. 1986. 'Making up People', in T. Heller, M. Sosna and D. Wellberry (eds), *Reconstructing Individualism*. Stanford, CA: Stanford University Press, pp. 222–36.

Karlsson, B.G. 2003. 'Anthropology and the "Indigenous Slot": Claims to and Debates about Indigenous Peoples' Status in India'. *Critique of Anthropology* 23(4): 403–23.

Kertzer, D.I. 1997. 'The Proper Role of Culture in Demographic Explanation', in G.W. Jones, R.M. Douglas, J.C. Caldwell and R.M. D'Souza (eds), *The Continuing Demographic Transition*. Oxford: Clarendon Press, pp. 137–57.

Kertzer. D.I., and D. Arel. 2002. 'Censuses, Identity Formation, and the Struggle for Political Power', in D.I. Kertzer and D. Arel (eds), *Census and Identity: The Politics of Race, Ethnicity, and Language in National Censuses*. Cambridge: Cambridge University Press, pp. 1–42.

Kreager, P. 1997. 'Population and Identity', in D.I. Kertzer and T. Fricke (eds), *Anthropological Demography: Toward a New Synthesis*. Chicago: University of Chicago Press, pp. 135–74.

Macassa, G. 2004. *Poverty and Health in Different Contexts: Social Inequalities in Child Mortality in Mozambique and Nineteenth-century Stockholm*. Stockholm: Kavolinska Institutet.

Martinez Cobo, J.R. 1987. *Study of the problem of discrimination against indigenous populations, vol. 5: conclusions, proposals and recommendation*. New York: United Nations.

Mitchell, J. 2007. 'History', in B. Carson, T. Dunbar, R.D. Chenhall and R. Bailie (eds), *Social Determinants of Indigenous Health*. Crows Nest: Allen and Unwin, pp. 41–64.

Nobles, M. 2002. 'Racial Categorisation and Censuses', in D.I. Kertzer and D. Arel (eds), *Census and Identity: The Politics of Race, Ethnicity, and Language in National Censuses*. Cambridge: Cambridge University Press, pp. 43–70.

Parkinson, A. 2007. 'The International Polar Year 2007–2008: The Arctic Human Health Legacy', *Alaska Medicine* 49(2): 43–45.

Saugestad, S. 2008. 'Beyond the "Colombus Context": New Chellenges as the Indigenous Discourse is Applied to Africa', in H. Minde (ed.), *Indigenous Peoples: Self–determination, Knowledge, Indigeniety*. Delft: Eburon Delft, pp. 157–73.

Scott, J. C. 1998. *Seeing Like a State. How Certain Schemes to Improve the Human Conditions Have Failed*. New Haven and London: Yale University Press.

Scott, S., and C.J. Duncan. 2002. *Demography and Nutrition: Evidence from Historical and Contemporary Populations*. Malden, MA: Blackwell.

Sköld, P. 1992. *Samisk bosättning i Gällivare 1550–1750*. Umeå: Centre for Arctic Research.

Snipp, C.M. 1997. 'The Size and Distribution of the American Indian Population: Fertility, Mortality, Migration, and Residence', *Population Research and Policy Review* 16: 61–93.

Szreter, S., H. Sholkamy and A. Dharmalingam. 2004. 'Contextualising Categories: Towards a Critical Reflexive Demography', in S. Szreter, H. Sholkamy and A. Dharmalingam (eds), *Categories and Contexts: Anthropological and Historical Studies in Critical Demography*. Oxford: Oxford University Press, pp. 3–56.

Taylor, J. 2009. 'Indigenous Demography and Public Policy in Australia: Population or Peoples?' *Journal of Population Research* 26: 115–30.

Taylor, J., and M. Bell. 2004. 'Introduction: New World Demography', in J. Taylor and M. Bell (eds), *Population Mobility and Indigenous Peoples in Australasia and North America*. London: Routledge, pp. 1–10.

Thornton, A. 2001.'The Developmental Paradigm, Reading History Sideways, and Family Change'. *Demography* 38(4): 2001, 449–65.

Thornton, R. 1997. 'Aboriginal North American Population and Rates of Decline, ca. A.D. 1500–1900', *Current Anthropology* 38(2): 310–15.

Tuhiwai Smith, L. 1999. *Decolonising Methodologies: Research and Indigenous Peoples*. Dunedin: University of Otago Press.

Urla, J. 1993. 'Cultural Politics in an Age of Statistics: Numbers, Nations, and the Making of Basque Identity', *American Ethnologist* 20: 818–43.

Wright, R. 2002. 'Historical and Anthropological Perspectives on the Formation of Cultural Identity', *Ethnohistory* 49(3): 703–14.

1

FRACTIONAL IDENTITIES: THE POLITICAL ARITHMETIC OF ABORIGINAL VICTORIANS

Len Smith, Janet McCalman, Ian Anderson, Sandra Smith, Joanne Evans, Gavan McCarthy and Jane Beer

Miss *LB* has been a domestic for years, quite capable and clean. Of late, due to infirmity of years she has had a light position looking after an aged person, but now she must relinquish work altogether at the age of 62. She is thoroughly civilised and no different from another woman only for the colour of her skin. She is 3/4 black, I should say, perhaps scarcely that. She was sent by the Board of Protection of Aborigines to the pension office with a view to getting an old age pension as she would have received had she even been 50 per cent white. She was refused on the grounds that the blood predominance was aboriginal. She came sobbing to me and I assured her that I would take up her case for we have a half promise that there will be an alteration to the law to enable approved aborigines to obtain the rights of whites. Meanwhile I told her I would try to get her State assistance which she is entitled to if she resumes an Aboriginal status in Framlingham aboriginal station, or as a native put it to me last night, "if she returns to the ashes of the campfire".

—Secretary of the Aborigines Uplift Society,
Mr APA Burdeu, to the Archbishop of Melbourne, July 1939.

The debate over the size of the Aboriginal population of Australia on the eve of the European invasion has been complicated by the nation's unsavory 'history wars'. The smaller the number of original inhabitants, the lower is the implied number of colonial casualties and the more defensible appears the claim that a people of the plough had a right to convert a seemingly empty land into a food basket for the Empire. However, as scholars have come to understand the complexity of Aboriginal society and its management of plant and animal food resources, they have also gained a new appreciation of the land's carrying capacity. Indeed, the belated discovery of women's significance as food gatherers has revealed the extent to which Aboriginal people were reliant on the gathering of the vegetable and invertebrate food resources to be found in previously un-appreciated abundance throughout the continent, as well as the extent to which they systematically managed those resources by fire, aquaculture, and proto-agriculture. Smith has estimated that this so–called 'terra nul-lius' would have supported around 1.6 billion human lives past infancy during an estimated 70,000 years of human occupation before British colo-nisation – scarcely an empty land that belonged to no one (Smith 2002; Windschuttle 2002; Macintyre and Clark 2003; Manne 2003).

The Colonial Decline of the Aboriginal Population

There has been considerable variation in the estimates of the original pop-ulation of Australia before European colonisation. It is said that Arthur Phillip, the first British Governor, estimated the population of the whole continent when it was annexed in 1788 to be around 1 million, although there is now a dispute over whether this estimate was ever made. Later estimates by explorers and government officials were based on observa-tions of concentrations of people whose numbers may already have de-clined because of introduced diseases. In 1930, A.R Radcliffe-Brown, who reviewed the available literature on settler observations, frontier violence, and introduced disease, determined the original population to be at least 250,000 and possibly in excess of 300,000. Subsequent archaeological re-search that has rewritten modern understandings of Aboriginal society, ecological practice, and food gathering, now makes an estimate of 1 mil-lion in 1788 seem implausibly low for a land mass of such a size and vari-ety of resources (Broome 2005; Mulvaney 2002).

A similar profusion of estimates about the size of the Victorian population emerged both in 1788 and in 1835, when the first settlement was established at Port Phillip. Until recently, a consensus had developed, based on Radcliffe-Brown's work, that about 15,000 people occupied the area south of the Murray River before the British occupation. However, that figure must be considered an absolute minimum, given the evidence of decline until 1850, summarised by Barwick and others (Barwick 1971).

Since then, the work of Butlin (1983), Lourandos (1997) and Campbell (2002) has resulted in a substantial increase in the supposed population. The southeast corner of the Australian continent was probably the most densely populated part of Aboriginal Australia, with sufficient food supplies to support a semi-sedentary society and economy along the Murray River and parts of the western basalt plain. This population was affected by two successive smallpox epidemics around 1788 and 1829 that swept across the southeast ahead of the colonial frontier: Curr (1883), Smyth (1878) and numerous others reported that the initial epidemic reduced the tribes as far away from Sydney as the Murray estuary by half. Broome (2005) argues that the figure of 15,000 must refer to the population at the founding of the colony in 1835, and that if each epidemic resulted in 50 per cent mortality, the precolonial population must have been about 60,000. Hence, by the time that the colonial capital of Melbourne was formally settled in 1835, the Aboriginal population had already fallen by 75 per cent (Barwick 1971; Butlin 1983; Webb 1984; Lourandos 1997; Campbell 2002). Figure 1.1. portrays our tentative reconstruction of the colonial population decline and its subsequent recovery.

Just eighteen years later, in 1853, official counts placed 1,907 Aborigines and 6.5 million sheep in Victoria, but the European invaders were quickly making up the human deficiency; half a million gold seekers surged into the colony in a decade. Because the entire colony was closely settled, from 1835 onward the Aborigines were restricted in their movements and alienated from their hunting and foraging lands. They were subject to high mortality, not only from tuberculosis, syphilis and other diseases, but also from settler violence. Births were few, and the population went into a rapid decline (Smith 1980).

By the time of Australian Federation in 1901, 1.2 million whites and 652 Aborigines, by official calculation, lived in Victoria, plus 11 million sheep and 1.6 million cattle. The colonisation of Victoria was arguably the most rapid and most catastrophic colonial dispossession of the nineteenth century. In the course of a single human lifespan, the authorities could be confident that the 'native population' in Victoria was fading away. In 1993, when the 'last of the tribe', Mary Angeline Morgan, died, racial purists could claim that Aboriginal Victoria had disappeared into the mists of time (Pepper and De Araugo 1985: 262).

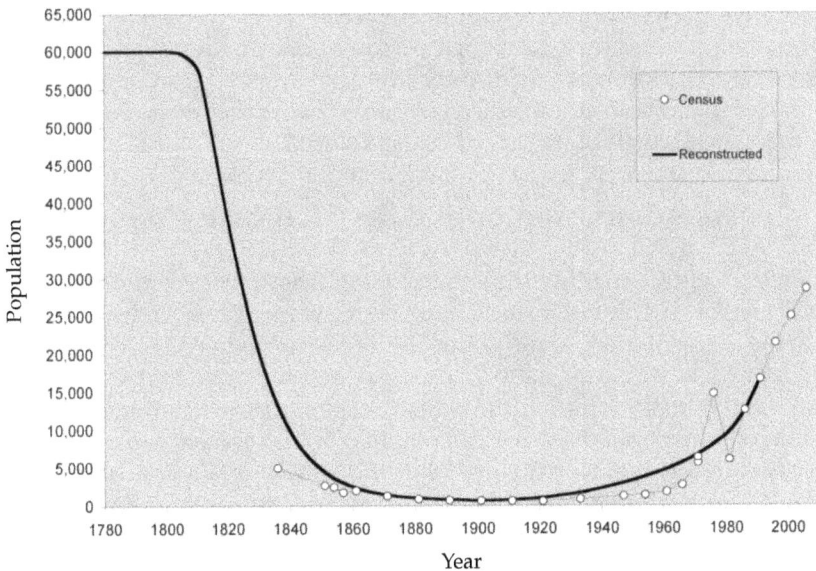

Figure 1.1 Victorian Aboriginal Population, 1780–2001

Victorian Distinctiveness

The immense wealth found in Victoria's goldmines lured more educated and prosperous immigrants during the 1850s. Almost all of them paid their own way; and for a time, the colony had the highest level of literacy in the British Empire. Of the half a million who came in the 1850s, half of them settled permanently – among them physicians, scientists, artists and artisans with progressive views who were keen to build a better society. Australasia's first medical society and professional medical journal were established in the 1850s, as were a Royal Society for those with scientific interests, as well as a new university, a public library, a public museum, and a host of voluntarist welfare, health and educational institutions. Victorians prided themselves on building a democracy that realised many of the Chartists' principles – a protectionist political economy benefiting, both manufacturers and workers, a strong civic and intellectual culture, and a progressive native administration (Serle 1977; Davison 1978, 2001: 52–53).

The colonial government had been quick to establish rationing stations, missions and even schools. George Augustus Robinson was appointed Chief Protector of Aborigines in 1839 in the hope of preventing the disastrous depopulation that had occurred in Van Diemen's Land. A protectorate existed until 1849. A Select Committee in 1859 led to the formation of a Central Board to Watch Over the Interests of Aborigines, which by 1862 superintended seven reserves and twenty-three small camping places. Victoria's 1869 Act, which established safe havens to protect the remnants of tribes from the excesses of settlers, became the model for legislation in the rest of the country decades later. It also marked, however, the beginning of coercive native administration in Australia. From that point forward, Aboriginality – and by extension, a person's status under the Act – came under the jurisdiction of a magistrate. The act controlled Aborigines' place of residence, movement outside the reserves, work contracts, money and children's welfare (Broome 2005: 120–32, 146–52).

Native Administration and the 'Half-caste Problem'

When the Central Board for the Protection of Aborigines replaced the earlier Board for Aborigines in 1869, its objective was to protect native people from the abuse of settlers, and about half of the surviving Aborigines were collected together on its stations. Our research indicates that the protection that the Board afforded the station residents was certainly effective. The half of the population that did not live on the reserves seems to have left few identifiable descendants; only a handful of families are known to have survived outside the Board's protection. But even though many of their lives were saved, the station residents were clearly not protected from interactions with settlers (Broome 2005: 146–65).

The circumstances and intimate details of relations between white men and Aboriginal women in colonial Victoria will probably always remain largely hidden from historians. Existing accounts derive from censorious third parties, who saw the situation in terms of prostitution, exploitation and depravity; they give little insight into the personal and social dynamics of the 'union of the races', as the Select Committee coyly termed it. What is known, however, is that more and more Aboriginal women living on the Board's stations began to bear children whose fathers were white. The 'union of the races' proceeded so rapidly that on stations controlled by the Board, 'half-castes' outnumbered 'full-bloods' by the late 1880s. The majority of mixed-race children, if they survived, became the responsibility of their mothers to be raised on the stations as Aborigines (Victoria Parliament Select Committee 1859, ; Protection Board Report 1889; Barwick 1971: 299).

These 'part-Aboriginal' people living as Aborigines caused great concern to the colonial government and the emerging colonial society. They challenged both the policy and fiscal basis of native administration. The assumption was that the Aborigines would gradually disappear in the face of the superior British civilisation and that the Board's budget, never adequate, would reduce in concert with the native population. To official and popular objections that people of mixed descent should not be receiving protection or relief, were added calls for a reduction in the cost of maintaining the stations and complaints that the reserves were occupying land that could be made available to settlers (Barwick 1971: 289–91).

Legislating Aboriginality: Fractional Identity and Fractional Citizenship

These concerns were addressed by the Victorian *Aborigines Protection Act 1886*, known generally as the 'Half-caste Act', and described in the 1887 Protection Board Report as 'a measure for merging the half-castes among the general population of the colony'. The new Act sought to accelerate the 'natural historical process' of assimilation, absorption, and therefore disappearance, of Aboriginal Victoria from the human story, by simply declaring – in the name of economy and the peoples' own best interest – that persons of mixed descent were not Aborigines and were not entitled to live on stations nor receive aid as a right. With certain provisos, upon reaching maturity these people were to leave the reserves and become members of the general community, to 'make their own way, with occasional assistance from the Board'. This policy set the pattern for the solution of the 'half-caste problem' throughout Australia, for the next eighty years. Aboriginal people were divided into 'full-bloods', who remained entitled to full rationing on the Aboriginal reserves, and those of fractional Aboriginality, who were denied access to life and support on the reserves, no matter how close their ties of kinship and association to those permitted to remain (Broome 2005).

This political arithmetic of race spawned elaborate charts of 'blood predominance', and racial theorising waxed and waned in response to international intellectual and political tides (Anderson 2002). As Broome points out, the 'fractions' varied from Act to Act in Victoria: In 1886, 'half caste' meant any degree of mixed blood, but according to the 1916 regulations, those with one-eighth or more of white blood had to leave the stations, implying that only those less than one-eighth white were Aboriginal and authorised to stay on reserves. The *Aboriginal Act 1928* stated that the Board could not expend money on 'octoroons' and 'quadroons', meaning that only people less than one-quarter white were to be deemed Aboriginal (Broome 2005: 203).

In 1956, the state government established an inquiry into the operation of the 1928 Act, conducted by Charles McLean, a retired magistrate. Despite being instructed to investigate those of one-quarter descent or more, McLean in his report recognised that all Victorians of Aboriginal descent were suffering from deprivations and discrimination and urged the government to adopt a wider definition. Hence, the new 1957 Act, which abolished the Board, reverted to the 1886 definition – that is, any admixture of Aboriginal blood (ibid.: 186, 203, 244, 314–16).

Regulation of the Family

Australian native policy was distinctive in its 'animal husbandry' approach to assimilation – in the Australian context, meaning the physical assimilation and disappearance of the Aboriginal people – which was based on a combination of the separation of caste groups, the regulation of marriage, and the removal of children. In theory, the 'Victorian solution' since 1886 had sought the absorption and eventual disappearance of a 'dying race' through the dilution of 'blood' and the encouragement of miscegenation. Indeed, marriages that might 'strengthen the blood' were to be discouraged and even prevented (Ellinghaus 2002). In practice, doing so meant that a 'fractional Aboriginal identity' was insufficient to justify support as an Aboriginal person, but sufficient to deny equality, both legal and cultural, with whites. Aboriginal veterans from both world wars, for instance, found that their equality on the battlefield evaporated once they returned to claim their veterans' entitlements. As Barwick recorded, people bitterly recalled, 'We were too black to get work or State Relief, and too white to get help from the Board' (Barwick 1971: 291).

Despite the passage of the 1886 Act, the objective of making people of mixed descent disappear into the general population was accepted neither by Aborigines nor by whites. Those 'half-castes' expelled from the reserves after the adoption of the Act, and thereby thrust into the terrible economic conditions of the 1890s depression, had to compete for work and survival with thousands of unemployed urban and rural people. Far from 'merging with the general population of the colony', they found that the 'general population of the colony' was unwilling to accept them. Unable to find work or accommodation, most of them were relegated to shanty settlements on the margins of the reserves or nearby towns. As Broome (2005) pointed out, however, many of those entitled to receive support fled the reserves because of the oppressiveness of the regime. Even when the Board was enabled in 1910 to give assistance to people other than those of full descent, few chose to return to the reserves, though most were living in poor conditions nearby (Barwick 1963; Broome 2005).

The 'Invisible Aborigines'

Despite being told by the Board and the law that they were not Aborigines, people not living on the reserves knew whether they were Aborigines or not, as did the local authorities and white people who in daily life discriminated against them as such. But, since they were progressively excluded from the Board's population statistics, they appear not to have recorded themselves as Aborigines in the censuses conducted by the colonial state and Australian statistical authorities. Instead, they joined a reservoir of statistically invisible Aborigines that developed for 100 years as a direct product of Victorian native administration (Smith 1980).

In 1921, the Victorian census count of Aborigines reached its lowest point, just 586, and, as late as 1961, it numbered fewer than 2,000. But in 2001, in the first Australian census of the new millennium, almost 30,000 people in Victoria affirmed that they were of Aboriginal origin. Natural increase in a 'closed' population without any source of external growth from immigration cannot explain this extraordinary recovery, and it would require a higher level of family formation than is indicated in any historical record. The inescapable inference is that the source of growth was a hidden population that was not officially Aboriginal in the eyes of the law or the authorities. Smith pointed to the re-emergence of these previously invisible people in the census counts since 1966 when he reviewed the population history of the Victorian Aborigines in 1980 (ibid.).

The process accelerated in 1971 when, for the first time, the Australian census invited people to identify themselves as Aboriginal rather than as some racial fraction. Not surprisingly, as indigenous identity became less stigmatised, the number of Aboriginal people nationwide grew rapidly with each subsequent census – nowhere more so than in Tasmania and Victoria, states where the Aboriginal population was officially 'extinct'. In Victoria, the process produced amazing growth rates of almost 20 per cent per year for several decades. In the 1960s, an Aboriginal political movement emerged, increasingly framed around such values as autonomy, self-determination and land rights (Burgmann 2003).

This political organisation coincided with a resurgent interest among Aboriginal peoples in Aboriginal arts, culture and heritage, especially in Victoria. Aboriginal people resisted the categorisation of caste that the authorities had deployed in the interest of racist administrative policy, reasserting clan and regional identities in its place. In this new social milieu, the statistical recognition of Aboriginal people in population counts was accompanied by an insistent politics that demanded the recognition of a continuous, albeit colonised, historical presence.

Genealogical Identity

Aboriginal Victorians, even those not officially counted as Aboriginal or situated on reserves, had retained their identity, their community and their culture. They defined Aboriginality as they always had, as a matter of cultural identification and community recognition. The glue that bonded them was genealogy and 'country'. Barwick found in the 1960s that most of the older adults had a genealogical knowledge that was 'extraordinarily vast'; they could 'reconstruct the complete history of their own families and, indeed, most of the cognate stocks of the same home region, dating back to the founding couples born in the 1850s or earlier' (Barwick 1971). By the 1960s, the descendant population had entered its seventh generation. Researchers turned to these genealogies and memories when they began to explore Victorian Aboriginal family and population history in the 1930s as well as in the 1960s. Genealogy offered a key to finding a people who were supposed to have disappeared and whose defining characteristic – their race – had been removed from the contemporary record (ibid.: 296–97).

Given all the foregoing, what we would like to do next is demonstrate how Aboriginal Victorians both survived and regrouped. By doing so we wish to shed light on the disappearance and subsequent re-emergence of invisible Aborigines by studying the genealogies of those Aborigines living today – reconstituting the Aboriginal population and combining family histories with information contained in the colonial censuses and vital registrations, and in the Board's censuses. Out of respect for the privacy of Aboriginal people and their ancestors, we do not identify people by name but reconstruct their demographic history from sources in the public domain. This method is made possible by the remarkable historical record of colonisation created by the government of the new colony and the statisticians who established what was arguably the most sophisticated system of vital registration in the nineteenth-century Anglophone world.[1]

Sources and Methods

In 1853, the colony of Victoria appointed William Henry Archer acting Registrar General and Government Statist. He was a disciple of William Farr, the pioneering epidemiologist and statistician who led the General Register Office of England and Wales for four decades. Archer put Farr's principles into practice. Henceforth, the registration of births, deaths and marriages mandated a full record of kinship, social position, and geographical identification. Moreover, a uniform nosology regulated the certifications of death, including as many as four contributing or allied morbidities with estimates of their duration. Moreover, all death certificates had to be completed by registered medical practitioners, not undertakers.

The colony was divided into registration districts, each with its own trained deputy registrar. Aboriginal births, deaths and marriages were recorded along with those of whites. In many cases, the registrars took pains to record the white biological fathers on birth certificates as well as the social Aboriginal fathers, documenting for posterity the sexual exploitation of Aboriginal women by some of Victoria's most prominent early colonists and the apparent legitimacy accorded to it. The colonial censuses conducted under the direction of Archer, and later H.H. Hayter, are also unique in directly documenting the decline of the indigenous population as it was occurring. The statistical data on the Victorian Aboriginal population are, therefore, of extraordinary quality and quantity: census estimates of the population are available from 1836 to 1841, and full counts thereafter (Eyler 1979; Smith 1980; Hopper 1986; Larson 1994).

While the Aborigines were being counted in the colonial censuses, the Aborigines' Protectorate and the Board for the Protection of Aborigines were conducting their own censuses. Robinson, the first Protector appointed in 1838, was instructed to take a complete census of the Aboriginal population – the number in each family, and the age, name, sex and tribe of each individual. The first attempt in 1839 was only partly successful, but subsequent years, particularly after 1851, saw numerous censuses undertaken and published in the Board's reports. In contrast to the colonial censuses, these censuses preserve many of the individual records, and this study has incorporated them into its database.

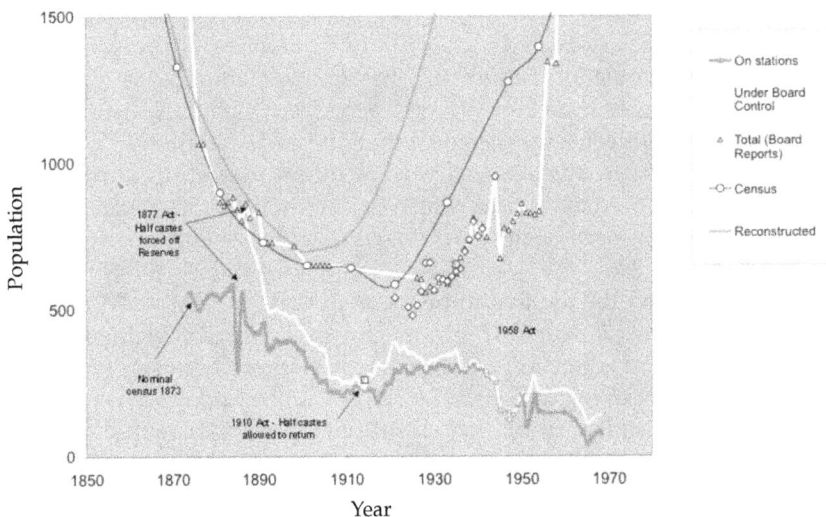

Figure 1.2 Subgroups of Victorian Aboriginal Population

As forced assimilation increasingly became the Board's policy, its statistics included more and more distinctions and fractional divisions within the population – 'full-bloods', 'half-castes', and 'quarter-castes' – and showed separate figures for those living 'on stations', 'under the control of the Board', and 'in contact with the Board'. Remarkably, the Board also provided an enumeration of those deemed not to be Aborigines at all. Figure 1.2 reveals the changes over time in these different populations. Because most of these totals derive from lists with the names of the individuals involved, they are reliable.

Reconstituted Identities:
The Koori Health Research Database

The basis of this chapter's research – a population reconstituted from genealogical records of the current Victorian Aboriginal population – is informed by the work of many researchers working over a long period. This research carefully traced the spouses and children of all identified individuals forward in time and their parents and siblings backward in time. In 1938/9, Norman Tindale collected genealogies of people from the Cummeragunga and Lake Tyers mission stations, that are now held at the South Australian Museum. Hamilton Hendry recorded some families from Lake Tyers in the 1950s, and Alan West and Aldo Massola, curators at the Museum of Victoria, collected oral histories and genealogies in the 1960s. Archival sources include the papers of John Bulmer (1833–1913) and A.W. Howitt 1830–1908), both now held by Museum Victoria.

The major contributions after Tindale came from Barwick, who began work on Aboriginal Victorians in 1960, and from Alick Jackomos at the Australian Institute of Aboriginal and Torres Strait Islander Studies (AIATSIS). Barwick collected extensive oral histories and combed the reports of the Protection Board and the mission stations to construct detailed genealogies. She had limited access to Victorian birth, death and marriage certificates for the confirmation of identities and dates, but her genealogies were available, in part, to other researchers at Museum Victoria. Barwick died prematurely in 1986, and until 2005, her full archive of drafts, research notes, and genealogies remained with her widower and daughter. In 2004, the Australian Research Council (ARC) provided funds that enabled the archive to be indexed online by Anne McCarthy, of the eScholarship Research Centre at the University of Melbourne, in preparation for the collection's donation to the State Library of Victoria and its eventual opening for general scholarly and community use.

Since 1987, Sandra Smith, an Aboriginal genealogist, has worked in the Aboriginal Heritage programme at Museum Victoria, collating and checking these sources of family history and entering them into a genealogical database. The Museum uses this resource to provide a confidential family history service to members of the Victorian Aboriginal community attempting to re-establish family connections. In 1999, an ARC grant enabled the employment of research assistants to collect information from the records of Victorian Aboriginal welfare administration in the Australian archives, as well as other historical sources, and to incorporate them into the Museum's genealogical database. Funds from the ARC grant covered the cost of accessing the birth, death and marriage certificates of individuals in the reconstituted genealogies, and permitting the information in the genealogies to be checked. Other documentary sources – such as police, court and prison records – served to validate and enrich the genealogical data.

The grant also funded the creation of the Koori History Research Database (KHRD) by Joanne Evans and Gavan McCarthy of the eScholarship Research Centre at Melbourne, who used their own software. The KHRD takes family data from the genealogical database, disaggregates it into individual records, reconciles multiple references to individuals, and incorporates them in a normalised relational database. This database is flexible, fully searchable for both individuals and families, largely free of duplications, and exportable into statistical databases for epidemiological and demographic analysis. The material from the Barwick archive, particularly the genealogies and census lists of individuals, will be consulted in depth as a final source for the genealogical and historical data collated in the KHRD. When she died, Barwick was still reconstructing the ancestral Aboriginal population based on her genealogies. The availability of the KHRD database and the indexing of Barwick's archive allow us finally to finish her work.

Reconstituting Victoria

In combination with the historical statistical sources, the quantitative evidence from this study's analysis of the population reconstituted from the genealogies brings clarity to two central aspects of Victorian Aboriginal population history: the colonial decline, and the disappearance and re-emergence of the invisible Aborigines. Figure 1.3, which compares the population reconstituted from the genealogies with the numbers derived from the colonial and Protection Board censuses, has two striking features, one of them expected and the other a complete surprise. The first is the direct, unprecedented documentation of the size and evolution of the invisible Aboriginal. The second is the fact that the current Victorian Aboriginal population seems to be descended from the approximately 500 individuals collected on the Board's reserves in the 1870s. The other 500 to 1,000 people recorded by the Board and the colonial census as living outside the reserves appear to have left scarcely any descendants except a handful of families who, significantly, had some land of their own. Even they were in contact with the Board and in receipt of assistance from time to time. Eventually, some of these families married back into the Aboriginal community under the Board's control (Broome 2005: 156–65)

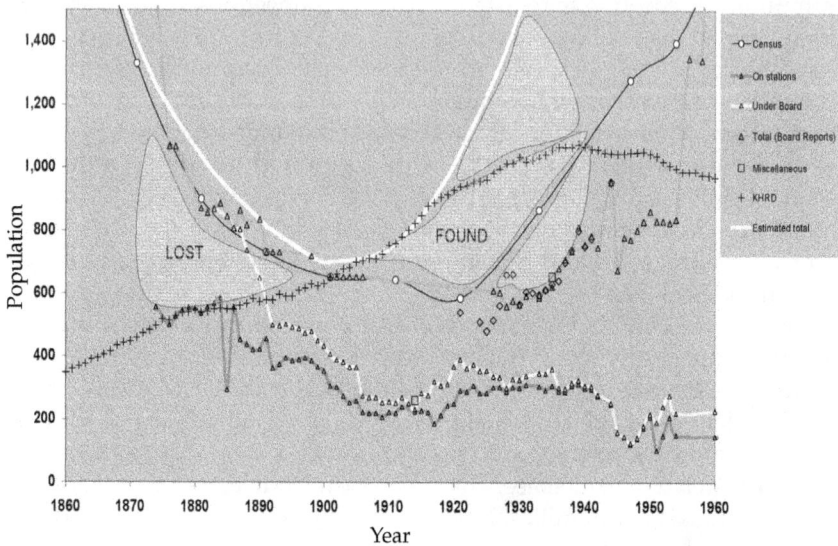

Figure 1.3 Evidence from KHRD of the Movement of Victoria's Aborigines into and out of the Census and Protection Board Populations

The Emergence of the Invisible Aborigines from the Shadows

Smith has argued that only the existence of a substantial group of invisible Aborigines, excluded from the Aboriginal population until the abandonment of assimilation policies, could explain the rapid growth in the census population since the 1960s (Smith 1980). He further argued that the size of the gap between the population before and after the period in which the policy flourished – as revealed by past census and Board statistics and the hypothetical population ancestral to the current census Aboriginal population – implied that the invisible Aborigines must have diverged from the known Aborigines a long time ago. The KHRD data now provide the first explicit evidence that Smith was correct: in Victoria, the census population began to fall below the population ancestral to today's Aborigines in the 1890s, during the era of forced assimilation, and the gap widened as more and more people of mixed descent joined the invisible group. The KHRD also reveals that the population reached its lowest level of about 900 in the 1890s, rather than the low point of fewer than 600 in 1921 indicated by the census. Twice as many appear to have become statistically invisible by that time.

Smith's analysis was based on the 1971 census, which enumerated fewer than 6,000 Aborigines in Victoria. Given that the Aboriginal population in 2001 stood at about 30,000, the emergence of previously invisible people has clearly continued apace. Unfortunately, the KHRD becomes progressively less complete after 1921. Although it includes all known deaths, because it excludes births from 1921 (records of which are not available to the public), the process of rejoining the enumerated population cannot be documented in detail. That it occurred is certain, however, as witnessed by the explosive growth of the Aboriginal population since 1966.

From the 1880s to the 1950s, when the Victorian authorities continued to promote the policy and mythology of absorption, striving to keep the recognised population to an absolute minimum, the reservoir of invisible Aborigines was growing at the rate of about 3 per cent a year. As Figure 1.3 shows, the agreement between the Board's figures and the censuses between 1891 and 1921 indicates that the great number of 'part-Aborigines' that the KHRD reveals to have been excluded from the Board's figures were also excluded from the census; they were either not enumerated or, more likely, they were not identified as Aborigines – by themselves or by the census enumerators. Since the Board's figures remain well below the census figures from 1921 to 1954, clearly not all people of mixed descent accepted the Board's dictum that they were not Aborigines, at least not on the census form. Even without the births, the KHRD population remains substantially higher than either the censuses or the Board's figures during this period.

The effect of government race policy on the figures is particularly striking when the McLean Commission marked the end of assimilation policy in 1957. Once Victoria's substantial Aboriginal population gained official recognition, and the government came to accept responsibility for all persons of Aboriginal descent, both the census and Board figures showed an immediate, dramatic climb. Just as the Board's estimates led the way down, they also led the way up, and the census quickly followed. Between 1954 and 1971, the census population and the Board's figures more than quadrupled; the number enumerated at the census continued to grow at almost 20 per cent a year until 1961. The Board's estimates were based on complete records of all Aboriginal families and they represented nearly complete counts of the total number of persons who acknowledged Aboriginal descent (McLean 1956/7; Felton 1981).

The Colonial Decline

The population reconstructed from the genealogies also adds to information about the colonial decline. These painstaking forward and backward-looking genealogies are highly unlikely to have omitted substantial numbers of people. Yet, surprisingly, if the genealogies are correct, the entire current population of Aboriginal Victorians is descended from that half of the population that the Board collected at its stations in 1863.

What happened to the other half of the population that appears to have left no descendants at all? Who were they? The obvious interpretation is that, not being under the Board's protection, they were killed by settlers or they

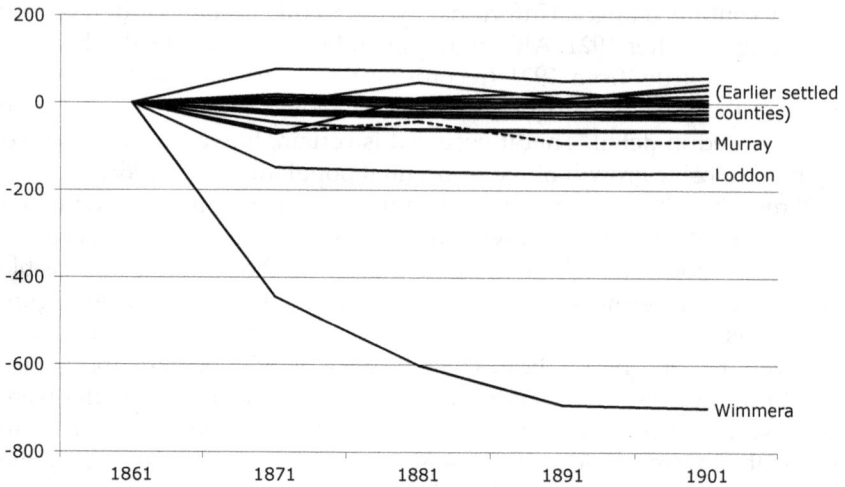

Figure 1.4 Changes in Aboriginal Population in Counties, Censuses 1861 to 1901

died because they lost access to their traditional economic resources. Critchett (1990), Clark (1995) and Elder (2003), among others, have documented the extent to which these outcomes occurred in Gippsland and the Western District. But the people who left no descendants could also have been the parents or childless siblings of Aborigines under the Board's protection, or they might have been beyond the Board's reach precisely because they were unmarried, childless, or without living relatives.

Partial answers to these questions appear in the rich colonial censuses, which from 1856 include counts of the Aboriginal population. Every census contains extremely detailed information on the geographical distribution of the population. Preliminary examination of the populations by land divisions in the censuses from 1861 to 1901 – aggregating divisions as necessary to obtain a consistent time series – reveals that the people outside the Board's protection who left no descendants were not the scattered parents or childless relatives of those protected by the Board (see Figure 1.4). Rather, they were whole populations in the frontier regions – particularly in the Wimmera, the last-settled part of the colony. Within three decades, they had disappeared from the administrative record. Whether they died out entirely or were absorbed into other Aboriginal communities across colonial and state borders remains an open question.

Conclusion

The population reconstitution outlined above resolves longstanding uncertainties about the fate of Aboriginal people in Victoria in the colonial and postcolonial era. The findings would not have been possible without the integration of genealogically based family reconstitutions and official census returns. The reconstitution confirms that the resurgence of Aboriginal Victoria during the late twentieth century was the result of the rejection of fractional identity and invisibility by Aboriginal people themselves. They had never disappeared; they had been rendered invisible only by legislative fiat. The other, more startling, finding – that the surviving population is descended almost entirely from those under the protection of the colonial state – invites a revision of the historiography of reserves and Aboriginal protection, at least in Victoria. After the completion of white settlement, the protective legislation and the structures that it generated undoubtedly became instruments of oppression and control. One interpretation of the findings herein might be that during the frontier period, the Protection Board played a benevolent, protective role more in keeping with their name. Nonetheless, the fact that the Board extended protection to the remnants of the population only after their lands had been taken and settlement had been consolidated may well indicate that it was simply another agent of dispossession.

Notes

1. The research in this article was funded by the Australian Research Council and supported by the Museum of Victoria. We also thank Nicholas Knight and Kate Naughton for data entry and the Registrar of Births, Deaths and Marriages, Victoria, for access to the records.

References

Anderson, W. 2002. *The Cultivation of Whiteness: Science, Health and Racial Destiny in Australia.* Melbourne: Melbourne University Press.

Barwick, D. 1963. 'A Little More Than Kin: Regional Affiliation and Group Identity among Aboriginal Migrants in Melbourne', Ph.D. dissertation. Canberra: Australian National University.

——— 1971. 'Changes in the Aboriginal Population of Victoria, 1863–1966', in D.J. Mulvaney and J. Golson (eds), *Aboriginal Man and Environment in Australia.* Canberra: Australian National University Press, pp. 288–315.

Briscoe, G., and L.R. Smith (eds). 2002. *The Aboriginal Population Revisited: 70,000 Years to the Present.* Canberra: Aboriginal History Monographs.

Broome, R. 2005. *Aboriginal Victorians: A History since 1800.* Sydney: Allen and Unwin.

Burgmann, V. 2003. *Power, Profit and Protest: Australian Social Movements and Globalisation.* Sydney: Allen and Unwin.

Butlin, N.G. 1983. *Our Original Aggression.* Sydney: Allen and Unwin.

Campbell, J. 2002. *Invisible Invaders: Smallpox and Other Diseases in Aboriginal Australia, 1780–1880.* Melbourne: Melbourne University Press.

Clark, I.D. 1995. *Scars in the Landscape A Register of Massacre Sites in Western Victoria, 1803–1859.* Canberra: Aboriginal Studies Press.

Critchett, J. 1990. *A Distant Field of Murder: Western District Frontiers, 1834–1848*. Melbourne: Melbourne University Press.

Curr, E.M. 1883. *Recollections of Squatting in Victoria, Then Called the Port Phillip District (from 1841–1851)*. Melbourne: George Robertson.

Davison, G. 1978. *The Rise and Fall of Marvellous Melbourne*. Melbourne: Melbourne University Press.

——— 2001. 'Gold–rush Melbourne', in I.D. McCalman, A. Cook and A. Reeves (eds), *Gold: Forgotten Histories and Lost Objects of Australia*. New York: Oxford University Press, pp. 52–66.

Elder, B. 2003: *Blood on the Wattle: Massacres and Maltreatments of Aboriginal Australians since 1788*. French's Forest, NSW: New Holland.

Ellinghaus, K. 2002. 'Taking Assimilation to Heart: Marriages of White Women and Indigenous Men in Australia and North America, 1870s–1930s,' Ph.D. dissertation. Melbourne: University of Melbourne.

Eyler, J.M. 1979. *Victorian Social Medicine: The Ideas and Methods of William Farr*. Baltimore, MD: Johns Hopkins University Press.

Felton, P. 1981, 'No Reliable Records', M.A. thesis. Sydney: University of Sydney.

Hopper, J. 1986. 'The Contribution of W.H. Archer to Vital Statistics in the Colony of Victoria', *Australian Journal of Statistics* 28: 124–37.

Larson, A. 1994. *Growing Up in Melbourne: Family Life in the Late Nineteenth Century*: Canberra: Demography Programme, Australian National University.

Lourandos, H. 1997. *Continent of Hunter–gatherers: New Perspectives in Australian Prehistory*. Cambridge: Cambridge University Press.

Macintyre S.F., and A. Clark. 2003. *The History Wars*. Melbourne: Melbourne University Press.

McLean, C. 1956/7. 'Report upon the Operation of the Aborigines Act 1928 and the Regulations and Orders Made Thereunder'. Victorian Parliamentary Papers, No. 18. Melbourne: Government Printer.

Manne, R. (ed). 2003. *Whitewash: On Keith Windschuttle's Fabrication of Aboriginal History*. Melbourne: Black Inc.

Mulvaney, D.J. 2002. 'Difficult to Found an Opinion: 1788 Population Estimates', in G. Briscoe and L. Smith (eds), *The Aboriginal Population Revisited: 70,000 Years to the Present*. Canberra: Aboriginal History Monographs, pp. 1–8.

Pepper, P., and T. De Araugo. 1985. *The Kurnai of Gippsland*. Melbourne: Hyland House.

Serle, G. 1977. *The Golden Age: A History of the Colony of Victoria 1851–1861*. Melbourne: Melbourne University Press.

Smith, L.R. 2002. 'How Many People Had Lived in Australia Before it Was Annexed by the English in 1788?', in G. Briscoe and L. Smith (eds), *The Aboriginal Population Revisited: 70,000 Years to the Present*. Canberra: Aboriginal History Monographs, pp. 9–15.

————— 1980. *The Aboriginal Population of Australia*. Canberra: Australian National University Press.

Smyth, R.B. 1878. *The Aborigines of Victoria: With Notes Relating to the Habits of the Natives of Other Parts of Australia and Tasmania*. Melbourne: Government Printer.

Victoria Parliament. 1859. 'Select Committee on the Aborigines: Report'. Melbourne: Government Printer.

————— 1889. 'Report of the Board for the Protection of Aborigines'. Government Printer.

Webb, S. 1984. 'Intensification, Population and Social Changes in South-eastern Victoria: The Skeletal Evidence', *Aboriginal History* 8: 154–72.

————— 1995. *Palaeopathology of Aboriginal Australians: Health and Disease across a Hunter–gatherer Continent*. Melbourne: Cambridge University Press.

Windschuttle, K. 2002. *The Fabrication of Aboriginal History, I: Van Diemen's Land 1803–1847*. Paddington, NSW: Macleay Press.

2

BUILDING ETHNIC BOUNDARIES IN NEW ZEALAND: REPRESENTATIONS OF MAORI IDENTITY IN THE CENSUS

Tahu Kukutai

Introduction

Defining ethnic boundaries for official purposes is an inherently political task, but one deemed necessary in many multiethnic states.[1] The definition of indigenous identity for official purposes is especially contentious, given the intrinsic link between indigeneity, and claims to territory and self-determination.[2] Although indigenous rights may be enshrined constitutionally or by treaty, the matter of who qualifies as indigenous for state recognition and reward is largely determined by bureaucratic rules and classifications. Official demographic sources, and the national census in particular, are important forums where indigenous identities are constructed and circumscribed. As the flagship of enumeration, the census is an influential site of inclusion and exclusion where the state selectively acknowledges collective identities within its borders. For this reason, among others, the census is deeply implicated in a nation's social and political order (Hochschild and Powell 2008). To understand how official enumeration practices reflect and constitute indigenous identities, this chapter focuses on the census in New Zealand – home to the indigenous Maori. Like other national contexts examined in this book, New Zealand has particular features that make it fruitful for an exploration of indigeneity.

Among the white-settler states of North America and Oceania, New Zealand alone possesses an indigenous 'majority' minority.[3] Indeed, for much of the nation's history, Maori were the only demographically significant ethnic minority in an otherwise Anglo-dominant society. Consequently, the development of ethnic classification and enumeration in New Zealand has been heavily influenced by efforts to count Maori, a legacy that still endures. This chapter traces the varied ways in which Maori identities have been defined and circumscribed vis-à-vis the census, and describes some of the conflicting imperatives that underpinned those efforts. In addition to providing an historical analysis of state enumeration strategies, I also address contemporary issues associated with counting Maori. One recurring issue is whether there ought to be a single statistical definition of who is Maori, or what constitutes the Maori population (Pool 1991; Kukutai 2004; Durie 2005). The census presently collects data on Maori ethnicity, descent and tribal affiliation; statutory definitions of Maori are based on descent; and *iwi* (tribes) define membership on the basis of *whakapapa* (genealogical ties). The differences are not merely conceptual. As I show, different criteria yield Maori groups of different sizes and socio-demographic characteristics, with the potential to generate substantively different conclusions about Maori demographic, socio-economic and cultural characteristics. This is important because the use of ethnic statistics in policy formulation and statutory contexts has symbolic and material consequences.

To that end, the Maori example illustrates the perspective, widely accepted within the social sciences, that identity categories and the groups they seek to describe, are neither natural nor objective, but are historical and political constructions (Nobles 2000; Kertzer and Arel 2002; Rallu, Piché and Simon 2006). Moreover, when deployed for official purposes, these constructions often reflect prevailing race logics and state imperatives, at odds with the criteria that groups use to define themselves (Morning and Sabbagh 2005). To better appreciate these points, a brief discussion of sociological perspectives on ethnic boundaries and categorising practices follows.

Boundary Building in Official Statistics

The sociological understanding of ethnic boundaries owes much to the seminal work of Fredrik Barth (1969). Ethnic boundaries may be understood as cognitive frameworks that individuals use, often unconsciously, to make distinctions between 'us' and 'them'. These frameworks are built from abstract rules, norms and beliefs, but are given institutional form through legal and political action. Barth's observations that ethnic groups lack an objective basis, and that boundaries tend to endure in spite of extensive interactions across them, have been influential in shaping accounts of ethnic processes (e.g., Gans 1979; Alba and Nee 2003). More recently, scholars have moved beyond Barth's largely individualist account of boundary building to examine the role of institutions – and especially the state – in forging, preserving and dismantling ethnic boundaries (e.g., Nagel 1994; Cornell and Hartmann 1998; Hochschild and Powell 2008).

One of the ways the state creates and sustains ethnic boundaries is through the use of official ethnic categories and schemas. As Nagel notes, 'Ethnic boundaries determine who is a member and who is not and designate which ethnic categories are available for individual identification at a particular time and place' (Nagel 1994: 154). Ethnic categories not only enable the statistical depiction of collective identities, but also portray a particular vision of social reality that often privileges the discourses of the dominant group. Historically, there are many examples of official data used to portray indigenous peoples in ways that supported colonial narratives. Popular accounts include the inexorable demographic decline of native peoples, and their transformation of heathen tribesman into docile, civilised subjects (see below). Statistical classifications of indigenous peoples have also worked in tandem with legal and other bureaucratic definitions, the latter often devised to delimit group membership through the imposition of prescriptive criteria (Snipp 1997; Kauanui 2005). In the mainland United States, for example, government bureaucracies implemented 'blood' measures to determine which individuals qualified as tribal members with access to targeted 'Indian' resources. Blood racialisation has been similarly used in Hawaii where, in order to qualify for a homestead lease from the Department of Hawaiian Homelands, individuals have to 'prove' that they have at least a 50 per cent Hawaiian blood quantum (Kukutai 2004). By codifying indigeneity in prescriptive ways, legal and other bureaucratic conceptualisations of race have served to provide a material basis to otherwise abstract schemas. In New Zealand, blood quantum has been employed in statistical and legal definitions of Maori, but has its own unique contours. These are discussed in the following account of how Maori identities have been represented in the census.

Maori in the New Zealand Census: Quantifying the Quantum Maori

Maori are New Zealand's indigenous people and first settlers. Archaeological evidence suggests that the ancestors of present day Maori voyaged in several disparate waves from south-east Asia, via eastern Polynesia, finally settling in New Zealand sometime in the late 13th century (Howe 2003). Foreign whalers and traders were present from the late eighteenth century, but systematic settlement did not begin until after the Treaty of Waitangi – signed between Maori chiefs and representatives of the British Crown in 1840.[4] The vast majority of 'European'[5] migrants originated from the British Isles, which begat a settler populace one historian has described as 'better Britons' (Belich 1996).

Maori were quantified and qualified from the earliest days of the colony. Today the term Maori, meaning 'normal' or 'ordinary', is used unreflectively, obscuring the fact that Maori, like 'American Indian' and 'Australian Aboriginal', is a modern appellation borne from the expediencies of cross-cultural contact. Prior to the arrival of Europeans in New Zealand, indigenous identities were founded on genealogical ties, which connected the individual to an eponymous ancestor or ancestors via the kinship network of *whanau* (family), *hapu* (sub-tribe) and tribe (Brougton 1993).

Given the centrality of kinship to New Zealand's indigenous inhabitants, tribal references were curiously absent from the first official enumeration of Maori taken between 1857 and 1858. Instead, the published report reveals an attempt to describe a corporate supra-tribal identity, with the terms Maori, Native and Aboriginal used interchangeably (Fenton 1859). Enumeration was more intuitively structured around tribal membership in the 1874 national census, but with some limitations. Inter-tribal partnering meant most Maori were linked to various tribes through genealogical ties, yet individuals were only enumerated as members of the tribe with which they resided. Though enumerating individuals by tribal residence made logistical sense, it also reflected official interest in monitoring the growth and mobility of tribes following violent clashes with government forces during the 1860s. Ongoing tensions throughout the nineteenth century meant many Maori viewed census taking with some suspicion, with 'rebel' tribes especially resistant to enumeration (e.g., Registrar General 1892: 118). After the 1901 census, the collection of tribal data was abandoned until its resurrection nearly a century later.

Individuals of mixed Maori–European 'blood' were documented in the census from the outset. Initially, blood was expressed through the 'half-caste' label,[6] employed to describe the progeny of Maori and European unions. The designation was not a state invention – the historical record shows it was already in colloquial usage well before 1874 – but appropriation by public officials granted it substantial scientific and ideological legitimacy. In addition to distinguishing half-castes from 'full-bloods', further boundaries were drawn between half-castes who lived as Maori, and those who lived as European. At the time it was not entirely clear how this determination was to be made,[7] although a critical factor appeared to be residence in a separate nuclear household, versus the traditional communal setting of the *pa* (Maori village). As Maori were separately enumerated from the rest of the population until 1951, the distinction based on mode of living fitted the collection strategy.[8] Maori and half-castes living as members of tribes were excluded from the *Census Act 1877* and, for half a century thereafter, were excluded from published figures on the 'general' population.[9] Like half-castes, Maori wives of European men were also distinguished from 'pure-bred' Maori. These women were counted as part of the Maori population, even though many were enumerated with their husbands, using the same schedule and enumerators. Interestingly, none of the census reports contain data on Maori husbands of European wives, though it defies belief that no such pairings existed.

Despite the biological language of blood and the undeniable 'colour consciousness' of Europeans (Ballara 1986), phenotypical distinctions were absent from statistical determinations of race. The published reports of sub-enumerators make no reference to the use of skin colour, or other sorts of phenotypical traits, to differentiate Maori from European half-castes. Legal determinations were similarly indifferent to physical markers of

race. Under the *Native Land Amendment Act 1912*, a 'Native' could volun-
tarily apply to be declared European, so long as he or she possessed pro-
ficiency in the English language, had obtained a specified minimum level
of education, and had the means of deriving a sufficient income (Meredith
2006).[10] The possession of European blood as a necessary but insufficient
condition for Europeanisation reflected colonial policies of assimilation,
which viewed racial and cultural amalgamation as complementary, if not
synonymous, processes. From a policy perspective, the principal consideration was the adoption of idealised European preferences and behaviours,
rather than looking like a European (Ward 1973).[11] The latter was probably
a moot point, given the implicit assumption, evident in census reports,
that the collective 'whitening' of Maori would inevitably occur through
intermarriage and assimilation processes.

Indeed, census reports reveal how colonial identity categories were underpinned by racial reasoning that could be both fluid and contradictory.
Belich (2001) has identified three dominant strands of race thinking in Victorian New Zealand, centred on stereotypes of 'Black' (permanently inferior), 'White' (convertible), and 'Grey' (dying) savages. Reports from the
late nineteenth and early twentieth century were peppered with observations of Maori shortcomings, but their inferiority as a people was neither
irredeemable, nor permanent. To the contrary: Maori – and half-castes in
particular – were generally portrayed as worthy candidates for Europeanisation, and trumpeted as a superior type of native (Ward 1973; Belich
1996). According to Sorrenson (1975), this faith in Maori adaptability was
a central reason for the continued existence of assimilation as the dominant form of native policy, long after other colonies had abandoned it for
segregation and reserve-land policies. Not only were half-castes symboli-
cally important in state narratives proclaiming the virtues of assimilation,
they also played a central role in the account of Maori demise. Initially
this was expected to occur as a consequence of European disease and vices
(Newman 1881; Belich 1996); and then through biological absorption. As
the Under Secretary of Native Affairs observed in 1906: 'It is an idea of
many people that the ultimate fate of the Maori race is to become absorbed
in the European. Whether any tendency is shown in this direction must
be gathered from the increase or decrease in the number of half-castes'
(Registrar General 1907: lv).

Over time, blood quantum was extended from half-caste to embody
a dazzling array of racial designations. The 1926 Maori census form instructed respondents: 'If of full blood write "Maori," if not, write "Half-
caste," "Three-quarter-caste," &c., as the case may be' (Statistics New Zealand 2006). The question was extended to the general population a decade
later, with successive census reports documenting increasingly detailed
mixes. A survey on racial 'miscegenation' in the 1951 census reveals how
embedded the system of blood racialisation had become, with tabulations
on mixed race children spanning Maori full bloods, to those deemed one-

eighth Maori and seven-eighths European. The admission by census takers that blood measures lacked scientific validity, and its rejection as a method of racial enumeration elsewhere, make its lasting appeal in New Zealand appear anachronistic (see Census and Statistical Office 1927, vi: 1).[12] The link between blood quantum and racism meant sustained efforts to racially quantify Maori also risked undermining the government's claim of exemplary Maori–European race relations. It begs the question: Why was blood quantum so embedded in New Zealand's census?

One possible explanation rests with its raison d'être and usage. In the United States and South Africa, blood measures were explicitly used within a legal framework devised to sustain a grossly unequal racial order. In New Zealand, the statistical deployment of blood quantum reflected its usage in legal definitions of Maori, but was not tied to an explicit system of discrimination.[13] For the most part, blood quantum was largely used to incorporate rather than exclude Maori, albeit that incorporation was assumed to occur on European terms, and to the latter's advantage.[14] Nevertheless, by decoupling blood quantum from overt discrimination, its statistical usage could be posited as a socially meaningful (albeit, scientifically dubious), system of tracking racial boundaries and Maori 'progress' toward the European norm.

Although blood quantum was not used to overtly discriminate against Maori, restrictive measures aimed at non-European 'race aliens' included some by default. From 1916 to 1951 the 'race alien' designation was used to categorise individuals with any degree of non-European blood. The term was tied to legislation that aimed to restrict the entry of 'coloured' migrants, particularly Chinese, but included individuals with Maori and/or European blood within its definition.[15] This leads to the anomalous practice of designating Maori-Europeans as Maori or European; but applying a 'one drop' rule to Maori with racial heritage other than European. Although their number was few – the 1926 report on race aliens listed nine Indian-Maori, nine Japanese-Maori, and thirty-nine Polynesian-Maori – the fact of their enumeration indicates the bureaucratic preoccupation with tracking inter-racial mixing. It also reveals a double standard towards minorities: official discourse may have welcomed the racial amalgamation of Maori and European, but miscegenation with race aliens was to be studiously avoided. This sentiment was evident in the 1921 census report, which noted the importance of racial purity in New Zealand, and warned that the coalescence of the white and coloured races was 'not conducive to improvement in racial types' (Census and Statistical Office 1923, vi).[16]

The statistical treatment of race aliens underscores how racial boundaries in the census could be manipulated to meet state imperatives. Consequently, classifications frequently appeared to be ad hoc and arbitrary. In 1916, for example, Maori-European half-castes living as Europeans were included 'somewhat diffidently' with race aliens (Census and Statisticsal Office 1923). From 1926, following the abandonment of the mode of living distinction, all half-caste Maori-Europeans were counted solely in the Maori population. After the term 'other races' replaced race alien in 1956, Maori with non-European heritage were subjected to the usual half or more rule, except when the non-European race was Polynesian. Individuals with Maori and any degree of Polynesian heritage were counted only in the Maori population until the 1966 census, reflecting the assumption of a common pan-Polynesian culture (Department of Statistics 1967, vii). Those charged with the task of navigating these complex rules were not immune to its vagaries, with sub-enumerators' reports expressing frustration with the somewhat arbitrary nature of the rules they worked with.

By recognising the social fact of miscegenation, official classifications in New Zealand had the potential to legitimate the blurring of racial boundaries. However, this potential was never fully realised because various rules were applied to interpret blood quantum in ways that solidified, rather than transcended, the notion of separate races. Though individuals were enumerated as multiracial, and their number listed in published reports, statistical rules were used to allocate them back to mutually exclusive race groups. Consequently the bifurcated paradigm of Maori and European races remained intact, despite the explicit recognition of mixed race individuals. The motivation to fit people into discrete groupings was informed not just by racial reasoning but also the pragmatic concerns of bureaucrats. As Hochschild and Powell note, racial taxonomies in national censuses are subject to multiple influences including the dominant group's racial ideology, state disciplinary control, and bureaucratic conservatism (Hochschild and Powell 2008: 65). In the case of Maori-Europeans, allocating individuals to one group simplified the data in ways that permitted comparisons between groups for policy and political purposes. This was not a 'problem' unique to the time. The issue of how to count people who transcend the 'tick one box' paradigm of ethnic enumeration continues to challenge modern statistics agencies (Callister, Didham and Potter 2005; Morning and Sabbagh 2005).

Given these complexities, the question arises of how Maori responded to official efforts to quantify their identities. Unfortunately, little has been written about this issue, and it is one of the gaps deserving of further inquiry. That being noted, the pattern of responses to blood quantum, and the insights of ethnographic work, suggest many Maori did not interpret the blood quantum measure in the way that officials intended.[17] Many more people identified themselves as Maori full-bloods than was biologically possible, given historic levels of Maori–European coupling.[18] Rather than compute complex fractions, individuals with Maori heritage appeared to respond on the basis of cultural identification (Metge 1964), or gave only a rough approximation of blood (Census and Statistical Office 1946, viii: iv).

From the 1960s onwards, as Maori cultural revitalisation and political activism gained momentum, Maori organisations became more vocal in their criticism of quantum measures as offensive and burdensome to complete (Statistics New Zealand 1999). The impetus to change the statistical designation came with the *Maori Affairs Amendment Act 1974* that effectively removed blood requirements from statutory definitions. In 1976 the underlying concept in the census was changed from race to ethnic origin, and a decade later all references to fractions were abandoned, paving the way for a new era of ethnic enumeration.

Multiplying the Dimensions of Maori Identity in the Modern Census

In the last fifteen years there have been major changes to how Maori identity has been treated in the census. This can be seen in Table 2.1, which documents the changing concepts, definitions and classifications used to statistically define Maori. The key change has been the replacement of a system based on racial origins with one employing ethnic group identification. Statistics New Zealand defines an ethnic group as people who have some or all of the following characteristics: a common proper name; one of more elements of a common culture which need not be specified, but may include religion, customs, or languages; unique community of interests, feelings and actions; a shared sense of common origins or ancestry, and a common geographic origin (Statistics New Zealand 2004).

Table 2.1. Changes in Statistical Concepts, Definitions and Classifications of Maori

Census	Basic Concept	Measurement	Definition of Maori
Up to 1921[a]	Race	Degree of blood	Maori race: Person of more than 1/2 Maori blood; half-caste living as a Maori
			Maori descent: Person of any degree of Maori blood.
1926–1971[b]	Race	Degree of blood	Maori race: Person of 1/2 or more Maori blood.
			Maori descent: Person of any degree of Maori blood.

1976	Ethnic origin	Degree of ethnic origin	Maori ethnic origin: Person of 1/2 or more Maori ethnic origin; person of Maori race or a descendant with unspecified degree of Maori ethnic origin.
	Race or descent	Race or descent	Maori descent: Person of any degree of Maori ethnic origin; person of Maori race or a descendant with unspecified degree of Maori ethnic origin.
1981	Ethnic origin	Degree of origin	Maori ethnic origin: Person of 1/2 or more Maori ethnic origin.
			Maori descent: Person of any degree of Maori ethnic origin.
1986	Ethnic origin	Ethnic origin	Solely Maori ethnic origin: Person of Maori ethnic origin alone.
			Maori ethnic origin or descent: Person of Maori ethnic origin, either alone or in combination
1991–2006	Ethnic group	Ethnic group	Maori Ethnic Group: Person who specified Maori as the sole ethnic group or as one of several ethnic groups.
	Descent	Descent	Maori descent: Person who specified descent from a Maori.
	Tribe	Tribal affiliation	Tribal member: Person who specified a tribal name.

Notes: (a) Excluded Maori with non-European blood, 1916–1951; (b) Included Maori with any degree of Polynesian blood, 1956–1966

Although the definition refers to common origins, the reference to 'shared sense' averts a rigid conception of concrete, historically determined ties. The subjective basis of ethnicity is reinforced in the census help notes that direct respondents to answer on the basis of the 'ethnic group or groups (cultural groups) you belong to or identify with'. This fits with the egalitarian notion of 'ethnic options' (Waters 1990), and marks a significant departure from the negative connotations associated with the nomenclature of blood and race. In 1991 a question on Maori descent was introduced to meet legal require- ments for determining electoral representation and, for the first time since 1901, a question on tribal affiliation was included.[19]

These shifts in the representation of Maori identity grew out of dramat- ic political changes in New Zealand that reflected those occurring in many other western, multicultural states, in response to civil rights movements and the proliferation of 'new social movements', including indigenous rights. Maori political activism was critical in forcing the shift from as- similation and integration policies to those supporting Maori cultural and political rights. During the late 1980s and throughout the 1990s, official discourses emphasised biculturalism, and the notion of Maori and Euro- pean as parallel, equal cultures. The reinstatement of tribal enumeration in the census coincided with a process of 'retribalisation', in which tribes emerged as state-mandated corporate actors able to receive and adminis- ter financial settlements from the Crown for historical wrongdoings (Rata 1999). After more than a century of using blood quantum to define Maori, the collection of official statistics endeavoured to be more responsive to minority needs and sensitivities. The apogee was a hierarchical system of post hoc prioritisation devised to allocate individuals who reported multi- ple ethnic groups, into one group. Prioritisation was ostensibly a method- ological tool to simplify the analysis of complex ethnic data, but was also clearly influenced by politics. This was evident in the rationale that the method ought to favour smaller groups that were historically disadvan- taged in statistics, with Maori receiving the largest demographic bonus (Allan 2001).[20] Ethnic boundaries were still being constructed in official statistics – only the motivations and nomenclature had changed.

The Shifting Size of Maori Identity Categories

One of the consequences of including various kinds of Maori markers in the census means several kinds of Maori identity categories can be iden- tified. Drawing on results from the 2006 census, various parameters are shown in Figure 2.1.

The largest and most inclusive group is the Maori descent group. This is the group that meets statutory definitions of Maori based on descent. Only persons of Maori descent can enrol in a Maori electorate, lodge a claim with the Waitangi Tribunal, or apply for certain kinds of educational scholarships. The use of descent is meant to function as an objective filter of group membership but, in practice, proof of descent is rarely required. To date, Maori descent data has not been widely used in research or policy because it is not deemed to be a determinant of social inequality, nor a meaningful measure of identity.[21]

The Maori Ethnic Group (MEG) is the second largest group. It is the reference group used for administrative and policy purposes, and for census tabulations and media releases. Ethnic identification is regarded as a better measure of identity than descent, at least in terms of gauging 'lifestyle, expectations, affiliations, and aspirations' (Durie 2005: 33). Figure 2.1 shows a considerable overlap between Maori descent and Maori ethnic groups – that is, they contain many of the same people. However, the relationship between ethnicity and descent is asymmetrical. Of the 643,977 persons who recorded Maori descent in the 2006 census, about one in five did not record Maori ethnicity. Ethnic identification, however, was closely coupled with acknowledging Maori descent. The vast majority of people who recorded Maori ethnicity, also recorded Maori descent.[22]

The MEG can be further divided into individuals who identify solely as Maori and those who choose it as one of several ethnicities. In 2006, the former constituted just over half of the MEG. Like the reportage of full blood, exclusive Maori ethnic identification does not mean an individual is exclusively Maori in terms of ethnic heritage. Most Maori have a non-Maori (usually European) ancestor, sometimes a non-Maori parent, but only some opt to acknowledge it. Among people of Maori descent, the reportage of exclusive Maori ethnicity would seem to be a subjective expression of ethnic orientation, attachment, and/or attribution by self and others. The lack of an explicit 'mixed' category on the census makes it difficult to know what people mean when they record Maori as one of several ethnic groups. Such people might see themselves as belonging to several different ethnic groups, or it may be an expression of a unique blended identity.

Tribal affiliation provides other criteria with which to construct boundaries. Tribe comes closest to approximating classical Maori conceptions of group membership based on *whakapapa*. Karetu (1990) has described *whakapapa* as the glue that connects individuals to a specific place or places, and locates them within a broader network of kin relations. *Whakapapa* also endows certain rights in terms of land succession and usufruct rights in Maori land. Historically, residence near one's ancestral land was closely tied with *whakapapa*, but urbanisation and labour market transformations means that the majority of Maori now live outside their tribal area (Statistics New Zealand 2002).

From the three criteria of ethnicity, descent and tribal affiliation, a 'core' Maori group can be constructed that comprises people who identify themselves exclusively as Maori by descent, ethnicity and tribe. In 2006, the core numbered 243,642, about one third of the broadest parameter based on descent alone. Group size matters, particularly where it is tied to the

Maori descent (643,977)

Ethnic Maori (565,329)
(Maori only =298,395)

Tribal Maori
(535,233)

Core Maori (exclusive ethnicity, descent, tribe)
(N=243,642)

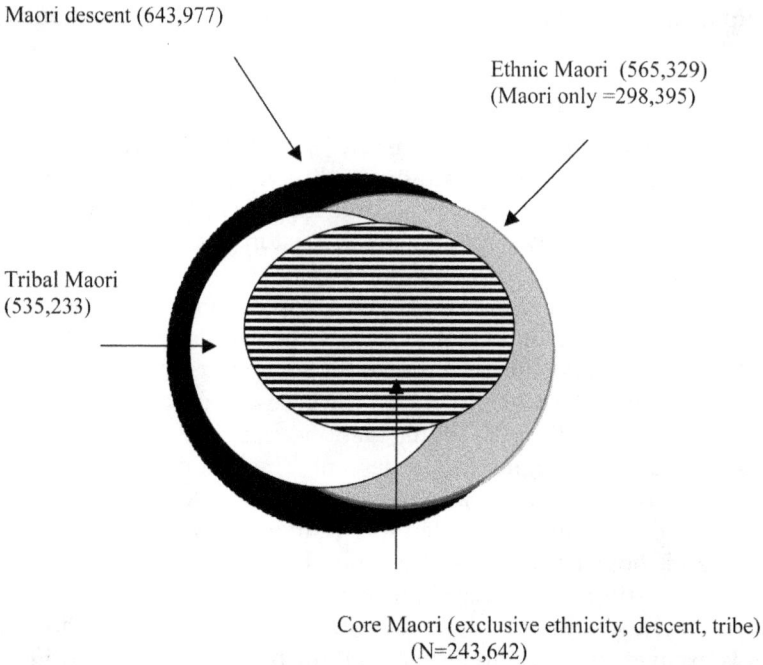

Figure 2.1 Maori Group Parameters, 2006 New Zealand Census of Population and Dwellings

allocation of resources, group rights and constitutional arrangements. But it is not just group size that is influenced by the statistical criteria used to define who is Maori – group characteristics are also affected, a matter to which we now turn.

The Characteristics of Maori Identity Categories

So far this chapter has concentrated on the statistical construction of Maori identity in the census as a form of political boundary-making. Less attention has been paid to the characteristics of the groups that those boundaries enclose. For many scholars, the ethnic content of group boundaries is seen as less important than the factors that motivate or impede processes of ethnic boundary building. Barth (1969), for example, believed documenting collective ethnic traits was ultimately a fruitless exercise given the inherently subjective and unstable nature of ethnicity. Yet, acknowledging the subjective and socially constructed nature of ethnicity and ethnic groups does not render the concept of ethnicity meaningless, nor make it any less 'real' in the social worlds that people inhabit. In New Zealand, the routine collection of ethnic data and its usage in academic and policy analyses means ethnic enumeration has tangible consequences. It is thus important to understand how the criteria used to statistically define Maori not also only influences group size, but also the collective profile in terms of socio-economic, demographic and cultural characteristics..

Much of the research that has employed Maori ethnicity as an independent variable has done so to document or explain ongoing Maori disadvantage in the stratification system. Decades of research have shown that Maori, as well as other Pacific peoples (such as Samoans and Tongans) fare worse on nearly every social and economic indicator than other New Zealanders. On average, Maori are poorer, less educated, less healthy and more economically vulnerable than their European counterparts (Te Puni Kokiri 2000; Kukutai 2004; Callister 2007). However, intra-group differences are also important, with recent research indicating that people who identify exclusively or primarily as ethnic Maori tend to be more disadvantaged than those who have a secondary or mixed Maori ethnic affiliation (Kukutai 2004). These within-group differences are illustrated in the table below which compares the groups shown in Figure 2.1 across several key socio-demographic and cultural indicators. To enable a broad comparative context, a non-Maori category is also included.[23]

Comparing the largest descent group and the smallest core group, obvious differences are apparent across most indicators. However, the most pronounced differences are between two groups of similar size: multi-ethnic and core Maori (see the shaded columns). The former group has a much smaller proportion of members who speak Maori, or who live in areas where Maori are over-represented. It has a younger age structure, and a much more favourable socio-economic profile. Of all the groups, it is closer in characteristics – with the exception of age – to the non-Maori comparator. The opposite is true of the core group. Core Maori are more likely to engage with symbols of Maori ethnicity – such as living among, taking a partner among, and speaking Maori – and have poorer outcomes in terms of employment and education. The close coupling of sole Maori ethnic identification with descent and tribal affiliation accounts for the similar profiles between the overlapping monoethnic and core groups.

The comparison of these groups might lead one to conclude that stronger Maori identity is causally implicated in poorer outcomes. There are several problems, however, with inferring such a relationship from the data in Table 2.2. First, if the purpose of using ethnicity as an independent variable is to capture the effects of ethnic group attachment – or, more specifically, variation in the strength of attachment– one needs to attempt to measure attachment directly at the individual level. Measurement of the latent multi-dimensional construct of individual ethnic identity is substantively different from allocating individuals to groups constructed using basic measures of ethnic identification.[24] Second, ethnic group comparisons imply there is something about group membership that matters, either intrinsically or because of the value or costs attached to group membership in the social system. The categories used here, such as sole

Table 2.2. The Diverse Content of Maori Group Boundaries, 2006 New Zealand Census of Population and Dwellings

Indicator	Maori descent n=643,977	MEG n=565,329	Maori ethnicity alone n=298,395	Multi-ethnic Maori n=266,934	Tribal Maori n=535,233	'Core' Maori n=243,642	Non-Maori n=3,294,834
Median age	23.4	22.7	28.7	17.7	23.9	29.5	38.1
Legal partner[a]	36.8	33.5	19.4	40.5	36.2	31.2	51.7
Has a non-Maori partner[b]	58.9	48.4	36.1	64.9	53.2	35.4	94.1
No formal qualification[c]	40.6	43.4	50.0	33.2	40.2	47.8	22.7
Male unemployment rate[d]	7.8	8.7	10.3	6.5	8.3	10.2	4.4
Can speak Maori[e]	20.6	24.4	34.6	13.0	24.1	36.4	0.1
Lives in TLA with at least 20% ethnic Maori[f]	36.0	38.5	45.6	30.5	38.1	46.4	15.2

Notes on Table 2.2: All age standardised rates use the 2001 Total NZ Population. (a) People aged 20 years and older in a legal marriage, standardised; (b) Restricted to people aged 20 years or older in a partnership; (c) People aged 15 years and older, standardised; (d) Men aged 15 – 64 years, standardised; (e) All ages; (f) Territorial Land Authority is a standard geographic unit used in analysis.

Maori, mixed Maori and core Maori, are statistical creations based on aggregated individual-level data, rather than 'real world' concrete groups. Third, causal pathways cannot be determined by bivariate analysis – other factors associated with ethnicity may explain why individuals in the core Maori group appear to be more disadvantaged.

Nevertheless, the comparisons point to several problems of undertaking ethnic analysis based on census categories and aggregations derived from them. Though their usage might be helpful for providing macro-level insights, it also runs the risk of reifying categories, and concealing variation within those categories. The construction of ethnic groups in official statistics, and comparisons between them, are ultimately constrained by the categories used to describe them, and such categories are inevitably historically contingent and politically conceived.

Maori: A Single Definition?

An issue that has arisen in recent years is whether it is desirable or even possible to institute a standard definition of Maori for use across legal, statistical and bureaucratic contexts. Policy makers generally agree ethnic definitions and classifications should reflect the views of those to whom they are applied. This implies that concrete groups exist independently of ethnic categories, and that consensus exists within them about what the critical makers of identity are. Among Maori, at least, there is a wide range of views on what makes a person Maori and what distinguishes Maori as a people. These range from somewhat exclusive notions based on meaningful participation in Maori networks and cultural and linguistic competence, to simply having a Maori ancestor.

Like Barth (1969), I hold that there is no essential ethnic core, or objective ethnic group boundary. The Maori ethnic (or descent, or tribal) group is not a timeless, fixed entity characterised by immutable, inherited traditions. However, in many societies it is the belief in ethnicity (or race, or culture), both self-perceived and ascribed by others, that makes it real, irrespective of its subjective foundations. Given problems of subjectivity, and the heterogeneity shown in Table 2.2, it is clear that the question of how to define who is Maori for official purposes is a difficult one. One approach might be to define an inclusive boundary, and then use other markers of Maori identity to examine heterogeneity within that boundary. As Kaufmann (2000) has argued, all groups hold ideas about their symbolic boundary, and symbolic core. The symbolic boundary is the most inclusive parameter, and is typically delimited by the idea of putative descent in the form of race or ancestry. By contrast, the symbolic core comprises the group's 'ethnic mythomoteur' – for example, symbols, myths, images and so on – which represents the group's ideal type and thus tends towards exclusivity (ibid.: 1106).

For Maori, *whakapapa* is an important boundary symbol and manifests loosely as Maori descent, and more exclusively as tribal affiliation. Tribal affiliation, though important for many Maori, is not accessible to all. One outcome of the very rapid urbanisation of Maori from the 1950s was the fragmentation of rurally based tribal networks. It is questionable whether detribalised Maori should be defined out of the Maori population because of these historical forces. However, when tribes define their own constituencies, it makes sense that *whakapapa* is used. This is the case with tribal registers, which typically require applicants to furnish details of their *whakapapa* ties to the tribe, typically by naming two generations of ancestors, and their sub-tribal or *marae* (communal meeting place) affiliations. Ethnicity is the criteria currently used in the majority of statistical and policy formulations affecting Maori. But, for reasons noted above, there is a strong case for amending existing statistical and statutory definitions of Maori to reflect both ancestry and ethnicity.

Some have questioned whether identities, including those based on indigeneity, should receive political recognition, particularly where substantial resources are at stake. It is beyond the scope of this chapter to advance arguments for or against ethnic enumeration. Rather, where ethnic and, more specifically, indigenous identities are counted, the more important task is to interrogate the basis upon which different categories of indigeneity have been constructed, and their implications for empirical research on how indigeneity intersects with other social dimensions, such as inequality and self-determining aspirations.

Conclusion

The representation of ethnic identities in the census is a complex and often contentious task. This is especially so in the case of indigenous peoples, whose unique legal and political status confers rights and resources on them that are unavailable to other minorities. Though the goal of the census is to objectively count subjective identities, this chapter has shown that ethnic enumeration is less the product of dispassionate, scientific inquiry, than a process of negotiation informed by myriad motivations. In New Zealand, ethnic complexity has long posed a challenge to officials who, for more than a century, sought to delineate clear boundaries between Maori and Europeans, through the prism of blood quantum, and in ways that reflected state imperatives and prevailing race logics. Though scientifically and morally disputed, the legacy of blood racialisation still lingers in public and political discourses, where it is not uncommon for Maori rights and sense of peoplehood to be challenged on the premise that no Maori full-bloods exist. Nowadays, the representation of Maori identities in the census is more flexible and inclusive, with multiple criteria used to define Maori. Though this might better fit egalitarian notions of self-identification, it has created a new 'problem': different criteria yield Maori groups of different sizes and sociodemographic characteristics, with the potential to generate substantively different conclusions when used in ethnic analysis.

As this chapter has shown, how Maori is defined produces varied results in so far as who qualifies as Maori in certain contexts. The discourses invoked in defining Maori have rarely been neutral, but ones where individual and group rights have been, and continue to be, vigorously debated and contested. In this respect Maori are not unique. Wherever there is ambiguity about racial and ethnic group boundaries, there will be disagreements about how these divisions are drawn. In the twenty-first century Maori identity reflects the subjective outcomes of political consciousness and choice, the presumed objectivity reality of biological and cultural origin, and structural constraints that condition the opportunities to access and express identity. These discontinuities and inconsistencies, while conceptually messy and analytically challenging, reflect the inherently fluid nature of ethnicity, changing socio-political forces, and shifting paradigms of thinking about ethnicity.

Notes

1. I use 'ethnicity' broadly to refer to socially defined differences based on race, culture, origins, skin colour, ancestry and so on, but revert to the specific term 'race' to emphasise its importance in a particular context.
2. Political non-dominance, cultural distinctiveness and prior occupation of a particular geographic area are routinely invoked as defining features of indigenous peoples. It should be noted, however, that there is no definitive definition of indigeneity, either within the social sciences (Kuper 2003), or the international political community. For example, the *Declaration on the Rights of Indigenous Peoples*, adopted by the United Nations General Assembly in 2007, does not contain a definition of indigeneity. Instead, Article 33 notes that "Indigenous peoples have the right to determine their own identity or membership in accordance with their customs and traditions" (United Nations General Assembly 2007).
3. In the 2006 census, ethnic Maori represented 14.6 per cent of the New Zealand population. By comparison, American Indians comprised 1.5 per cent of the total United States population in the 2000 census, and Canadian and Australian Aboriginals comprised 3.3 and 2.3 per cent of their respective national populations in 2006.
4. The 1840 Treaty, signed by representatives of the British Crown and Maori tribes, guaranteed Maori the protection of their interests, and the rights and privileges of British subjects. In the English language version, Maori ceded sovereignty to the Crown in return for these guarantees; in the Maori language version, signed by the chiefs, only *kawanatanga* (governance) was ceded. The Treaty was not embedded in the New Zealand constitution and its terms were routinely flouted until 1975, when the Waitangi Tribunal was established to investigate and make recommendations on issues relating to the wrongful alienation of Maori land and other natural resources. Although the tribunal's rulings are not binding on government, its decisions have resulted in significant settlements involving land and cash.
5. The nebulous label 'European' was primarily a racial descriptor of white settlers rather than a referent to a common geographic origin. Guidelines for the race question in the 1936 census advised: 'All persons of "white" race should enter

"European", irrespective of whether they are of New Zealand, English, Scottish, Irish, French, United States, or other origin or nationality' (Statistics New Zealand 2006). The colloquial Maori term *Pakeha* was also used to describe the British settler population and their descendants, but was not instituted in official statistics.

6. Quotations are employed for first usage of historical terms and concepts such as 'half-caste', 'blood', 'native' and 'miscegenation' to indicate that they are not neutral descriptors, but terms bound to a particular historical context.

7. There appeared to be considerable confusion in the field on how to make this distinction. The 1906 report noted: 'There is no very defined rule to guide the Enumerators and sub-enumerators in deciding what half-castes should be classified as "living as Europeans" and "living as Maoris" respectively' (Registrar General 1907: lv).

8. The Maori census was carried out by officers of the Native Department, and was taken over several days. From 1926, attempts were made to make the Maori census more comparable with the general census by limiting the enumeration to one night and allowing Maori to self-report in the same manner as the rest of the population, albeit with fewer items. The Maori and general censuses were merged in 1951, as officials considered Maori had reached a stage of development where special measures were no longer required (Census and Statistical Office 1953, i). It is worth noting that Maori in the South Island had been enumerated with Europeans since the 1920s, the rationale being that most were living in European fashion and their number was too small to warrant the cost of separate enumeration.

9. The term 'general' often operated as a synonym for European or 'non-Maori' in statistics and in law, with successive census reports using all three terms interchangeably. Until 1975, the general electoral seats in parliament were called European seats.

10. The earlier *Maori Land Act 1909* defined a 'Native' as a person 'belonging to the Aboriginal race of New Zealand, and includes a half-caste and a person intermediate in blood between half-castes and persons of pure descent from that race'. Most statutory definitions, either historically or more recently, have been based on a biological notion of blood, or the looser criteria of descent. For example, the *Maori Representation Act 1867*, which provided for limited Maori enfranchisement, defined Maori as: 'a male Aboriginal native inhabitant of New Zealand at the age of twenty-one years and upwards and shall include half-castes.' The *Maori Social and Economic Advancement Act 1945* had the more inclusive definition of: 'a person belonging to the aboriginal race of New Zealand, and includes any person descended from a Maori.' The *Births and Deaths Registration Act 1951* reverted to the more exclusive definition of 'a person belonging to the aboriginal race of New Zealand; and includes a half caste and a person intermediate in blood between half castes and persons of pure descent from that race.' See Hunn (1961) for an overview of the multiple legal definitions of Maori in operation at the time.

11. Scholars have noted that the European desire for Maori to assimilate not only reflected an innate belief in the benefits of adopting a 'superior' civilised culture, but was inextricably linked to economic imperatives, notably the individualisation of Maori land. As Meredith argues: 'colonial officials were concerned to establish British law, and through that law, secure social control and gain access to the land. Persuading Maori to embrace European habits, customs, and English language was one measure of getting them to accept

the law' (Meredith 2006: 106). He notes the explicit effect of being declared a European under Section 17 of the *Native Land Amendment Act* was the Europeanisation of the applicant's land – in effect, the removal of protective mechanisms extended to Maori land.

12. In the United States the terms 'quadroon' (one quarter Black) and 'octoroon' (one eighth Black) were only used in the 1890 census; while the term 'mulatto' (all degrees intermediate between half and fully Black) was abandoned in the early twentieth century. Morning and Sabbagh (2005: 58) argue the substitution of those terms with the singular term 'Negro' reflected the 'post civil war hardening of one drop rule', rather than enlightened racial thinking on the part of bureaucrats. As noted earlier, blood quantum was applied to American Indians and Native Hawaiians for particular purposes – usually involving resources – but not in the national census.

13. There were some circumstances in which blood was used to determine rights and access to resources. One was voting rights. Under the *Maori Representation Act 1867*, Maori electoral representation was guaranteed though the establishment of four separate Maori electorates. After the introduction of a Maori electoral roll in 1947, half-castes were given the choice of enrolling on the Maori or general electoral roll, but Maori (half or more) were restricted to voting in Maori electorates until 1975. There was, however, considerable elasticity in how blood quantum was interpreted by officials tasked with policing the definitions and individuals affected by it.

14. 'Incorporation' is, of course, a loaded term. The incorporation of Maori into a European dominated polity was vigorously resisted by many Maori, and welcomed by others (Ward 1973; Belich 2001). Though the intention of policies of incorporation may have been benevolent, the results in terms of cultural loss, social dislocation and economic inequality defied the stated ideal of an inclusive society. However, the statistical usage of blood was not an explicit tool in effecting those outcomes.

15. Statutes aimed at restricting non-European migrants included the *Chinese Immigrants Act 1881*, the *Immigration Restriction Act 1908*, and *Undesirable Immigrants Exclusion Act 1919*. The Chinese, in particular, were a target of racist policies, including poll taxes, and marked out for special attention in early statistics. Although Chinese were counted as part of the general population, their number was separately identified in national summaries. Like Maori, Chinese were also the subject of official interest in miscegenation. The 1896 census, for example, made a special note of distinguishing half-caste and pure-bred Chinese.

16. The term 'coloured people' was clearly aimed at non-European immigrants. Although Maori were not seen as white, nor were they routinely described as coloured. An exception was the report on the 1857/8 census, in which the term was used in contradistinction to the 'white' (i.e., settler) population, and in the context of a discussion about global colonisation. Similarities were drawn between 'red Indians' and Maori as colonised coloured peoples (Fenton 1859).

17. Meredith's insightful account of Europeanisation under the *Native Land Amendment Act* also raises questions about the disconnection between official discourses of race, and interpretations of membership within Maori communities. He argues that the decision of Maori to Europeanise was largely an instrumental one, undertaken in response to particular social and economic conditions. As such, their European identities in law ought to be seen as 'situational' rather than 'cultural' (Meredith 2006: 146–47).

18. To illustrate, the ratio of Maori to half-castes in the 1921 census was almost 7:1 (49,635 Maori; 3,116 half-caste Maori; 4,236 half-caste European). However, a survey of 814 men of the New Zealand Maori Pioneer Battalion undertaken by the Maori anthropologist Peter Buck in 1919 reported that almost half had European "blood". Buck's survey of 4,500 children in Native schools a few years later found a similar proportion was mixed Maori-European (Buck 1924; Census and Statistical Office 1927, xiv: 4).
19. The opportunity to increase Maori political representation came with the change from a first-past-the-post to a mixed-member-proportional system in 1996. The determination of electoral boundaries depends, in part, on the size of the Maori descent population (Kukutai 2004). At the last election in 2008, there were seven Maori seats and sixty-three general electorate seats and fifty list seats.
20. Maori were at the top of the prioritisation schedule, so that individuals who reported Maori ethnicity in conjunction with some other ethnic group were counted only as Maori. The schedule then prioritised Pacific peoples, Asians, other non-European groups, and 'Other European' ethnicities respectively, with New Zealand European as the residual. This system was dispensed with after the 2001 census. For more on the analytical implications of using prioritised and non-prioritised data, see Callister, Didham and Potter (2005).
21. In 2006, the question relating to descent asked: "Are you descended from a Maori (that is, did you have a Maori birth parent, grandparent, or great-grandparent, etc.)"
22. For a similar comparison using 2001 census data, see Kukutai (2004).
23. Statistics New Zealand's practice of counting multiethnic people in all of their reported groups means that people who identified as Maori and some other group will be counted in several of the sub-groups shown below.
24. There is also the problem of endogenity. That is, groups are constructed on the basis of presumed strength of Maori ethnic attachment using identification markers, then an attempt is made to account for intra group variation across other kinds of ethnic markers.

References

Alba, R., and V. Nee. 2003. *Remaking the American Mainstream: Assimilation and Contemporary Immigration*. Cambridge, MA: Harvard University Press.

Allan, J. 2001. *Review of the Measurement of Ethnicity: Classifications and Issues*. Wellington: Statistics New Zealand.

Ballara, A. 1986. *Proud to be White? A Survey of Pakeha Prejudice in New Zealand*. Auckland: Heinemann.

Barth, F. 1969. *Ethnic Groups and Boundaries*. Boston, MA: Little, Brown.

Belich, J. 1996. *Making Peoples: A History of the New Zealanders, from Polynesian Settlement to the End of the Nineteenth Century*. Auckland: Penguin.

—— 2001. *Paradise Reforged: A History of the New Zealanders, from the 1880s to the Year 2000*. Auckland: Penguin.

Broughton, J. 1993. 'Being Maori', *New Zealand Medical Journal* 106(968): 506–8.

Buck, P. 1924. 'The Passing of the Maori', *Transactions and Proceedings of the New Zealand Institute* 55: 362–75.

Callister, P. 2007. *Special Measures to Reduce Ethnic Disadvantage in New Zealand: An Examination of Their Role.* Wellington: Institute of Policy Studies, Victoria University of Wellington.

Callister, P., R. Didham and D. Potter. 2005. 'Analytical Frameworks in Ethnic Analysis: Using Non–prioritised Data for Research on Ethnic Intermarriage – A Research Note', *New Zealand Population Review* 32(1): 49–67.

Census and Statistical Office. 1923. 'Results of a Census of the Dominion of New Zealand 1921, Vol. 6'. Wellington: Government Printer.

——— 1927. 'Dominion of New Zealand Population Census 1926, Vol. 6'. Wellington: Government Printer.

———. 1946. 'Dominion of New Zealand Population Census 1945, Vol. 8'. Wellington: Government Printer.

———. 1953. 'New Zealand Population Census, Vol. 1'. Wellington: Government Printer.

Cornell, S., and D. Hartmann. 1998. *Ethnicity and Race: Making Identities in a Changing World.* Thousand Oaks, CA: Pine Forge Press.

Department of Statistics. 1967. 'New Zealand Population Census 1966, Vol. 7'. Wellington: Government Printer.

Durie, M. 2005. *Nga Tai Matatu: Tides of Maori Endurance.* Melbourne: Oxford University Press.

Fenton, F.D. 1859. *Observations on the Aboriginal Inhabitants of New Zealand.* Auckland: New Zealand Government.

Gans, H. 1979. 'Symbolic Ethnicity: The Future of Ethnic Groups and Culture in America', *Ethnic and Racial Studies* 2: 1–20.

Hochschild, J., and B.M. Powell. 2008. 'Racial Reorganisation and the United States Census 1850–1930: Mulattoes, Half–breeds, Mixed Parentage, Hindoos, and the Mexican Race', *Studies in American Political Development* 22: 59–96.

Howe, K.R. 2003. *The Quest for Origons: Who First Discovered and Settled New Zealand and the Pacific Islands?* Auckland: Penguin.

Hunn, J.K. 1961. *Report on Department of Maori Affairs: With statistical supplement, 24 August 1960.* Wellington: Government Printer.

Karetu, T. 1990. 'The Clue to Identity', *New Zealand National Geographic* 5: 112–17.

Kauanui, K. 2005. 'The Multiplicity of Hawaiian Sovereignty Claims and the Struggle for Meaningful Autonomy', *Comparative American Studies* 3(3): 283–99.

Kaufmann, E. 2000. 'Liberal Ethnicity: Beyond Libernal Nationality and Minority Rights', *Ethnic and Racial Studies* 23(6): 1086–1119.

Kertzer, D., and D. Arel (eds). 2002. *Census and Identity: The Politics of Race, Ethnicity and Language in National Censuses.* Cambridge: Cambridge University Press.

Kukutai, T. 2004. 'The Problem of Defining an Ethnic Group for Public Policy: Who is Maori and Why Does it Matter?' *Social Policy Journal of New Zealand* 23: 86–108.

Kuper, A. 2003. 'The Return of the Native', *Current Anthropology* 44(3): 389–402.

Meredith, P. 2006. 'Pakeha by Law: The Europeanisation of Maori, 1912–1931', *New Zealand Universities Law Review* 22: 103–147.

Metge J. 1964. *A New Maori Migration: Rural and Urban Relations in Northern New Zealand*. Wellington: Victoria University Press.

Morning, A., and D. Sabbagh. 2005. 'From Sword to Ploughshare: Using Race for Discrimination and Antidiscrimination in the United States', *International Social Science Journal* 57(183): 57–73.

Nagel, J. 1994. 'Constructing Ethnicity: Creating and Recreating Ethnic Identity and Culture', *Social Problems* 41(1):152–76.

Newman, A.K. 1881. 'A Study of the Causes Leading to the Extinction of the Maori', *Transactions of the Proceedings of the New Zealand Institute* 14: 459–77.

Nobles, M. 2000. *Shades of Citizenship: Race and the Census in Modern Politics*. Stanford, CA: Stanford University Press.

Pool, I. 1991. *Te Iwi Maori*. Auckland: Auckland University Press.

Rallu, J., V. Piché and P. Simon. 2006. 'Demography and Ethnicity: An Ambiguous Relationship', in G. Caselli, J. Vallin and G. Wunsch (eds), *Demography: Analysis and Synthesis. A Treatise in Population Studies, Vol 3*. Boston: Elsevier.

Rata, E. 1999. A Political Economy of Neotribal Capitalism. Lanham, MA: Lexington Books.

Registrar General. 1892. 'Results of a Census of the Colony of New Zealand'. Wellington: Government Printer.

——— 1907. 'Results of a Census of the Colony of New Zealand 1906'. Wellington: Government Printer.

Snipp, C.M. 1997. 'Some Observations about Racial Boundaries and the Experiences of American Indians', *Ethnic and Racial Studies* 20(4): 669–89.

Sorrenson, M.P.K. 1975. 'How to Civilise Savages: Some "Answers" from Nineteenth-century New Zealand', *New Zealand Journal of History* 19(2): 97–110.

Statistics New Zealand. 1999. 'Measuring Maori Ethnicity in the New Zealand Census', unpublished paper. Wellington: Social Policy Division.

——— 2002. '2001 Census of Population and Dwellings: Iwi'. Wellington: Statistics New Zealand.

——— 2004. 'Report of the Review of the Measurement of Ethnicity'. Wellington: Statistics New Zealand.

Te Puni Kokiri. 2000. 'Progress Towards Closing Social and Economic Gaps Between Maori and Non-Maori: A Report to the Minister of Maori Affairs'. Wellington: Te Puni Kokiri.

Ward, A. 1973. *A Show of Justice: Racial 'Amalgamation' in Nineteenth Century New Zealand*. Auckland: Auckland University Press.

Waters, M. 1990. *Ethnic Options: Choosing Identities in America*. Berkeley, CA: University of California Press.

3

COUNTING INDIANS:
CENSUS CATEGORIES IN LATE COLONIAL AND
EARLY REPUBLICAN SPANISH AMERICA

Steinar A. Saether

Estimating the size of indigenous populations in Latin America and accounting for their demographic development is a most difficult – if not impossible – task. The most renowned part of the debate about native demographic history in the Americas has concerned the magnitude of the demographic collapse following the European conquests of the sixteenth and seventeenth centuries.[1] Although less publicised, the more recent demographic history of indigenous groups is also teeming with unanswered questions, lacunae of knowledge, broad speculations, intriguing case studies and perspectives which have the potential of altering our way of conceiving the history of Latin America, and not only the indigenous part of it.

If the sixteenth and seventeenth centuries are problematic for demographers, so is the period between 1750 and 1850. Yet this is a crucial period if we are to understand the development in the long run of indigenous populations. Part of the problem is of course that Spanish America in the mid eighteenth century was already a very diverse region in ethnic terms, where the social interactions between individuals and groups had varied considerably since the arrival of the first Europeans and Africans in the fifteenth century. Another part of the problem is that most, but not all, of this area ceased to be Spanish between 1810 and 1830, and subsequent census taking practices varied greatly, making meaningful comparisons of data complicated.

Apart from all this, scholars intending to do quantitative work on indigenous populations in Spanish America confront even more fundamental problems: the possible meanings of racial and ethnic terms used in demographic sources. Although the terms *indio* and *indígena* appear in many of the eighteenth and nineteenth-century censuses, their use is far from uniform. For demographers and others interested in quantitative aspects of indigenous populations, it is essential to understand the reasoning behind the categories which appear in the sources. However, this is easier said than done, partly because the praxis employed by census takers varied with time and space, and partly because most contemporary scholars using these kinds of sources have neglected the study of census and parish record formation and tended to jump straight to their more or less credible results.

Demographers and social historians have produced a substantial number of studies of late colonial and early republican Spanish America. Since the 1970s there has been a plethora of studies on topics such as family and household composition, sexuality, marriage patterns, and race. Typically, these studies have been geographically limited to individual towns, cities or provinces, although there are also examples of comparative studies within larger regional or national boundaries, the vast majority of them dealing with the late colonial period, typically from the 1770s to 1810.[2] As noted by McCaa, a large portion of these studies have been modelled on the work of Peter Laslett and the Cambridge Population Group (McCaa 2000). However, there is a lack of studies with a broader geographical perspective. Few studies incorporate both colonial and national periods, and there is an obvious need for studies on how censuses and parish records were formed. In other words, there are many local studies on race and ethnicity based on censuses and parish records, but in sum these add up to a very fragmented whole.

Here, the object is threefold. An overview of the ethnic categories used in censuses during the period 1750 to 1850 is provided; some tentative explanations for the variation in the census categories employed are proposed; and, finally, some suggestions for further research are made. Many of the examples included concern the Caribbean provinces of Colombia, but efforts have been made to compare patterns disclosed in the Colombian material with results published by scholars who have worked on other Latin American areas. In this manner, it is hoped that the Colombian material may illustrate some general Latin American trends, and that the differences are useful to test the validity of explanations comparatively.

The period treated here covers roughly the century between 1750 and 1850. For most of Latin America it corresponds to the late colonial and early republican periods – Spain and Portugal lost almost all their American dominions between 1810 and 1830. For historians interested in the use of ethnic and racial categories in censuses and parish records, it is a key period, since the patterns of classification formed then served as a foundation for subsequent census systems.

The problem with this period is not primarily a dearth of primary demographic material. Goyer and Domschke's impressive handbook of national population censuses (Goyer and Domschke 1983) convinces the reader that Latin America – or at least parts of it – has been rather well served by good censuses since the 1780s. Nor is the quality of the censuses necessarily poor. Obviously, census quality depends on bureaucratic expertise and competence, and they are costly and require a certain level of state development. It is not surprising; therefore, that Chile is the country with the earliest and most developed use of censuses in the nineteenth century. There, nationwide censuses were conducted in 1831–1835, 1843, 1865, 1875, 1885 and 1895. In Mexico and Argentina, where the first fifty years of independent rule were fraught with upheaval, the first censuses date from 1869 and 1895 respectively. If we are to believe Goyer and Domschke, no reliable censuses were carried out in Bolivia, Paraguay and Ecuador until 1950. In Colombia, surprisingly good censuses were conducted in 1825, 1835 and 1843, but only partial ones in the tumultuous second half of the nineteenth century. Cuba, which remained a Spanish colony until 1898 and hence escaped the civil strife common in other parts of the hemisphere, has a particularly good series of nineteenth-century censuses. In other words, scholars interested in estimating the size of indigenous populations in Latin America would do well to select their countries of study with great care.

Furthermore, they should not be overly optimistic about finding easily usable statistics on indigenous populations, even from the countries where censuses were regularly conducted. In a simple but thought-provoking appendix, Goyer and Domschke (ibid.: 636–641) present a list of the variables included in national censuses between 1950 and 1980. The large majority of states with an Iberian colonial past display a remarkable tendency: ethnic or racial categories are absent from the censuses. This is in stark contrast to virtually all islands, territories or states which had been under British, French, Danish or Dutch dominion, for instance in the Caribbean. There, racial or ethnic categories seem to have been a constant element in censuses during the twentieth century.

During the last 250 years, censuses in Latin America seem to have undergone five distinct periods. It is important to identify these as they will lead to a better understanding of the censuses, their background, and especially the nature of racial and ethnic terms employed in them. The first period covers the decades from about 1725 to 1800, when a range of standardised censuses were completed in Spanish America, associated with the new Bourbon dynasty in Spain and their so-called 'second conquest' of America. The second period covers the first decades of republican rule from 1820 to the 1860s, where new governments with varying results attempted to carry out censuses, often – but not always – based on a radically different view of how society was composed. In this second period, an important characteristic of most censuses conducted in the independent republics was the exclusion of racial and ethnic categories altogether, or a territorialisation of race which implied that all inhabitants of often marginal or peripheral areas were defined *in toto* as, for instance, indigenous or black. A third period, covering the last decades of the nineteenth century and the first half of the twentieth, saw most Latin American states develop modern census taking procedures, again including categories of ethnicity, race or colour. In the second half of the twentieth century, the general tendency in Latin America seems to have been a generalised scepticism towards the use of such categories in censuses, and then in the late 1980s and 1990s the categories again reappear, presumably as a consequence of the widespread renaissance of indigenous identities and cultures.

This broad tendency is of interest for several reasons. It suggests that categories employed in censuses are there for particular reasons, and not merely automatic reflections of actual social divisions. Thus, the initial and rather casual reading of Goyer and Domschke's useful work above raises some intriguing questions about demographic sources and ethnic categories in Latin America. The first concerns the relationship between the state and the censuses it conducts. To what extent are censuses based on the nature of state bureaucracy? This question not only involves the capacity of the state to actually count the inhabitants of a given territory, but also the possible uses of the censuses. For instance, Centeno (1997, 2002) has demonstrated that Latin American states during the nineteenth century depended far less than European states on direct taxation. We might assume that censuses are particularly important for states that either depend on taxation or wish to increase the level of taxation of its inhabitants. As we shall see, the issue of taxation had important consequences for the way in which indigenous populations were counted in different Latin American states.

Another question concerns the ways in which society was conceptualised by bureaucrats, and how they viewed the position of ethnic groups within or in relation to the state. The apparent absence of ethnic categories in twentieth-century Spanish American censuses noted by Goyer and Domschke may not be entirely accurate. But it nevertheless indicates that there are important cultural differences in how bureaucrats across Latin America perceived the composition of their societies, differences which in turn are reflected in the censuses and parish records. Were all inhabitants citizens? Should everyone be counted, irrespective of their juridical and political relation to the state that administered the census? Interestingly, Latin American states adopted somewhat different positions on these questions, a tendency which implies that their common Iberian colonial past in itself is not sufficient to explain differences in how censuses were recorded. Indeed, several factors may explain the categories used in demographic sources, some of which will be explored below: the state's strength and ability to form comprehensive censuses, the conceptualisation of society, the fiscal needs of the state, and popular responses and reactions to census taking.

Censuses in Late Colonial Spanish America

In Colombia, as in the rest of Spanish America, the first comprehensive censuses – as opposed to mere headcounts – were conducted in the eighteenth century, and are intimately associated with the so-called Bourbon reforms. The replacement of the Habsburg dynasty and the Bourbon succession to the Spanish throne led to the introduction of a series of administrative, judicial, military and financial reforms in part modelled on those attempted in France during the second half of the seventeenth century.[3] In Spain, comprehensive censuses were conducted between 1713 and 1720, and again in 1755, these two preceding the three most renowned ones, that of ministers Aranda (1768), Floridablanca (1787) and Godoy (1797). The Spanish American censuses followed a few years behind the Spanish ones, and seem to have been completed largely for the same reasons. While a general census of Peru was attempted between 1725 and 1740 (Pearce 2001), and a reputedly excellent census of Mexico City was conducted in 1753 (Seed 1982), the best-known censuses covering most of Spanish America are the ones carried out in 1776–1778 and 1793–1795. In addition to these, there were several partial ones, on separate provinces and vice-royalties. As Jiménez de Gregorio (1968) and Dopico and Rowland (1990) note, the late eighteenth-century Spanish censuses were formed with four particular objectives in mind: first, from an 'enlightened' absolutist perspective, the number of inhabitants was seen as the inner strength of the state and thus important to quantify in order to conceive of policies to enhance it; secondly, to count the number of taxable subjects in order to improve and make more efficient taxation; third, and very closely related to the second objective, to identify the number of clergy exempted from taxation; and fourth, to identify the number of nobles exempted from taxation. Apparently military concerns were not paramount for the formation of these censuses. Separate and local head counts were formed in cities across the Spanish empire for recruitment to militias and regular companies. Often, these motives went together, as noted for instance by Rodney Anderson regarding the Revillagigedo census (Anderson 2003).

Although the Spanish American censuses were modelled on the Spanish ones, there were important differences between them, especially concerning the social categories employed. The 1786 Floridablanca census, widely regarded as the best of the eighteenth-century Spanish ones, contains the following variables for each individual: sex, age, civil status and occupation. Civil status was conceived as single, married or widow(er), while the occupation category was of utmost importance as the number of clergy and hidalgos ('nobles') were noted with particular care, as they were exempt from taxation.[4] In Spanish America, however, the taxation system was in many respects different from the one that operated on the Iberian peninsula. The number of hidalgos was minute, but over the course of more than two centuries of colonial rule in the Americas a highly complex mosaic of taxes and exemptions had developed. One of the principal tasks of the bourbon reformers was to simplify and make more efficient the collection of taxes.[5]

One of the principal sources of income for the Spanish monarchy from Spanish America was the *tributo*, a poll tax, payable by Indian males aged eighteen to fifty residing in Indian pueblos. Only Indians were subject to this tax. On the other hand, Indians were exempted from military service and some other taxes, notably the *alcalaba*, a sales tax. Given the fiscal importance of the *tributo*, it was vital for the Spanish Bourbons to count the number of Indians in Spanish America, and thus 'Indian' was a separate category in late eighteenth-century censuses (TePaske 1990). Just like in Spain, the actual counting was done by parish priests who set up so-called *padrones*, usually recording the name, sex, civil status, age, racial or ethnic category, and sometimes occupation. The racial and ethnic categories used at this basic level could be extremely varied. Either a civil or ecclesiastical servant calculated the total sums of the province or bishopric. At this level, the racial or ethnic terms were more standardised. Commonly, tables were set up which included the total of males and females within four or five different social, ethnic, or racial groupings. The most common of these were *blancos* or *españoles* ('whites'), *libres* ('free people'), *libres de varios colores* ('free people of various colours'), *libres de todos los colores* ('free people of all colours'), *mestizos* or *castas* ('mixed race'), *esclavos* (slaves) and finally *indios* (Indians), but even in the imperial censuses' ethnic categories tended to vary considerably between administrative units.

For demographers interested in using the census results, it is essential to keep in mind that Indians residing in Spanish cities or those groups which were not effectively under Spanish colonial rule were not counted. On the Caribbean coast of Colombia, for instance, the Guajiro Indians (today called Wayúu) were not counted in the 1793 census, except for the small minority of them who had been settled in missions or tributary villages near the city of Riohacha (Polo Acuña 1998; Saether 2005a, 2005b). The reason for this exclusion was mostly due to the fact that the Spanish authorities had no effective control over the Guajira peninsula, and no parish ministers or government secretaries could form the *padrones*. Understandably, unconquered Indian communities throughout the Americas were not counted in the eighteenth-century censuses, although Spanish authorities laid claim to land from Tierra del Fuego in the south to San Francisco in the north. Large indigenous communities such as the Mapuches south of the Bio-bio river in Chile, the Wayúu, Cuna, Misquitos, and Apaches, and almost all the groups of the Amazon basin, are only some of the most well-known examples of those not counted in the Spanish colonial censuses. The *indios* counted in the late colonial censuses actually tended to be the ones who conformed the closest to the ideal Indian in Spanish law: a person of native or indigenous descent, who lived in a designated Indian *pueblo*, spoke Spanish, was a devout Catholic, and paid the *tributo* twice a year in money or in kind. The colonial census category *indio* must be seen primarily as a juridical and fiscal category which responded to the administrative needs of the Spanish monarchy and in most instances is not translatable to modern concepts of indigenousness.

Furthermore, the reactions of those counted towards ethnic or fiscal categorisation is essential for understanding the result of the censuses. Precisely because of the *tributo*, many individuals sought by various means to be identified as non-Indians when the *padrones* were set up, while over-zealous bureaucrats were interested in including as many as possible in this category. Several authors working on different regions of colonial Spanish America have noted the relation between mobility and escape from *tributo* exactions. Martin Minchom (1994), for instance, studied a series of lawsuits from Quito on 'Declarations of mestizo'. The large majority of these cases are from the years after 1776, precisely when the Bourbon government attempted to make *tributo* collection more efficient and when the first imperial censuses were conducted. Pejoratively called *cholos*, the litigants studied by Minchom were principally individuals from the Indian pueblos of the highlands who had migrated to Quito, adopted Spanish dress, and claimed to be mestizos rather than Indians. They were, they argued, not obliged to pay the *tributo*. In order to distinguish between Indians and mestizos, the Quito authorities called in witnesses to testify on the reputed 'Indianness' of the individual in question. As the examples provided by Minchom show, frequently the witnesses themselves did not agree on the classification of individuals nor on the criteria to be used to distinguish Indians from non-Indians, while dress, colour, genealogy, language, occupation were among those frequently used. Interestingly, in the cases discussed by Minchom, the authorities often ended up granting the litigants non-Indian status. As Minchom acknowledges, the number of cases actually reviewed in this time-consuming process was probably very small compared to the number of Indians who had migrated to Quito. This indicates again that the 'ethnic' labels used in colonial censuses are problematic and must be approached with care.

To conclude from this that late colonial censuses generally are of little value and seriously underestimate the number of tribute-paying Indians would be erroneous. Arij Ouweneel (1991) has argued that the censuses generally, and in particular the counts of tributaries in central Mexico, are quite reliable because tribute payment was a condition for having access to a plot of land administered in commons in the *pueblos de indios*. Since access to land depended on being registered as a tribute payer, town residents had a strong economic incentive to be counted. Indeed, the association between pueblo residence, access to communal lands and tribute payment was so strong that non-Indians living in Indian towns in censuses and headcounts were frequently listed as Indians. Even runaway slaves of West African origin were able to form a *pueblo de indios* north of Puebla in central Mexico with the Crown's recognition (ibid.: 541). More commonly, outsiders moved to the Indian towns, sometimes marrying there and – at least in some of the sources – were subsequently counted as Indians. This implies again, that the term 'Indian' in the late colonial census must be seen primarily as a juridical and fiscal category and should not be understood as a meaningful synonym for indigenes in any modern sense of the term.

In addition to migration, social mobility and individual negotiation over ethnic classification, an important reaction or response to census taking in the colonial period was open revolt. The late colonial period was characterised by a wave of local and regional rebellions, provoked in the majority of cases by the Bourbon bureaucratic zeal for implementing new administrative reforms.[6] In some instances, the rebellions were explicit responses to census-taking practices. For instance, in Riobamba, Ecuador, peasants revolted against an attempt of conduct a census in the 1760s, and in several towns in Peru in the late 1770s rural inhabitants succeeded in preventing censuses being carried out, based on the fear that the census would imply their inclusion in the class of tribute payers (Cahill 1990; Campbell 1972; Moreno Yáñez 1995). Although census taking itself did not necessarily imply that people of partial African descent would be classified as Indians, nor that they would have to pay the normal tribute, this seems to have been the conclusion drawn by the rebels. The extension of a poll tax was seen to be a charge against their honour, and the denigration felt towards the new tax policy played an important role in these rebellions.

The close relation between tribute, access to land and 'Indianness' may help explain some of the geographical variation in the use of the term *indio* in censuses. The percentage of the population defined as 'Indians' in the colonial censuses varied substantially, and hence also the different provinces' dependence on tribute. Ouweneel (1991: 541) notes that in Mexico during the eighteenth century roughly 80 per cent of the population were defined as Indians, and about 85 per cent of these lived in *pueblos de indios*. There, as in the Andean highlands, tribute comprised an important and increasing source of Crown revenue, although other types of revenue –such as the *alcabala* (sales tax), taxes on mining and crown monopolies on tobacco and *aguardiente* – were rising faster as commerce grew and taxation became more efficient. In the vice-royalty of New Spain, by far the most valuable part of the Spanish dominions in America, tribute revenue rose from 1 million pesos yearly in the 1770s to about 1.6 million between 1800 and 1809, while commercial taxes exceeded on average 4.8 million pesos yearly between 1780 and 1809, and the monopolies provided almost 10 million pesos a year in the final decades of colonial rule in Mexico (Burkholder and Johnson 2008: 335–36). In the central and southern Andean highlands, tribute was more important than in Mexico, but even here by the end of colonial era tribute represented less than 10 per cent of total revenue (Klein and Barbier 1988: 46).

In other areas of Spanish America, however, tribute was of lesser importance. In the Caribbean Colombian province of Santa Marta, for instance, the 1793 census listed a total of 47,100 persons of which only 8,632

(18.33 per cent) were classified as Indians.[7] Of these, 760 lived outside the *pueblos de indios* of the province, the majority in small 'Spanish' towns and hamlets in rural areas. Around the city of Santa Marta, there remained six such pueblos at the end of the colonial period with a combined population of 2,499, of which 2,241 (89.7 per cent) were classified as Indians in the 1793 census. In the 1780s the annual tribute exacted from these towns oscillated between 800 and 1000 pesos, which represented less than 2 per cent of the revenue for this small local branch of the royal exchequer.[8] Genealogical surveys of the inhabitants of these towns before independence suggest that the vast majority of them were descendants of the native inhabitants of the area, and thus – unlike the Mexican towns studied by Ouweneel – non-Indians had not migrated to the pueblos. This difference may be explained by the relative abundance of cheap land in Santa Marta: becoming a tribute-paying Indian was not a prerequisite for access to agricultural plots here.

As in the rest of the vice-royalty of New Granada, the majority of the population were categorised as *libres* ('free people') or *libres de todos los colores* ('free people of all colours'). In the 1793 census of Santa Marta, 29,036 persons (61.65 per cent) were classified as *libres de todos los colores*. Possibly because of the popular violent reactions in Peru, the Bourbon reformers did not attempt to extend tribute to non-Indians in New Granada, or establish new poll taxes for those groups. This, in turn, may be part of the explanation of why there seems to have been less popular resistance against the colonial censuses in New Granada than in Peru.

The different categories employed in the late colonial Spanish American censuses seem, therefore, to reflect to a large extent the slightly different taxation systems in place in the different administrative regions of Spanish America. In the Aymara-speaking and coca-producing Yungas valleys north of La Paz, Herbert S. Klein (1979) has shown that both the late colonial censuses of 1786 and 1803 and the early republican censuses of 1829 and 1839 distinguished between three types of Indians – *yanaconas*, *originarios* and *agregados* – and an additional category for non-Indians, *mestizos* or *cholos*. The distinction made between different types of Indians in these censuses was clearly related to the tribute system in place there. The *indios originarios* here resemble the tributary Indians in the colonial censuses of Santa Marta. The *originarios* are those who were identified as an original member of an *ayllu*, the traditional community groups of the area. They had access to land held in common by the *ayllu*, and paid the full tribute. The *agregados* were newcomers or outsiders who were associated with an *ayllu*, resided in the community, paid a reduced tribute fee, and did not enjoy the same rights to land administered by the *ayllu*. The *yanaconas* were landless peons working on coca-producing haciendas owned by non-Indians and paid the lowest tribute rate to the state. Again, in order to better understand the variation in ethnic categories used in Spanish American censuses, one has to be aware of the close relationship between census categories, tribute obligations and access to land.

Censuses in the New Republics

Independence from Spain marks a fundamental break in the way in which ethnic and racial categories were recorded in censuses and parish records, at least in Colombia. In 1821 the Congress of Cúcuta not only abolished the Indian tribute, it also stated that the term *indio* should be replaced by *indígena* in official documents, and that communal lands should be privatised. Although tribute payment was re-established by Bolivar's decree in 1827 as a *contribución personal* ('personal contribution'), it was again abolished in 1831 after Bolivar's death and the separation of Venezuela and Ecuador from Colombia (Safford 1991: 12–13). Since tribute was abolished when the early republican censuses of 1825, 1835 and 1843 were undertaken, there was little need to differentiate between Indians and non-Indians. In fact, these censuses are much simpler than the late colonial ones in that they only contain two social categories, *libre* (free) and *esclavo* (slave). With the abolition of the slave trade, a 'free-womb' law enacted in 1821, and several manumission decrees thereafter, the number of slaves decreased rapidly until the final abolition of slavery in 1851. Therefore, the early republican Colombian censuses conveniently portrayed the vast majority of the population as simply 'free'. The 1843 census of Santa Marta province, for instance, lists a total of 45,678 inhabitants, of whom 44,594 (97.6 per cent) are listed as free.

Following the above line of reasoning concerning the relationship between census categories and taxation systems, the disappearance of the Indians from the Colombian censuses makes sense as a consequence of the abolition of tribute. This explanation is further corroborated by the continuation of colonial categories in those republics where tribute remained. As already noted, the categories used in the Bolivian censuses on the Yungas valleys studied by Klein were not changed. On the contrary, there the late colonial and early republican census categories were identical (Klein 1979: 320). In Ecuador, tribute was not abolished until 1857, and it should come as no surprise that in the Ecuadorean censuses Indians remained a category until 1846, the year of the last census before the abolition of tribute (Van Aken 1981: 457).

Obviously, the economic conditions of the new republics played a central role in determining whether tribute was to be retained or not. Van Aken notes that in the Audiencia of Quito on the eve of independence, tribute constituted more than one-third of tax revenues (ibid.: 441). By the 1850s, with the expansion of the cacao trade out of Guayaquil, the *contribución personal* only constituted 8.5 per cent of total revenues for the Ecuadorean state. The reduced importance of the Indian poll tax for government finances, according to Van Aken, opened the way for the final dissolution of tribute in 1857 (ibid.: 450–452). In neighbouring Peru, following the guano boom beginning in the 1840s, tribute was also abolished in the 1850s, but possibly reinstated later in the nineteenth century when the Peruvian state again found itself in dire economic straits

(Cahill 2002: 166–67). Meanwhile in Bolivia, tribute continued well into the 1860s partly for economic reasons, and partly because the state lacked the resources to conduct cadastral surveys needed for a proposed taxation system based on property (Platt 1987; Klein 2003: 107).

However, the fiscal needs of states are not sufficient to explain why the tribute and Indian categories in censuses were retained or abolished. Just as in the colonial period, popular demands and resistance to state policies also played an important role. In Santa Marta, Governor José Ignacio Díaz Granados explained in 1831 that the inhabitants of the former tributary towns around the city reacted vehemently against the *contribución personal* introduced by Bolivar in 1827. They refused to pay it, stating that they abhorred such a system and that they preferred to pay normal taxes as ordinary citizens of Colombia (Saether 2005b: 77). In Bolivia on the other hand, Tristan Platt (1987: 286) found that the inhabitants of Chayanta province saw no contradiction between paying tribute and being citizens. On the contrary, they insisted on paying tribute, presumably because their control of agricultural land depended on its continuation.

In addition to the material interests of states and communities, the categories employed in the republican censuses reflect to some extent the ways in which elites (and possibly, in some indirect ways, peasants) conceptualised society, both the way they thought of their existing societies and how they thought society should ideally be. Van Aken explains the justification for the abolition of tribute in Ecuador:

> Urbina's Minister of Finance, Francisco Pablo Icaza, set forth in typically liberal terms the government's rationale for ending capitation. He saw the traditional impost as a 'barbarous' legacy of colonial times, inconsistent with the concept of justice. Not only was the tax not 'proportional,' as required by the Ecuadorian Constitution, but it was so burdensome, said the minister, that it 'enslaved' the impoverished Indian. Capitation deprived the Indian of all incentive to work and produce and encouraged him to turn to alcohol for solace, alleged the administration's spokesman, with obvious exaggeration. Repeal of the personal contribution, said Icaza, would set the Indian free, provide him with economic incentive, and turn him into a useful and productive 'citizen' (the liberal reformer's fervent hope). It is apparent from the minister's arguments that the goal of tribute repeal in 1857 was the social integration of the Indian into the dominant Hispanic society – the same goal envisioned earlier by General San Martin and by the Congress of Gran Colombia. (Van Aken 1981: 453)

The liberal ideas of society, informed by Enlightenment philosophy, evident in the citation above corresponds well with the attitudes analysed by Frank Safford (1991) for early republican Colombia. The dominant view among creole elites in early republican Colombia favoured the transformation of former tribute-paying Indians into ordinary citizens, and called for the abolition of all vestiges of the old colonial order. Although conservative opinions also existed within the newly established republics, this does not invalidate the claim that the ideal of most politicians was to create a liberal, republican and national order where legal and political equality was a primary objective. This fundamental world-view is important in order to understand why Peruvian, Bolivian and Ecuadorean governments abolished tribute when economic circumstances permitted.

The new republican conceptualisation of the nation also implied an important transformation with respect to the spatial dimensions of race and ethnicity. Various authors have recently shown that concepts of race and ethnicity in the new republics became territorialised. Nancy Appelbaum, for instance, holds that 'nineteenth-century Colombians organised racial hierarchy in their national space. They created an interregional geography of race and status that privileged certain places and peoples within the nation as white, modern, and progressive while denigrating others as backward and inferior' (Appelbaum 1999: 632). Concurrent with this view are some very interesting aspects of the republican censuses. While former tribute-paying Indians became 'free' in the censuses, the native groups that had resisted Spanish domination and remained uncounted in the colonial censuses appeared in special appendices of the republican censuses of Colombia as *indígenas salvajes* ('savage Indians'). In 1826, the Colombian congress decreed that 'independent and uncivilised indigenous tribes' should be registered. The following nineteenth-century censuses list *indígenas* summarily for each province, though numbers often seem to be based on rough estimates. In 1835, 111,130 persons and in 1843, 184,230 persons were included in this new category.

In this manner the republican censuses conveyed a very different vision of Colombian Indianness from that of the colonial censuses. In fact, hardly any individual counted as Indian in the late colonial censuses would have been defined as indigenous in the early republican ones. Conversely, probably very few of those enumerated as 'uncivilised Indians' in the early republican censuses would have been included at all in the late colonial ones. Thus the meaning of the terms *indio* and *indígena* went through a fundamental transformation. Furthermore, the Indians envisioned in republican censuses were now only found in the peripheral and marginal spaces of national territory, by definition devoid of civilisation.

There is a need for further studies of Latin American censuses and the way in which ethnic and racial categories have been employed in them. In order to understand the categories used, a wide variety of different perspectives needs to be taken into account. We have noted how taxation systems, government capacity, elite attitudes and popular resistance all come into play in how the censuses depict ethnic groups. Further studies on how censuses were actually carried out, debates surrounding censuses, the uses which bureaucrats had in mind when undertaking them, the reactions of those counted – all these may enhance our ability to use the massive amount of demographic material available. Finally, more comparisons of censuses across colonial and republican administrative divisions would be useful.

Notes

1. See Henige (1986, 1993, 1999), Borah (1992), Brooks (1993), McCaa (1995) and Cook (1999).
2. See, e.g., Martinez-Alier (1974), McCaa (1982, 1984, 1994, 2000), Seed (1988), Lavrín (1989), Miller (1990), Gootenberg (1991), Gutiérrez (1991), Kuznesof (1991), Stavig (1995), Stark (1996), Meisel Roca and Aguilera Díaz (1997), Matos Rodríguez (1999), Twinam (1999) and Barickman (2004).
3. See, e.g., Rípodas Ardanaz (1977), Brading (1983), Fisher, Kuethe and MacFarlane (1990), Miller (1990), Fisher (1992), McFarlane (1993, 2005), Bakewell (1997) and Saether (2003).
4. See 'Real Orden de 25 de julio de 1786'. Retrieved 15 April 2008 from from: http://www.logro-o.org/pub/censo1817.htm.
5. See Brading (1983), Fisher, Kuethe and MacFarlane (1990), Miller (1990), McFarlane (1998a) and Saether (2005a).
6. See Phelan (1978), Loy (1981), McFarlane (1984, 1989, 1995, 1998b), Stern (1987), Fisher, Kuethe and MacFarlane (1990) and Van Young (1993).
7. See 'Indiferente general 1527: "Padrón que manifiesta el numero de personas habitantes en esta provincia de Sta Marta con distincion de clases, sexos, edades, y estados, inclusos parvulos"', AGI.
8. For summaries of the royal treasury accounts of Santa Marta between 1780 and 1810, see Santa Fe 1207, AGI.

References

Archives

AGI – Archivo General de Indias, Seville.

Published Sources

Anderson, R. 2003. 'Guadalajara Census History: 1600–1850.' Retrieved 15 April 2008 from: http://www.fsu.edu/~guadalaj/english/censuses/censuses.htm.

Appelbaum, N. 1999. 'Whitening the Region: Caucano Mediation and "Antioqueño Colonisation" in Nineteenth-century Colombia', *Hispanic American Historical Review* 79(4): 631–64.

Bakewell, P. 1997 'Eighteenth-century Spanish America: Reformed or Deformed?' in *A History of Latin America*. Oxford: Blackwell, pp. 254–93.

Barickman, B.J. 2004. 'Revisiting the *Casa-Grande*: Plantation and Cane-farming Households in Early Nineteenth-century Bahia', *Hispanic American Historical Review* 84(4): 619–59.

Borah, W. 1992. 'The Historical Demography of Aboriginal and Colonial America: an Attempt at Perspective', in W.M. Denevan (ed.), *The Native Population of the Americas in 1492*. Madison, Wisc. : Univ. of Wisconsin Press, pp. 13–34.

Brading, D.A. 1983. 'Tridentine Catholicism and Enlightened Despotism in Bourbon Mexico', *Journal of Latin American Studies* 15: 1–22.

Brooks, F.J. 1993. 'Revising the Conquest of Mexico: Smallpox, Sources and Populations', *Journal of Interdisciplinary History* 24(1): 1–29.

Burkholder, M.A., and L.L. Johnson. 2008. *Colonial Latin America*. 6th ed. Oxford: Oxford University Press.

Cahill, D. 1990. 'Taxonomy of a Colonial "Riot": The Arequipa Disturbances of 1780', in J.R. Fisher, A.J. Kuethe and A. McFarlane (eds), *Reform and Insurrection in Bourbon New Granada and Peru*. Baton Rouge: Louisiana State University Press, pp. 255–91.

———— 2002. 'The Cacique Network and Tribute Administration', in *From Rebellion to Independence in the Andes: Soundings from Southern Peru, 1750–1830*. Amsterdam: Aksant Academic, pp. 153–68.

Campbell, L.G. 1972. 'Black Power in Colonial Peru: The 1779 Tax Rebellion of Lambayeque', *Phylon* 33(2): 140–52.

Centeno, M.A. 1997. 'Blood and Debt: War and Taxation in Nineteenth-century Latin America', *American Journal of Sociology* 102(6): 1565–1605.

———— 2002. *Blood and Debt: War and the Nation-state in Latin America*. University Park: Pennsylvania State University Press.

Cook, N.D. 1999. 'Numbers from Nowhere: The American Indian Contact Population Debate', *Journal of Interdisciplinary History* 30(3): 516–20.

Dopico, F., and R. Rowland. 1990. 'Demografía del Censo de Floridablanca: Una Aproximación', *Revista de Historia Económica* 8(3): 591–618.

Earle, R. 1993. 'Indian Rebellion and Bourbon Reform in New Granada: Riots in Pasto, 1780–1800', *Hispanic American Historical Review* 73(1): 99–124.

Fisher, J. 1992. 'Iberoamérica Colonial', in M. Lucena Salmoral (ed.), *Historia de Iberoamérica*. Madrid: Editorial Cátedra, pp. 551–657

Fisher, J., A.J. Kuethe and A. McFarlane (eds). 1990. *Reform and Insurrection in Bourbon New Granada and Peru*. Baton Rouge: Louisiana State University Press.

Gootenberg, P. 1991. 'Population and Ethnicity in Early Republican Peru: Some Revisions', *Latin American Research Review* 26(3): 109–57.

Goyer, D.S., and E. Domschke. 1983. *The Handbook of National Population Censuses: Latin America and the Caribbean, North America, and Oceania*. Westport, CT: Greenwood.

Gutiérrez, R. 1991. *When Jesus Came the Corn Mothers Went Away: Marriage, Sexuality and Power in New Mexico, 1500–1846*. Stanford, CA: Stanford University Press.

Henige, D. 1986. 'Primary Source by Primary Source? On the Role of Epidemics in New World Depopulation', *Ethnohistory* 33(3): 293–312.

———— 1993. 'Counting the Encounter: The Pernicious Appeal of Verisimilitude', *Clahr* 2(3): 325–61.

———— 1999. 'Born to Die: Disease and New World Conquest', *Journal of Interdisciplinary History* 30(1): 109–11.

Jiménez de Gregorio, F. 1968. 'La Población de las Islas Canarias en la Segunda Mitad del Siglo XVIII', *Anuario de Estudios Atlánticos* 14: 127–301.

Klein, H.S. 1979. 'The Impact of the Crisis in Nineteenth Century Mining on Regional Economies: The Example of the Bolivian Yungas, 1786–1838', in D.J. Robinson (ed.), *Social Fabric and Spatial Structure in Colonial Latin America*. Ann Arbor: University Microfilms International, pp. 315–38.

——— 2003. *A Concise History of Bolivia*. Cambridge: Cambridge University Press.

Klein, H.S., and J.A. Barbier. 1988. 'Recent Trends in the Study of Spanish American Colonial Public Finance', *Latin American Research Review* 23(1): 35–62.

Kuznesof, E.A. 1991. 'Sexual Politics, Race and Bastard-bearing in Nineteenth-century Brazil: A Question of Culture or Power?' *Journal of Family History* 16(3): 241–60.

Lavrín, A. (ed.) 1989. *Sexuality and Marriage in Colonial Spanish America*. Lincoln: University of Nebraska Press.

Loy, J.M. 1981. 'Forgotten Comuneros: The 1781 Revolt in the Llanos of Casanare', *Hispanic American Historical Review* 61(2): 235–57.

McCaa, R. 1982. 'Modelling Social Interaction: Marriage, Miscegenation and the Society of Castes in Colonial Spanish America', *Historical Methods* 15(2): 45–66.

——— 1984. 'Calidad, Clase, and Marriage in Colonial Mexico: The Case of Parral, 1788–90', *Hispanic American Historical Review* 64(3): 477–501.

——— 1994. 'Marriageways in Mexico and Spain, 1500–1900', *Continuity and Change* 9(1): 11–43.

——— 1995. 'Spanish and Nahuatl Views on Smallpox and Demographic Catastrophe in Mexico', *Journal of Interdisciplinary History* 25(3): 397–431.

——— 2000. 'Familias y Género en México: Crítica Metodológica y Desafío Investigativo para el Fin del Milenio', in V.M. Uribe and L.J. Ortis (eds), *Naciones, Gentes y Territorios*. Medellín: Universidad de Antioquia, pp. 103–38.

McFarlane, A. 1984. 'Civil Disorders and Popular Protests in Late Colonial New Granada', *Hispanic American Historical Review* 64(1): 17–54.

——— 1989. 'The "Rebellion of the Barrios": Urban Insurrection in Bourbon Quito', *Hispanic American Historical Review* 69(2): 283–330.

——— 1993. *Colombia before Independence: Economy, Society and Politics under Bourbon Rule*. Cambridge: Cambridge University Press.

——— 1995. 'Rebellions in Late Colonial Spanish America: A Comparative Perspective', *Bulletin of Latin American Research* 14(3): 313–38.

——— 1998a. 'Identity, Enlightenment and Political Dissent in Late Colonial Spanish America', *Transactions of the Royal Historical Society* 8: 309–35.

——— 1998b. 'The Politics of Rebellion in New Granada, 1780–1810', in H.-J. König and M. Wiesebron (eds), *Nation Building in Nineteenth*

Century Latin America: Dilemmas and Conflicts. Leiden: CNWS, pp. 199–217.

—— 2005. 'Autoridad y poder en Cartagena de Indias: La Herencia de los Austrias', in H. Calvo Stevenson and A. Meisel Roca (eds), *Cartagena de Indias en el siglo XVIII*. Cartagena: Banco de la República, pp. 221–59.

Martinez-Alier, V. 1974. *Marriage, Class and Colour in Nineteenth-century Cuba*. Cambridge: Cambridge University Press.

Matos Rodríguez, F.V. 1999. 'Spatial and Demographic Change in Nineteenth-century San Juan, Puerto Rico, 1800–1868', *Journal of Urban History* 25(4): 477–513.

Meisel Roca, A., and M. Aguilera Díaz. 1997. 'Cartagena de Indias en 1777: Un Análisis demográfico', *Boletín Cultural y Bibliográfico* 34(45): 21–57.

Miller, G.M. 1990. 'Bourbon Social Engineering: Women and Conditions of Marriage in Eighteenth-century Venezuela', *Americas* 46: 261–90.

Minchom, M. 1994. *The People of Quito, 1690–1810: Change and Unrest in the Underclass*. Boulder, CO: Westview Press.

Moreno Yáñez, S. 1995. *Sublevaciones Indígenas en la Audiencia de Quito: Desde Comienzos del Siglo XVIII Hasta Finales de la Colonia*, 4th edn. Quito: Ediciones de la Pontificia Universidad Católica del Ecuador.

Ouweneel, A. 1991. 'Growth, Stagnation, and Migration: an Explorative Analysis of the *Tributario* Series of Anáhuac, 1720–1800', *Hispanic American Historical Review* 71(3): 531–77.

Pearce, A.J. 2001. 'The Peruvian Population Census of 1725–1740', *Latin American Research Review* 36(3): 69–104.

Phelan, J.L. 1978. *The People and the King: The Comunero Revolution in Colombia, 1781*. Madison: University of Wisconsin Press.

Platt, T. 1987. 'The Andean Experience of Bolivian Liberalism, 1825–1900: Roots of Rebellion in Nineteenth-century Chayanta (Potosí)', in S. Stern (ed.), *Resistance, Rebellion, and Consciousness in the Andean Peasant World, 18th to 20th Centuries*. Madison: University of Wisconsin Press, pp. 280–333.

Polo Acuña, J. 1998. 'Aspectos Históricos de Riohacha durante el Periodo Colonial', *Historia Caribe* 2(3): 33–49.

Rípodas Ardanaz, D. 1977. *El Matrimonio en Indias. Realidad Social y Regulación Jurídica*. Buenos Aires: FECIC.

Saether, S.A. 2003. 'Bourbon Absolutism and Marriage Reform in Late Colonial Spanish America', *Americas* 59(4): 475–509.

—— 2005a. *Identidades e Independencia en Santa Marta and Riohacha, 1750–1850*. Bogotá: Instituto colombiano de antropología e historia.

—— 2005b. 'Independence and the Redefinition of Indianness around Santa Marta, Colombia, 1750–1850', *Journal of Latin American Studies* 37(1): 55–80.

Safford, F. 1991. 'Race, Integration and Progress: Elite Attitudes and the Indian in Colombia, 1750–1870', *Hispanic American Historical Review* 71(1): 1–33.

Seed, P. 1982. 'Social Dimensions of Race: Mexico City, 1753', *Hispanic American Historical Review* 62(4): 569–606.

————— 1988. *To Love, Honor, and Obey in Colonial Mexico: Conflicts over Marriage Choice, 1574–1821*. Stanford, CA: Stanford University Press.

Stark, D.M. 1996. 'Marriage Strategies Among the Eighteenth Century Puerto Rican Slave Population: Demographic Evidence From the Pre-plantation Period', *Caribbean Studies* 29(2): 185–212.

Stavig, W. 1995. '"Living in Offence of Our Lord": Indigenous Sexual Values and Marital Life in the Colonial Crucible', *Hispanic American Historical Review* 75(4): 597–622.

Stern, S. 1987. 'The Age of Andean Insurrection, 1742–1781: A Reappraisal', in S.J. Stern (ed.), *Resistance, Rebellion, and Consciousness in the Andean Peasant World, 18th to 20th Centuries*. Madison: University of Wisconsin Press, pp. 34–93.

TePaske, J.J. 1990. 'The Royal Treasury Accounts of Spanish America', *European Review of Latin American and Caribbean Studies* 49: 122–25.

Twinam, A. 1999. *Public Lives, Private Secrets: Gender, Honor, Sexuality, and Illegitimacy in Colonial Spanish America*. Stanford, CA: Stanford University Press.

Van Aken, M. 1981. 'The Lingering Death of Indian Tribute in Ecuador', *Hispanic American Historical Review* 61(3): 429–59.

Van Young, E. 1993. 'Agrarian Rebellion and Defense of Community: Meaning and Collective Violence in Late Colonial and Independence-era Mexico', *Journal of Social History* 27(2): 245–69.

4

THE CONSTRUCTION OF LIFE TABLES FOR THE AMERICAN INDIAN POPULATION AT THE TURN OF THE TWENTIETH CENTURY

J. David Hacker and Michael R. Haines

Substantial qualitative evidence indicates that the American Indian population of the United States suffered high mortality in the five centuries after contact with European populations (Thornton 2000). Comprehensive and reliable age-specific mortality data, however, are not available until after 1955, when the U.S. Public Health Services assumed responsibility for Indian healthcare (Shoemaker 1999: 8). Rough estimates of life expectancy before that date suggest very high mortality rates. In 1940, American Indian life expectancy at birth for both sexes combined is estimated to have been 51.6 years, 12.6 years lower than that of the white population and 1.5 years lower than that of the black population. Infant mortality rates in 1944 is estimated to have been 135 per 1,000, approximately three times higher than that of other races (Snipp 2006: 746, 744).

This chapter constructs new life tables for the American Indian population in the late nineteenth and early twentieth centuries, thus pushing back the availability of age-specific mortality and life expectancy estimates nearly half a century. Because of the lack of reliable vital registration data for the American Indian population in this period, the life tables are constructed using indirect census-based estimation methods. Infant and child mortality rates are estimated from the total number of living children each woman has given birth to and the total number of those children still living reported in the 1900 and 1910 censuses. Adult mortality rates are inferred from the infant and child mortality estimates using model life tables. Adult mortality rates are also estimated by applying the two-census method of Preston and Bennett (1983) to the 1900 to 1910 intercensal period.

As other chapters in this collection emphasise, there is a complex relationship between aboriginal identity, its measurement in demographic sources, and demographic analyses. Although no other source on the American Indian population at the turn of twentieth century approaches the richness and comprehensiveness of the American Indian censuses, potential problems in the enumeration likely bias the estimation of mortality. As discussed below, errors reporting age and marital duration in the census likely imparts substantial bias in mortality estimates derived from both the surviving children and the two-census method. In addition, difficulties in defining individuals as belonging to an American Indian 'race' present a major challenge to the estimation of mortality with two-census methods, which assumes that the American Indian population was closed to migration. Federal assimilation policy strongly encouraged American Indians to assimilate into the general population, where they were less likely to be identified as Indian. Thus individuals descended in whole or part from the pre-contact Indian populations of North America may have 'migrated' across racial categories between the two censuses.

The 1890, 1900 and 1910 Indian Censuses

The enumeration of American Indians on special forms in the 1890, 1900 and 1910 censuses grew out of aspirations of the U.S. federal government to better manage the nation's Indian population and to measure the impact of its assimilation policies (Jobe 2004). Neither a complete count of American Indians nor an enumeration of their social, economic or demographic characteristics was required. Although the U.S. Constitution mandated a census every ten years to apportion representatives in Congress, it specifically noted that only 'taxed' Indians – that is, Indians severing tribal relations and living among the general population – counted towards congressional representation. As a result, the vast majority of Indians living in the United States before 1890 were not enumerated by a census.[1] It was not until the 1940s that all Indians were considered 'taxed' and routinely enumerated (ibid.).

The first attempt to truly count and collect demographic information for all Indians of the United States was made with the 1890 census. Of the total 248,253 Indians enumerated, 58,806 were 'Indians taxed' and 189,447 were 'Indians not taxed'. As in earlier censuses, distinguishing between 'taxed' and 'non-taxed' Indians proved difficult. According to the census report:

> Indians taxed and Indians not taxed are terms that cannot be rigidly interpreted, as Indian citizens, like white citizens, frequently have nothing to tax. Indians subject to tax and Indians not subject to tax might more clearly express the distinction. Indians taxed have so far become assimilated in the general population that they are not exempt from tax by reason of being Indians. Indians not taxed are remnants of uncivilized tribes or bodies of Indians untaxed by reason of specific treaties or laws controlling their relation to the national government, as the Six Nations of New York and the Five Civilized Tribes of Indian Territory (Census Bureau 1894: 131).[2]

A more difficult problem for the Census Bureau and other federal agencies was defining who was an 'Indian' and what defined membership of a tribe. Prior to the nineteenth century, most tribes adhered to a kinship model in which biological children and individuals marrying or adopted by a member of the tribe were considered members or citizens of the tribe. During the nineteenth century, however, the federal government increasingly relied on a race-based definition that focused on an individual's degree of 'Indian blood'. In *United States v. Rogers* (1846), for example, the U.S. Supreme Court ruled that a white person living in the Cherokee territory and married to a Cherokee tribal member – though considered a citizen of the Cherokee nation by tribal law – was not an Indian for jurisdictional purposes. Passage of the *General Allotment Act 1887* furthered the move towards a blood quantum definition of Indian identity. To implement the policy, Congress passed an act in 1894 that gave Indians denied an allotment the ability to file a federal lawsuit, provided that the person was 'in whole or in part of Indian blood or descent'. Federally imposed racial definitions were eventually adopted by Indian tribes. Today, most tribe memberships have an explicit blood quantum standard (Spruhan 2006).

The 1890, 1900 and 1910 censuses were thus taken during a period of changing definition of 'Indian.' In practice, the census definition was based on enumerator observation and respondent answer, leading to problems of identification. As the 1890 census report noted, 'Enumeration would be likely to pass by many who had been identified all their lives with the localities where found, and who lived like the adjacent whites without any inquiry as to their race, entering them as native born whites' (Census Bureau 1894: 131). According to the same report, some non-Indians were likely to be counted as

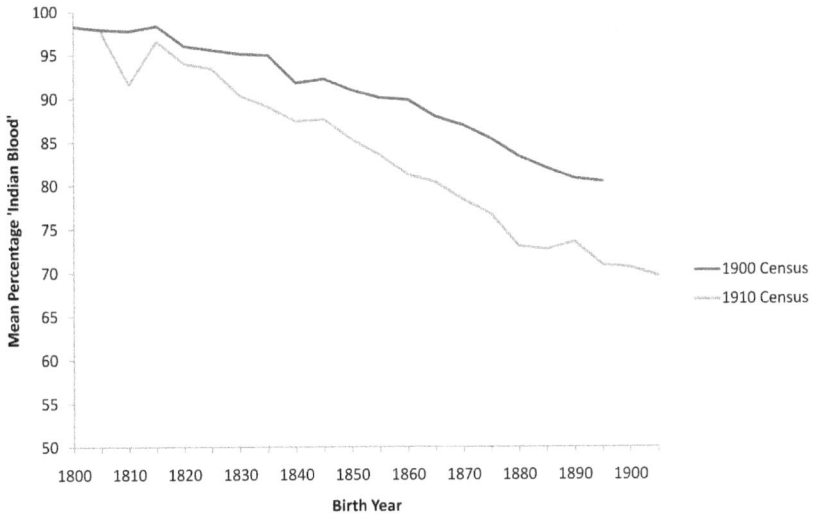

Figure 4.1 Mean Percentage 'Indian Blood' by Birth Year
Source: Ruggles et al. 2008.

Indians: 'On the other hand, certain legal and proprietary claims lead persons of very slight Indian blood connections, or even pure whites by birth, to call themselves Indians by heredity or acquired right, and there are those of pure white blood who wish to be called Indians, in order to share in pecuniary advantages, who are not acknowledged by any tribes' (ibid.: 131).

The inclusion of a special census question in the 1900 and 1910 censuses on an individual's proportion of 'Indian blood' reflects the growing emphasis on blood quantum by the federal government and an attempt to avoid some of the ambiguity of defining an Indian. The 1910 census report on American Indians, for example, noted that 'all persons of mixed white and Indian blood who have any appreciable amount of Indian blood are counted as Indians, even though that proportion of white blood may exceed that of Indian blood' (Census Bureau 1915: 10). Figure 4.1, which plots the mean percentage of Indian blood by birth cohort in the 1900 and 1910 Indian Census Integrated Public Use Microdata Series (IPUMS) samples, suggests that the new emphasis led to a greater number of individuals of mixed decent being counted as Indian in the 1910 census.[3]

In addition to the Census Bureau's acknowledged difficulties measuring race and tax status, Shoemaker (1992) contends that cultural differences between enumerators and Indians created special challenges for the 1890, 1900 and 1910 census enumerations. Family structure varied tremendously among tribes and was often at odds with the patriarchal family structure dominant among enumerators. In many Indian societies, 'fathers', 'mothers' and other identified kin were equivalent to what Euro-Americans would call aunts, uncles, unrelated individuals or fictive kin. Although Shoemaker suspects that most Indians and enumerators recognised these cultural differences and accounted for them on the census forms, we cannot be entirely certain. Indians may have also been reticent to share some information with the federal government. Indian parents concerned about the possibility of losing their children to government-run boarding schools had a potential incentive to hide children. Parents whose children were eligible for allotments, on the other hand, might have counted deceased children and pregnancies in the hope of acquiring additional acreage (ibid.). In addition to challenges noted by Shoemaker, the Census Bureau took a dim view of the quality of many of the questions unique to the 1910 Indian enumeration. 'Inquires were also made on the special Indian schedule as to graduation from educational institutions, allotments, residence on own lands, and whether living in civilized or aboriginal dwellings,' noted the Bureau's report on the 1910 enumeration, 'but the answers were so deficient or manifestly inaccurate as to render the results of little or no value' (Census Bureau 1915: 9).

Despite these problems, we have no other source on the American Indian population comparable in coverage and scope to the 1900 and 1910 censuses. For the most part, enumerators were chosen for their familiarity with particular tribes and appear to have been diligent in their effort

(Johansson and Preston 1978; Shoemaker 1992). In her study of five Indian tribes, Shoemaker (1999: 108) noted that enumerators were usually mixed-blood Indians, white men married to Indian women, or employees of the Bureau of Indian Affairs who were familiar with the language and the culture of the groups they enumerated, thus minimising the potential for misunderstandings and error.

The 1900 and 1910 American Indian IPUMS Samples

Although the Census Bureau collected data in 1890, 1900 and 1910, it lacked the necessary funds to analyse the 1900 data. The Bureau was able to publish brief analyses of the 1890 and 1910 data, but like other census publications of the era these included only a few dozen cross tabulations. The creation of microdata samples from the original returns allows the analysis of data in a much more sophisticated way. Unfortunately, the original manuscript returns of the 1890 census were destroyed in a fire. The 1900 and 1910 censuses are thus the first surviving censuses to enumerate all American Indians in a systematic manner. These returns were sampled and transcribed at the Minnesota Population Center, then coded and released to the public on the IPUMS website between 2005 and 2008 (Ruggles et al. 2008).

The 1900 and 1910 Indian IPUMS samples are 1-in–5 samples of all households in the Indian census. Indians living outside reservations among the general population – approximately 6 per cent of the total number of Indians in 1900 and 7 per cent in 1910 – were enumerated in the regular census schedules and are not included in the high density Indian sample.[4] The 1900 high-density Indian sample includes 45,651 individuals identified as members of 226 unique tribal groups. The 1910 sample includes 48,724 individuals of 225 unique tribes.

The diversity of the American Indian population is not easily summarised. Table 4.1 tabulates the samples by sex, year and major tribal group, a classification scheme used by the 1990 census and the IPUMS project.[5] The Cherokee and Sioux nations had the most members in both census years, each representing about 11 per cent of the sampled population in 1900. There was a noticeable drop in the number of Sioux in 1910 relative to other groups, however, perhaps reflecting sampling variability, changes in census coverage, or differential fertility and mortality.

Constructing Life Tables Using Information on Child Survivorship

Demographers have developed indirect methods of fertility and mortality estimation for populations with poor or nonexistent vital registration systems. One of the most commonly used indirect methods is the Brass method for estimating child mortality from census or survey data on child survivorship (United Nations 1983: 73–96; Preston, Heuveline and Guillot

Table 4.1. Number of American Indians in the 1900 and 1910 Indian IPUMS Samples, by Sex and General Tribal Group

General Tribal Group	1900 Sample				1910 Sample			
	Number of Males	Number of Females	Both Sexes	Percentage of total	Number of males	Number of females	Both Sexes	Percentage of total
Apache	600	667	1,267	2.8%	590	568	1,158	2.4%
Blackfoot	173	198	371	0.8%	242	228	470	1.0%
Cherokee	2,316	2,497	4,813	10.5%	2,895	2,703	5,603	11.5%
Cheyenne	312	392	704	1.5%	278	269	547	1.1%
Chickasaw	359	390	749	1.6%	437	475	912	1.9%
Chippewa (Ojibwa)	1,682	1,589	3,271	7.2%	1,760	1,651	3,411	7.0%
Choctaw	1,119	1,149	2,268	5.0%	1,411	1,341	2,752	5.6%
Creek	601	652	1,253	2.7%	685	658	1,343	2.8%
Iroquois	816	754	1,570	3.4%	821	728	1,549	3.2%
Kiowa	111	111	222	0.5%	108	154	262	0.5%
Navajo	1,280	1,186	2,466	5.4%	2,023	1,975	3,998	8.2%
Osage	153	172	325	0.7%	158	141	299	0.6%
Paiute	502	502	1,004	2.2%	353	378	731	1.5%
Pima	420	399	819	1.8%	406	397	803	1.6%
Potawatomie	142	115	257	0.6%	263	210	473	1.0%
Pueblo	1,352	1,207	2,559	5.6%	1,147	1,038	2,185	4.5%
Seminole	163	155	318	0.7%	154	150	304	0.6%
Shoshone	416	351	767	1.7%	343	361	704	1.4%
Sioux	2,461	2,607	5,068	11.1%	1,814	1,783	3,597	7.4%
Tohono O'Odham	354	347	701	1.5%	360	358	718	1.5%
Puget Sound Salish	216	210	426	0.9%	225	253	478	1.0%
All Others	7,735	6,718	14,453	31.7%	8,531	7,896	16,427	33.7%
Total, all Tribes	23,283	22,368	45,651	100.0%	25,004	23,720	48,724	100.0%

Source: Ruggles et al. 2008.

2001: 224–55). The method requires data on the total number of live births that a married woman had in her life and how many of those children survived. Fortunately, these questions were included in the 1900 and 1910 censuses (Preston and Haines 1991; Haines and Preston 1997).

The Brass method transforms the proportion of deceased children among women of different age or marriage duration categories into a standard life table parameter, q_x, the proportion of children dying before reaching age 'x'. The exposure of children to the risk of dying can be proxied with three different approaches. The 'age model' uses women's age, the 'duration model' uses women's marriage duration, and the 'surviving children' method uses ages of the surviving children. Very roughly, for example, the proportion of deceased children among women aged 20 to 24 and women married for 10 to 15 years correspond to the proportion of children dying before age 5. Adjustments are made for age-specific and marital duration specific fertility schedules. Unfortunately, the estimating procedure for the surviving children method would not converge on a solution in the computer program designed for the approach for the American Indian population. The cause is likely age misstatement among children. Results are thus reported only for the age and marital duration models.

Age misstatement appears to have been common in the American Indian census among adults as well. Figures 4.2 and 4.3 suggest a much higher level of age and marital duration 'heaping' problems in the Indian population than in the nation's native-born white population. Age and marriage durations for the American Indian population ending in a 5 or 0 – ages 40, 45, 50 and so on – are clearly over-reported, while age and marital durations ending in other digits are under-reported. There are, for example, approximately three times as many American Indians aged 40 as there are aged 39 or 41. If age-heaping errors are small random rounding errors – that is, true ages are normally and tightly distributed about the reported age – the resulting bias in indirect mortality estimates will be modest. Shoemaker (1999) has estimated life expectancy of five selected Indian tribes in 1900 with alternative age categories – age 38 to 42, 43 to 47 and so on – and found very small differences in the results. However, if the rounding is systematic – for example, an increasing tendency to round up true ages with increasing age – the bias will be more severe.

The results from indirect child mortality estimation methods applied to the original 1900 and 1910 IPUMS samples and to the new 1900 and 1910 American Indian IPUMS samples are given in Tables 4.2 and 4.3. The sample universe includes currently married women in the 1900 and 1910 Indian censuses with spouse present, and valid age, martial duration, number of children born, and number of children surviving data. The 1910 sample is further restricted to women in their first marriage (a question on the number of times each married individual had been married was added in the 1910 census). The tables show the corresponding q_x value for each age and marriage duration category, the number of children born used

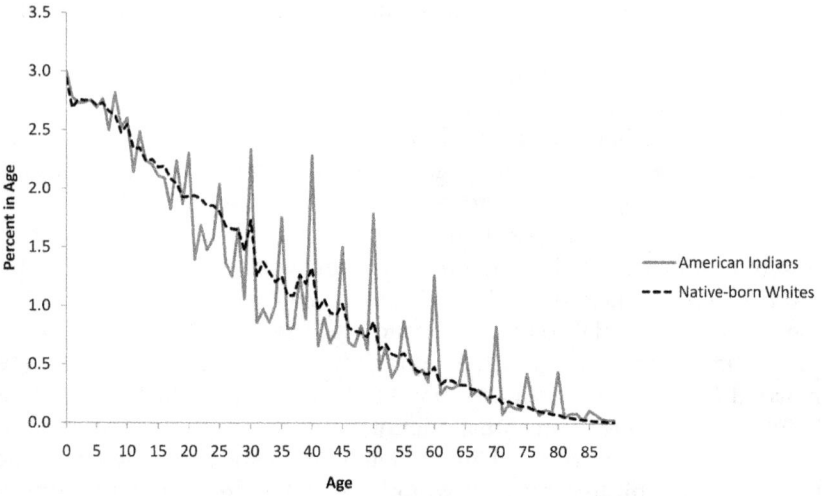

Figure 4.2 Age Distribution of the American Indian and Native-born White Populations of the United States in 1900
Source: Ruggles et al. 2008.

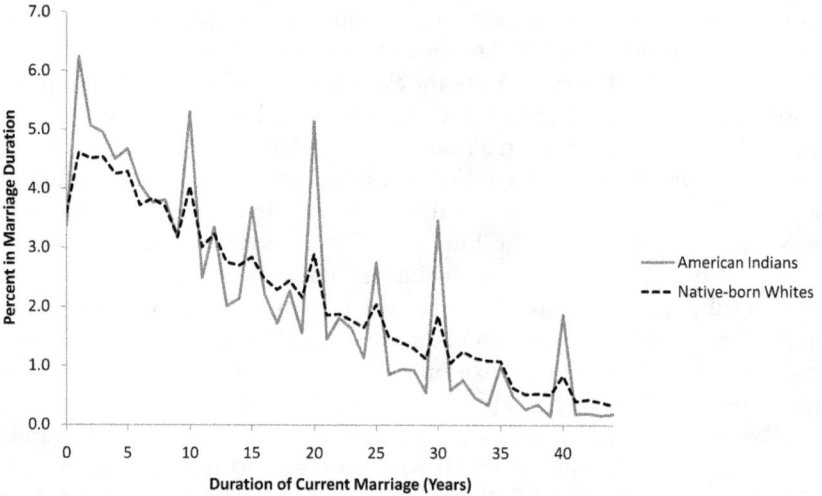

Figure 4.3 Duration of Current Marriage, American Indian and Native-Born White Women in 1900
Source: Ruggles et al. 2008.

to make the estimate, the relevant date in the past to which the estimate applies, and the expectation of life at birth, e_0, indicated by that level of child mortality in the model West life table system (Coale and Demeny 1966). Model West was chosen because it fit the American experience in 1900 very well (Preston and Haines 1991: 49–87).

Figure 4.4 plots the implied model West life expectancies by method of construction, census sample, and date to which each estimate applies. Most estimates are between 35 and 45 years. Estimates made with the 1910 census sample using the age and duration methods closely correspond. Those made with the 1900 sample, however, do not. The likely reason is the lack of information on remarriage in 1900. When mortality is high, as it was in the American Indian population, there is a good deal of widowhood and potential remarriage of widows. Thus, older women who have had more children and a longer period of exposure to risk of child death would be included in the shorter marriage durations. This problem was largely eliminated in 1910 by limiting the sample to women in their first marriage. A partial solution for the problem in the 1900 duration model was to select women who were younger than age 35 at the estimated time of marriage (age minus duration of current marriage), which is why estimates of longer marriage durations are not included in Table 4.2.[6]

The 1900 age model and the 1910 age and marital duration models suggest rapid trends towards higher life expectancies in the years preceding the census. Although mortality was falling for the white population (ibid.), there are several reasons to be sceptical of the American Indian results. First,

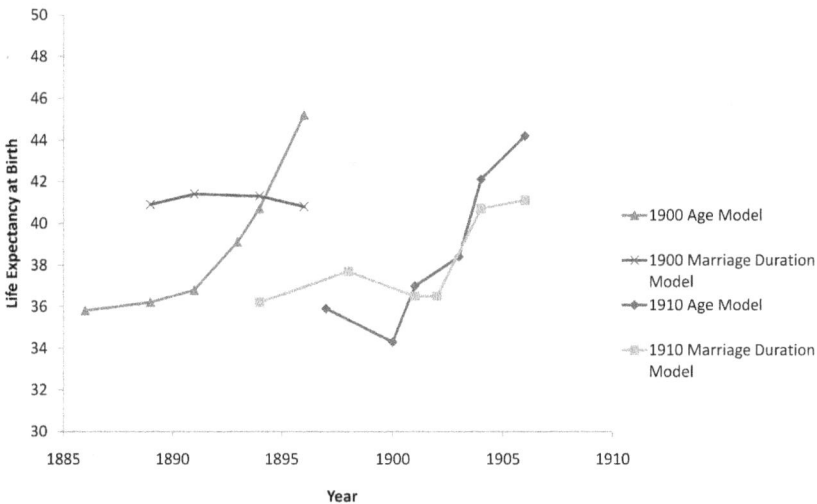

Figure 4.4 Life Expectancy at Birth: Indirect Estimates from the 1900 and 1910 American Indian Censuses

Table 4.2. Estimates of Child Mortality in the Late Nineteenth Century United States by Race Using the Age and Marriage Duration Estimation Methods

AGE MODEL	Age Groups						
	15–19	20–24	25–29	30–34	35–39	40–44	45–49
	q(1)	q(2)	q(3)	q(5)	q(10)	q(15)	q(20)
				q(i)			
Total	0.15332	0.17664	0.16438	0.17736	0.20662	0.21983	0.26076
White	0.16168	0.15176	0.15109	0.16705	0.19512	0.20920	0.24755
Black	0.13090	0.26216	0.21502	0.25164	0.27776	0.29367	0.34327
American Indian	0.07770	0.20713	0.26780	0.30932	0.36201	0.38869	0.41898
Reference Date							
Total	1899.7	1898.5	1896.7	1894.6	1892.1	1889.4	1886.4
White	1899.7	1898.6	1896.9	1894.8	1892.5	1889.8	1886.8
Black	1899.9	1898.5	1896.2	1893.4	1890.4	1887.3	1884.3
American Indian	1898.2	1896.5	1894.7	1893.0	1891.3	1889.3	1886.7
Implied Life Expectancy at Birth, e(0)							
Total	44.5	46.5	49.8	50.0	48.7	48.6	46.5
White	43.2	49.8	51.5	51.1	49.8	49.6	47.7
Black	48.2	36.4	43.8	42.2	41.7	41.7	39.3
American Indian	62.6	45.2	40.7	39.1	36.8	36.2	35.8

DURATION MODEL	Duration of Marriage						
	0–4	5–9	10–14	15–19	20–24	25–29	30–34
	q(2)	q(3)	q(5)	q(10)	q(15)	q(20)	q(25)
				q(i)			
Total	0.14722	0.15514	0.18234	0.19496	0.21885	0.25267	0.27768
White	0.12926	0.13949	0.17267	0.19234	0.21101	0.24398	0.26915
Black	0.28021	0.26441	0.25096	0.22168	0.27879	0.32477	0.35960
American Indian	0.30060	0.26617	0.28591	0.30809	0.31930	–	–
Reference Date							
Total	1899.3	1897.2	1894.8	1892.4	1889.6	1886.5	1883.5
White	1899.2	1897.1	1894.8	1892.4	1889.8	1886.6	1883.6
Black	1899.3	1897.4	1894.8	1891.8	1888.8	1885.8	1883.1
American Indian	1899.0	1896.6	1894.2	1891.9	1889.0	–	–
Implied Life Expectancy at Birth, e(0)							
Total	50.4	50.9	49.5	49.4	48.7	47.2	47.1
White	52.9	53.0	50.5	50.1	49.4	48.0	47.8
Black	34.6	38.5	42.3	47.2	43.0	40.8	40.3
American Indian	35.0	40.8	41.3	41.4	40.9	–	–

Source: Indirect estimates based on the original public use micro sample of the 1900 U.S. Census of Population and are from Preston and Haines (1991), chapter 2. The estimates for the American Indian population are based on the IPUMS sample of the American Indian population from the 1900 U.S. Census of Population (Ruggles et al. 2008). Coale & Demeny (1966) Model West is used in all cases.

Table 4.3. Estimates of Child Mortality in the Late Nineteenth Century and Early Twentieth Century by Race Using the Age and Marriage Duration Estimation Methods

AGE MODEL	15–19 q(1)	20–24 q(2)	25–29 q(3)	30–34 q(5)	35–39 q(10)	40–44 q(15)	45–49 q(20)
				q(i)			
Total	0.02795	0.10727	0.13950	0.17215	0.19298	0.21983	0.24128
White	0.02740	0.09415	0.12361	0.15605	0.17785	0.20379	0.22559
Black	0.03172	0.16472	0.22150	0.26631	0.28831	0.33625	0.34450
American Indian	0.04179	0.19206	0.23032	0.29048	0.33056	0.38164	0.38629

Reference Date

Total	1907.6	1905.9	1904.2	1902.7	1901.2	1899.5	1896.9
White	1907.7	1905.9	1904.2	1902.7	1901.1	1899.4	1896.8
Black	1907.6	1906.0	1904.4	1902.9	1901.6	1899.9	1897.3
American Indian							

Implied Life Expectancy at Birth, e(0)

Total	70.2	56.1	53.0	50.9	50.1	48.5	48.2
White	70.7	58.1	55.1	52.6	51.7	50.2	49.7
Black	69.2	47.7	43.1	40.7	52.8	52.1	51.0
American Indian	66.5	44.2	42.1	38.4	37.0	34.3	35.9

DURATION MODEL	0–4 q(2)	5–9 q(3)	10–14 q(5)	15–19 q(10)	20–24 q(15)	25–29 q(20)	30–34 q(25)
				q(i)			
Total	0.12882	0.14615	0.16490	0.18479	0.20981	0.22518	0.24815
White	0.11107	0.13386	0.15473	0.17635	0.20170	0.21660	0.23353
Black	0.24088	0.23237	0.24353	0.26359	0.28037	0.32328	0.36964
American Indian	0.32947	0.23909	0.26649	0.33587	0.35407	0.36373	0.41242

Reference Date

Total	1908.9	1906.6	1904.2	1901.8	1899.0	1898.6	1892.5
White	1908.9	1906.6	1904.2	1901.8	1899.0	1895.6	1892.5
Black	1908.9	1906.7	1904.3	1902.0	1899.4	1896.0	1892.9
American Indian							

Implied Life Expectancy at Birth, e(0)

Total	52.8	52.1	51.5	51.0	49.6	49.7	49.7
White	55.5	53.7	52.7	51.9	50.4	50.6	51.0
Black	38.4	41.9	43.1	43.1	42.9	41.0	39.6
American Indian	29.6	41.1	40.7	36.5	36.5	37.7	36.2

Source: Indirect estimates based on the original public use micro sample of the 1900 U.S. Census of Population and are from Preston and Haines (1997), chapter 2. The estimates for the American Indian population are based on the IPUMS sample of the American Indian population from the 1900 U.S. Census of Population (Ruggles et al. 2008). Coale & Demeny (1966) Model West is used in all cases.

Table 4.4. American Indian Life Tables Circa 1894

Age	qx	lx	dx	Lx	Tx	ex
0	0.2028	100000	20279.9	86412.4	3788442	37.88
1	0.1152	79720	9184.9	294558.6	3702029	46.44
5	0.0314	70535	2216.5	347134.6	3407470.6	48.31
10	0.0227	68319	1553.0	337711.0	3060335.9	44.80
15	0.0316	66766	2113.0	328546.2	2722624.9	40.78
20	0.0448	64653	2899.3	316015.6	2394078.7	37.03
25	0.0497	61753	3068.1	301097.2	2078063.1	33.65
30	0.0572	58685	3355.2	285039.0	1776965.9	30.28
35	0.0672	55330	3720.6	267349.6	1491926.8	26.96
40	0.0819	51610	4226.9	247480.9	1224577.3	23.73
45	0.0975	47383	4621.6	225359.5	977096.4	20.62
50	0.1254	42761	5363.0	200397.9	751736.9	17.58
55	0.1578	37398	5902.2	172234.8	551339.0	14.74
60	0.2148	31496	6765.6	140565.4	379104.2	12.04
65	0.2858	24730	7068.7	105979.8	238538.8	9.65
70	0.3857	17662	6812.2	71277.5	132559.0	7.51
75	0.5194	10849	5635.2	40159.1	61281.4	5.65
80	1.0000	5214	5214.2	21122.3	21122.3	4.05

Age	qx	lx	dx	Lx	Tx	ex
0	0.1737	100000	17368.6	88710.4	4060664	40.61
1	0.1148	82631	9486.1	305491.6	3971953	48.07
5	0.0330	73145	2411.6	359697.3	3666461.6	50.13
10	0.0257	70734	1820.6	349116.7	3306764.3	46.75
15	0.0341	68913	2351.0	338687.6	2957647.6	42.92
20	0.0430	66562	2860.3	325659.2	2618960.0	39.35
25	0.0483	63702	3079.6	310809.4	2293300.8	36.00
30	0.0546	60622	3312.9	294828.1	1982491.4	32.70
35	0.0604	57309	3462.4	277889.7	1687663.3	29.45
40	0.0659	53847	3548.9	260361.4	1409773.6	26.18
45	0.0733	50298	3684.6	242277.8	1149412.2	22.85
50	0.0957	46613	4459.8	221916.8	907134.4	19.46
55	0.1237	42153	5212.5	197735.8	685217.7	16.26
60	0.1789	36941	6609.4	168181.0	487481.9	13.20
65	0.2424	30332	7353.5	133273.7	319300.9	10.53
70	0.3449	22978	7924.6	95078.3	186027.2	8.10
75	0.4730	15053	7120.4	57465.6	90948.9	6.04
80	1.0000	7933	7932.9	33483.3	33483.3	4.22

Source: Ruggles et al. 2008. Estimates are derived on the Children Surviving Age Model, Women age 30–34 years, and the Model West System.

Table 4.5. American Indian Life Tables Circa 1904

Age	qx	lx	dx	Lx	Tx	ex
0	0.2093	100000	20925	85980.2	3706367	37.06
1	0.1195	79075	9451.6	291272.1	3620387	45.78
5	0.0325	69623	2262.3	342461.2	3329114.9	47.82
10	0.0235	67361	1583.2	332847.3	2986653.7	44.34
15	0.0327	65778	2147.7	323520.0	2653806.4	40.34
20	0.0463	63630	2943.7	310791.5	2330286.4	36.62
25	0.0513	60686	3113.1	295649.5	2019494.9	33.28
30	0.0590	57573	3398.7	279369.8	1723845.4	29.94
35	0.0694	54175	3759.5	261474.3	1444475.6	26.66
40	0.0844	50415	4255.5	241436.7	1183001.3	23.47
45	0.1002	46160	4626.3	219232.0	941564.6	20.40
50	0.1286	41533	5340.2	194315.5	722332.6	17.39
55	0.1612	36193	5833.6	166380.9	528017.1	14.59
60	0.2189	30359	6645.7	135182.7	361636.2	11.91
65	0.2904	23714	6887.4	101349.9	226453.5	9.55
70	0.3908	16826	6576.1	67691.1	125103.5	7.44
75	0.5250	10250	5381.8	37796.4	57412.5	5.60
80	1.0000	4868	4868.4	19616.1	19616.1	4.03

Age	qx	lx	dx	Lx	Tx	ex
0	0.1794	100000	17940.5	88338.7	3975388	39.75
1	0.1192	82059	9780.4	302427.6	3887049	47.37
5	0.0342	72279	2469.7	355221.4	3584621.6	49.59
10	0.0267	69809	1862.8	344390.2	3229400.1	46.26
15	0.0353	67947	2398.9	333736.0	2885009.9	42.46
20	0.0444	65548	2912.6	320457.2	2551274.0	38.92
25	0.0500	62635	3128.7	305354.0	2230816.8	35.62
30	0.0565	59506	3359.7	289133.2	1925462.8	32.36
35	0.0624	56147	3501.2	271981.1	1636329.6	29.14
40	0.0679	52646	3576	254288.1	1364348.5	25.92
45	0.0753	49070	3693.3	236114.9	1110060.4	22.62
50	0.0982	45376	4454.7	215744.9	873945.5	19.26
55	0.1266	40922	5180	191658.2	658200.6	16.08
60	0.1829	35742	6538.5	162362	466542.4	13.05
65	0.2470	29203	7214.3	127980	304180.4	10.42
70	0.3504	21989	7703.9	90684.4	176200.5	8.01
75	0.4789	14285	6840.7	54322.8	85516	5.99
80	1.0000	7444	7444.2	31193.2	31193.2	4.19

Source: Ruggles et al. 2008. Estimates are derived on the Children Surviving Age Model, Women age 30–34 years, and the Model West System.

the estimates rise very rapidly, approximately ten years in the ten years prior to each census. Given the lack of modern medicine and public health measures for the American Indian population at the time, the increase is too rapid to be accepted uncritically. Second, the estimates derived from the 1900 and 1910 samples do not agree with each other in years in which they overlap. The age model, for example, suggests a life expectancy at birth of approximately 45 years centred about 1896 using the 1900 census data and an estimate of 36 centred about 1897 using the 1910 census data. Third, the similar pattern of rapidly increasing life expectancy using both the 1900 and 1910 samples suggests that a similar bias was at work in each census. It is impossible to be specific about the causes of the bias, but misstatement of mother's age, martial duration and number of times married, identification of a mother's sociological instead of biological children, number of children born and number of children surviving recall errors, or even deliberate misstatement of the number of children born and children surviving information are all possible sources of bias.

Given the problem of unknown remarriage in the 1900 duration model, and the potential problem of defining marriage and its duration in the American Indian population, it is probably best to focus on results for the age model. But given the wide range of implied life expectancies and the potential for age misstatement and other forms of bias, which estimates are best? The value of q_1, estimated from the child survivorship data reported by mother's aged 15 to 19, is clearly too high to be believed. Implied life expectancy at birth estimated using the 1900 sample is almost 63 years, 20 years greater than that for the white population. In addition to the many possible biases listed above, the estimate of q_1 also suffers from a relatively short exposure of children to the risk of dying and a corresponding small number of child deaths. At the other extreme, the value of q_{20}, estimated from the child survivorship data reported by mother's aged 45 to 49, may be biased by the increasing tendency of older Indian women to misreport their age and children survival data.

The value of q_5, estimated from data reported by women aged 30 to 34, is probably a good compromise between avoiding the fewer cases of child mortality reported by younger women and the potential of age misstatement and memory recall errors associated with elderly mothers. It is also less sensitive to the choice of model life table (ibid.: 49–87). The q_5 estimate applies on average to about 1893/4 in the 1900 sample and about 1903/4 in the 1910 sample. These results imply an expectation of life at birth for the American Indian population overall of 39.1 years in the early 1890s and 38.4 years in the early 1900s. In contrast, the data imply an e_0 of 50 to 51 years for the white population and of about 42 years for the black population in 1893/4 and an e_0 of 52 to 53 years for the white population and of about 43 years for the black population in 1903/4. Thus the American Indian population was at a very serious mortality disadvantage to the majority white population and even at a slight disadvantage to the black population.

Although valuable, the child mortality data reported in Tables 4.2 and 4.3 apply to a limited part of the life span. A life table, which summarises the algebraic relationships between all age groups and mortality, survivorship, and life expectancy, is more valuable. Life tables have numerous applications in the study of mortality, fertility, migration and population growth, and are especially useful tools for the study of populations covered by a census but lacking a vital registration system, such as the American Indian population. When combined with indirect methods, life tables can be used to estimate vital rates or project populations from census age distributions and estimate age-specific fertility rates from census microdata samples.

Table 4.4 is a life table for the male and female American Indian population circa 1894, and Table 4.5 is a life table for the American Indian population circa 1904. Both tables were constructed by fitting the implied life expectancy at birth from the age model for Indian women aged 30 to 34 years to the model West life table system. At a given level of mortality, the model assumes that female mortality is lower than that for males. Thus, life expectancy circa 1894 is estimated to be 37.9 years at birth for Indian males, and 40.6 years for Indian females. The implied infant mortality rates are very high: about 203 infant deaths in the first 12 months per 1,000 live births for Indian males and 174 per 1,000 for Indian females. The survivorship column, l_x, indicates that less than half of all Indian males survive to 45 years of age and less than half of all Indian females to 50 years of age.

Constructing Life Tables Using Two-Census Methods

Availability of the IPUMS samples of the American Indian population also allows the use of two-census methods to evaluate adult survival of the American Indian population in the intercensal period.[7] Two-census methods have been a standard tool of demographers since the nineteenth century. Although there are well-known pitfalls in using two censuses to estimate mortality – including the problems created by differential enumeration, migration, age-reporting errors, and lack of population stability – newer methods help minimise bias from these sources. Preston and Bennett's census-based method for estimating adult mortality (Preston and Bennett 1983) does not depend on a model life table system, the survival of kin, or assumptions of population stability. The method relates the number of individuals at any two ages through age-specific growth rates and age-specific mortality rates and requires only age distributions in two census years and an assumption of a closed population.

The extent to which the American Indian population was not a closed population is probably the largest source of error. Despite some movements of individuals across the Canadian and Mexican borders, international migration appears to have been negligible relative to the total size of the population. The larger problem appears to be individuals who moved across racial categories between the two censuses. Although we cannot be sure about the size and direction of this migration, there is good reason to believe that it ran it both directions. The federal government's assimilation policies between 1880 and 1920 encouraged American Indians to learn English, shift from traditional subsistence strategies to farming, wear 'citizen's clothing', and become U.S. citizens (Hoxie 1984). Continuing intermarriage of the American Indian population with whites and blacks furthered the trend towards assimilation and produced children of mixed ancestry (see Figure 4.1). These pressures no doubt caused some individuals of full or partial Indian ancestry who were enumerated as Indians in the 1900 census to be enumerated as non-Indians in 1910. If there were substantial numbers of such individuals, estimates of mortality based on two-census methods would be biased upwards. The revised 1910 census instructions strongly encouraging enumerators to record the race of individuals having full or partial American Indian ancestry as Indians, however, probably resulted in racial migration in the opposite direction and biased estimates of mortality downwards (Nobles 2002).

Table 4.6 presents the application of Preston and Bennett's census-based procedure (Preston and Bennett 1983) to the combined age distribution of American Indians in the general 1900 IPUMS and 1900 Indian IPUMS samples and the age distribution of the American Indian population published by the Census Bureau for the 1910 census (Census Bureau 1915).[8] Life expectancy estimates for both sexes are provided for ages 10 and over. At age 10, American Indian males could expect to live an additional 37.3 years. The corresponding figure for American Indian females is 34.9 years. Higher male life expectancy, which reaches a peak differential of almost 4 years at age 30, is unusual. The vast majority of modern populations have a sex mortality differential in favour of females at all ages. It is nonetheless possible that American Indian females in the early twentieth century suffered higher mortality than American Indian males. High fertility in the American Indian population was likely associated with high maternal mortality rates and a greater susceptibility to opportunistic infections such as tuberculosis (Kippen 2005). Indeed, the American Indian population suffered from endemic tuberculosis, which historically took a higher toll among females, especially women in their childbearing years (Puranen 1991; Shoemaker 1999; Jones 2004). Alternatively, sex differentials in age reporting errors, race reporting errors, and census coverage may have led to the unusual results.

The results using Preston and Bennett's procedure indicate much lower life expectancies at younger ages than implied by the number of children born and number of children surviving data (the difference at age 10 is −7.5 years for males and −11.9 for females). If the results are fitted to model West, the age 10 estimates suggest an e_0 in the low 20s. At higher ages, however, estimated life expectancy improves rapidly relative to the model. At age 25, the corresponding model West life expectancy for American Indian males is 35 years, at age 45 it is 48 years, and at age 65 almost 70 years. The internal

Table 4.6. Application of the Preston-Bennett Method to the American Indian Population, 1900–1910

Start of age interval (x)	Average annual growth rate $5r_x$	Sum of age-specific growth rates S_x	Stationary population in interval $5L_x$	No. surviving to age x in stationary population, l_x	Stationary population above age x, T_x	Estimated life expectancy at age x, e_x	Implied-Model West life exp. at birth, e_0
Males							
0	0.0186	-	-	-	-	-	-
5	0.0129	0.03216	17,869	-	-	-	-
10	0.0143	0.09995	16,772	3,464	129,261	37.3	24.9
15	0.0159	0.17527	16,191	3,296	112,489	34.1	25.7
20	0.0037	0.22414	13,890	3,008	96,297	32.0	28.0
25	0.0093	0.25652	11,450	2,534	82,407	32.5	35.5
30	0.0123	0.31056	10,002	2,145	70,957	33.1	45.0
35	0.0204	0.39248	10,413	2,042	60,955	29.9	46.3
40	0.0025	0.44984	9,520	1,993	50,542	25.4	43.2
45	−0.0051	0.44349	8,187	1,771	41,021	23.2	48.0
50	0.0163	0.47152	7,309	1,550	32,835	21.2	55.2
55	0.0193	0.56040	5,943	1,325	25,526	19.3	63.4
60	0.0150	0.64612	5,936	1,188	19,583	16.5	67.5
65	0.0290	0.75603	4,221	1,016	13,647	13.4	69.6
70	0.0116	0.85744	3,490	771	9,426	12.2	76.2
75	0.0026	0.89299	2,378	587	5,935	10.1	-
80	−0.0382	0.80403	1,921	430	3,557	8.3	-
85+	-	0.73468	1,636	356	1,636	4.6	-
Females							
0	0.0180	-	-	-	-	-	-
5	0.0142	0.03551	17,665	-	-	-	-
10	0.0111	0.09885	15,946	3,361	117,372	34.9	21.1
15	0.0180	0.17173	15,170	3,112	101,426	32.6	22.5
20	0.0076	0.23581	12,948	2,812	86,256	30.7	24.1
25	0.0032	0.26292	11,433	2,438	73,308	30.1	28.0
30	0.0090	0.29361	9,642	2,108	61,875	29.4	32.7
35	0.0151	0.35394	9,458	1,910	52,232	27.3	35.0
40	−0.0053	0.37843	8,782	1,824	42,774	23.5	32.2
45	−0.0007	0.36346	6,930	1,571	33,992	21.6	36.4
50	−0.0034	0.35314	6,438	1,337	27,062	20.2	44.3
55	0.0141	0.37974	4,750	1,119	20,625	18.4	52.5
60	0.0069	0.43216	4,771	952	15,875	16.7	63.5
65	0.0173	0.49273	3,361	813	11,104	13.7	66.6
70	0.0087	0.55770	3,060	642	7,743	12.1	74.8
75	−0.0184	0.53325	2,114	517	4,683	9.1	-
80	0.0071	0.50500	1,397	351	2,569	7.3	-
85+	-	0.47170	1,172	257	1,172	4.6	-

Source: Ruggles et al. 2008; U.S. Bureau of the Census 1915.

inconsistencies in the age pattern of mortality strongly suggest census coverage errors, age reporting errors (especially at older ages), the lack of a closed population, or some combination of these factors.

Preston and Bennett hypothesise a scenario in which the second census is less complete, with coverage errors constant by age (Preston and Bennett 1983: 94–98). Under such a scenario, the set of intercensal growth rates are too low and estimated life expectancy will be too low, with proportionally greater bias at lower ages. Such a scenario is consistent with the results, but not with the instructions of the Census Bureau in 1910 to count all individuals of partial Indian ancestry as Indians. It is also possible that errors in coverage – whether from migration, race reporting errors or under-enumeration – will be concentrated at younger ages. Mixed race American Indians, for example, may be more likely to be reported as Indians when living as children in the household of an Indian parent than when living in their own household.[9] Under a scenario in which a mixed-race individual is more assimilated than their American Indian parent – perhaps speaking English, practising a non-traditional Indian occupation, and having a non-Indian spouse – race reporting errors were probably common.

Conclusions

This chapter has attempted to carry out a demographic analysis using the 1900 and 1910 American Indian censuses, the first surviving censuses that attempted a comprehensive enumeration of all American Indians living in the United States. Several life tables were constructed, which should prove useful in future analyses. Confidence in the accuracy of the results, however, is low, especially in the results obtained by two-census methods. Age reporting errors are clearly present in the data and internal inconsistencies in the results suggest the presence of various types of bias.

Difficulties census enumerators faced in assigning 'race' is problematic, especially in the estimation of mortality with two-census methods, which assumes that the American Indian population was closed to migration. The early twentieth century was a period of great change for the American Indian population, with coercive federal assimilation policies encouraging the division of collective tribal land, its allotment to individuals and families, the education of Indian children in specialised boarding schools, and the granting of citizenship to the majority of Indians living in the borders of the United States. American Indians were increasingly intermarrying with the nation's white population and census evidence suggests that individuals identified as Indians were increasingly of mixed-race decent. Given these challenges, consistently assigning individuals to the same race in each census would be a major challenge. Internal age inconsistencies in the mortality estimates reported above strongly suggest that substantial numbers of individuals identified as American Indian in one census 'migrated' across racial categories in earlier or subsequent censuses.

Despite these difficulties, the demographic evidence indicates that the American Indian population suffered from substantial mortality in the late nineteenth and early twentieth centuries. Life expectancy at birth was probably about 40 years, substantially lower than the white population and even lower than the black population. With proper care, the American Indian censuses can be used for a great variety of demographic analyses. They thus represent a valuable resource in the study of American Indian demography.

Notes

1. The Bureau of Indian Affairs collected various data on the Indian population in the nineteenth century, but the coverage and quality of these data varies enormously (Jones 2004). Various attempts to count Indians were made in earlier censuses, but these relied on a large number of estimates. Of the 383,712 Indians reported by the 1870 census to be living in the United States, for example, more than 68 per cent were estimated (Thornton 1987: 212–13).
2. See also the comments of F.A. Walker, Superintendent of the Census of 1870, who complained about 'the absence of any constitutional, legal, or judicial definition of the phrase "Indians not taxed" within the Constitution or the census law of 1850' (Walker 1872: xii).
3. A greater tendency to report non–Indian ancestors and differential mortality among the population counted as Indian in 1900 may also play some role. Hacker and Haines (2005) document much lower infant and childhood mortality among Indians reporting higher percentages of white blood in 1900.
4. Indians enumerated in the general census can be found in the regular 1900 and 1910 IPUMS samples, which are 1 per cent density samples. These individuals can be weighted appropriately and added to the high density sample to conduct analyses requiring the complete population, such as two–census mortality estimation.
5. For example, the classification scheme considers individuals identified as Apache, Jicarilla Apache, Lipan Apache, Mescalero Apache, Payson Apache and White Mountain Apache as members of the general group 'Apache'. Although culturally related and all located in the American Southwest, the various Apache groups speak different, though related, languages.
6. There are other potential problems in using the duration approach. The use of marriage duration as a proxy for the exposure to risk of childbearing assumes, first, that marriage is the appropriate situation in which almost all childbearing occurs and, second, that remarriage is not common. The first assumption is reasonable for the white population of the United States in 1900 but may not be true for the American Indian population.
7. Two–census methods often rely on published age distribution methods. Because the 1900 results were never published, the 1900 IPUMS sample is needed to provide the necessary age distribution.
8. The 1900 census samples were weighted to reflect a national population of 237,196 American Indians. Each individual in the general 1900 IPUMS sample identified as an Indian received a weight of 102.224 while those in the American Indian oversample received a weight of 5.111.
9. See M.G. Merli's application of the Preston and Bennett method to two successive censuses in Vietnam in his analysis of similar types of age–specific errors and analysis of their potential causes (Merli 1998).

References

Census Bureau. 1894. 'Report on Indians Taxed and Not Taxed in the United States (except Alaska)'. Washington, DC: Government Printing Office.

—— 1915. 'Indian Population in the United States and Alaska, 1910'. Washington, DC: Government Printing Office.

Coale, A.J., and P. Demeny. 1966. *Regional Model Life Tables and Stable Populations*. Princeton, NJ: Princeton University Press.

Hacker, J.D., and M.R. Haines. 2005. 'American Indian Mortality in the Late Nineteenth Century: The Impact of Federal Assimilation Policies on a Vulnerable Population', *Annales de Démographie Historique* 110(2): 17–45.

Haines, M.R., and S.H. Preston. 1997. 'The Use of the Census to Estimate Childhood Mortality: Comparisons from the 1900 and 1910 United States Public Use Samples', *Historical Methods* 30(2): 77–96.

Hoxie, F.E. 1984. *A Final Promise: The Campaign to Assimilate the Indians, 1880–1920*. Lincoln: University of Nebraska Press.

Jobe, M.M. 2004. 'Native Americans and the U.S. Census: A Brief Historical Survey', *Journal of Government Information* 30(1): 66–80.

Johansson, S.R., and S.H. Preston. 1978. 'Tribal Demography: The Hopi and Navaho Populations as Seen Through Manuscripts from the 1900 U.S. Census', *Social Science History* 3(1): 1–33.

Jones, D.S. 2004. *Rationalizing Epidemics: Meanings and Uses of American Indian Mortality Since 1600*. Cambridge, MA: Harvard University Press.

Kippen, R. 2005. 'Counting Nineteenth-century Maternal Deaths: The Case of Tasmania', *Historical Methods* 38(1): 14–25.

Merli, M.G. 1998. 'Mortality in Vietnam, 1979–1989', *Demography* 35(3): 345–60.

Nobles, M. 2002. 'Racial Categorization and Censuses', in D.I. Kertzer and D. Arel (eds), *Census and Identity: The Politics of Race, Ethnicity, and Language in National Censuses*. Cambridge: Cambridge University Press, pp. 43–70.

Preston, S.H., and N.G. Bennett. 1983. 'A Census-based Method for Estimating Adult Mortality', *Population Studies* 37(1): 91–104.

Preston, S.H., and M.R. Haines. 1991. *Fatal Years: Child Mortality in Late Nineteenth Century America*. Princeton, NJ: Princeton University Press.

Puranen, B. 1991. 'Tuberculosis and the Decline of Mortality in Sweden', in R. Schofield, D. Reher and A. Bideau (eds), *The Decline of Mortality in Europe*. Oxford: Clarendon Press, pp. 97–117.

Ruggles, S. et al. 2008. *Integrated Public Use Microdata Series: Version 4.0.* Machine–readable database. Retrieved 3 March 2008 from http://usa.ipums.org/usa/index.shtml. Minneapolis: Minnesota Population Center.

Shoemaker, N. 1992. 'The Census as Civilizer: American Indian House-hold Structure in the 1900 and 1910 U.S. Censuses', *Historical Methods* 25(1): 4–11.

———— 1999. *American Indian Population Recovery in the Twentieth Century*. Albuquerque: University of New Mexico Press.

Snipp, C.M. 2006. 'American Indians', in S.B. Carter et al. (eds), *Historical Statistics of the United States: Earliest Times to the Present. Vol. 1, Part A: Population*. New York: Cambridge University Press, pp. 715–77.

Spruhan, P. 2006. 'A Legal History of Blood Quantum in Federal Indian Law to 1935', *South Dakota Law Review* 51(1): 1–50.

Thornton, R. 1987. *American Indian Holocaust and Survival: A Population History Since 1492*. Norman: University of Oklahoma Press.

———— 2000. 'Population History of Native North Americans', in M.R. Haines and R.H. Steckel (eds), *A Population History of North America*. New York: Cambridge University Press, pp. 9–50.

United Nations. 1983. 'Indirect Techniques for Demographic Estimation'. New York: United Nations.

Walker, F.A. 1872. 'Report of the Superintendent of the Ninth Census', in U.S. Bureau of the Census, 'The Statistics of the Population of the United States'. Washington, DC: Government Printing Office, pp. ii–xlix.

5
THE ABORIGINAL POPULATION AND THE 1891 CENSUS OF CANADA

Michelle A. Hamilton and Kris Inwood

Introduction

As more national censuses are being sampled and digitised, scholars are examining the social, political and geographical context of enumeration in order to interpret historical enumeration data.[1] The construction of questions for the census schedules, the instructions to enumerators, the physical process of enumeration, and the tabulation of results influenced the type of information collected, the accuracy with which it was recorded, and the probability that several sectors of the population were over or undercounted or distorted.[2] Regarding indigenous populations, Alterman (1969: 293–96) and Jobe (2004) have shown that political policies shaped the efforts to enumerate Native Americans in the United States, as Watts (2003) has for the Aborigines of Victoria, Australia. Shoemaker (1992) and Hollos (1992) have discussed how censuses designed by non-indigenous groups inadvertently distorted cultural structures, such as household characteristics. Meanwhile, Hull (1984: 147), Forbes (1990: 2) and Jobe (2004: 76) have also observed that fluctuations in the political climate of enumerated indigenous peoples led them decide whether or nor to self-identify as indigenous, and this affected the reported numbers of these peoples.

As yet, however, no comprehensive treatment of the relationship between Aboriginal peoples and the historical Canadian enumeration process is available.[3] Hamilton (2007) has assessed the colonial relationship between the census, Aboriginal communities and the Department of Indian Affairs (DIA), and analysed methodological problems of using the enumeration data between 1851 and 1916. Following Alterman's comments on the enumeration of Native Americans (Alterman 1969: 296–99), Curtis has identified the various difficulties encountered by Canadian census authorities between 1841 and 1871, including the remote or treacherous terrain through which some enumerators had to travel, the frustrations of tracking nomadic groups, the problem of communicating with peoples who were unfamiliar with either French or English, and Aboriginal resistance (Curtis 2001: 108–9, 127, 154, 192–94). Dunae (1999: 230–32, 236) has also recognised similar issues during the 1891 census of the province of British Columbia. Examining the 1911 census of the Northwest Territories, Ruppert (2009) meanwhile sees these elements as part of the production of a population, as distinguished from the construction of a population; the latter occurs when the state renders social relations into statistical categories in order to govern the population.

Here we consider the geographic and cultural factors that affected the enumeration of Aboriginal peoples in 1891, the extent of coordination at an administrative level between the DIA and the Census Bureau (which was lodged within the Department of Agriculture), and the manipulation and use of census data for colonising purposes. All of these factors affect the accuracy of the information recorded in 1891. Our work arises in the context of a project to create a public use sample of the original enumeration data from the 1891 national census at the University of Guelph (see Inwood and James 2005).

The Canadian Enumeration of Aboriginal Peoples, 1851–1891

The first 'national' censuses in Canada are often considered to be the 1851/2 and 1861 enumerations of the older-settled areas in what is now the provinces of Ontario and Quebec. The variety of information gathered for each person in the 1850s included a column in which to mark 'Indians if any' (Gagan 1974: 358).[4] In 1861, the census schedules group 'coloured', 'mulatto', and 'Indians' together (ibid.: 362). The instructions given to the enumerator state 'In this column mark a figure (1) every coloured person's name, i.e. negro or negress. This was much neglected last census, and the number of coloured persons was not ascertained. If Mulatto, mark M after his or her name – thus, (1)M; and if Indian, mark 'Ind'' (cited in ibid.: 364).[5]

By 1871 the Canadian census extended to the provinces of Nova Scotia and New Brunswick as well as Ontario and Quebec. The question about race had evolved to an identification of 'origin'. The instructions stated that, 'Origin is to be scrupulously entered, as given by the person questioned; in the manner shown in the specimen schedule, by the words English, Irish, Scotch, African, Indian, German, French, and so forth' (Department of Agriculture 1871: 23). The only other instruction given to enumerators about the origin question was a caution that 'Canadian' was not considered an acceptable response.[6] This origin category was repeated in 1881. In both years the simplest way to acknowledge Aboriginal identity was to identify oneself as an 'Indian' in response to the question about origin. Interestingly, no instruction of a general nature was given about the Aboriginal population. Although enumerators were not told to include or exclude Indians, the instructions clearly implied that at least some Aboriginal peoples would be enumerated. For example, 'wigwam' was included in the possibilities of dwelling types and 'Indian' was explicitly recognised as an acceptable response to the question about origin. But none of this conveys a general strategy for inclusion or exclusion of particular Aboriginal peoples who spent some or all of their year in territory over which the Canadian government claimed sovereignty.

Uncertainty about the enumeration of Aboriginal communities arose in part because in each census more and more territory was subject to enumeration. The 1851/2 and 1861 censuses, for the most part, encompassed territory settled for some time by Europeans and their descendents. In this area most Aboriginal peoples had lived for at least a generation, often much longer, alongside Euro-Canadians. Admittedly, some Aboriginal communities in eastern and central Canada still lived substantially apart from their Euro-Canadian neighbours, and indeed some communities did not accept the authority of the Canadian state. Nevertheless, there had been a long history of interaction and a basis for shared communication that at least made possible census-like information gathering. Enumerators were unlikely to overlook Aboriginal communities, and language would not likely have impeded communication between Aboriginal peoples and Canadian enumerators.

The expansion of the census to more northerly parts of Ontario and Quebec in 1871, and in the 1880s to some parts of western Canada, meant that enumerators began to encounter many more Aboriginal communities which had limited experience of dealing with Europeans and Euro-Canadians. The lack of a shared language was a not uncommon barrier to enumeration. Some of the northern and western Aboriginal groups were difficult to find because they lived by design and/or accident much further from the centres of Euro-Canadian society. Indeed, to the extent that the enumeration was conducted on the *de jure* principle of customary or usual residence, census staff might not have known how to enumerate those Aboriginal peoples who were nomadic. The territorial pretensions of the Canadian state clearly would have encouraged the enumeration of anyone living in the expanded area, but in practice this was becoming increasingly difficult to implement.

The 1891 Census

In 1891 the census was expanded to include even more northern and western areas that had not previously been enumerated or settled by many (if any) European descendents. Thus the challenge of enumerating the Aboriginal population became more complex. By 1891, Canada consisted of seven provinces – British Columbia, Manitoba, Ontario, Quebec, New Brunswick, Nova Scotia, Prince Edward Island – five provisional districts – Alberta, Athabasca, Assiniboia, Saskatchewan, Keewatin – and the Northwest or 'unorganised' Territories. Some of these areas had been ceded by Aboriginal peoples through treaties with the British or Canadian governments, while in others, non-native settlement had forced out the indigenous occupants with no agreement of any kind. In the older-settled provinces, reserves had been set aside for Aboriginal peoples, a process which continued as new treaties were negotiated. The Métis, those of mixed native and European descent, were also dislocated by the arrival of European immigrants and land speculators as the Canadian government prepared to fully open up the north-west areas for settlement. In the late 1860s and early 1870s, they had been forced to move from Manitoba into the Saskatchewan region. In 1885, in the face of increased European immigration and anticipating further loss of land, many of the Métis took up arms in an unsuccessful rebellion. In the end, the Canadian government issued scrip (certificates which acted as a cash settlement or which could be used to purchase land elsewhere) to the Métis, or allowed them to take treaty as legal Indians. The status and residency of mixed-race people was thus especially complex and in flux at the time of the 1891 census.

To implement the 1891 census, the Department of Agriculture appointed fourteen chief census officers, under which operated census commissioners, who trained the 4,300 district enumerators (Department of Agriculture 1891a: 3; Department of Agriculture 1891c: 3). Anyone who refused to answer questions could be charged under section eighteen of the 1879 *Census Act* which set out a penalty between five and twenty dollars.[7] Nine schedules, of which only the nominal return is extant, recorded statistics on the living, the dead, education, public institutions, real estate, agricultural products and livestock, industrial establishments and natural resources.

Unlike previous censuses, the 1891 enumeration did not include a column to identify 'origin'. The Department of Agriculture's Statistical Branch reported in its 1892 yearbook that, 'No particulars of "origin" were taken in 1891, and very wisely so, as they were of no specially instructive value and only tended to perpetuate race distinctions' (Department of Agriculture 1893a: 104). The 1891 census officials, however, did tabulate numbers for different ethnicities of immigrants based on a column for the recording of the birthplace of parents. The inclusion of this column, and another to specifically identify French-Canadians, was considered to be a solution to the previous problem of people giving their origin as 'Canadian', which was not thought to be an appropriate response (Gaffield 2007: 425). The latter column only confused Aboriginal enumeration as census takers expressed uncertainty over the inclusion of the western French-speaking Métis in this category, whereas in the censuses of the mid 1880s this group had been given a separate designation (see Department of Agriculture 1886: 11; 1887: xiii–xiv; 1893b: xviii). In the province of British Columbia, Chief Census Officer George Sargison later came to have second thoughts because he believed that a way to distinguish Aboriginals on the census schedules was necessary for statistical purposes.[8]

Although the manual for enumerators in 1891 gave no specific instructions regarding the enumeration of Aboriginal peoples, it is possible to make some inferences based on the execution of earlier and later Canadian censuses. A variety of approaches had been used in 1881. Information for Aboriginal groups that had negotiated treaties was simply transferred from the annuity payment records of the DIA, while the eastern part of the 'unorganised' territories was regularly enumerated through house-to-house visits. But for most of the 'unorganised' territories, the 1881 census report admitted that the enumeration of the resident Aboriginal population was 'almost impossible' (Department of Agriculture 1882: xiv). In some parts of the west outside treaty areas, census officials simply based their estimate on earlier enumerations. Population estimates for the northern and interior parts of British Columbia, for example, were taken from one of the 1871 census reports written by Joseph-Charles Taché, the Deputy Minister of Agriculture and Statistics (Taché 1876: lii–lxxxiv), who based his numbers upon earlier censuses conducted by missionaries, explorers and the Hudson's Bay Company. This estimate was considered to be fairly accurate because a check between the regularly enumerated areas in 1881 and the estimates of the same areas for 1871 proved to be similar. The 1881 report suggested, however, that reliable information about birth, death and other categories was unobtainable for much of the Aboriginal population of western Canada (Department of Agriculture 1882: xiv; 1884: v).

A desire to monitor increased migration to Manitoba, Saskatchewan, Alberta and Assiniboia during the early 1880s prompted a special enumeration of these areas between 1884 and 1886. Fearing that Aboriginal peoples might misunderstand the purpose of these western censuses, census staff once again obtained information from the files of the DIA for those living within treatied territory. The Manitoba census report noted that, quite apart from the fragile political context of race relations at this time, some reliance on the IDA was unavoidable due to the nomadic nature of natives and a dearth of non-natives who could speak Aboriginal languages (Department of Agriculture 1887: xii). Outside treaty areas, enumeration was conducted through household visits (Department of Agriculture 1886: xvi). In 1901, the census instructions specifically stated, for the first time, that DIA officials should facilitate census taking, or conduct the enumeration themselves (Department of Agriculture 1901: 6). Robert Hamilton Coats, the Dominion statistician, felt this to be a wise strategy particularly in the north or in sparsely settled areas. As well, for those natives living on reserves, Indian agents could be employed as enumerators since they held the knowledge required to answer the census questions, and supposedly, the 'confidence' of their wards. Indians, Coats asserted, had always been suspicious of people making personal enquiries about their affairs.[9]

Accordingly, it seems likely that the 1891 enumeration relied partly on the efforts of the DIA. One British Columbia census commissioner stated that the DIA had not been consulted about the taking of the census, nor had they made any reference to the DIA's own census returns.[10] This, however, is not entirely true as cross-checking the list of enumerators with the Indian agents of 1891 indicates that several agents were the enumerators of the reserves they managed.[11] Moreover, in British Columbia the Chief census officer personally provided lists of Aboriginal groups taken from DIA reports for each district, in order to inform enumerators of the groups each could expect to encounter.[12]

Manitoba officials also appear to have coordinated their efforts with the DIA in 1891. This is suggested by the fact that treaty and non-treaty natives were enumerated differently in this province. The Manitoba enumeration schedules for each district contain treaty Indian tallies which generally only list numbers of male and female natives and the total population. These tallies cannot be summaries of each district because the numbers often exceed the total number of individuals enumerated within that district. Further, in some cases families within the regular enumeration schedules have been annotated as 'non-treaty Indians'. Thus it seems that the natives who lived on treaty-allocated reserves were not enumerated through regular household visits, and that the tallies were likely taken from DIA records. In contrast, an examination of the 1891 census manuscripts for Alberta and Assiniboia shows that reserves were simply not enumerated at all. Indian agents, interpreters and farm instructors appear on the census but there is no accompanying native presence. In Saskatchewan, however, it appears that reserve or treaty Indians were included in the regular enumeration process, as evident from the presence of Aboriginal style names and occupations (Fortier 2006a: 4–6).[13]

The Department of Agriculture also made other arrangements for Aboriginal enumeration in northern and isolated areas in 1891. Secretary H.B. Small wrote to Anglican Bishop John Horden of Moose Factory requesting that he assist in the enumeration, either personally or through other missions at Moose Factory and Rupert's House (both Hudson's Bay Company trading posts).[14] Small also asked the Reverend Father Prevost, who had helped in earlier enumerations, to do the same with the Roman Catholic missions in the Hudson's Bay Company's trading area.[15] Small even provided a list of geographical places where Aboriginal peoples often congregated. Missionaries also assisted unofficially. For example, in British Columbia, Frederick Greer consulted several registers of vital statistics kept by these local officials (Department of Agriculture 1891b: 6, 9). In British Columbia, Hudson's Bay Company staff conducted enumerations in the northerly region of the Liard River and its tributaries, at Fort St John, Fort

McLeod, along the Peace and Parsnip Rivers, and in the north-western corner of the Westminster district.[16]

Challenges of Aboriginal Enumeration

Whether Indian agents, missionaries or others employed by the Department of Agriculture, enumerators faced geographic, linguistic and cross-cultural challenges during the census taking of the Aboriginal population. For the first time, the vast provisional districts were traversed by the enumerator, and it was these and other northern and remote areas that proved particularly problematic. Enumerators remarked that it was difficult to find Aboriginal groups, which were often dispersed and moving as they pursued their seasonal subsistence activities. As one contemporary commentator noted, many areas were also geographically difficult to access.

> A steamer of enumerators on board traversed the deep indents of the Pacific coast line as far as Alaska, thence to Queen Charlotte's Islands ... Pack-horses were required in the mountain region of the same Province ... through the valleys which ran among the hills of the Rockies. Dog-trains were a necessity in Saskatchewan. To obtain the population on the northern slope of the height of land in Ontario and Quebec a canoe expedition started from the head waters of the Lievre River, to go by lake and river and portages to Albany River, at James Bay. Camping outfit and canoes were needed ... in the Nipissing District ... The enumerators in Manitoba had now to foot it, now to go by buck-board, and now by boat ... Many townships in Algoma had to be taken by slow and toilsome pedestrianism. For the north shore of the Gulf of St. Lawrence a schooner had to be chartered, the enumerators put on board and dropped at different points till the Straits of Belle Isle were reached, from which point the schooner was directed to the Isle of Anticosti.[17]

In British Columbia, Captain John Martley suffered a broken arm when his horse fell crossing a mountain, and Eric Duncan was forced to go on foot over much of his district since horse travel was impractical (Duncan 1979: 42; Dunae 1999: 230–32). A census taker of the Lake Manitoba area lost his way for eight days, apparently surviving only because he killed and ate his horse.[18] Enumerators of northern and coastal British Columbia also experienced problems when travelling by water. Frederick Greer wrote in his diary that it was difficult to travel on the Naas River due to constant downpours, strong tides and heavy winds. In some cases, he had to pull his boat up rivers rather than paddle it. One day, Greer made three portages for his provisions and blankets, each time pulling his boat on a line (Department of Agriculture 1891b: 6–7). The steamer the *Islander* foundered, causing some original census manuscripts to be lost and the need for re-enumeration.[19] Other situations made enumeration difficult. Greer remarked on the constant 'clouds' of mosquitoes and blackflies, which made travel unpleasant. Near the North Pacific cannery, a landslide buried part of the Aboriginal workers' camp the morning Greer arrived, killing ten people (Department of Agriculture 1891b: 7, 6). Such challenges likely deterred enumerators from completing their task.

Indeed, after the census numbers were released, British Columbia's politicians complained that their population total was inaccurate, partly for the above reasons. In reply, the Dominion Statistician, George Johnson, stated that one area that the politicians claimed to have been missed was in fact in the Yukon district, not in British Columbia, though the natives there may have indeed frequently crossed over the border.[20] But Aboriginal groups within the headwaters of the Stewart, Pelly, Francis and Liard Rivers, an area outside the province, traded within British Columbia, and they had been enumerated as part of the province. Thus the nomadic nature of northern Aboriginals was not accounted for consistently. Another area, Johnson observed, was indeed left out, and although he described this area as 'unexplored' he justified this decision by stating that few natives lived there. If there was a large Aboriginal presence, he argued, the Hudson's Bay Company would have established forts in this area, and therefore he would have asked the Company to enumerate them.

The challenges of interpretation also hampered the enumeration process. As revealed through the legal case of Chief Dokis (below), interpreters could not always successfully communicate with native groups, which in some cases were suspicious of the motives of the census takers. In British Columbia, Frederick Greer relied upon Aboriginal interpreters to explain enumeration to coastal communities but these interpreters quit on grounds of overwork and little pay (Department of Agriculture 1891b: 6–10). Greer also encountered problems with those, many of them older people, who did not understand Chinook, the trading language of the west.[21] While the 1891 manual of instructions stated that enumerators were to record the answer given by the individual, not an answer shaped by the enumerator's understanding (Department of Agriculture 1891c: 6), this must have been a difficult task for those that did not understand Aboriginal languages. Indeed, numerous manuscripts simply have 'Indian' recorded in the name column, sometimes with the sex indicated, and often little else (Fortier 2006b: 3).

Beyond linguistic interpretation, 1891 enumerators must have found it difficult to fit elements of Aboriginal culture into the classificatory scheme of the census. Earlier, during the 1885 census of the Northwest Territories, enumerators who consulted the records of Indian agents noted that some polygamous wives had been labelled as widows because only one woman could be assigned to the head of a household, while the other wives and their children lived separately. Many 'marked as widows ... were not widows but wives, but neither agent nor any one else could say whose wife' (Department of Agriculture 1886: xvi), a situation which posed problems for enumerators who were charged with recording individuals as part of households, according to their instruction).[22]

The census was also supposed to link households with the property that each occupied. In 1891, British Columbia Chief Officer George Sargison and his commissioners decided 'Indian Tenancy' needed to 'be confirmed to what each individual occupies'.[23] Yet this would prove difficult in some areas, if tribal or band protocol did not necessarily specify individual occupation. For example, in conducting a DIA census, W.H. Lomas of the Cowichan Agency in British Columbia noted that it was difficult to assign families to specific bands or villages. Many people, he reported, owned shares in ranches in several villages through both their father's and mother's lineages, and often moved between them (Department of Indian Affairs 1892: 115).

For those enumerators or census officials who relied upon the records of the DIA to fill out their forms rather than household visits, it is quite possible that they inadvertently omitted Aboriginal individuals. This is because individuals listed on the DIA census or treaty payment records reflected those with a legal Indian status, and not necessarily everyone who lived on a reserve or in an Aboriginal treaty area. By the 1880s, the system of making payments to those who had taken treaty forced the government to define, in a relatively precise and legally binding manner, who would be regarded as an Indian for this purpose. Chapter 43 of the *Act Respecting Indians* 1886 defined an 'Indian' to be a male of Indian blood reputed to belong to a band, the child of such a person, and any woman who was or had been married to an Indian. The law also outlined ways in which Indian status could be gained or lost, and the superintendent general of the DIA or an individual Indian agent possessed the power to determine who was a legal Indian or who shared in treaty annuities. By 1891, Aboriginals judged intelligent enough to exercise the privileges of enfranchisement could apply to become full citizens of Canada but this rescinded their legal Indian status.[24] A non-Aboriginal woman who married an Aboriginal man became, by law, an Indian. In contrast, an Aboriginal woman who married a non-Aboriginal man or a non-treaty Indian lost her official government status as an Indian, although she retained her share in treaty payments if her band permitted. The child of an Aboriginal mother and a white father did not receive Indian status since in the eyes of the state ancestry was traced through the father, irrespective of whether or not the Aboriginal band was matrilineal. The DIA could also exclude any illegitimate child who had not shared in band money for over two years at any time, or any individual who had resided in another country for over five years without the consent of the superintendent general.[25] The latter was of some importance since in the late nineteenth century Aboriginal peoples, particularly those whose traditional territories had been divided by the Canada/United States border, often crossed this boundary to join fellow band members or to seek employment. Officials could also revoke treaty payments to an Aboriginal man who deserted his family or a childless woman who left her husband to live 'immorally with another man'.[26]

It is thus quite possible for the census to have overlooked individuals who continued to live on a reserve after their official status was revoked by the government. Indian agents would not have considered them Indians, and their names would not have appeared on annuity payment lists. If the census enumerator did not conduct house-to-house visits on a reserve, these individuals would not likely have been enumerated.

Government policies also legislated who was legally considered Métis. As white settlers moved into the northwest in the 1860s, the government offered heads of Métis families and their children scrip to be used to purchase land, or money scrip as a cash settlement. The majority of Métis chose money scrip because the areas in which they lived were marginally suitable for farming, and because they distrusted the government to settle land claims. But taking scrip implied an abandonment of legal Indian status. An 1888 amendment to the *Indian Act* stated that no 'half-breed' of Manitoba who had taken scrip could be called an 'Indian'; no Métis head of family, with the exception of a widow who had already taken treaty, could be considered an Indian or entitled to treaty rights; and any Métis individuals who had previously taken treaty were allowed to withdraw from it and such withdrawal affected any unmarried minor children.[27] Thus such people would not appear in treaty Indian tallies, in treaty payment records or likely live on reserves, and would blend into the non-native demographic records. In contrast, some Métis individuals moved onto reserves, possibly because the government refused to respond to requests for land grants, and thus may have appeared in census records as Indian if they had taken treaty.[28]

Aboriginal Suspicion and Resistance

The inescapable challenges of geography, language and cross-cultural communication were further complicated by the inherently paternalistic attitude of the government and the response of Aboriginal peoples, which often took the form of suspicion and sometimes quiet resistance. The Department of Agriculture feared in the mid 1880s that the western censuses would 'excite' those native peoples who did not understand the 'real object' of the census and would instead perceive a 'wrong and mischievous motive' (Department of Agriculture 1886: xvi). In 1891, at one British Columbia cannery, an industry that employed many natives, Ronald Green found a group of workers who were diffident and reluctant to cooperate. Apparently, the Chinese employees at the cannery had told their Aboriginal co-workers that the enumerators were really poll tax collectors, a tax which the Chinese themselves had to pay. With no magistrate to legally enforce the *Census Act*, Green took an alternative approach. He informed them that, while he did not personally care whether their names were recorded, he was leaving that night and 'anyone not on the list might as well be dead' and would not be able to apply for government assistance in the future. According to Green's diary, these untruths coerced Aboriginal workers to provide him with the necessary information.[29]

Perhaps because of these difficulties, at another community Green visited a couple of weeks later, he met with the chief first, a tactic used by some enumerators to gain approval from village leaders, and thus hopefully of the remaining residents. But Green still encountered problems. After he fell through the porch steps of one house, cutting and bruising his leg, the native owner demanded he be compensated. In Port Essington, Green also experienced 'unusual trouble'. The local Aboriginal group demanded that he explain the purpose of the census at 'every place' and refused to cooperate until they had discussed the matter in private amongst themselves.[30] In the same province, enumerator Frederick Greer found that he received many enquiries from Aboriginal peoples about his purpose. Some asked to be paid for their information, or for information they gave about families away hunting or berry-picking. Greer noted that it was 'almost an impossibility' to learn the numbers of dwellings and canoes because of people's suspicion. In one spot, elders asked if Greer had been told 'to find out how many of them there were, and then the Government would do away with them to get their land'. Greer responded that, in fact, it was just the opposite: the government, once in possession of their names, would 'do them good and protect them' (Department of Agriculture 1891b: 6–7).

The case of Michel D'Aigle, or Chief Dokis, of northern Ontario illustrates not only linguistic challenges, but also the suspicion with which Aboriginal peoples met enumerators. George B. Mills, the enumerator, first visited the eldest son of Chief Dokis, whose wife gave him the desired information, but Dokis's other two sons and his wife refused to cooperate until they consulted the chief. Consequently, Mills asked Dokis to meet him the next morning, but when he did not arrive Mills asked one of Dokis's sons to fetch him. Neither returned, so Mills visited the family camp. Although Mills explained twice that by law Dokis was bound to answer his questions, the chief steadfastly refused to do so. Mills stated that Chief Dokis fully understood the nature and purpose of the census enumeration and even that Dokis remembered the last census and the name of the 1881 enumerator. After a day and a half of persistence, only one of the chief's sons answered Mills's questions. As a result, Mills had warrants issued and sent constables to apprehend Dokis and his uncooperative son. Despite this, Mills said, he was willing to settle the matter if only the men would provide him with the required information. Dokis refused again and instead paid Mills's board for the time spent in his camp and other fees, a total of $26.60, and even shook his hand.[31]

After Dokis's appearance before a magistrate, Justice of the Peace Joseph Michaud of Sturgeon Falls wrote to the DIA. Dokis, Michaud explained, had been suspicious of the enumerator and, in particular, the interpreter, who had previously acted as part of a party that had pressed Dokis and his band to sell timber rights.[32] The interpreter's presence during the attempt to take the census led Dokis to assume this issue was being raised again. Michaud believed that Dokis was simply trying to protect the interests of his people, and, moreover, could not understand the interpreter, who hardly spoke French and no Aboriginal languages. In contrast to Mills's claim, Michaud also stated that the Dokis band knew nothing about census enumeration. Consequently, Michaud requested that DIA remit Dokis the paid fine.[33] At first, the Department simply replied that it could not interfere since the law had been broken,[34] but eventually Deputy Superintendent General of Indian Affairs Lawrence Vankoughnet wrote to Deputy Minister of Agriculture John Lowe and asked that Dokis be reimbursed due to the circumstances.[35]

The Department of Agriculture then began its own enquiry into the matter and contacted the district Census Commissioner William Hogarth. Hogarth reported that he had heard nothing about this situation until the Reverend Mr Huntington, another supporter of Chief Dokis, informed him of the situation.[36] Hogarth stated that the approximate $26 was the amount of expenses incurred by Mills and his assistant and thus the fine had been directly paid to Mills, yet Mills had charged the Department of Agriculture for this time and expenses too. Hogarth also inferred that this was not the first charge against Mills, and thus suggested that the DIA should reimburse Dokis and that census officials should take the doubly charged expenses out of Mills's salary. Hogarth ordered a deduction of $52.10 from Mills's wage for seven days off at Sturgeon Falls and the amount of the fine.[37]

Throughout late summer and early autumn, Michaud pressed the DIA for resolution of this 'gross injustice,' and even threatened to bring the matter before Parliament in Ottawa.[38] By late August the Department of Agriculture agreed not to pursue the case, but continued to enquire about the paid fine.[39] The last existing correspondence on the matter is Mills's report, stamped received on 22 September 1891, protesting the remittance of the fine; there is no indication whether Chief Dokis ever received reimbursement. During his investigation, Hogarth reported that Dokis had told him that he had not understood the purpose of the census, and that if he had he would have complied.[40] This statement, however, may have been a subterfuge to hide Dokis's real resistance to the presumption of the Department of Agriculture to record information concerning his band. Either way, this legal case certainly demonstrates the difficulties in cross-cultural communication inherent in census taking.

The government instruction that Indian agents should enumerate their own reserves or assist others in order to ease the process was not necessarily fruitful. The relationship between agents and Aboriginal groups was one frequently marked by suspicion, avoidance and resistance, whether passive or overt. The problems encountered by Indian Agent E.D. Cameron of the Six Nations of the Grand River in Ontario during the DIA's own enumeration in 1891 are suggestive. Cameron was forced to hire

Chief A.G. Smith to assist him since his first round of visits to record information achieved little. Many, he reported, seemed afraid of providing information or refused outright to cooperate. Some believed that this census would result in location tickets which provided inheritance rights for the children of holders, but which stipulated private ownership, thus removing the land from the reserve and overall band control. As both a person of influence in the community and the interpreter for the DIA office, Smith could explain the purpose of the census. Cameron also noted that he himself was a stranger to the Six Nations because he had acted as their agent for less than a year. While his arrangement with Chief Smith may have resulted in obtaining the necessary information, the Six Nations certainly did not welcome the enumeration, as evidenced by Cameron's complaint that no one provided him with any food during the entire day, a distinct lack of hospitality unusual in native communities. The Dominion enumerators who took the 1891 census on the Six Nations reserve could not have met with much more welcome nor would have Cameron's presence encouraged them to be cooperative.[41] Of course, non-Aboriginal individuals also resisted enumeration, particularly since there seemed to be widespread suspicion that the information would be used to increase taxes, but the resistance of Aboriginal peoples must be seen as part of their struggles against colonialist policies.

The Census and Colonial Policies

The DIA used census information to track its native wards. In 1871, the Department admitted that it had discovered the existence of some previously unknown bands in Ontario and Quebec 'through the agency of the person who collected the data' of the decennial census (Department of Indian Affairs 1872: 38). Since these groups did not receive treaty annuities, it concluded, they had had no inducements to report themselves to department officials. The 1871 annual report was thus adjusted to include these groups (ibid.: 39). Likewise, in 1891 and in 1911 the Department amended its own internal census of the 'Nomadic Indians' in the provinces of Ontario and Quebec according to the Dominion census (see Department of Indian Affairs 1872: 323; 1911: xxii).

The Canadian government also used census numbers to justify their colonial policies. For example, although British Columbia's politicians had argued that the native population was decreasing whenever issues of land claims and larger reserves had been raised, the government later suggested that the 1891 census had undercounted this group when it was negotiating for an increased provincial subsidy, which was based on population totals (Dunae 1999: 236). In response, Dominion Statistician George Johnson assumed a process of native extinction and thus a decrease in numbers. He stated that the Department of the Interior had calculated in 1873 that the number of Aboriginal peoples in British Columbia stood at

28,000. The 1881 national census recorded it at 25,661 and thus the number 23,257 taken in 1891 appeared justified. The claim that approximately another 12,000 people should be added to the population total represented a 38% increase which Johnson found improbable.[42]

Politicians who believed that the 1891 census undercounted Aboriginal peoples in British Columbia discounted Johnson's theory of decrease because they believed that the teaching of Christian missionaries and the 'beneficence' of the DIA meant that some groups were actually increasing in number.[43] Perhaps there was a slight decrease overall, but not on the scale that Johnson suggested. The Department of Agriculture explained both the decrease and increase in Aboriginal populations. While British Columbia, Alberta, Assiniboia, Saskatchewan and Manitoba had experienced a decline in Aboriginal numbers, there was an overall increase of 60 per cent across Canada, according to one census bulletin (Department of Agriculture 1891b: 4). The Department judged such an increase of the Aboriginal population shown by the 1891 census as the 'strongest possible evidence of the wisdom of the policy pursued by the Government' (Department of Agriculture 1892: 85). Much of the increase occurred within the Aboriginal groups of eastern Canada because they had been under government supervision longer, the Department suggested. Similar assimilation policies implemented in the northwest in the 1890s would also result in a population increase in these areas in the future (ibid.: 85).

Conclusion

During the late nineteenth century, Canadian census authorities attempted to better understand Aboriginal communities, just as Aboriginal communities undoubtedly improved their own understanding of the Canadian state and its information-gathering activities. Unfortunately, the perceptions and understandings of Aboriginal communities are not easily recovered from historical sources. What the Canadian census authorities learnt is more readily visible.

The 1891 census was the first attempt to enumerate large parts of western Canada. The difficulties encountered and strategies adopted in 1891 led to a considerable change in the enumeration practices employed in 1901, when the question about 'origin' was reintroduced and, interestingly, defined much more clearly than in 1871 or 1881:

> Among whites the racial or tribal origin is traced through the father, as in English, Scotch, Irish, Welsh, French, German Italian, Scandinavian, etc ... [I]n the case of Indians the names of their tribes should be given, as 'Chippewa,' 'Cree,' etc. Persons of mixed white and red blood – commonly known as 'breeds' – will be described by addition of the initial letters 'f.b.' for French breed, 'e.b.' for English breed, 's.b.' for Scotch breed and 'i.b.' for Irish breed ... Other mixtures of Indians besides the four above specified are rare, and may be described by the letters 'o.b.' for other breed. If several

races are combined with the red ... they should also be described by the initials 'o.b.' (Department of Agriculture 1901: paragraph 53).

A second and even more explicit question about race provided further clarity:

> The races of men will be designated by the use of 'w' for white, 'r' for red, 'b' for black and 'y' for yellow. The whites are, of course, the Caucasian race, the reds are the American Indian, the blacks are the African or negro, and the yellow are the Mongolian (Japanese and Chinese). But only pure whites will be classed as whites; the children begotten of marriages between whites and any one of the other races will be classed as red, black or yellow, as the case may be, irrespective of the degree of colour' (ibid.: paragraph 47).

In 1901 it was also made clear that those Indians who had taken treaty were to be enumerated, and for the first time it was explicitly suggested that the regular Department of Agriculture enumerators should not take the census of Aboriginal communities:

> In the enumeration of inmates of asylums, hospitals, penitentiaries and educational or other institutions, as well as of Treaty Indians ... it will generally be found advantageous to employ officials and other agents in place of the regular enumerators. In every such case the commissioner for the district will be notified, and he will be required to withdraw the schedules dealing with the particular subjects from the regular enumerators and to inform them accordingly (ibid.: paragraph 9).

Even the category of religion explicitly allowed the return of 'pagan'.[44] Previously some enumerators returned pagan as a religion even though the discussion of the question in their instructions clearly presumed a response from among the various Christian churches. Undoubtedly Aboriginal identification in the 1901 census continued to reflect much of the complexity identified above for 1891. Nevertheless, the changes in enumeration practice introduced in 1901 probably reduced the ambiguity of Aboriginal identification. Census authorities were learning from experience about how to represent Aboriginal communities in a social inventory that was fundamentally inappropriate to the extent that it was designed by and for European-derived societies. The Aboriginal peoples were also learning about the scope, purpose and impact of this information gathering as part of their adaptation to the expansion of a European-derived presence in the Americas.

Notes

The authors would like to acknowledge the assistance of Chelsea Jack, Jean Dalgliesh, Ashley Fortier, Wesley C. Gustavson, Benjamin Hoy and Forrest Pass. Michelle Hamilton's research and writing was assisted by a Postdoctoral Fellowship, funded by a Canada Research Chair in Rural History at the University of Guelph. The 1871 and 1891 Census of Canada projects were funded by the Canadian Foundation for Innovation and the Ontario Ministry of Research and Innovation.

1. See, for e.g., Inwood and Reid (1995), Ruggles and Menard (1995), Ruggles, Sobek and Gardner (1996), Hall (1999), Baskerville and Sager (2000), Dillon (2000, 2002), Sager (2001), Darroch (2002), Hacker (2003), Clubine-Ito (2004), Mandemaker and Dillon (2004) and Gaffield, ed. (2007).
2. See, for e.g., Brookes (1976), McInnis (1981), Galois (1983), Dunae (1999), Bradbury (2000), Buck et al. (2000), Gaffield (2000), Curtis (2001) and Inwood and Reid (2001).
3. In Canada, the term Aboriginal includes First Nations (or native peoples) and the Métis, those of mixed European and Aboriginal descent.
4. For a historical survey of the changing categories for various ethnicities in Canada, see Kralt (1990) and White, Badets and Renaud (1993).
5. Gagan found the original instructions for 1851/2 in the William Camber Papers, Archives and Research Collections Centre, University of Western Ontario, London, Ontario, and for 1861 in the *Hamilton Weekly Spectator*, 10 January 1861.
6. 'That Census', *Canadian Illustrated News*, 6 May 1871, 3(18): 288.
7   *An Act Respecting Census and Statistics*, 1879, 42 Vict., ch21, s16, p185.
8. G. Sargison to E.H. St Denis, 6 March 1891, in Sargison Letter book, 1890–1900, p.89. MS.2454, BCA.
9. R.H. Coats, 'The Census of Indians', n.d., in files by R.H. Coats and H. Marshall. SC/LAC.
10. R.E. Gosnell to T. Davie, 21 April 1893. Correspondence, file 1, box 3, AG/BCA.
11. These are John Beattie (Western Superintendency, Ontario), James Martin (Maniwaki, Quebec), Charles Beckwith (King's County, New Brunswick), W.H. Lomas (Cowichan Agency) and Harry Guillod (West Coast Agency, British Columbia). At least two native individuals, Solomon Loft of Tyendinaga and William Wawanosh of the Chippewas of Sarnia, acted as enumerators for their own communities.
12. See correspondence in Sargison Letter book, 1890–1900, MS.2454, BCA: G. Sargison to J.S. Bennet, 8 April 1891, p.123; Sargison to J.S. Bennet, 16 April 1891, p.137; Sargison to R.E. Gosnell, 8 and 9 April 1891, pp.123–24; Sargison to M. Bray and W.K. Leighton, 9 April 1891, p.125; and Sargison to John Stevenson, 10 April 1891, p.126. Sargison also talked with a Mr A.W. Hewson of Victoria, British Columbia, allegedly an authority on Aboriginal peoples of the province, and suggested that enumerators confer with him.
13. One exception of treaty Indians regularly enumerated in Assiniboia can be found in the 1891 census, District 199, Sub-district C4, 5–6, Reel 426.
14. H.B. Small to Bishop Horden, 9 April 1891, p.76. Vol.1586, T–125, L/DoA/ LAC.

15. H.B. Small to Reverend Prevost, 9 April 1891, p.77. Vol.1586, T–125, L/DoA/ LAC.
16. G. Johnson, 'Re. Census of British Columbia', 25 September 1893, pp.3–5. Correspondence, 1894, file 2, box 3, AG/BCA.
17. 'How the Census Was Taken', *Qu'appelle Progress,* 17 September 1891, p.4.
18. *Edmonton Bulletin,* 9 May 1891, p.1.
19. A.N. Blue, 'Memo by Dr Blue on the Censuses of 1901 and 1891', p.11. SC/ LAC.
20. G. Johnson, 'Re. Census of British Columbia', 25 September 1893, pp.2–3. Correspondence, 1894, file 2, box 3, AG/BCA.
21. 'An Indian Census Man's Adventures', *Gazette,* Montreal, 30 December 1891, p.1.
22. Shoemaker (1992: 6, 7) noted the same problem in the United States.
23. G. Sargison, Notebook, 1883–1891, p.66–7. MS.0367, BCA.
24. See the *Act to Amend and Consolidate the Laws Respecting Indians 1880,* chapter 28.
25. See *Act Respecting Indians 1886,* chapter 43.
26. See *Act to Amend the 'The Indian Act' 1887,* chapter 33.
27. See *Act to Further Amend 'The Indian Act' 1888,* chapter 22.
28. For an example of Métis who took treaty, see Reimer and Chartrand (2004: 579).
29. R.E. Green, 'Diary of Journey to Port Simpson and Queen Charlotte Islands', 7 and 8 July 1891. MS.2453, BCA.
30. R.E. Green, 'Diary of Journey to Port Simpson and Queen Charlotte Islands', 21 and 24 July 1891. MS.2453, BCA.
31. G.B. Mills, 'Report', 22 September 1891. Docket 80352, Vol.701, DMS/DoA/ LAC. See also 'Form of Information or of Complaint on Oath'. Docket 80351, Vol.701, DMS/DoA/LAC.
32. J. Michaud to R. Sinclair, 9 July 1891. Docket 79421, Vol.693, DMS/DoA/LAC. For more about the Dokis band and timber rights, see Angus (1989).
33. J. Michaud to DIA, 1 September 1891. Docket 80352, Vol. 701, DMS/DoA/ LAC. and J. Michaud to DIA, 2 July 1891. Docket 79421, Vol.693, DMS/DoA/ LAC.
34. R. Sinclair to J. Michaud, 8 July 1891. Docket 79421, Vol.693, DMS/DoA/ LAC.
35. L. Vankoughnet to J. Lowe, 13 July 1891. Docket 79421, Vol.693, DMS/DoA/ LAC.
36. W. Hogarth to G. Johnson, 15 July 1891. Docket 79421, Vol.693, DMS/DoA/ LAC.
37. W. Hogarth to G. Johnson, 15 July 1891. Docket 79421, Vol.693, DMS/DoA/ LAC and W. Hogarth to G. Johnson, 24 August 1891. Docket 80351, Vol.701, DMS/DoA/LAC.
38. J. Michaud to L. Vankoughnet, 15 August 1891. Docket 79975, Vol. 698, DMS/ DoA/LAC.
39. L. Vankoughnet to J. Lowe, 31 August 1891. Docket 80042, Vol.699, DMS/ DoA/LAC.
40. M. Dokis to W. Hogarth, 4 August 1891. Docket 80351, Vol.701, DMS/DoA/ LAC.
41. E.D. Cameron to L. Vankoughnet, 19 November 1891. File 115 111, Vol.2565, C–11240, RG 10, DIA/LAC.

42. G. Johnson, 'Re. Census of British Columbia', 25 September 1893, p.1. Correspondence, 1894, file 2, box 3, AG/BCA.
43. 'Re. Census of British Columbia', 1893? Correspondence, 1894, file 2, box 3. AG/BCA.
44. The Census Office's instructions state: 'The classification of the people by their religious faith must not ignore any church, or denomination, or form of belief, saving in the case of a church or denomination whose identity has been lost by union or otherwise. There is no State Church in Canada, and if a person is not a member of or does not adhere to or favour any one church or denomination he must not be classed with one or another. If he is an agnostic, or a non-believer, or a pagan, or a reincarnationist, or whatever his relationship to religion may be, he should be so classed' (Department of Agriculture 1901: 14).

References

Archives

AG/BCA – Attorney General, British Columbia, GR–0429. British Columbia Archives, Victoria, British Columbia.

BCA – British Columbia Archives, Victoria, British Columbia.

DIA/LAC – Department of Indian Affairs. Library and Archives Canada, Ottawa.

DMS/DoA/LAC – General Correspondence, Deputy Minister and Secretary, 1852–1920, Department of Agriculture, RG 17 A–I–1. Library and Archives Canada, Ottawa.

L/DoA/LAC – Correspondence, Department of Agriculture General Letter books, 1852–1894, Department of Agriculture, RG 17 A–I–2. Library and Archives Canada, Ottawa.

SC/LAC – Census Files, Statistics Canada, Office of the Dominion Statistician, Vol.1417, RG 31. Library and Archives Canada, Ottawa.

Other Sources

Alterman, H. 1969. *Counting People: The Census in History*. New York: Harcourt, Brace and World.

Angus, J.T. 1989. 'How the Dokis Indians Protected Their Timber', *Ontario History* 81(3): 181–200.

Baskerville, P., and E. Sager (eds). 2000. 'The Canadian Families Project', *Historical Methods* 33(4), special issue.

Bradbury, B. 2000. 'Single Parenthood in the Past: Canadian Census Categories, 1891–1951, and the "Normal" Family', *Historical Methods* 33(4): 211–17.

Brookes, A.A. 1976. '"Doing the Best I Can": The Taking of the 1861 New Brunswick Census', *Histoire Sociale* 9: 70–91.

Buck, I. et al. 2000. 'Reconstructing the Geographical Framework of the 1901 Census of Canada', *Historical Methods* 33(4): 199–205.

Clubine-Ito, C. 2004. 'Multilevel Modeling for Historical Data: An Example from the 1901 Canadian Census', *Historical Methods* 37(1): 5–22.

Curtis, B. 2001. *The Politics of Population: State Formation, Statistics, and the Census of Canada, 1840–1875*. Toronto: University of Toronto Press.

Darroch, G. 2002. 'Semi-automated Record Linkage with Surname Samples: A Regional Study of "Case Law" Linkage, Ontario 1861–1871', *History and Computing* 14(1/2): 153–83.

Department of Agriculture. 1871. *Manual Containing "The Census Act" and the Instructions to Officers Employed in the Taking of the First Census of Canada*. Ottawa: B. Chamberlin.

—— 1882. *Census of Canada 1880/81*, Vol. 1. Ottawa: MacLean, Roger and Co.

—— 1884. *Census of Canada 1880/81*, Vol. 2. Ottawa: MacLean, Roger and Co.

—— 1886. *Census of the Three Provisional Districts of the North-west Territories 1884/5*. Ottawa: MacLean, Roger and Co.

—— 1887. *Census of Manitoba 1885/6*. Ottawa: MacLean, Roger and Co.

—— 1891a. *Census of Canada, 1891: Bulletin 1*. Ottawa: S.E. Dawson.

—— 1891b. *Census of Canada, 1891: Bulletin 5*. Ottawa: S.E. Dawson.

—— 1891c. *Manual Containing "The Census Act", and the Instructions to Officers Employed in the Taking of the Third Census of Canada (1891)*. Ottawa: Brown Chamberlin.

—— 1892. *Statistical Year-book for 1891*. Ottawa: Government Printing Bureau.

—— 1893a. *The Statistical Year-book of Canada for 1892*. Ottawa: Government Printing Bureau.

—— 1893b. *Census of Canada, 1890/91*. Ottawa: S.E. Dawson.

—— 1901. *Fourth Census of Canada: Instructions to Officers*. Ottawa: S.E. Dawson.

Department of Indian Affairs. 1872. *Annual Report 1871*. Ottawa: I.B. Taylor.

—— 1892. *Annual Report 1891*. Ottawa: S.E. Dawson.

—— 1911. *Annual Report*. Ottawa: C.H. Parmelee.

Dillon, L.Y. 2000. 'International Partners, Local Volunteers and Lots of Data: The 1881 Canadian Census Project', *History and Computing* 12(2): 163–76.

—— 2002. 'Challenges and Opportunities for Census Record Linkage in the French and English Canadian Context', *History and Computing* 14(1/2): 185–212.

Dunae, P.A. 1999. 'Making the 1891 Census in British Columbia', *Histoire Sociale* 31(62): 223–39.

Duncan, E. 1979. *Fifty-seven Years in the Comox Valley*, 2nd edn. Courtenay: Comox Books.

Forbes, J.D. 1990. 'Undercounting Native Americans: The 1980 Census and the Manipulation of Racial Identity in the United States', *Wicazo Sa Review* 6(1): 2–26.

Fortier, A. 2006a. 'Aboriginal Presence in the 1891 Canadian Census: Notable Regional Variations', unpublished paper. University of Guelph.

——— 2006b. 'The Challenges and Utility of Studying Aboriginal Presence in the 1891 Canadian Census', unpublished paper. University of Guelph.

Gaffield, C. 2007. 'Language, Ancestry, and the Competing Constructions of Identity in Turn-of-the-century Canada', in E.W. Sager and P. Baskerville (eds), *Household Counts: Canadian Households and Families in 1901*. Toronto: University of Toronto Press, pp. 420–33.

——— (ed). 2007. 'Canadian Century Research Infrastructure', *Historical Methods* 40(2), special issue.

——— 2000. 'Linearity, Nonlinearity, and the Competing Constructions of Social Hierarchy in Early Twentieth-Century Canada: The Question of Language in 1901', *Historical Methods* 33(4): 255–60.

Gagan, D.P. 1974. 'Enumerator's Instructions for the Census of Canada 1852 and 1861', *Histoire Sociale* 7(14): 355–65.

Galois, R.M. 1983. 'Mapping the British Columbia Census 1881', *Association of Canadian Map Librarians Bulletin* 47: 26–36.

Hacker, J.D. (ed). 2003. 'Building Historical Data Infrastructure: New Projects of the Minnesota Population Center', *Historical Methods* 36(1), special issue.

Hall, P.K. (ed). 1999. 'IPUMS: Integrated Public Use Microdata Series', *Historical Methods*, 32(3), special issue.

Hamilton, M.A. 2007. '"Anyone Not on the List Might As Well Be Dead:" 7 Aboriginal Peoples and the Censuses of Canada, 1851–1916', *Journal of the Canadian Historical Association* 18(1): 57–79.

Hollos, M. 1992. 'Why Is It Difficult to Take a Census in Nigeria?' *Historical Methods* 25(1): 12–19.

Hull, J. 1984. '1981 Census Coverage of the Native Population in Manitoba and Saskatchewan', *Canadian Journal of Native Studies* 4(1): 147–56.

Inwood, K., and K. James. 2005. 'Une resource numérique pour l'analyse historique: le recensement canadien de 1891', *Cahiers québécois de démographie* 34(2): 315–29.

Inwood, K., and R. Reid. 2001. 'Gender and Occupational Identity in a Canadian Census,' *Historical Methods* 34(2): 57–70.

——— (eds). 1995. 'Use of Census Manuscript Data for Historical Research', *Histoire Sociale* 28(56), special issue.

Jobe, M.M. 2004. 'Native Americans and the U.S. Census: A Brief Historical Survey', *Journal of Government Information* 30: 66–76.

Kralt, J. 1990. 'Ethnic Origins in the Canadian Census, 1871–1986,' in S.S. Halli, F. Trovato and L. Driedger (eds), *Ethnic Demography: Canadian Immigrant, Racial and Cultural Variations*. Ottawa: Carleton University Press, pp. 13–29.

McInnis, R.M. 1981. 'Some Pitfalls in the 1851–1852 Census of Agriculture of Lower Canada,' *Histoire Sociale* 14(27): 219–31.

Mandemaker, K., and L.Y. Dillon. 2004. 'Best Practices with Large Databases on Historical Populations', *Historical Methods* 37(1): 34–38.

Reimer, G., and J.-P. Chartrand. 2004. 'Documenting Historic Métis in Ontario', *Ethnohistory* 51(3): 567–607.

Ruggles, S., and R.R. Menard (eds). 1995. 'The Minnesota Historical Census Projects', *Historical Methods* 28(1), special issue.

Ruggles, S., M. Sobek and T. Gardner. 1996. 'Distributing Large Historical Census Samples on the Internet', *History and Computing* 8(3): 145–59.

Ruppert, E.S. 2009. 'Becoming Peoples: "Counting Heads in Northern Wilds"', *Journal of Cultural Economy* 2(1–2):. 11–31.

Sager, E.W. (ed). 2001. 'New Perspectives in Canadian Families', *Journal of Family History* 26(2), special issue.

Shoemaker, N. 1992. 'The Census as Civilizer: American Indian Household Structure in the 1900 and 1910 U.S. Censuses', *Historical Methods* 25(1): 4–11.

Taché, J.-C. 1876. *Censuses of Canada, 1665 to 1871*. Ottawa: I.B. Taylor.

Watts, R. 2003. 'Making Numbers Count: The Birth of the Census and Racial Government in Victoria, 1835–40', *Australian Historical Studies* 34(121): 26–47.

White, P.M., J. Badets and V. Renaud. 1993. 'Measuring Ethnicity in Canadian Censuses', in *Challenges of Measuring an Ethnic World: Science, Politics and Reality*. Washington, DC: United States Government Printing Office, pp. 223–69.

6

'IN THE NATIONAL REGISTRY, ALL PEOPLE ARE EQUAL': SAMI IN SWEDISH STATISTICAL SOURCES

Per Axelsson

Introduction

Sweden has a long and well-known history of population statistics as well as one of the world's most eminent and all-inclusive collections of statistical information on its population. As long ago as 1749 a system for annually collecting and presenting population statistics, the *Tabellverket,* was created, offering an overview of demographic events from all 2,500 parishes in Sweden, and tax registers, parish registers and different administrative books had been kept prior to 1749 (Sköld 2004: 7–8). During the eighteenth century, nearly all countries lacked information on ethnic groups, but the Swedish parish registers from that time contain ethnic markers, and in the early nineteenth century, a specific category for the Sami population was created in the *Tabellverket*. The national census that began in 1860 continued to count the Sami population, and this continued up until the end of the Second World, which marked the end of registering people's ethnic affiliation. In contrast to many other countries, Sweden today has no separate statistical information regarding ethnicity, not only concerning its only recognised indigenous population but also concerning other ethnic groups. The Swedish state has legislated that registering information such as ethnicity may harm a person's integrity, and such registration is therefore regulated by law.[1]

One of the largest post-war demographic examinations of the Sami was conducted in the mid 1970s, and the official report – which was concerned with support for Sami language and culture – opened with the words, 'In the national registry, all people are equal' (SOU 1975:11). Owing to the lack of population statistics on ethnic identities, the author of the report had recourse to reindeer herding registers, from between 1965 to 1971. People who were active or had been active reindeer herders were listed and then genealogies were constructed to create 'the Sami population of Sweden'. This also meant that those without any connection to reindeer herding – the majority of the Sami population – was left out.

Although Sweden may have avoided some problems of discrimination and the misuse of statistics, not registering ethnicity also creates problems for a country. Sweden was recently criticised by the UN Special Rapporteur on Indigenous Issues, Paul Hunt. He stated that the absence of facts about the size and distribution of the Sami population generates problems – for instance concerning health issues among the Sami or other ethnic populations. As Hunt writes: 'If they do not know the scale and nature of the problem, how can they devise the most appropriate interventions? If an intervention were introduced, how would they know whether or not it was effective?' (Hunt 2007: 30).

Historians, sociologists and anthropologists, among others, have shown that ethnic enumeration is a complex procedure, and over the years countries have dealt with this issue differently. Focusing on the statistical history of the Swedish Sami population, this chapter addresses some of the crucial and difficult questions of historical, social and cultural factors that have had a bearing on how a dominant administrative structure has dealt with the statistical construct of an indigenous population. It investigates how Sweden dealt with the enumeration of the Sami population from approximately 1750 until 1945, when ethnic registration ended.[2] Three sources of Swedish population statistics will be examined: the parish registers, the *Tabellverket*, and the censuses. The focus is not on the validity of the sources; rather, it is on addressing the question of how categories have been constructed, exploring the creation of the statistical identity of Sweden's indigenous Sami population, the context of how this identity was created, and investigating what caused the categories to change over time.

A Note on the Statistical Sources

Historical demographic research on the population of the Swedish Sápmi region has been intensified lately due to the creation of new research infrastructures. The Nothern Inland Population Database available at the Demographic Data Base, Umeå University, has digitised eighteenth and nineteenth-century parish registers in Sápmi. The database covers approximately 150 years, from 1750 to 1900, and the records include every individual in the parishes, Sami or non-Sami. This is also the time period during which the area was colonised by largely Swedish settlers and the Sami population changed from a majority to a minority. The Demographic Data Base has also digitised the *Tabellverket* and made it available online. The *Tabellverket* covers the period 1749 to 1859 and contains aggregated population statistics, but it is non-nominal. In addition, the 1900 Swedish census is another demographic source that has been newly released and made available through the Minnesota Population Center.[3] The census contains Sami markers as well. Given these new initiatives, it is important to elucidate why we have these ethnic categories, how they have been constructed, and how they have changed over the years. The ethnicity displayed in the material could be understood using the theoretical tools provided by Fredrik Barth's work on cultural boundaries (Barth 1969) and Pierre Bourdieu's concept of habitus (Bourdieu 1977). This tells us that those members of the clergy with a Swedish background and education were the people defining 'them', the Sami. We cannot be certain that the people designated as 'Sami' actually felt that they belonged to a Sami population. We can only accept the fact that the clergy at the time thought of them as Sami. It is worth underscoring that it is the Swedish state that, over the years, has made several attempts to define and estimate the size of the Sami population. A census has never been initiated and undertaken by the Sami population themselves.

Previous Research

The field of indigenous studies is steadily growing. In the Nordic countries alone, there are several established research centres focused on the Sami and indigenous issues. This chapter draws on material from research on indigenous populations and demography.

It seems as if demographic research, historically as well as at present, tends to have a specific section explaining the extra set of issues and concerns that occur when dealing with statistical information on indigenous populations. Geographer Bruce Newbold pointed out that one basic problem pervading all data sets 'is the definition of Indigenous identity, with it becoming increasingly complicated to define for statistical purposes who is Indigenous, and who is not' (Newbold 2004: 123). It is fair to say that researchers have to be aware of, and acknowledge the limitations and complexity involved in, defining indigenous populations for statistical purposes. Yohannes Kinfu and John Taylor described these difficulties in relation to statistics on Australian indigenous populations as: 'the variable manner in which States, Territories and the Commonwealth attempt to enumerate and categorise Indigenous people, and the choices made by respondents to such overtures. In the not-so-distant past, the politics of such data collection served to exclude, devalue or deter Indigenous representation in official statistics' (Kinfu and Taylor 2005: 234).

When working with demographic sources on indigenous peoples, there are some important questions and issues that need consideration. It is important to understand the historical context of not only how the demographic sources were constructed – Who is counted? Who is not? Who did the counting and for what purpose? – but also the complexity within the indigenous population – How do the indigenous people define themselves? Are there sub-groups? Also, researchers need to be aware of the long (sometimes bleak) history of Western research on indigenous communities and the problems that this has caused them. The fact that I may not be part of the population I am studying also means that I may lack an understanding of the habits or cultural traits that are important to my analysis.

That said, indigenous studies – whether pursued from an insider or outsider perspective, whether based on demography or not – is an important field, and analyses should be distributed and discussed in a dialogue between indigenous peoples and research communities.

Kertzer and Arel have stated that before the emergence of modern states, collective identities were not thought to be of great importance. Now and again, the state needed some assessment of its population for taxes and conscription, 'yet [it] remained largely indifferent to recording the myriad cultural identities of its subjects. As a result, there was little social pressure on people to rank-order their localised and overlapping identities. People often had the sense of simply being "from here"' (Kertzer and Arel 2002: 2).

Regarding previous research on the ethnic enumeration of populations in Sweden, there have been several important contributions. In their book on the history of the Sami in Norway, Sweden, Finland and Russia – the traditional Sápmi area – Lars Ivar Hansen and Bjørnar Olsen (2006) discussed how the Sami have been identified and named in historical times. The authors emphasised the complexity of establishing ethnic identities in the past as well as the importance of recognising that the source materials we know of have been collected by men of the clergy and of the state using labels and categories that were comprehensible to them at that point in time. In Swedish statistical material prior to the mid twentieth century, the word *Lapp* is most commonly used to describe the Sami people. This term seems to derive from regions east of Sweden in Russia. The first written evidence in the Nordic countries is from the thirteenth century, and from Sweden in the fourteenth. Other early names include *Finn* or *Skridfinn*, and the Sami self-chosen *Šämä* (ibid.: 45–49; see also Hansen, this volume). However, they are not commonly used in the Swedish material.

Historian Peter Sköld has written extensively on the history of Swedish population statistics, especially focusing on the events during the eighteenth and nineteenth centuries. On the basis of mercantilist ideas, the size of a nation's population was a key question in the mid eighteenth century. To get a picture of how to best rationalise and increase the Swedish population, a group of influential Swedish scientists established the *Tabellverket*. Sköld has emphasised the role that the clergy had in carrying out the footwork and compiling the data. But the existence of a medical organisation and a central administrative system were also important factors in creating the early Swedish national population registers (Sköld 2001, 2004).

Historian Henrik Höjer (2000) has also studied how national statistics helped to shape the representation of Sweden as a country. Population statistics played a major role. At the beginning of the nineteenth century, the mercantilist standpoint emphasising the advantages of a large and growing population, still was a central idea to nation states in Europe. However, Höjer found that around the 1830s, the perspective shifted to a Malthusian standpoint. The significance of quantity was replaced by the importance of the quality of a nation's population, and through statistics it was possible to discern categories that could define the quality of the nation and its population. Statistical categories that focused on the morals and physical well-being of the country's population were created. In the 1850s, the influential public officer and statistician Carl Edvard Ljungberg discussed the distinctive Swedish character and underlined the importance of a homogeneous population. According to Ljungberg, the population of Sweden was almost pure and unmixed, but it was important to confirm this with statistics to identify and count other populations within Sweden, such as Jews, Gypsies and Sami. Höjer argued that categorising these 'other people' was a new trait in population statistics, implying the introduction of a new, more biological and ethnic way of regarding the population (ibid.:172–80).

Rogers and Nelson's (2003) study of statistical categories in Sweden suggests that information about the Sami first became available in 1805. They argue that the state needed more information on agricultural production, and thus included the Sami owing to their reindeer herding, fishing and hunting activities. They also highlight that occupational categories were modified and updated. Rogers and Nelson put forward the notion that the control of land and other resources played a part in including three categories of Sami in the national statistics.

Both Ulf Mörkenstam (1999) and Lennart Lundmark (2002) have written extensively on Swedish policy towards Sami, and also touched upon the subject of statistics. During the nineteenth and first half of the twentieth century, Swedish politicians considered the Sami to be a lower human race. This perspective led to discrimination against the Swedish Sami population in several respects over the years. One example is the reindeer herding law of 1928, where the Swedish parliament decided that only those involved in reindeer husbandry were Sami, thereby excluding Sami with other occupations; in fact, the majority of Sami are not reindeer herders. As a result, those Sami not involved in reindeer husbandry lost their rights to fish and hunt in areas where their ancestors had lived. They also lost their Sami identity and became neither Sami nor Swede. The 'real' Sami was defined as a nomadic reindeer herder.

Lundmark emphasises that the statistics have also been affected by Sweden's Sami policy. The officials of the Swedish state decided who was to be counted as Sami. Categories changed over the years, and this brought about several problems. Lundmark underlined, for instance, that in the 1920 census, mixed marriages were considered a problem. As a result, Statistics Sweden decided that all children should be assigned the ethnicity of their father. This policy was reconsidered in the 1930s, when

Statistics Sweden discussed the concept of half-breeds (Swedish-Sami, Sami-Swedish), though the category was never used as there was no census undertaken in 1940 due to the strained Swedish economy. In 1945 the next census was undertaken, but in light of the events of the Second World War officials wished to avoid talk about race or tribes. Instead, Statistics Sweden decided only to count Sami-related topics of importance to school and industry, and to omit details of who was Sami and who was not (Lundmark 2002: 150).

Previous research has not made any longitudinal study or comparison of the different statistical sources on the Sami population. The following section will further introduce and examine three sources of Swedish population statistics: the parish registers, the *Tabellverket*, and the censuses. For the nineteenth century, there exists demographic information on the Sami population in the northernmost counties of Sweden, for instance in five-year reports sent to the king.[4] However, these statistics are clearly based on the parish registers or *Tabellverket*, and consequently the five-year reports and other additional sources have been left out of the present investigation.

Parish Registers

Parish registers have long served for purposes other than the clerical. In 1686, a law was introduced regulating the practice of keeping parish registers. During the annual house-to-house meetings lists, named catechisation registers, had one important aim to enable the clergy to monitor the Christian beliefs of parishioners, as well as their moral behaviour and literacy. Parish registers also included lists of birth, marriages, migration and deaths and also served the Swedish state as a means for regulating taxes and enabling the recruitment of soldiers. As Sören Edvinsson notes, by keeping parish registers, 'the clergy became state employees, administering many duties demanded by the central authorities. And when the government wanted national population statistics from the middle of the eighteenth century, the parish registers were naturally used' (Edvinsson 2000: 233). During the late nineteenth century there were several other important changes concerning how the registers were kept, with new categories being added and others being changed or dropped. The state's increasing demand for statistical information on a variety of areas led to the creation of Statistics Sweden, which started its work in 1860. And with the *Church Law* of 1894, new forms were sent out and the catechetical registers came to an end. Nevertheless, until 1973 the Swedish population registers were based on information from the parish registers (Wannerdt 1982: 46–47).

The instructions to the clergy in 1686 concerning the keeping of parish registers do not mention the Sami population, and although there are Sami identity markers in the parish registers in the eighteenth century, it is obvious that it was not until the *Church Law* of 1894 that practical instructions on how to record Sami were published. The clergy were then ordered to note *Främmande stam*, 'foreign tribe', with the 'language at home' being decisive if nothing else determined whether or not a person belonged to a 'tribe'. A footnote in the *Church Law* reads: 'Spoken language must generally be considered as a solid ground for judgments of a person's tribe, although it may be that a great many Lappish families use the Finnish language as their spoken language' (Beskow 1894: 31).

The state also sought information on the Finns and Jews in the same manner. The Swedish Church specified that language was crucial to distinguishing the ethnicity of the Sami population. At the same time, however, the wording above suggests that people could use another spoken language regardless of their 'tribe'. It is very likely that the responsibility for determining the ethnicity of parishioners fell on the shoulders of local clergyman.

In the seventeenth and eighteenth century, Härnosand and Piteå were the two northernmost dioceses of Sweden, and they covered the Sápmi area. In Härnosand, there are records of clergymen from the area having thirteen meetings between 1664 and 1750, and in Piteå seven meetings were held prior to 1750 (Söderlind 1958). The records of these meetings, synodal acts, have been investigated in order to locate texts about the Sami population.[5] We know that people like Pehr Högström, a Christian missionary famous for his writings about the Sami and Sápmi, were active in the 1740s. Moreover, in the first half of the eighteenth century, the Church started missionary schools for Sami in order to convert them to Christianity.[6] Despite this, prior to 1750 there are very few passages in these synodal acts that speak of the Sami population. But in 1755, a very interesting account is found in the synodal act from Piteå: 'Dean Solander asked if a specific column in the table of the numerousness of the population could not be established for the Lapps, so that the High Powers could see their growth' (ibid.: 214). The request of Dean Carl Solander (1699–1760), pastor and member of the Swedish Parliament, was soon granted. Henning Johansson argues that 1757 marks the first real attempt to estimate the Sami population, as can be seen in the primary tables of the *Tabellverket*, but Johansson did not believe the statistics were very reliable (Johansson 1975: 322). But Solander's suggestion indicates, nonetheless, that the Sami seem to have been included in mercantilist thinking at the time, and also that Solander thought it possible to identify members of the Sami population.[7]

It can be argued that the Swedish Church had rather good knowledge of each individual they considered Sami by the middle of the eighteenth century. Through taxes, Christian missionaries and the school system, the Church had kept a record of the Sami population, probably since the seventeenth century or earlier (Johansson 1975: 322–23; Sköld 2004: 7). For instance, based on the traditional Sami *Siida* system, the state created a system of *Lappbyar*, or 'Sami villages', to enable tax collection from the Sami (Sköld 1992: 23). In 1746, the first *Lappförsamling*, 'Sami parish', was created that exclusively contained Sami people. Föllinge Lappförsamling was a non-territorial administrative construction for registering Sami in the parish of Jämt-land and parts of Kopparberg County. Over the following hundred years there were several administrative changes, and at the end of the eighteenth century there were four 'Sami parishes' in Sweden (Thomasson 1956: 7–12).[8] These non-territorial parishes need to be further investigated to obtain a clearer picture of their history and actual purpose, but we can conclude that the clergy treated the Sami in the southern parts of northern Sweden as a single population. After another series of administrative changes, the Sami parishes were abolished in 1942 (Rumar 2007: 12).

Although it is not systematic, the clergy left information allowing to-day's researchers to discuss and examine the Sami identity markers they used in several ways. Besides the special Sami parishes, inclusion of the word *Lapp* is the most prominent indicator of Sami ethnicity in the sourc-es. Most often these terms are found in the name column or field of occu-pation, but also in the column where the clergy noted information about the person, such as economic, social, legal or moral characteristics, as well as in the mortality records. As a consequence, not only are nomadic Sami included in this ethnic category, but so too are those Sami who are in the process of adopting a more settled lifestyle. Geographical information is also available, and the Sami population often lived in places that were restricted to them, the 'Sami villages', which gives us an additional way of identifying Sami ethnicity. Moreover, family names reveal heritage. There are certain Sami family names entered in the registers that can be traced over many generations (Sköld and Axelsson 2008).

The bottom line here is that the clergy had no column for registering the Sami in the parish registers of the eighteenth and nineteenth century. However, in the early parish registers of northern Sweden we find the Sami identity markers mentioned above. It is largely up to the individual researcher to judge how best to use these.

Swedish National Statistics: The *Tabellverket*

In the middle of the eighteenth century, the Swedish state – influenced by the mercantilist regime, which feared Sweden was becoming underpopu-lated, by numerous wars and epidemics – established what was to become the world's oldest continuous set of national population statistics, the *Tabellverket*. The work was lead by the Swedish Royal Academy of Science, and a group known as the Table Commission was formally established by the king in 1756. Instead of collecting data through taking censuses, the clergy and their ecclesiastical registers were used (Sköld 2001: 87; 2004). The *Tabellverket* began in 1749 and consisted of two statistical serials that focused on different demographic aspects of the Swedish population. It was not a nominal census, and at first contained four tables in two differ-ent forms.[9] One form concentrated on mortality and registered all births, baptisms, marriages, deaths and burials in Sweden. Another part contained information about the composition of the population according to age, sex, marital status, occupation, social group, estate, other household details, remarks and sporadic information. There were changes in the nomenclature over the years, for instance concerning causes of death, and the *Tabellverket* was in use until it was replaced by Statistics Sweden in 1860 (Sköld 2004).

Keeping Kertzer and Arel's argument in mind, it is appropriate to ask: When did the need to identify Sami identity in the Swedish population statistics actually arise? As discussed earlier, in some records on occupations and social groups, information on the Sami population already existed in 1757. The statistics were organised in columns and rows, where 'Lapp' shared the same row as 'prisoners' and 'poor people'. Consequently, this makes the data difficult to interpret. Henning Johansson (1975: 322) noted that the numbers are very unreliable and that definitions of Sami identity seem to differ. From 1760 to the turn of the eighteenth century, the 'Lapp/prisoner/poor category' has the same design. The synodal act of 1755 where Dean Solander suggested the inclusion of a specific category for the Sami is the only historical account that I have come across which discusses the creation of a category for Sami people. Nonetheless, it is interesting that these three categories of people are grouped together, given that they seem to have very little in common.

In 1805, a small section for Sami occurred in the population form (see Figure 6.1). There are three subcategories: reindeer herders, non-reindeer herders, and vagabonds/hired hands. The reason for this, Rogers and Nelson (2003: 65) suggest, is that the state needed more information on agricultural production, and thus included the Sami owing to their reindeer

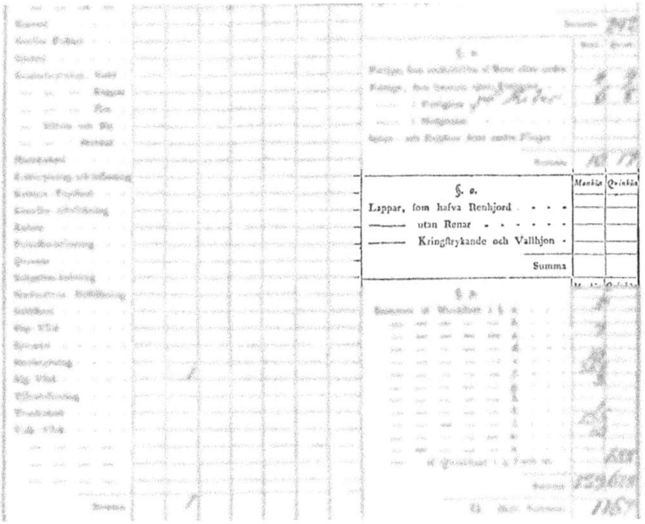

Figure 6.1 Population Form from 1805

herding, fishing and hunting activities. Rogers and Nelson also point out that the occupational categories were changed and updated. Finally, they suggest that the control of land and other resources could have played a part in including three categories of Sami in the national statistics.

The instructions given by the Table Commission actually hint at a fourth reason for including the Sami in the national statistics of 1805. In the instructions for the tables regarding social division, occupation and estate, prior to 1805 it reads: 'every person can be included several times in this table, on the basis of the manifoldness of the person's work'.[10] This indicates that one person could have had many occupations registered in the statistics. The occupational columns were not added up and adjusted in relation to the table, counting the number of people distributed by age, sex and marital status. This, then, allowed the clergy to not register people in the occupational categories if they did not fit into the categories of the printed forms. This circumstance was regulated in the instructions regarding the occupational form of 1805: 'In addition no one will be noted down more than once in this table, or for more than one occupation'.[11] In addition to not being registered more than once, starting in this year the tables regarding social division, occupation and estate were added up and had to be in accord with the tables for age, sex and marital status. Consequently, the printed forms of 1805 had to contain a more varied selection of occupations enabling everyone to be counted. Thus, the Sami population was made into an occupational category, which further was divided into reindeer herders, non-reindeer herders, and vagabonds and hired hands.

Starting in 1825, the data on the Sami population are presumed to be more accurate, although it was stressed by the national statistics office that:

> The information that Tabellverket contains about the Lapps cannot be claimed to be of the same completeness and reliability as the account for the settled population ... although it carries an unmistakable testimony, that neither the State nor the Church has neglected to increasingly follow the traces of these nomads of the polar area ... [T]he knowledge we thereby have of the number of Lapps on the Scandinavian peninsula is unquestionably more developed than the knowledge other states and countries have of their tribal ancestors.[12]

In addition to believing that they had the best knowledge in the world concerning 'the nomads of the Polar area', it is evident that the statisticians pictured the Sami as exclusively nomadic. Furthermore, it is interesting to note that the statistical reports speak of the Sami and Finnish 'race', but the columns are categorised as 'nationality' or 'tribe'. Rogers and Nelson state that the concept of race became increasingly 'important' after the turn of the twentieth century (Rogers and Nelson 2003: 66).

The Censuses

The first Swedish nominative census took place in 1860, and with the exception of Stockholm they were all based on the parish registers, a practice that continued until 1945 (Sköld 2001: 291–93). In a document written by the Table Commission in 1857, it is obvious that there were serious plans to carry out a de facto census of the entire country, but the parish registers, especially the catechetical registers, were reliable sources and were believed to include almost every aspect covered by foreign censuses. Another argument for not carrying out a de facto census was that it was expensive and that there might be problems in registering any Sami nomads who were moving their herds (Berg 1857: 6, 46).

The Table Commission consisted of only a handful of people and had experienced difficulties meeting the state's increasing demands for more complete statistical information. Already in the early nineteenth century there were discussions of restructuring the administration, but it was not until 1853/4 that Parliament decided to vote for a reorganisation of the *Tabellverket*, and in August 1858 the Swedish Statistical Bureau (later Statistics Sweden) began their work (Kock 1958).

The form for the first census in 1860 contained fifteen columns. The census was organised by household, and information was collected on sex, year of birth, social status, and whether the person had been vaccinated against smallpox. The most informative column was the one that recorded a person's name. This column was also supposed to contain information on occupation, social group, disabilities and nationality – if the respondent was foreign. Clearly one of the nationalities that the Statistical Bureau had in mind was the Sami people, but in the Sápmi area Finns, as well as Russians and Norwegians, were frequently listed. Until the census of 1900, information about the Sami was mainly entered in the name column.[13] There were also special instructions to register people of foreign nationalities, focusing particularly on, 'the Finnish and Lappish tribes by using the note: *Finne* and *Lapp*'.[14]

By the time of the 1900 census, changes in the nomenclature had occurred. The section on occupation, disability and foreign nationalities was divided so that each factor had its own column. Also, nationality was replaced by *stam* ('tribe'). This way of keeping records ended after the 1930 census.[15] It is worth mentioning that during work on preparing the data files of the 1900 census, it became clear that those who filled out the form did not always use this new column. For instance, in some regions *Lappbyar* or the word *Lappar* was used as a heading in the name column, and people were listed below.

As noted in the 1894 *Church Law*, language became the decisive factor for establishing 'foreign tribe', and it is obvious that this system was carried over to the 1900 census when the concept of 'tribe' was introduced. In an article from 1913, the head of the Statistical Bureau, Edvard Arosenius, expressed his worries that an increasing number of people reported their language to be Swedish instead of Sami. He stated that the system offered the undesired possibility that Sami people were being registered as Swedish. Therefore, the census of 1910 also used surnames to delineate Sami origin (Arosenius 1913). In the instructions for the 1920 census, the Statistical Bureau used the word *ras* (race) instead of *stam* (tribe), and also suggested that using language to establish 'race' was no longer a viable solution. They wrote that in the 'northernmost part of the country, Swedes, Finns and Lapps have lived side by side for a long time' and that 'Lapps had largely changed their own language to Swedish or Finnish'.[16] Therefore the Statistical Bureau concluded that statistics should be based not on language but on *ras karaktäristik* (race characteristics) and the nomadic way of life.[17]

Further revisions were made for the 1930 census, and a new 'tribe concept' was introduced for the collection of statistics on the Sami and Finnish populations. The Statistical Bureau wanted to differentiate between *hel Lapp* (full-blooded Sami) and *halv Lapp* (half-blooded Sami). Initially, they made a distinction between Sami people in the two northernmost counties of Sweden, the inhabitants in the Sami parishes of Jämtland, and finally all other people registered as Sami living elsewhere in Sweden. According to the Statistical Bureau, the 'real Sami population' consisted of the nomadic people registered as belonging to a 'Sami village', and their ancestors. In the introduction to the 1930 census, it is also mentioned that a form was sent out

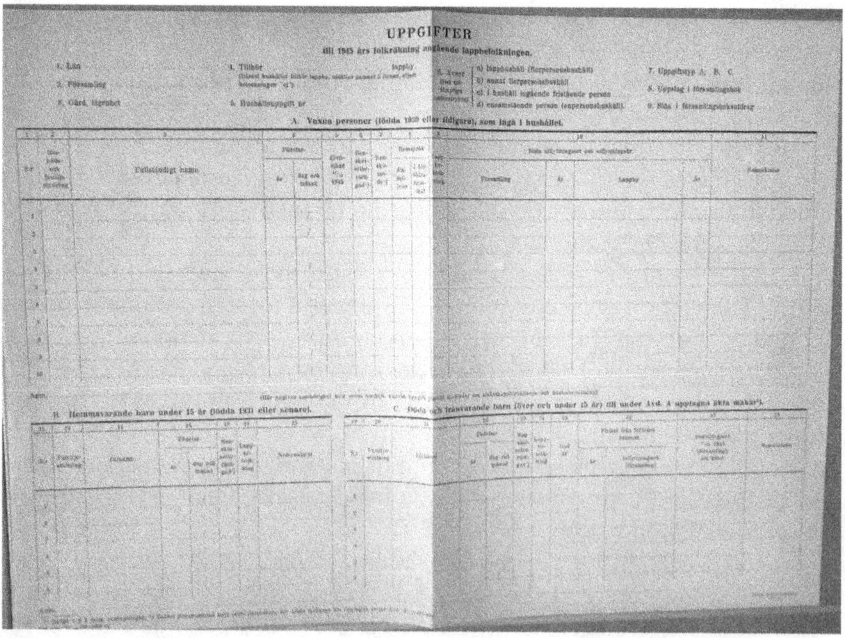

Figure 6.2 The Last Official Sami Census 1945

to investigate what language was used at home, but there are no accounts of this published in the census, other than as a tool for defining ethnicity.[18]

The 1930 census established that the 'real Sami' were the reindeer herder. This view corresponds with the Sami reindeer herding law of 1928, where the nomadic reindeer-herding Sami were considered to constitute *the* Sami population. Thus, Sami with other occupations or ways of living were no longer considered to be Sami (Mörkenstam 1999: 142–45). However, examining an official report from the early 1940s, Lundmark found that the 'tribe' concept of the 1930 census was criticised for not matching the standards of the 1928 reindeer herding law regarding who was a Sami and who was not (Lundmark 2002: 149). There was also a plan to carry out a census in 1940 – which would have been even more complex – but it was abandoned for economic reasons (ibid.: 150).

The end of the Second World War also marked the end of the last Swedish effort to register the Sami population in a census. A special part of the 1945 census was devoted entirely to the demography of the Sami. Although this was fifteen years after the previous census, it must be remembered that the State Institute for Racial Biology had already carried out its own enormous demographic investigation of the Sami (Wahlund 1932). In the introduction to Wahlunds work, it is carefully explained that the previously used 'tribe concept' was not applicable due to 'racial mixture and other circumstances'.[19] The instruction to local administrators was that they should define the Sami population on the basis of one of two criteria: either those entitled to herd reindeer, or those who used Sami as their home language. Lundmark notes that in 1945 interest in distinguishing 'races' had naturally diminished, given the outcome of the Second World War (Lundmark 2002: 150). In one respect, the censuses from 1860 and 1945 mark the rise and fall, respectively, of the cultural hegemony that had defined Sami as a 'lower human race', the unquestionable peak of this hegemony being in the 1930 census and in the thorough investigations carried out by the State Institute for Racial Biology.

Concluding Remarks

It is clear from the first local parish registries up to the later national population statistics that registering some kind of ethnicity, a division between peoples, was a practice of value to those collecting the information: the clergy and the Swedish state. Ethnic enumeration has often been associated with the rise of nationalism during the nineteenth century (Höjer 2000: 172–80; Kertzer and Arel 2002: 2–7), but as we have seen, gathering information on 'the Lapps' was part of the parish records and national statistics of the eighteenth century, although the arguments put forward for collecting this information shifted, from religious to societal and scientific positions. Following the Second World War, Sweden decided to discontinue ethnic enumeration, and the reason for this could be traced to how these demographic records were used for research based on racist ideas. There was also the question of the difficulties inherent in determining the actual boundaries of a racial category. For instance, mixed marriages were a great problem for ethnic classification (Lundmark 2002: 149–50).

Instead, since the Second World War, Swedes have known about the indigenous Sami, but not about the size of the population. And as Paul Hunt so rightly pointed out, this also is a problem. Our knowledge about the size of the Sami population is based on a mid 1970s report stating that there were at the time approximately 17,000 Sami in Sweden, and they projected that the Sami population would be 20,000 by the year 2000 (SOU 1975: 100). This number is still frequently cited in official reports and presentations on the Sami (e.g., Ministry of Agriculture 2004). However, these estimates must be handled with care because Sami society is very complex. Since 1993, there has existed a Swedish Sami Parliament that has not confined itself to a defining Sami exclusively in terms of people connected to reindeer herding. To be included in the electoral register, a person needs to consider themselves Sami, speak a Sami language, have lived in a Sami household, or have a parent or grandparent who speaks or spoke a Sami language. When researchers at the Southern Lapland Research Department constructed a database of the Sami population in 2002, they used reindeer-herding registers and included the registers held by the Sami Parliament, ending up with a Sami population of almost 42,000. This suggests that the Sami population is more than twice the size of that officially recognised by the Swedish government (Hassler 2005: 26–28; Axelsson and Sköld 2006).

These new statistics could have wide implications; for instance, for the political actions taken by the Swedish government to preserve and support the Sami people. Although an active Sami movement has in several ways challenged traditional and well-established views of the Sami and their culture, still it is the Swedish state that through policies and legislation possesses the power to identify and define the Sami and their society in many areas of common interest (Lantto and Mörkenstam 2008: 40–41). Due to Hunt's complaint about how Sweden handled Sami health issues (Hunt 2007), the National Union of the Swedish Sami (SSR) have sent a letter to the Swedish Ministry of Agriculture requesting a census of the Sami population. However, at the time of writing we do not know whether it will be accepted, and, if it is, how such a census would be designed and carried out.

Notes

1. See Personuppgiftslag 1998:204 § 13.
2. This chapter draws on my article published in Berichte zur Wissenschaftsgeschichte and ; Axelsson P. 2010 'Abandoning "the Other": Statistical Enumeration of Swedish Sami, 1700 to 1945 and Beyond', Berichte

zur Wissenschaftsgeschichte 33, (3): 263–279. Copyright Wiley-VCH Verlag GmbH & Co. KGaA. Reproduced with permission.

3. For further information on the databases, see the Demographic Data Base at www.ddb.umu.se, and the materials available from the Minnesota Population Center at www.nappdata.org/napp/.
4. For example. Kongl. Maj:ts befallningshafvandes över Norrbotens län till Kongl.Maj:t år 1828 afgifne Fem-ÅrsBerättelse 1829, Stockholm.
5. According to Nils Söderlind, much of the oldest chapter material has been destroyed by wars and fires. The acts mentioned are the only ones left from this period that can tell us something about the clergy and their work (Söderlind 1958: 133).
6. For an account about a 'Lapp' and a 'Lapp maid' at one of these schools, see Söderlind (1958: 173). On Högström and the missionaries, see Hallencreutz (1990)
7. Indeed, in 1764 the clergy appear to have wanted to encourage helping those Sami in need; see the extract of the synodal act in Söderlind (1958: 226).
8. See also Norrlands (1995).
9. Between 1749 and 1773 there was also a summary form.
10. Retrieved 1 December 2010from: http://www.ddb.umu.se/material/tabellverk/tabellverkets-originalformular/
11. Retrieved 1 December 2010 from: http://www.ddb.umu.se/material/tabellverk/tabellverkets-originalformular/
12. Sveriges Officiella Statistik (1851–1855) Serie A, I, del 3, p.69.
13. See Statistiska Centralbyrån (1860–1890).
14. Svensk författningssamling n:o 64: Kongl. Maj:ts kungörelse 4 November 1859.
15. See Statistiska Centralbyrån (1900–1930). In the research project 'Home, Hearth and Household', we are making use of the Swedish censuses of 1900 and 1890.
16. Statistiska Centralbyrån (1920: 23).
17. Statistiska Centralbyrån (1920: 27–28).
18. Statistiska Centralbyrån (1930).
19. Statistiska Centralbyrån (1945: 2).

References

Arosenius, E. 1913. 'Lappar och Finnar i Sveriges Tre Nordligaste Län år 1910', *Statistisk Tidskrift*: 264–73.

Axelsson P. 2010 'Abandoning "the Other": Statistical Enumeration of Swedish Sami, 1700 to 1945 and Beyond', *Berichte zur Wissenschaftsgeschichte* 33(3): 263–79.

Axelsson, P., and P. Sköld. 2006. 'Indigenous Populations and Vulnerability: Characterizing Vulnerability in a Sami Context', *Annales de démographie historique* 111(1): 115–32.

Berg, T.F. 1857. *Plan för Insamlande af Uppgifterna till Sveriges Befolkningsstatistik 1857*. Stockholm.

Beskow, V. 1894. *Kyrkobokföringen och Dermed Sammanhängande Stadganden*. Stockholm.

Edvinsson, S. 2000. 'Sweden – Umeå – The Demographic Data Base at Umeå University: A Resource for Historical Studies', in P. Kelly Hall, R. McCaa and G. Thorvaldsen (eds), *Handbook of International Historical Microdata for Population Research*. Minneapolis: Minnesota Population Center, pp. 231–48.

Hallencreutz, C.F. 1990. *Pehr Högströms missionsförrättingar och övriga bidrag till samisk kyrkohistoria*. Uppsala: Svenska institutet för missionsforskning.

Hansen, L.I., and B. Olsen. 2006. *Samernas Historia fram till 1750*. Stockholm: Liber.

Hassler, S. 2005. 'The Health of the Sami Population of Sweden 1962–2002: Causes of Death and Incidences of Cancer and Cardiovascular Diseases', Ph.D. dissertation. Umeå: Umeå University.

Höjer, H. 2000. *Svenska siffror: Nationell Integration och Identifikation genom Statistik 1800–1870*. Hedemora: Gidlunds förlag.

Hunt P. 2007. 'Mission to Sweden: Report of the Special Rapporteur on the Right of Everyone to the Enjoyment of the Highest Attainable Standard of Physical and Mental Health', Report No. A/HRC/4/28/Add.2, United Nations General Assembly, Human Rights Council. New York: United Nations.

Johansson, H. 1975. 'Samerna i den Svenska Befolkningsutvecklingen', in T. Hägerstrand and A. Karlkvist (eds), *Forskare om Befolkningsfrågor: blandvetenskaplig bilaga till Ett folks biografi*. Stockholm: Samarbetskommittén för långtidsmotiverad forskning , pp. 322–23.

Kertzer. D.I., and D. Arel. 2002. 'Censuses, Identity Formation, and the Struggle for Political Power', in D.I. Kertzer and D. Arel (eds), *Census and Identity: The Politics of Race, Ethnicity, and Language in National Censuses*. Cambridge: Cambridge University Press, pp. 1–42.

Kinfu, Y., and J. Taylor. 2005. 'On the Components of Indigenous Population Change', *Australian Geographer* 36(2): 233–55.

Kock, K. 1958. 'Tabellkommission Försvinner: Statistiska Centralbyrån Kommer till', *Statistical Review* 7(9): 487–91

Lantto, P., and U. Mörkenstam. 2008.'Sami Rights and Sami Challenges: The Modernization Process and the Swedish Sami Movement, 1886–2006', *Scandinavian Journal of History* 33(1): 26–51.

Lundmark, L. 2002. *'Lappen är Ombytlig, Ostadig och Obekväm': Svenska Statens Samepolitik i Rasismens Tidevarv*. Bjurholm: Norrlands universitetsförlag.

Ministry of Agriculture. 2005. *The Sami, an Indigenous People in Sweden*. Stockholm: Ministry of Agriculture.

Mörkenstam, U. 1999. 'Om "Lapparnes Priviligier": Föreställningar om Samiskhet i Svensk Samepolitik 1883–1997', Ph.D. dissertation. Stockholm: Stockholm University.

Newbold, K.B. 2004. 'Data Sources and Issues for the Analysis of Indigenous People's Mobility', in J. Taylor and M. Bell (eds), *Population Mobility and Indigenous Peoples in Australasia and North America*. London: Routledge, pp.117–35.

Norrländsk Uppslagsbok, Vol.3. 1995. Umeå: Norrlands universitetsförlag.

Personuppgiftslag 1998:204. Svensk författningssamling.(Retrieved from internet 1 December 2010 from: http://www.riksdagen.se/webbnav/index.aspx?nid=3911&bet=1998:204)

Rogers, J., and M.C. Nelson. 2003. '"Lapps, Finns, Gypsies, Jews and Idiots': Modernity and the Use of Statistical Categories in Sweden', *Annales de demographie historique* 105(1): 61–79.

Rumar, L. 2007. 'Sakkunnigutlåtande i Mål T 879–5, Hovrätten för Nedre Norrland'. Retrieved 31 December 2008 from: http://www.lennartlundmark.se/internt/lennart.nsf/doc/003AE949/$FILE/sakkunnigutlatande_lars_rumar.pdf

Sköld, P. 1992. *Samisk Bosättning i Gällivare 1550–1750*. Umeå: Center för arktisk kulturforskning.

——— 2001. 'Kunskap och Kontroll: Den Svenska Befolkningsstatistikens Historia', Demographic Data Base report no. 17. Umeå: Almqvist and Wicksell.

——— 2004. 'The Birth of Population Statistics in Sweden', *History of the Family* 9: 5–21.

Sköld, P., and P. Axelsson. 2008. 'The Northern Population Development: Colonization and Mortality in Swedish Sápmi 1786–1895', *International Journal of Circumpolar Health* 67(1): 29–44.

Söderlind, N. 1958. *Norrländska Kyrkostadgar och Synodalakter före 1812*. Härnösand: Forum Thelogicum.

SOU 1975:100. *Statens Offentliga Utredningar'Samerna i Sverige. Stöd åt Språk och Kultur. Bilagor.'* Stockholm: Liber förlag.

Statistiska Centralbyrån. 1860–1945. 'Folkräkningen'. Stockholm: Statistiska Centralbyrån.

Sveriges Officiella Statistik. 1851–1855. 'Bidrag till Sveriges Officiella Statistik'. Stockholm.

Thomasson, L. 1956. *Om Lapparna i Jämtland och Härjedalen: Folkmängden och Dess Förändringar under ett Århundrade*. Uppsala: Acta Lapponica.

Wahlund, S. 1932. *Demographic Studies in the Nomadic and the Settled Population of Northern Lapland*. Uppsala: Almqvist and Wiksell.

Wannerdt, Arvid. 1982. *Den Svenska folkbokföringens historia under tre sekler*. Stockholm: Riksskatteverket.

7

The Registers of the 'Sami Tax' from 1600 to 1750, and Their Usefulness for Reconstructing Population Development and Settlement in Northern Nordland, Norway

Lars Ivar Hansen

Introduction

The first real, comprehensive census of Norway – in the sense that it recorded both sexes and people of all age groups – was undertaken in 1769. Prior to this, only two, more general, surveys of the population had been carried out – between 1664 and 1666, and in 1701 – but they only included the male population, and the last one only males over one year of age (see Dyrvik 1983). They also differed highly from region to region as to how exactly they registered the Sami population. Thus, when it comes to estimating population numbers and distribution before the middle of the eighteenth century one has to rely on tax registers and the information that might be drawn from them. In several local and regional analyses, the tendencies which can be read from tax registers have also been used in very skilful and successful ways in order to give a picture of population numbers and the diversity of living conditions over time in many parts of Norway (e.g., Lindbekk 1978; Nielssen 1990; Hansen 2003). But just how reliable are the tax registers when we are interested in charting the Sami population in these bygone centuries, and what challenges must we cope with? These are the main questions that I want to discuss in this chapter. In order to highlight the kind of problems that confront the researcher, I shall draw on examples from a recently completed research project.[1] During this project, seven scholars from the disciplines of archaeology, history and social anthropology focused on the complex cultural and ethnic structures of the population of northern Nordland County from the iron age to the present.

Over this time, the population of Nordland consisted primarily of Norwegians and Sami, with Kvens (people of Finnish descent) appearing more consistently and systematically in the sources from the second part of the nineteenth century onwards (Evjen and Hansen 2008). In the mid eighteenth century, the permanently settled Sami (known as the 'Sea Sami') may have made up between roughly 8 and 30 percent of the resident population, dependent on parish or region (Hansen 2008). In addition were the nomadic Sami, engaged in reindeer herding – many of them migrating between winter pastures in Sweden and summer pastures in Norway – and a substantial number of former nomadic Sami who were in the process of becoming sedentary on the Norwegian side of the border. These latter took up permanent settlement in the mountains, hillsides and outlying fields surrounding established settlements along the Norwegian coast, and practised livelihoods consisting of stationary reindeer herding, some minor animal husbandry, and participation in the fisheries (Storm, 2001; Hansen 2003, 2008).

Categorisation of Sami during the Seventeenth and Eighteenth Centuries

From the point of view of the Dano-Norwegian governmental authorities, the categorisation of these various groups of Sami underwent a distinct transformation at the turn of the eighteenth century. From medieval times through to the fifteenth, sixteenth and seventeenth centuries, the traditional and main distinction between different groups of Sami – as seen from the viewpoint of their neighbouring peoples – had been the dichotomy between so-called 'Finns' and 'Lapps': 'Finns', or 'Sea Finns', were the more or less stationary Sami population along the coast in the north and west, permanently attached to farmsteads and settlements in the fjords. 'Lapps', by contrast, were inland Sami, living under Swedish administration, some of whom had taken up reindeer-herding. It should be emphasised that these designations are imposed 'out-group' categories, used by outsiders to categorise a neighbouring people according to variations in traditional habitation area, ways of livelihood and lifestyle. The Sami had their own terms – *Samit*, *Same* and *Saemieh*, according to different Sami dialects – and are also known to have used specific, mutual designations relating to habitation area and landscape forms or livelihoods to refer to each other, such as 'upper people', 'sea people', and 'reindeer people'.

During the 1740s, however, a new, more specific terminology was developed by the Dano-Norwegian authorities due to the work of the border commissioner, Major Peter Schnitler, who was in charge of the preparatory investigations that were to result in the final border treaty negotiations between Sweden and Denmark-Norway at the turn of the century (see Schnitler 1929, 1962, 1983). Using a series of specific censuses and surveys collected from the various missionaries sent out to preach among the Sami, as well as extensive testimonies delivered by both Norwegians and Sami at local court meetings, he developed a new classification, dividing the Sami population into three groups: Firstly, there were the 'Settled Finns', who corresponded with the Finns or Sea Finns of the older classification. Secondly, there were the 'Community Lapps' or 'Parish Lapps', sometimes called 'Forest Lapps', who were Sami engaged in becoming sedentary. These were in a process of establishing new farmsteads and making clearances in the wood-clad valleys on the land between the fjords and sounds, and could also be found in the outlying areas stretching from already settled areas up into the mountain range. This group comprised mainly of former nomads, but possibly also some former Sea Finns. Subsequently, they became known in Norwegian as *markasamer*, 'outlying field Sami'. Finally, there were the 'Lapps', the transhumant reindeer-herding Sami. This group was further sub-divided into the 'Eastern Lapps', who migrated between winter camps and pastures on the Swedish side of the border to summer camps and pastures on the Norwegian side; and the 'Western Lapps', whose winter and summer camps and pastures both lay on the Norwegian side of the border.

In hindsight, it is obvious that Schnitler had a clear political agenda for 'streamlining' the categorisation with a view to serving the interests of the Dano-Norwegian state authorities in the forthcoming negotiations with Sweden. In the first place, the traditional, resident Sami population along the coast was represented as being quite as settled as the Norwegian population: thus, the stress on settlement in the specification 'settled Finns', as opposed to the unspecified older term 'Finns' and 'Sea Finns'. Next, it was useful to represent the group of former nomads who were in the process of settling as being firmly tied and attached to the settled communities along the coast so that no doubt could be cast on their state allegiance by the Swedish negotiators. While the missionaries had used the localisation of these new Sami dwellings as a decisive criterion, and spoke of 'district Lapps', 'district mountain Lapps' or even 'mountain Finns' (*fjellfinner*), Schnitler for his part insisted on standardising things with the terms 'Community Lapps' and 'District Lapps' (Hansen 2007; Evjen and Hansen 2008).

The rest of this chapter will be devoted to the problems attached to the task of making population estimates for the two main groups of Sami in the western coastal landscape – the traditional, 'Settled Sami' ('Sea Finns'), and the growing number of 'Community Lapps' during the eighteenth century – based on the available sources.

The Old Tax System

In order to understand the nature of the extant tax records, some features of the old tax system should be explained, both in relation to Norwegians and Sami. From the middle ages and onwards, the Crown had levied a so-called *leidang* tax, or 'conscription tax', on the Norwegian population. This tax had its origins in the old, medieval obligation to give military service when the king demanded, in times of war and tension. By the later part of the Middle Ages the obligation to muster men had already been partly replaced with a yearly tax, which in northern Norway was levied in yields of dried fish. In addition, constant appeals from the Dano-Norwegian government during the sixteenth century about extraordinary contributions, in the form of money in order to finance everything from royal weddings to wars, lead to the introduction of a new yearly land tax, levied in money. Subsequently, this yield was called contribution tax. Thus, during the seventeenth and eighteenth centuries the Norwegians paid two taxes: one in dried fish, and one in money. As for the Sami population, the more stationary and settled among them – the Finns or Sea Finns along the coast of Nordland, Troms and Finnmark – had paid the so-called 'Finn tax' to the Crown from the time in the early middle ages when the monarchy had defeated the north Norwegian chieftains and acquired their right to trade with and tax the Sami.

At the beginning of the seventeenth century, therefore, the situation was that the Norwegians paid two kind of taxes, while the Sami only paid one. But at this moment, during the reign of the Dano-Norwegian king Christian IV, the central government became aware of this situation and perceived it as an anomaly. To create a system that seemed parallel and balanced, they introduced a new tax for the Sami – the so-called *the so-called Finn leidang (Sami conscription)* – which was paid in dried fish. In this way, both peoples ended up with an analogous pair of taxes to pay,[2] albeit the yield from Sami taxes was lower than that from the taxation of Norwegians.

Now, these two parallel sets of taxes have been considered as being fairly good indicators of large-scale movements in population numbers and settlement for periods when more specific censuses and parish registers are lacking, and have also been seen as giving a fairly good picture of the relative population of Sami and Norwegians. A closer scrutiny of the tax registers for the northern part of Nordland County does, however, reveal that things are not so simple, and that several things have to be taken into account when one tries to use the tax registers as sources for reconstructing population numbers and settlement. The problem stems from the close connection between the levying of the 'Sami tax' ('Finn tax') and the property status of the farms on which people lived. Some of these farms were allodial, or freehold properties (known as *finneodel*); that is, they were not part of the general system of leaseholding which encompassed nearly all other farms in northern Norway. In short, what seems to have been decisive when it came to choosing between recording a person as 'Norwegian' or 'Sami' in the tax register was the legal status of the farm rather than the ethnic affiliation of the person who lived on it. Thus, for some periods, the tax records that apparently should register the Sami holders, do in fact contain a fair number of ethnic Norwegians. In order to highlight these circumstances, we need to briefly look at the institution of Sami allodial lands and their destiny.

The 'Sami Allodium'

According to the old land property system of the seventeenth and eighteenth centuries, nearly all peasant farmers had to be tenants in order to be able to cultivate land and dispose of their product. In northern Norway, almost all land was owned by one of the three great landowners: first, the Crown; second, certain institutions of the Church, which had been granted fiefs by the king after the confiscation of Church property due to the Reformation; and third, parts of the nobility and some rising burgesses. These landowners leased their land to tenants, and tenants were obliged to pay a yearly rent to the land owner. In addition to the rent, tenants also had to make an extra payment when a lease agreement was drawn up, this being known as the *første-bygsel*, 'earnest money' or 'entry fine'.

However, some of the settled Sami, cultivating farms in the coastal area, were exempted from this system, forming an anomaly in relation to the ordinary land-ownership system. As Knut Kolsrud (1947), one of the first scholars to investigate this phenomenon, observed, the institution of the 'Sami allodium' consisted of a kind of privilege granted to some but not all of the settled Sami, or Sea Sami, along the coast. Kolsrud states that the Sami took over their farms without paying any 'earnest money' (*bygselpenger*), and nor did they pay 'rent' (*landskyld*) or 'triennial fines' (*tredjeårstake*) for their farms, but rather 'an arbitrary tax' and *leidang*, paid in stockfish, each year. These taxes amounted to considerably less than the ordinary fees levied on leasehold tenants (ibid.: 24–26).

The term 'Sami allodial property', or *Finneodel*, which was constructed by Dano-Norwegian government officials, may seem strange since allodial property and the Norwegian odel institution have traditionally been viewed as typical agrarian phenomena, attached to traditional Norwegian farmsteads. The majority of the Sami were in contrast known to adapt ways of livelihood that combined a wider range of resources, and were also partly organised in other kinds of social units, such as siida collectives for instance. But a deeper investigation into how this institution functioned reveals that a comparison with the Norwegian *odel* institution is not so far-fetched. It appears that functionally and in practice these Sami landholders – occupying the special Sami allodial properties – enjoyed an analogous position to those freeholding farmers in southern Norway who possessed the right to lease (*bygselretten*) properties over which they held allodial rights (*odelsjord*); that is, they were *odelsbønder*, holders of allodial rights, or freeholders. The central point here is that the Sami holder and his kin held inheritance rights over their farms and clearings; they controlled who should succeed whom as holder of the clearing. This was in contrast to ordinary tenant farms, where this decision in principle lay with the king's bailiff or the representative of the bishop or the nobleman.

Pressure against the 'Sami Allodium'

But despite this situation, one can observe some unrest and uneasiness concerning the status of Sami allodial clearings, which came under pressure from Norwegian settlers who wanted to usurp the Sami and take over the holdings themselves. This process began in the last years of the seventeenth century. Kolsrud observed that prospective Norwegian settlers began to take an interest in the rent-exempted Sami clearings, and many of the allodial properties in Ofoten were sold to Norwegians – first to land owners and wealthy tradesmen, but later to ordinary Norwegian farmers (Kolsrud 1947: 27). The same tendency has later been charted by Alf Ragnar Nielssen in Tysfjord (Nielssen 1990; Nielssen and Pedersen 1994). Apparently, the Sami incumbents appear to have viewed their rights over their allodial properties in a manner which is more consistent with a modern conception of property, and which also encompassed the right to sell or dispose of the property to non-kin. Another way by which Sami allodial properties passed into Norwegian hands involved cases where farms had been left deserted for some years, either because the former incumbent had died or had moved to another place, and no heir or kin had come to claim the land.

Though the takeover of one of these Sami allodial properties – exempted from ordinary rent and entry fines, thus making them freehold farms with full rights – must have been an attractive option to many Norwegian settlers, the position of the government and authorities was crystal clear: in cases where Sami did not want to or could not prolong their special, ethnically defined relation to their property, they were to be considered Crown property. Consequently, they should be assessed for rent and incorporated into the regular system of leasehold property, and entered into the cadastral records, the *Matricules*. Thus, this process was also called 'matriculisation'.

Confusion in the Taxation Principles

Things got even more complicated in 1723 when the government ordered a general, all-encompassing new assessment of all landed property. The assessment was to include Sami allodial farms, and during 1724 they were all assessed for rent and incorporated into the official land registers. However, two years later the authorities went back on their decision, partly due to the intervention of the leader of missionary activities among the Sami, who sought to restrain the government from taking measures that would inspire Sami to leave Norway and take refuge on the Swedish side of the mountain range.

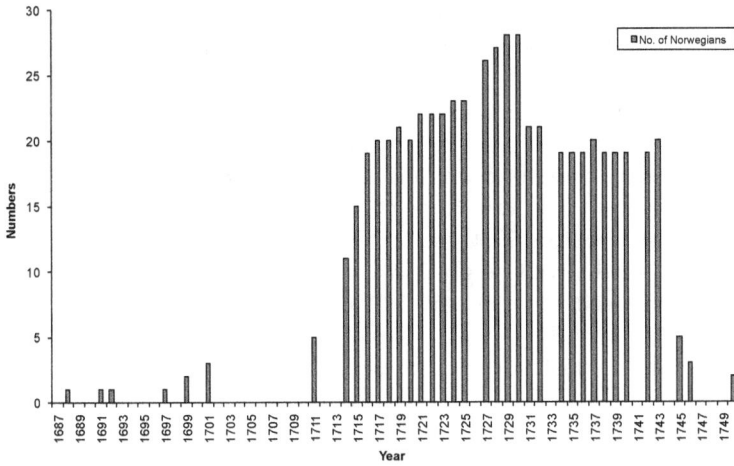

Figure 7.1 Number of Norwegian Tenants Registered in the 'Sea Finn Tax'

All this toing and froing led to a profound confusion among the local authorities and tax-collectors over how the holders of the Sami allodial farms should be taxed. According to the law and the logic of the system, incumbents of former allodial farms which had been assessed for rent and incorporated into the official land registers should have been excluded from the ranks of the payers of the 'Sami tax', and should have begun instead to pay the ordinary taxes that were collected from the Norwegian population; that is, the *leidang* and contribution *tax*. In the years immediately after 1724 this practice was implemented in some regions, but soon

Table 7.1. Sami Clearings Assessed for Rent 1724 (in Units of 'våger' = 18,52 kg Dried Fish)

Region	No. of farms	No. of holdings	No. of norw. tenants	Total rent	Rent pr. holding
Herjangen	12	17	11	10,26	0,60
Skjomen	14	19	4	6,95	0,37
Efjord	4	6	1	1,34	0,22
Skrovkjosen	5	8	2	2,01	0,25
Tysfjord	27	49	3	18,16	0,37
Sagfjord	8	14	1	3,52	0,25
Nordfold	12	13	2	5,61	0,43
Sørfold	7	14	2	5,43	0,39
SUM	89	140	26	53,28	

Source: Copies of rent assessments in the bailiffs' accounts of Salten, for the years 1724 and 1726, National Archives, Oslo.

afterwards holders of Sami allodial properties were again excluded from the Norwegian set of taxes, and registered once again as payers of the 'Sami tax'.

The overall result of this was that a number of those registered to pay the apparently *'Sami tax and conscription'* included a considerable number of Norwegian incumbents of Sami allodial farms. The number of these increased rapidly from a around three or so in about 1700 to over twenty in the 1730s. Shortly before 1730 the tax registers of the allegedly 'Sami' population contained twenty-eight Norwegian holders (see Figure 7.1). Thereafter it decreased, due to new initiatives by the local authorities, who took steps to have the farmsteads in question assessed for rent and incorporated in the cadastral records: twenty-two holdings were initially assessed in 1730, with a few in 1733/4, and finally three more holdings in 1737 (see Table 7.1).

Alternative Methods for Estimating the Sami Population

The above discussion necessarily leads us to the conclusion that the extant tax records cannot serve as a reliable base for calculating the size of the Sami population in the northern part of Nordland during the eighteenth century.[3] The ethnic affiliation of tax payers cannot be read from the names recorded in the 'Sami tax' registers. So what other options do we have?

In fact we seem to have only three: three male censuses of varying quality. The first of these is a census of 1701, and it contains details of male individuals over one year of age.[4] It appears, however, to be fairly good since it also includes some Sami cottagers who were not incumbents of proper farms units. The primary focus of this census is on the settled population along the coast, both Norwegians and the 'settled Finn' population. Thus, it does not contain any comprehensive information about the emerging group of 'community' or 'district Lapps' taking up settlements in the valleys and outlying fields. But with this in mind, it seems to give a fairly good basis for computing the number of households, in a way that clearly surpasses the quality of information in the tax registers.

The second source is another census, this one of the male Sea Sami population, conducted by the county court judge (*sorenskriveren*) at the request of Major Peter Schnitler in his role as border examination commissioner (reprinted in Schnitler 1929: 234–37). This census claims to describe the population in 1743, but compared with other sources it contains far too many individuals to be credible. A close scrutiny and comparison of the individuals mentioned in this census and the corresponding tax registers for the preceding and following years reveals that a large number of the people registered in the census – about 70 per cent – are never heard of again in later sources, simply disappearing after having been mentioned in the 1743 census. However, the census does contain names that had by then been associated with Sami allodial farms for a period of fifteen to twenty years.

Table 7.2. Last Time Mentioned in the Sources for Persons Registered in the 1743 Male Census

| | Numbers | Taxed for the last time | | | |
	1743	1743	Per cent	1745–50	Per cent
Only mentioned in the 'Sea Finn tax':	17	12	71	5	29
Mentioned both in the 'Sea Finn tax' and the 1743 male census:	80	21	26	59	74
Only mentioned in the 1743 male census:	118	84	71	33	28
Totals	215	117	54	97	45

Source: Registers from 'Sea finn tax and contribution' 1743–50, Bailiffs' accounts, Salten; Schnitler's Border examination protocols 1742–1745.

Table 7.3. Estimated Sea Sami Population 1701, ca. 1740 and 1762

| Region | 1701 | | | ca. 1740 | | | 1762 | | |
	No. of House-holds	Aver. House h Size	Estim. Popu-lation	No. of House-holds	Aver. House h size	Estim. Popu-lation	No. of House-holds	Aver. House h size	Estim. Popu-lation
Herjangen	14	5,15	72	7	5,19	36	6	5,22	31
Skjomen	18	4,70	85	23	4,82	112	19	4,94	94
OFOTEN	32	4,90	157	30	4,96	149	25	5,01	125
Efjord	8	3,45	28	7	4,01	28	6	4,56	27
Skrovkjosen	12	4,07	49	7	4,40	31	8	4,72	38
Tysfjord	55	4,17	229	63	4,11	259	60	4,04	243
TJELDSUND	75	4,07	306	77	4,12	317	74	4,16	308
Røttangen	34	3,25	110	24	3,85	92	22	4,44	98
Nordfold	17	3,62	62	13	3,93	51	20	4,24	85
Sørfold	16	3,71	59	11	3,89	43	26	4,06	105
FOLDA/HAM.	67	3,45	231	48	3,84	186	68	4,23	288
TOTALS	174		694	155		652	167		721

Sources: Male census of 1701, Salten bailiwick, vol. 19; Extraordinary tax of 1762, Salten bailiwick – both in the National Archives, Oslo. Schnitler's Border examination protocols 1742–45.

At the same time, it is an established fact that from 1739 until the early 1740s there were a number of bad harvests, and subsequently a great increase in mortality in Norway as a whole. The most obvious conclusion, therefore, would seem to be that the census of Sami individuals presented in 1743 represents a compilation of male persons who had been incumbents of Sami farms during a longer period – probably from the 1720s and onwards – and that the census does not in fact reflect the actual, living population of 1743. In fact, several of the individuals mentioned seem to have died in the two to five years immediately preceding 1743. Therefore, we have to use this source carefully, and identify those who were no longer alive in 1743 (Table 7.2).

The last relevant source consists of tax registers dating from the 'extraordinary tax' of the 1760s.[5] In contrast to the earlier, regular taxation registers, these lists from the second half of the eighteenth century include both males and females; however, they exclude children under twelve years of age. Thus, though we do not have to estimate the female part of the population, we must make an addition to allow for the unrecorded children, something which can be easily done adding the same proportion of under-twelves as is recorded in the total population census of 1769.[6] This method has served as the basis for establishing the figures rendered in Table 7.3.

Conclusions

At the outset of the eighteenth century, the resident Sea Sami population in the northern part of Nordland was about 700 persons. In the first part of the 1740s, this number fell to approximately 650, presumably due in part to the higher level of general mortality that occurred during those years. Over the next twenty years we see an increase to approximately 760 persons. For the sake of comparison, this means that the settled Sami population during the 1760s made up about 6 per cent of the total resident population in the northern part of Nordland. However, when we look at the separate regions and parishes, the Sami percentage of the population shows great diversity. The Sami share of the total settled population varies

Table 7.4. 'Finns and District Lapps' on Clearings 1762

Region	No. of Households	Ave. Household Size	Estimated Population
Leiranger fj.	10	4,56	46
Gildeskål fj.	13	3,62	47
Skjerstad fj.	35	3,94	138
Saltdalen fj.	19	4,66	89
Bodø fj.	24	4,23	102
TOTAL	101	4,17	422

Source: Extraordinary tax of 1762, Salten bailiwick, National Archives, Oslo.

from 10 per cent in regions such as Ofoten and Hamarøy to 14 per cent in Folda. The greatest population share is found in Tjeldsund (comprising Tysfjord or Divtasvuotna), where the settled Sami element makes up 30 per cent of the total resident population.

In the 1760s we also get more precise estimates of the population of former nomadic Sami, the 'Community' or 'District Lapps' who are in the process of becoming sedentary, settling on new farmsteads cleared in the outlying fields, the forest-clad valleys and on the isthmuses between established settlements along the coast. These former reindeer-herding nomads, who took up new ways of livelihood combining farming and fishing with stationary reindeer herding, consisted of more than 400 individuals; that is, a population totalling more than half of the former, settled Sami in the same area (see Table 7.4). In other words, they comprised an important part of the Sami population of Nordland, and at the same time to a certain degree made up for the apparent population reduction resulting from the 'Norwegianisation' process that for several centuries had taken place among the settled Sami of northern Nordland.

Returning to the question raised at the outset about the reliability of the tax registers as a means of charting population development, the conclusion has to be twofold. While the tax registers of the first half of the seventeenth century may give a fairly good indication of relative population movements and fluctuations, they cannot be used for this purpose when one moves one's focus to the first part of the eighteenth century. This is mainly due to the pressure on traditional Sami settlements and farms, exerted by other members of local communities – such as landowners, wealthy people engaged in trade, and ordinary Norwegian farmers – who wished to take over Sami allodial farms. For more than three decades of the first half of the eighteenth century, this led to a situation where a

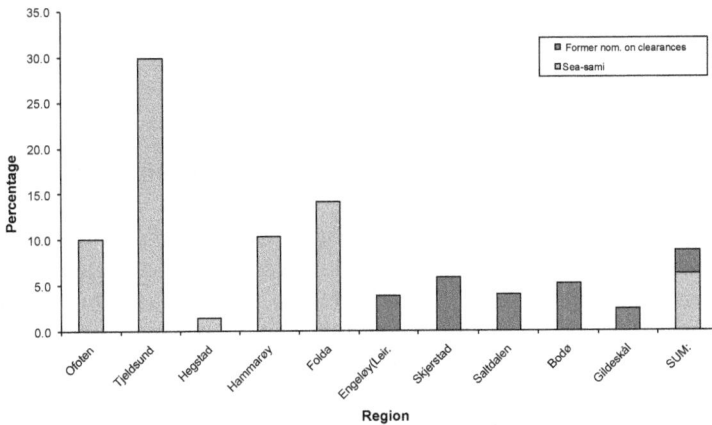

Figure 7.2 Relative Proportions of 'Sea Finns' and Former Nomadic Sami Dwelling on New Clearances (in Percentage of Total Population, incl. Norwegians)

substantial number of Norwegians appeared among the payers of the supposedly 'Sami tax'. When trying to estimate the Sami population for this period, one therefore has to rely on other censuses and surveys. Two censuses of the male population carried out in 1701 and 1743 contain substantial information, provided that they are used critically, and can be used alongside registers completed for the 'extraordinary tax' of the 1760s.

Notes

1. This project was entitled 'Ethnic Relations in the Northern part of Nordland County'.
2. From the last decades of the seventeenth century, the two 'Sami taxes' were levied at one and the same time, and were accounted for in the combined registers, under the double heading *Sjøfinneskatt & -leidang*, 'Sea Finns tax and conscription'.
3. For the seventeenth century, however, the registers of the 'Sami tax' seem to give a fairly good indication of population movements among the settled Sami, as long as one confines analysis to the household level; that is, one tries to compute the number of active households at any one time.
4. 'Manntallet [Male census]', 1701, The Chamber of Revenues, Salten bailiwick, vol.17, NNA.
5. 'Ekstraskatten [Extraordinary tax]', 1762, Salten bailiwick, NNA.
6. Norwegian National Census, 1769. This is available as a 1980 reproduction: Official Statistics of Norway, B 106, Central Bureau of Statistics, Oslo. This census, which for the first time charted both sexes, does not, however, contain information about ethnic affiliation for the northern part of Nordland county, and cannot be used for our purposes.

References

Archives

NNA – Norwegian National Archives, Oslo.

Other Sources

Dyrvik, S. 1983. *Historisk demografi: Ein innføring i metodane*. Bergen: Universitetsforlaget.

Evjen, B., and L.I. Hansen. 2008. 'Kjært barn – mange navn? Om forskjellige betegnelser på den Samiske befolkningen i Nordland gjennom århundrene', in B. Evjen and L.I. Hansen (eds), *Nordlands kulturelle mangfold: Etniske relasjoner i historisk perspektiv*. Oslo: Pax forlag, pp. 17–47.

Hansen, L.I. 2003. *Astafjord bygdebok, historie 2, Astafjord ca.1570–ca.1730*. Lavangen: Lavangen municipality.

——— 2007. 'Categorisation and Classification of Native Populations by State Authorities: The Case of the Sami in Nordland County, Norway, during the Seventeenth and Eighteenth Centuries', in L. Elenius and C.

Karlsson (eds), *Cross-cultural Communication and Ethnic Identities*. Luleå: Studies in Northern European Histories, pp. 286–97.

——— 2008. 'Den sjøsamiske befolkningen i Salten fogderi ca.1600–1760', in B. Evjen and L.I. Hansen (eds), *Nordlands kulturelle mangfold: Etniske relasjoner i historisk perspektiv*. Oslo: Pax forlag, pp. 51–86.

Kolsrud, K. 1947. *Finnefolket i Ofoten: Bidrag til finnernes bygdehistorie og etnografi*. Oslo: Etnografisk Museum.

Lindbekk, K. 1978. *Lofoten og Vesterålens Historie II*. The municipalities of Lofoten and Vesterålen.

Nielssen, A.R. 1990. *Lødingen, Tjeldsund og Tysfjords historie IV: Fra steinalderen til 1700-tallet*. Bodø: Lødingen, Tjeldsund and Tysfjord Municipalities.

Nielssen, A.R., and H. Pedersen. 1994. *Lødingen, Tjeldsund og Tysfjords historie V: Fra vidstrakt prestegjeld til storkommune*. Bodø: Lødingen, Tjeldsund and Tysfjord Municipalities.

Schnitler, P. 1929. *Grenseeksaminasjonsprotokoller, 1742–1745, Vol. 2*, ed. J. Qvigstad and K.B. Wiklund. Oslo: Kjeldeskriftfondet.

——— 1962. *Grenseeksaminasjonsprotokoller, 1742–1745: Vol. 1*, ed. Kr. Nissen. Oslo: Kjeldeskriftfondet.

——— 1983. *Grenseeksaminasjonsprotokoller, 1742–1745, Vol. 3*, ed. L.I. Hansen and T. Schmidt. Oslo, Kjeldeskriftfondet.

Storm, D. 2001. 'Markebygden i historien 1850–1990: Landskapsbruk og identitetsforvaltning', in T. Thuen (ed.), *Fortidsforståelser*. Kristiansand: Høyskoleforlaget, pp. 111–25.

——— 2008. *Gressmyrskogen – en bygd på Senja: Bosetningsmønstret i markebygdene 1700–1900*. Tromsø: Senter for Samiske studier, Universitetet i Tromsø.

8

VIEWING ETHNICITY FROM THE PERSPECTIVE OF INDIVIDUALS AND HOUSEHOLDS: FINNMARK DURING THE LATE NINETEENTH CENTURY

Hilde L. Jåstad

In Norway, historical sources which yield first-hand information about how different ethnic groups defined themselves are scarce. Second-hand information on the other hand is available in the population censuses undertaken from 1845 onwards.[1] The first part of this article gives a brief description of the source material, and in order to evaluate the strength of the ethnicity variable given in the population censuses a comparison is carried out with J.A. Friis's population table attached to his ethnographic map of 1861 and his estimate of the Sami population (Friis 1861: 1–5). In the second part of the article the focus will be on the instructions given to census takers and how they carried out their work in practice. There will also be a discussion of the usefulness of a reorganisation of census data into household units and how this strengthens our understanding of ethnic registration. A key finding here concerns the degrees of ethnic homogeneity and heterogeneity in households. The extent of mixed marriages, both in time and space, will also be an important issue for discussion. Mixed marriages can be a key variable in understanding social interaction between different ethnic groups.

Source Material

In contrast to the 1845 and 1855 censuses, which were founded on household units, the censuses from 1865 onwards were established on the enumeration of individuals. Based on the instructions issued to census takers between 1845 and the turn of the century, the impression is that ancestry was the most commonly used criteria for categorising ethnic identity, somewhat vaguely defined in the censuses up until 1865, but very distinct in the 1875 census. The 1855 instruction asked enumerators to record the 'Lapps or Finns and Kvens of the parish'. The 1865 census instructions were more comprehensive, specifically asking, for example, that resident Sami and nomadic Sami were to be reported separately. The instructions also stated that when 'mixed heritage' occurred, the parents' 'nationality' had to be reported as well. In the 1865 and 1875 censuses, a record of linguistic knowledge was also kept, whereas the census taker was instructed to specify whether or not the subject understood the Norwegian language. While there were no changes in the instructions concerning spoken language, the instructions became more complicated when it came to ethnic markers. As an example of this, the ethnicity of each parent had to be noted, and as a result the ethnic marker in the 1875 census could be made up of as many as sixteen combinations.

Thus, it may be correct to suggest that the 1855 instructions, and partly also the 1865 instructions, followed a kind of 'nationality criteria' which was fully developed in 1875; and further, that the 1855 instructions did not specifically define this but relied on identified differences between ethnic groups. Interestingly, some important changes occurred in this period, changes which dissolved the rather simple and well-arranged ethnic categorisation displayed in the enumeration form prior to 1875. What the census takers discovered, and what caused problems both schematically and statistically, was that Sami, Kven and Norwegians related to each other and acted together in several arenas, something which also led to mixed marriages. This 'mixture' caused a statistical challenge at the time. As early as 1855, mixed ethnicities were registered, and this was formalised in the 1865 census instructions, then fully cultivated in the earlier described sixteen combination scheme developed in 1875.

During the last part of the 1800s, the Norwegian linguist, theologian and author Jens Andreas Friis created two ethnographic maps of the two northernmost provinces in Norway, Troms and Finnmark (Friis 1861, Friis 1888). These maps show the ethnic and linguistic composition of the population in 1861 and 1888. The mapping was conducted at a household level, using three ethnic categories: Norwegian, Sami and Kven. When categorising the population by ethnicity, linguistic knowledge seems to have been an important criterion in Friis's work, in that the map contained detailed linguistic symbols. This observation is also strengthened by the fact that Friis sent the following instruction to the priest in Vardø parish in 1887 when revising the 1861 map:

> Nationality is defined by the language spoken in daily life by husband, housewife and the children in the home, unconcerned of clothing, heritage, etc. If, for example, Sami is the daily spoken language in the house, the family shall be marked and registered as a Sami family, even if one of the parents originally is of a different nationality. The same goes if there are other nationalities in question (cited in Hansen 1998: 47).

This means that in cases where the criteria of ancestry was difficult to decide – for example, when it came to mixed marriages – Friis designated the ethnic identity of a household on the basis of the actual language spoken in the house. This change of focus also led to a revision of the symbols that Friis used. An example of this is the omission of Friis's symbol for 'Sami household with Norwegian husband' in his 1888 map (Friis 1888: 6 bl). It is therefore not unreasonable to assume that Friis contributed to the later development of the census instructions, in that the linguistic criteria had its distinct breakthrough in the 1891 census with a special language-column in the questionnaire form.[2] Support for this view also comes from a document published in 1882 by the Statistics Norway. The document, a statistical survey of the 1875 census, emphasises Friis's thoughts on language – not only in his ethnographical maps but also from his fictional production – which were clearly used to define the ethnic composition of the northern population in the official statistics from the late nineteenth century (Kiær 1882: 144–154). In addition, the linguistic criterion was most likely politically motivated as well. Mapping linguistic knowledge was an important process in the ever-increasing political strategy of the Norwegian State aimed at weakening Sami culture and language. As Lars Ivar Hansen also notes, emphasis on linguistic criteria presents certain challenges, both with regards to the political pressure exerted by the Norwegian government in the late 1800s, but also with regards to whether or not it actually yields a deeper understanding of ethnic identity (Hansen 1998: 47). Hansen's view on this is that language may be a more distinct ethnic marker than ancestry, because language may define cultural identity more strongly than ancestry.

The 1855 Census and Friis's 1861 Map

The existence of Friis's 1861 ethnographic map provides a great opportunity for evaluating the strength of the ethnic registration in the population census, and this is done by a comparison between the population censuses before and after Friis's investigation was done. The results are presented at a household level. It is somewhat unclear if Friis defined 'family' as a kin related family unit or if he also included other non-related members of the household as well. In the 1855 census, the number of individuals on each farm was reported, and thus the household seems to be an appropriated basic unit for comparison. A comparison of the 1855 census and Friis's table, where parishes are separated into eastern and western Finnmark, can be seen in Figure 8.1.

As Figure 8.1 shows, the number of registered Sami household units clearly decreased, especially in western Finnmark, between 1855 and 1861. However, concerning those parishes where there were registered nomads in the 1855 census, it is fascinating to observe that the figure does not reveal the fact that the numbers Friis presented in 1861 deviate radically from the actual registration in 1855. A closer look at Kautokeino parish

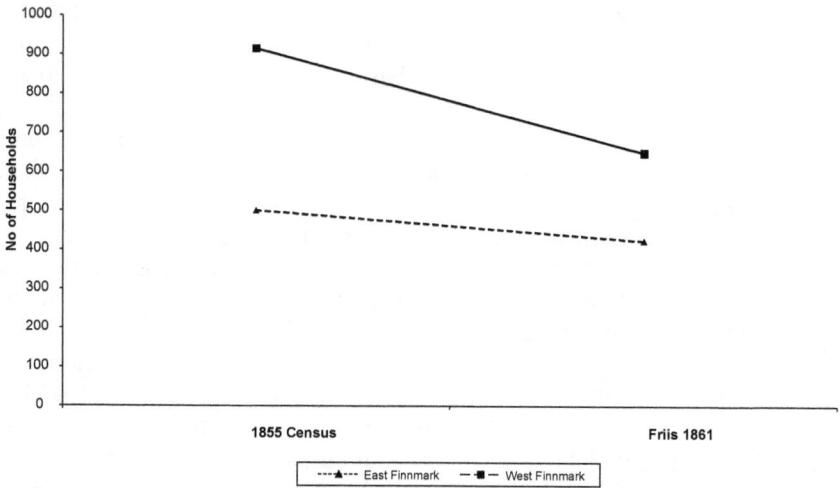

Figure 8.1 Sami Population in Eastern and Western Finnmark in 1855 and 1861

serves as a good example. In the 1855 census, Kautokeino contained 165 nomadic household units and 31 resident Sami households. In 1861 Friis claimed that there were only 24 Sami households in Kautokeino. A possible explanation to this may be that Friis, in addition to employing linguistic criteria, also categorised the population by way of dwelling type: earth hut or wooden house. Nomadic families lived in tents, and obviously did not fit into this system. Assuming that it was the priests who, to a certain extent, provided Friis with the basic material for the development of his maps (Hansen 1998: 47), it is reasonable to ask if it was the priest who forgot to report the nomads since their type of housing was a non existing option in the table, or if it was Friis who excluded them from his aggregates. In the tables which accompanied the maps, the term 'resident' was also used in parenthesis after the Sami. It is unknown if Friis added the term 'resident' as he finished his work on the table, or if it was a deliberate strategy to exclude the nomads from his ethnographic maps.[3]

During the period when the maps were published, the reindeer herders were victims of rather harsh public attacks. This was a consequence of several laws which benefited the Sami in particular. However, through a series of newspaper articles published in 1865, Friis stood up as a defender of the reindeer herders (see Hansen and Niemi 2001: 366). The exclusion of the nomads in the 1861 map therefore seems like a paradox, as it stands in contrast to his subsequent defence of the Sami. It may therefore be fruitful to visualise the map once more by adding to it the nomad household units recorded in the 1855 census (see Figure 8.2). As we can see, the registration of the Sami population remained somewhat stable between 1855 and 1861, and it is reasonable to suggest that this stability may strengthen the validity of the source material.

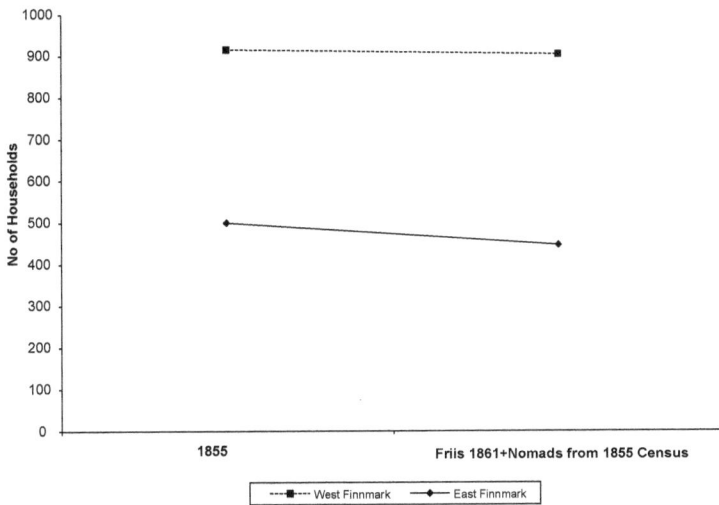

Figure 8.2 Sami Population in Eastern and Western Finnmark in 1855 and 1861, Including Nomads from the 1855 Census

The Sami Population in the 1865 Census

In contrast to the group-oriented ethnic registration of 1855, the 1865 census recorded actual individuals. The extent of ethnic registration in the 1865 census is such that ethnicity was recorded for every individual in ten of seventeenth parishes, a rate of more than 80 per cent. On the other hand, levels of recording ethnicity were rather low in five of the parishes, between 1 per cent and nearly 30 per cent. In total, ethnicity was registered in approximately 68 per cent of the total population in Finnmark.

By comparing registration of Sami ethnicity in the 1855 census and Friis's table from 1861 with the relevant data in the 1865 census, it is possible to get an impression of the extent of Sami registration in the 1865 census.

Figure 8.3 shows that the number of Sami households declined, especially in west Finnmark between 1861 and 1865. One way to interpret this is that the decrease was a result of the aforementioned missing ethnic markers in the 1865 census. Even if this is a fact which cannot be ignored, one must also keep in mind that the missing markers are quite equally distributed between parishes in east and west Finnmark. Furthermore, a comparison of Norwegian households between 1861 and 1865 shows a similar development: a decrease of 38 per cent. As discussed later, there was an increase in the number of mixed-marriages households between 1865 and 1875, combined with a more complex system of registering ethnicity at the individual level. This may also explain the decrease in the number of registered Sami households. A sensible strategy will therefore

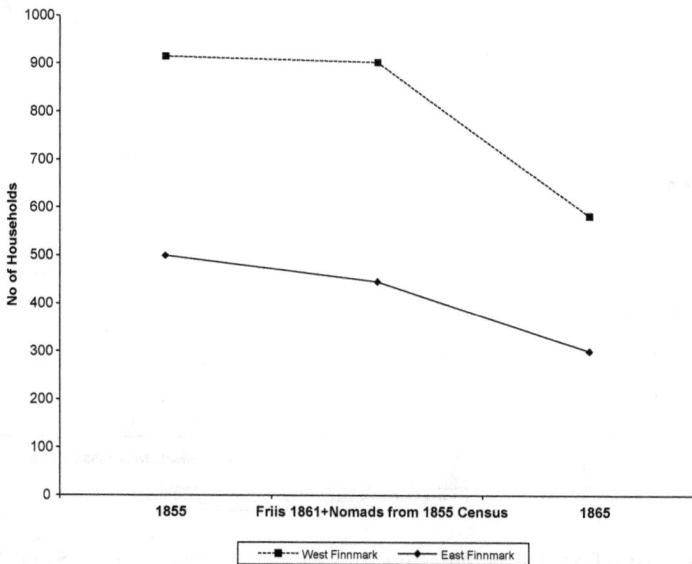

Figure 8.3 Extent of Sami Registration in Eastern and Western Finnmark in 1855, 1861 and 1865

be to examine the practice of the census takers in 1865, looking at whether or not this practice can in any way explain the downward tendency in the registration of the Sami households.

Three Different Criteria

Seen from a household perspective, the 1865 census was heavily influenced by a distinct ancestry criterion, and this is typically found in mixed-marriages households where several different combinations were used to express the children's heritage and ethnicity. A look at many examples reveals that a given person's complex genealogy could yield a rather complex ethnic marker. An interesting question in this context is how to identify the ethnicity of Elen Hansdatter, daughter of Kven Hanno Person and Gaia Olsdatter, who was half-Norwegian and half-Sami. In the census she and her siblings were marked as half-Kven, a quarter Norwegian and a quarter Sami. Use of the ancestry criteria is especially clear here, and it was fully employed in some parishes, though apparently less so in others.

In some parishes it seems that genealogy was less preferred to a system of registration that employed what one might call a cultural criterion. In the 1865 census from Tana parish, John Jakobsen, a Norwegian, was registered as married to a Sami woman. Despite this mixed marriage, the children were recorded as having Norwegian ethnicity. It is also interesting to observe a note recorded in the census concerning the housewife: 'Sami, but changed to Norwegian' (*lap, men gaaen over til norsk*). Does this registration suggest a kind of ethnic patriarchy, whereby the household head defined the ethnicity of the rest of the household? It is also interesting to ask if women who married men from different ethnic backgrounds were assimilated into their husbands' own ethnicity and culture. From a gender perspective there is no information which points in this direction, and there are in fact some examples which reveal an opposite tendency, whereby Arne Nilsen marked as 'Norwegian, but changed to Sami' and the children of his marriage with a Sami woman are marked as Sami.

Census registrations such as the one above were found in connection with every population group, independent of sex and ethnicity. What is interesting about these examples is the fact that they show us the cultural profile of the family, and that the cultural identity of the parents had quite a strong effect on the ethnicity of the next generation.

As I mentioned earlier, the use of the ancestry criterion reached its height in the 1875 census, and thus it is interesting to ask what then happened to individuals who, for example, were categorised as 'Norwegian, but changed to Sami'. In the 1875 census, Arne Nilsen appeared once again, and it is obvious that the cultural profile had disappeared from the registration, as he was recorded as having a Norwegian mother and father, and his children from his marriage with a Sami woman were recorded as having a Norwegian father and Sami mother. To what extent this also applies for the rest of the material remains to be seen.

Language is generally viewed as a strong marker of ethnicity, and it is therefore reasonable to ask to what extent a linguistic criterion was used in the 1865 census. However, no examples have been found which suggest that census takers, priest or other officials used the note concerning knowledge of the Norwegian language to determine ethnic identity. The general impression is that Sami ethnicity was registered independent of notes such as 'can speak Norwegian' or 'can speak some Norwegian'. Linguistic knowledge as a marker of ethnicity has not been found, even in mixed marriages, as we can see from the marriage of Sami fisherman Elias Mortensen and his Norwegian wife Sophie Sørensdatter: there are no notes concerning linguistic knowledge pertaining to Elias, but Sophie, who was Norwegian, 'does not speak Norwegian, lives like a Sami'. This despite of the fact that she kept her Norwegian ethnicity and that her children were registered as half-Sami and half-Norwegian.

The 1865 and 1875 Population Censuses

As has already been mentioned, the number of different ethnic categories defined in the census instructions reached their zenith in 1875 with sixteen different markers. However, the difference between what the formal instructions stipulated and what was actually registered by the census takers is significant. In the 1865 census fifty-five different ethnic markers were employed, while in 1875 this number increased to an astonishing seventy-one.[4] The fact that the registration practice challenged the boundaries of the registration scheme to such an extent is in itself interesting. The foregoing analysis showed clearly that in some wards census takers not only neglected the given instructions but also constructed their own systems of registration. These figures illustrates clearly that Finnmark was indeed quite a mixed ethnic society and that the construction of one common classificatory system may have seemed almost impossible. In what way is the registration complexity displayed when we organise individuals into household units?

Figure 8.4 shows households categorised in terms of the number of ethnic markers in each household; households with one ethnic marker dominated the picture with approximately 80 per cent in 1865. Looking at the 1875 census, homogeneous ethnic households still dominated, though one can also see that this group showed a downward tendency, and there was an increase in households with three different ethnic markers.

When comparing this figure with ethnic markers at an individual level, what becomes clear is that chaos gives way to order – despite there being 60 to 70 different ethnic markers, 70 to 80 per cent of households are ethni-

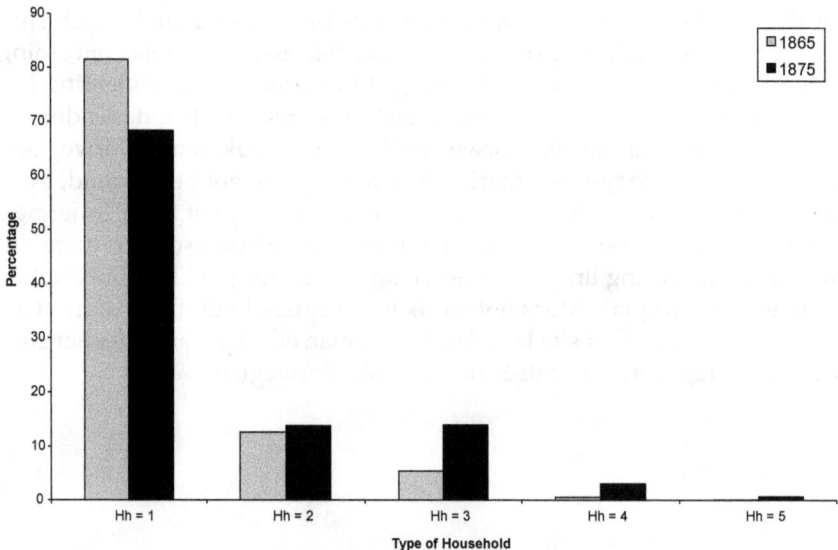

Figure 8.4 Number of Ethnic Markers in Each Household in Finnmark 1865 and 1875

cally homogeneous. In this context one may ask if this order was the result of the census takers' practices. Perhaps the census takers preferred to categorise households using just one ethnic marker? However, the number of different ethnic markers of each inhabitant is an obvious argument against this. When the census takers' enumeration was completed, census returns were looked over and authorized by higher authorities – such as the police or a priest – and ethnicity was one of four specific areas emphasised in this supplementary work. It is also worth mentioning that census takers in districts of mixed ethnic populations received higher salaries, which may have resulted in a more accurate registration in these areas.

The analyses presented above seem to indicate that household units maintained the characteristics of each ethnic group, unaffected by the ethnicity of each individual within the household. One wonders, therefore, whether or not this suggests that interaction between ethnic groups was not conducted or affected by individuals as such but by households, and that households were the basis by which ethnic markers – such as way of life, traditions, customs, habits, and so on – were maintained.

Mixed Marriages

Out of the approximately 2,700 households with known ethnic markers in Finnmark in 1865, 10 per cent contained mixed marriages. Comparing the extent of mixed marriages between the censuses, there was an increase to 15 per cent in 1875. In this context it would be important to identify any patterns concerning who married whom, and if some ethnic groups were more frequently involved in mixed marriages than others.

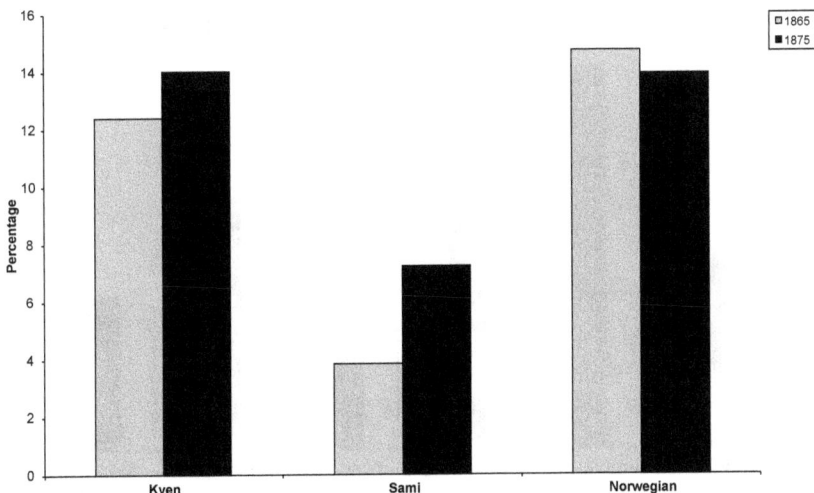

Figure 8.5 Mixed Marriages Categorized after Head of Households Ethnicity in Finnmark 1865 and 1875

By categorising mixed-marriage households in terms of the ethnic marker of the household head, we find that 13 per cent of all Kven households and 15 per cent of all Norwegian households were mixed in 1865. Compared to these figures it is interesting to observe that only 4 per cent of Sami households contained mixed marriages in 1865. Comparing the two censuses also reveals another interesting pattern. That is, while the numbers of mixed marriages in Norwegian and Kven households were remarkably stable, the number of mixed marriages in Sami households doubled from 1865 to 1875.

Evidence of marriages between Sami and non-Sami is known from folk literature, the old sagas, as well as from archaeological findings. Historians and archaeologists have for instance argued that relations between different groups of people during earlier times were maintained through marriages and trade (Hansen and Olsen 2004: 60). From the mid 1850s, however, this system of inter-ethnic relations was seen as a hindrance to the construction of the nation-state of Norway, and consequently the process of 'Norwegianisation' led to a ranking of ethnic identity (Mathisen 1993: 42).

When external conditions generated rank as an important element in inter-ethnic relationships, one's forbears' ethnicity – in particular, the 'Norwegianness' of one's genealogy – became part of each individual's assimilation strategies. Isolating 'Norwegian' forbears gave a person a 'factual' basis for appropriating Norwegian status, which they could not have done had marriage patterns been endogamous (Thuen 1989: 52–71). It is therefore important to ask if it is possible that the observed increase

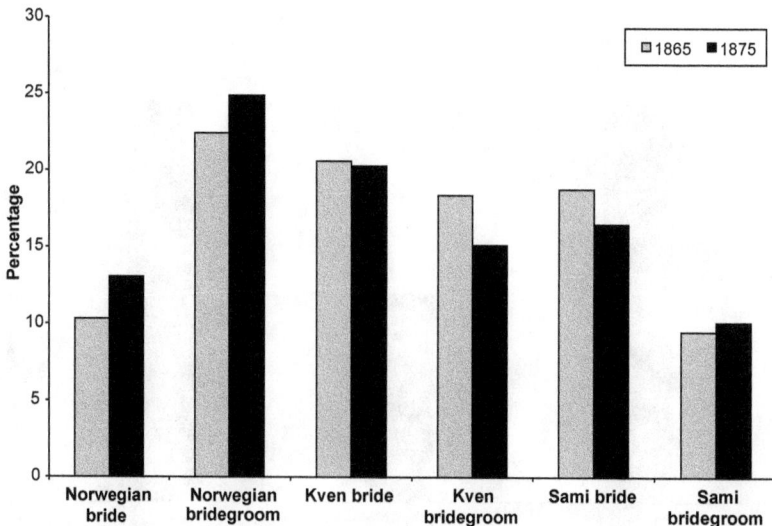

Figure 8.6 Number of Brides and Bridegrooms Distributed on Ethnic Categories in Finnmark 1865 and 1875

in mixed-marriages was a result of the Norwegianisation process. That is, was it part of people's strategies for obtaining national rather than a minority identity?

Given the assimilation theory described above, it should be of interest to look at actual marriage patterns and choices. For example, Norwegian men would be regarded a 'solid' choice for marriage by both Kven and Sami women; contrary, a Norwegian woman would seldom marry a Sami or Kven man.

Figure 8.6 shows the percentage of brides and bridegrooms in mixed marriages, by ethnic affiliation. Relatively to Sami and Norwegians brides and bridegrooms, we see that mixed marriages involving Kven, men and women are somewhat similarly represented, especially in the 1865 census. Contrary, a more diverge pattern is revealed when studying mixed marriages involving Sami and Norwegians: in 1865 there was approximately twice as many Norwegian husbands as there were Norwegian wives; and twice as many Sami brides as Sami husbands. This pattern is even more visible among mixed marriages that involved Norwegians in 1875.

By looking at the ethnic identity of partners in mixed marriages in 1865 (figure not shown here), the results show that Norwegian men married Kven women twice as often as Sami women. Kven men, meanwhile, did not have quite as clear an ethnic preference in cases of mixed marriage: 40 per cent of marriages were with Sami women, and 33 per cent were with Norwegian women. Sami men, on the other hand, were only found in about 5 per cent of all mixed marriages. In 36 per cent of these, Sami men married Kven women, and in 21 per cent of cases they married a Norwegian; in the remaining 43 per cent of cases the woman was of part-Sami ethnicity. This pattern is repeated in 1875 as well. However, the 1875 census also shows that only 11 per cent of Sami mixed marriages were with Norwegian women, and that in as many as half of the mixed marriages involving Sami men the women involved were part Sami.

This mixed-marriage patterns of twice as many Norwegian bridegrooms than Norwegian brides and twise as many Sami brides than Sami bridgrooms can be described as an inverse image and one can ask if it reflects the set of cultural preferences involving the choice of marriage partner operating at the time. Could it be that Norwegian men were the most attractive choice in marriage, and that the observed increase in mixed marriages in the Sami population was a result of an increasing number of Sami women marrying Norwegian or Kven men? Following this, one can also ask if it is possible that the observed increase in mixed marriages was a result of the Norwegianisation process. The Statistics Norway voiced similar thoughts in 1882:

> The Norwegians are the dominant people, as they are richer and more educated … Thus a woman, when she receives a proposal of marriage from a man belonging to a nationality regarded inferior to that of her own, will reject the proposal in fear of decreasing her reputation among her own

people. But it is also obvious that the situation is completely different if a man seeks for himself a wife from lower-ranking nationalities. This will not be a matter of him stepping down the social ladder, but rather a case of her stepping upwards (Kiær 1882: 148).

Analysing mixed marriages gives us an interesting insight into social interaction between ethnic groups, and perhaps the different patterns of marriage we have identified also reflect the fact that interaction was to some extent affected by the emphasised placed on ethnic relations by the authorities. However, if the pattern of mixed marriages observed can be considered a result of the Norwegianisation process initiated by the authorities, and that marital choices were made on the basis of appropriating Norwegian status, this does not explain why between 80 and 90 per cent of the inhabitants of Finnmark were registered as living in homogeneous ethnic households. The analysis of Sami mixed marriages might seem to indicate that some Sami employed marriage as a means of gaining Norwegian status. However, when one compares Norwegian, Kven and Sami marriage practices, and given the fact only 4 per cent of Sami marriages in 1865, and 7 per cent in 1875, were of the mixed kind, it becomes clear that 'becoming Norwegian' was not something that involved the majority of the Sami population.

Conclusion

This chapter has shown that the instructions given to Norway's census takers in Finnmark were not always carried out in the act of registration, and that registration practices varied between parishes. In some parishes it seems that an ancestry criterion was extensively used to record ethnic identity, while in other parishes one gets the impression that census takers used a cultural criterion as well as the ancestry criterion.

It is easy to imagine that the instructions issued by the authorities did not fit the population to be enumerated, and that census takers found it difficult to record information on ethnicity using either/or categories. This suggestion is strengthened by looking at registration practices on a parish level. It would seem that some parishes contained 'pure' Sami populations, while other parishes contained a large number of mixed marriages and ethnically mixed households.

Due to different registration practices and the continually changing registration instructions, this chapter has argued that it may be fruitful to define an understanding of ethnicity within an area or region by analysing the ethnic marker on different levels. By reorganising the censuses to show information on households units, and analysing the extent of ethnically homogeneous and heterogeneous households respectively, one can obtain a better understanding of ethnic interaction. In this context it was also important to discuss the practice of mixed marriage.

Notes

1. Both population censuses from 1845 and 1855 contain information about ethnicity, though at the household/farm level. Sometimes there is also some information in church registers, but this was not fixed by law.
2. The instructions for 1875 told census takers to register which language Finns, Sami, and people of mixed ethnicity usually spoke. This registration was done in an additional comment field. See Norges Offisielle Statistikk (1875).
3. However, in the revisions of his 1861 work, Friis mapped the routes between the winter and summer pastures of Sami nomads, and also included an approximation of the number of families and reindeer. These figures are not summarised in the attached population table (see Friis 1888: 6 Bl).
4. These numbers include other foreign nationalities as well.

References

Friis, J. A. 1861. Ethnografisk Kart over Finmarken. No. 1–5. 10 Bl. Udg. af Videnskabsselskabet i Christiania, med Bidrag af Oplysningsvæsenets Fond 1861–62.

——— 1888. Ethnografisk Kart over Finmarkens Amt. Udg. paa offentlig Bekostning. 1888. 6 Bl. Norges geograf. Opmåling.

Hansen, L.I. 1998. 'J.A. Friis' Etnografiske Kart over Troms og Finnmark', in H. P. Blankholm (ed.), *Ottar*, Tromsø: Tromsø Museum, pp.43–48.

Hansen, L.I., and E. Niemi. 2001. 'Samisk Forskning Ved et Tidsskifte: Jens Andreas Friis og Lappologien – Vitenskap og Politikk', in E. Seglen (ed.), *Vitenskap, teknologi og samfunn: En innføring i vitenskapens teori og praksis*. Oslo: Cappelen Akademisk Forlag, pp.350–77.

Hansen, L.I., and B. Olsen. 2004. *Samenes Historie fram til 1750*. Oslo: Cappelen Akademiske Forlag.

Kiær, N. 1882: *Bidrag til en Norsk Befolkningsstatistik*. Christiania: Det Statistiske Centralbureau.

Mathisen, P. 1993. 'Reconstructions of Relationships and Ethnic Boundaries', *Acta Borealia* 10(1): 37–44.

Norges Offisielle Statistikk. 1855. 'Folketelling'. Finnmark: National Archival Services of Norway.

——— 1865. 'Folketelling'. Finnmark: Norwegian Historical Data Centre.

——— 1875. 'Folketelling'. Finnmark: Norwegian Historical Data Centre.

Thuen, T. 1989. ' "Mixed" Descent and Ethnogenesis: Some Comparative Considerations of Contact Situations in the North', *Acta Borealia* 6(1): 65–83.

9

FINN IN FLUX:
'FINN' AS A CATEGORY IN NORWEGIAN
POPULATION CENSUSES OF THE NINETEENTH
AND TWENTIETH CENTURIES

Bjørg Evjen

The first population census in Norway took place in 1769, but it was not until 1801 that censuses were taken regularly. A plan was established to carry out a census every ten years, and to some extent the Norwegian authorities succeeded in this. In 1845 it was decided that ethnicity should be recorded as part of the census, but on a numeric level, and the household or family was entered as a whole. From 1865 onwards, censuses were recorded in a nominative fashion, and an ethnic label was designated to each household or family.

There was, however, no agreement on what designations should be used on the registration forms, a fact that has left challenges for demographic researchers who wish to analyse the multicultural population. This situation was caused by the different ways concepts were used, both in time and space, and by the Sami themselves and the authorities.

Several articles have been written which underline and analyse this problem, and attempt to find a simple way of using the different concepts lapp, finn or kven (Thorsen 1972; Torp 1986; Thuen 1989; Hansen 1994; Lie and Roll-Hansen 2001). Recent research has put a lot of effort into further discussing how ethnicity was registered in the censuses between 1845 and 1930 (Evjen and Hansen 2008).[1] In this article I want to focus on one aspect of the problem: the use of 'Finn' as a category in the censuses between 1865 and 1930.

Lapp, Finn, Kven and 'Mixed'

The main categories used in the censuses were *lap* (pl. *lappene*), *finn* (pl. *finner, finnene*), *kven* (pl. *kvener, kvenene*), and 'mixed'. The first two relate to the Sami population, and the third, Kven, to the descendants of an old migrant group from part of Finland. In addition to the different use in time and space mentioned above, the categories can also literally cause confusion as there is a certain resemblance between the common word for someone coming from Finland (a Finn) and for a member of the Sami population (a *finn*). 'Finn' is a thus a troublesome term in Norwegian demographic research, and it is this that is the focus of this chapter.

The use of these categories means that interpeting census records is problematic. The meaning of individual categories used at an official level changed several times during the course of the nineteenth century. In Nordland and southern Troms there was a clear distinction in eighteenth-century source material between Lapps and Finns. Lapp was used for nomads, while Finn was used for both the Sea Sami and the outlying rural population, the latter group also called 'rural Finns' in some areas. Towards the end of the eighteenth century this distinction is not so clear in the sources (Imsen and Winge 1999:366).

Before each census count, instructions were sent to the census takers that listed which categories should be used as a basis for recording the non-Norwegian population. In the years 1845, 1855 and 1865, these were 'Lapps or Finns and Kvens'. 'Lapps or Finns' must be interpreted as synonyms for the same group; otherwise there would have been a comma between them. In the instructions for 1865 there is a reference to some of the 'Lapps or Finns' being nomadic, and a stipulation that instances of this should be specifically noted. Those who were settled did not require specific mention. In northern Nordland, the Sea Sami population have constituted a large section of this settled population.[2] Others referred to as 'settled Lapps' had migrated from Sweden, and are also referred to in the source materials as 'rural Lapps'. The taking up of settled life was linked to, amongst other things, a bad year for reindeer herding on the Swedish side of the border (Berg 1975; Kvist 1989; Pedersen and Nielssen 1994).

Upon closer examination of the census returns for Tysfjord, it emerges that those listed were settlers in only a partial sense. The group consisted partly of regularly changing individuals. Some moved over the border to Sweden at irregular intervals, and others moved in and took their place, so that while the total numbers remained more or less stable the group was not comprised of the same individuals from one year to the next. The numbers from Tysfjord illustrate this. The number of individuals registered as 'Lapp settler' in Tysfjord increased in each census from 1865 to 1900. However, there was no fixed core to this group and there were frequent temporary moves back and forth across the border (Evjen 1998).

Looking in greater detail at the instructions for the census counts that followed in 1875, 1891 and 1900, the main categories were defined in a new fashion. Here it was stated in the list of non-Norwegian population categories that these were to be grouped as 'Kvens (Finns) or Lapps'. The category 'Finn' had, in other words, moved from being a synonym of Lapp to the equivalent of Kven.

One example shows that the categories were in a greater state of flux than is apparent here. In a report by A.N. Kiær, the head of the Norwegian Statistical Bureau, an entire chapter is devoted to the Lapp and Finn populations (see Kiær 1882: 144–55). Kiær chooses to employ the expressions 'Norwegian', 'Lappish/Lapp' and 'Finnish/Finn' as simplified categories. When the census takers wrote down *finn* in the ethnicity column, this was interpreted on Kiær's part as a person of Finnish origin. He abandoned the expression Finn and lumped the two, kven and finn, together as Kven, on the basis that they came from Finland (ibid.: 144). This was fine in certain areas, but in most cases in northern Nordland 'Finn' would denote a Sami who was not a reindeer herder but instead was either a Sea Sami or a 'rural Lapp'. Meanwhile, someone with Finnish roots would be designated 'Kven'. In the published statistics, the differentiation between Kvens and the Sea Sami population disappeared: they all became 'Kven' in 1875 and 1891, but 'Finn' in 1900. Kiær's decision led the statistics astray, at any rate in northern Nordland.

In the instructions for 1900 and 1910 matters were taken further: here the categories provided were *lf* as an abbreviation for 'Lapp settler', *ln* for 'Lapp nomad', *f* for 'Finn and Kven', and *b* for 'mixed'. Once again, the Finns were lumped in with the Kvens, and all of them designated as 'Finns'.

In 1920, 'Finn' was off the list of categories, and now only those of Sami and Kven extraction were mentioned in the instructions: 'For personnel who are sent to the Diocese of Hålogaland, to the rural areas of Trøndelag and to Solør, Vinger and Odal is added Question 17a on nationality and 17b on the language in daily use; this question should be filled out for all homes where there are persons of Lappish or Kven descent'.[3] In the official statistics, however, Finn and Lapp were both registered as 'Finn'.

Finally, in the instructions for the 1930 census, the last population count in which ethnicity – now called 'race' on the census form – was registered, the categories *sam* [sic] and *kven* were the only ones provided. For the first time the in-group name was taken in, although in a different form, since no one used *sam*. *Same* is the word used by the Sami people themselves. In a detailed explanation of how to compile the lists, it was stated that whether an individual was 'of Sami (Finnish) or Kven descent' should be recorded. The designation *finn* had thus not been abandoned, and many people continued to state that they were *finn*. This created statistical ambiguity, in that *finn* was now defined as the equivalent of the category *sam*.

What Is It About the 'Finn'?

Overall, it may be said that from 1845 to 1930 the authorities categorized the non-Norwegian section of the population as 'Kven' and 'Lapp', including both nomadic people and settlers. They were clearly more uncertain about the third category, 'Finn', which was referred to in all the instructions apart from those issued in 1920. The authorities did not employ this category in its own right, but lumped it in with 'Lapp' in the census counts for 1845, 1855, 1865 and 1930, and paired it with 'Kven' in 1875, 1891, 1900 and 1910. In the first two instances, 1875 and 1891, the common designation, according to the instructions, was to be 'Kven'; in the two final instances 'Finn', or *f*.

We can see firstly that this common designation makes it difficult to distinguish between 'Finn' and 'Kven' and that, secondly, the designation is not consistent. In addition in the original censuses one can also find combinations such as 'sea Finn', 'sea Lapp' and *lappfinn*. Not surprisingly, demographic research on issues of ethnicity has been reckoned to be almost impossible. Besides this, there is also the possibility of under-registration. Specific population numbers are therefore almost impossible to come by.

What is it about the 'Finn'? Who are, or were, they? The term *finn* is an old Norwegian word for Sami. In northern Norway, from ancient times, Finns were divided into groups according to their place of residence and cultural position, such as 'estate Finn', 'wilderness Finn', 'rural Finn', 'sea Finn', 'mountain Finn', 'eastern Finn', and so on. It has been stated that that the word 'Finn' was not used in northern Norway to refer to people from Finland; they were called 'Finlanders' or 'Kvens' (Imsen and Winge 1999: 111). The authorities in general came from the southern part of Norway where a 'Finn' was someone who came from Finland. Of course they must have known this, and 'Finn' and 'Lapp' were streated as synonyms in the censuses of 1845 to 1865, and in 1930. In the other censuses, hwoever, the term 'Finn' was used in such a way as to indicate the idea of being from Finland. The reason for this may have something to do with A. N. Kiær, who was in charge of national statistics and exerted considerable influence during this period. In his opinion, 'Finn' and 'Kven' referred to the same population group.

Thus the old meaning of 'Finn', linked to the Sami, was not employed in the censuses between 1865 and 1920, banished by administrative resolution. Since we know that a simultaneous Norwegianisation of society took place at precisely this time, this may explain why no one took steps to ensure that 'Finn' was used as it had previously been.

When the census takers came to register the ethnicity of a family with Sea Sami roots, and 'Finn' was not an option, the categories 'mixed' and 'Kven' were used. Is it possible to find examples of 'Sea Finns' crossing statistical boundaries between the *same* and *kven* categories in the aforementioned censuses, or were they entered in the 'mixed' category? The Sea Sami were the earliest Sami to become assimilated by the Norwegian population, and they achieved this to a greater extent han both the 'settled Lapps' and those concerned with reindeer herding. This is well documented for the Tysfjord area (Pedersen and Nielssen 1994). The question then is whether it is the Sea Sami, or 'Finns', who form the greater part of the 'mixed' category in the population censuses? In the areas of Tysfjord where a 'mixed' population was registered, people knew as late as the

1990s that this was exactly where the Sea Sami population had lived, and continued to live (Evjen 1998: 44–45). This strengthens the theory that the old Sea Sami population in northern Nordland formed a large proportion of those who were registered as 'mixed' in the census counts. A close study of the Sørfold area gives the same result.

The Kvens found in the population censuses for northern Nordland were not numerous. In Ofoten, in 1865, there were fourteen people who were designated thus. Of these, eleven had been born in Sweden, and nine of them were adults. In other words, they had not been on the Norwegian side of the border for long. However, this did not apply to everyone. One Kven who was born in Lødingen was a seventy-year-old unmarried woman. Her family must have been in the area prior to 1795.

In Tysfjord it emerged that Sami families called themselves 'Sami' in some contexts and 'Kven' in others. One explanation provided was that individual families could trace the migration of their relatives back to Østerbotten in Finland, and from there through Swedish Lapland and on to Tysfjord. They had both Sami and Kven ancestry and would sometimes choose to display one part of their family tree and sometimes another (ibid.: 46). This could lead to them being registered as 'Sami' in certain years and at other times as 'Kven'. However, there are also examples where the definition must lie with which definition was provided in the instructions for the census takers. If a family refereed to itself as *finn*, a census taker in the years between 1875 and 1910 could this to indicate that their ancestry linked them to Finland. For some people this was appropriate, but in areas where there had been a Sea Finn settlement from ancient times, the 'mixed' category was probably selected in these cases.

In northern Nordland, the 'Finns' belonged to the Sami section of the population. One exception should be mentioned, the wandering mining

Table 9.1. Definitions of 'Finn' in the Censuses from 1865 to 1970

1865	'finn' and 'lap' as one category, unclear use
1875	'finn' and 'kven' = 'kven'
1891	'finn' and 'kven' = 'kven'
1900	'finn' and 'kven' = 'finn'
1910	'finn' and 'kven' = 'finn'
1920	'finn' not mentioned
1930	'finn' og 'sam' = 'sam'
1946	no ethnicity
1950	language in designated areas
1960	no ethnicity
1970	'the Sami census' in designated areas, 'same' + 'finn' = 'same'

Sources: Instructions, given to the census-takers previous to every census, RHD, University of Tromsø.

Figure 9.1 Hilda and Richard visting a photographer in Bodø in the 1920s. Richard's family was registered as Norwegian in 1875, and as 'mixed' in 1900. Genealogic research showed that several of his ancestors were 'Finns', or Sea Sami. Combining genealogy and information from the censuses forms a method that may help to clear up the confusion surrounding this concept. (Photo: Bjøvg Evjen).

workers or navvies who were born in Finland and taken on as workers at the major industrial ventures in Sulitjelma or Narvik. A worker would be recorded in the census as a 'Finn' if they were in the area when the census count was carried out. Here, however, it is possible to check against the category of work and citizenship, and by this means separate out the vast majority of these from the old 'Finn' population of the area. In a study of ethnicity in northern Nordland, using population census material as the source, this has to be taken into account.

If we compare the instructions given to census takers with the categories used in the statistical bulletins of the Norwegian Staistical Bureau (NOS), we find the same use of categories in all instances except for the year 1920. Although *finn* was not mentioned in the instructions for that year, we find that *finn* and *lapp* are lumped together and filled in as *finn*.[4]

Cross-border Reindeer Herders

A greater part of the Sami who were concerned with reindeer herding in northern Nordland migrated between Norway and Sweden, with winter pastures on the Swedish side of the border. In the instructions for census takers, the stipulation that this group of nomadic Sami was to be particularly noted did not appear every year. However this did happen in 1865, when it was stated that 'in the case of Finns or Lapps, where they are nomadic, this circumstance should be noted'.[5] This was taken up again in 1900, and again in 1910: 'nomadic Lapps to be tallied according to where they are in residence at the time of the census count'.[6] The nomads could also be designated 'Finn', though generally in everyday speech. Further north, especially in Finnmark, they have continued to be called 'mountain Finns' right up to this day.

Here it should be added that the census was held in the middle of winter, when the greater part of the population was living peacefully at home. As a result, the great majority of Sami who were concerned with cross-border reindeer herding – a large majority of those based in northern Nordland – do not appear in the Norwegian statistics for nomadic Sami as they were at their winter pastures in Sweden when the census was taken.

The Swedish censuses do not provide much help in filling in the picture of how many reindeer-herding Sami lived in Nordland during the summer. The relevant part of the 1890 Swedish census, which might have been helpful in this matter, carried out by a priest throughout the year. The registration was thus not conducted over one or two specific days, as was the case on the Norwegian side. This makes it difficult to arrive at exact figures concerning cross-border reindeer herding. Here, other sources, such as the Lapp bailiff's reports, may help flesh out the census counts.

The nomads who emerge in these statistics are, in most cases, those who operated on the Norwegian side throughout the year. The category 'Lapp nomadic' is, in accordance with the instructions, registered in the statistics relating to all the censuses except for 1875.

Postwar Censuses

The incidents of the Second World War demonstrated where a focus on 'race' might lead. In the census of 1946 there was consequently no registration of 'race' or 'nationality'. In the 1950 census, questions were included about the everyday language spoken at home in most of the municipalities in the three northernmost counties. Studies have shown, however, that there was under-reporting on a major scale (Thorsen 1972; Aubert 1978: 15). In the 1960 census, the registration of Sami and Kven was omitted entirely. The most significant type of source material for ethnicity, dating back to 1845, was silent during these postwar years. Nor were any other sources produced that could fill the gap.

On the Sami side, this was perceived as a challenge that needed to be tackled. At the third Nordic Sami conference in Enare in 1959, a resolution was passed to undertake a demographic study of the Sami in Finland, Sweden and Norway. In the first two countries an attempt to document ethnicity was done, in 1962 and 1972/3 respectively (see Axelsson, this volume). In Norway in 1969, the sociologist Vilhelm Aubert was given the task of undertaking fieldwork that would serve as preparatory work for a possible Sami census linked to the ordinary national census of 1970. Aubert based his registration on local knowledge and selected individual census wards where the question of ethnic origin was to be registered. The registration was based on three questions concerning the use of the Sami language, and a fourth question enquired whether the interviewee considered themselves to be Sami.

Aubert writes: 'no attempt was made to chart another minority group in Northern Norway, namely the descendants of Finnish immigrants ... generally called Kvens ... A certain process of combination had occurred, amongst other things that the expressions Finn, sea Finn and mountain Finn had been used by the Sami' (Aubert 1978: 20). Aubert interpreted 'Finn' as part of the 'process of integration' that had occurred among Kven, and which had given the Sami the designation 'Finn'. In other words, the category was reckoned by Aubert to be part of the Kven category, as had been the case in the census counts between 1875 and 1910. The metamorphosis of the term 'Finn' had not ended with the 1920 census count. Kven, for their part, were missing from the statistics as early as 1930.

In northern Nordland in 1970, a total of 667 people from the chosen wards answered 'Yes' to the question of whether they considered themselves to be Sami. The choice of sample groups caused fluctuations. In Fauske, for example, no one answered 'Yes'. This was probably because members of the sample group who were reindeer-herding Sami were not included. This under-registration was also observed by Aubert himself: 'It is impossible to estimate how many people who should have been registered as having Sami features, strong or weak, but who fell outside the area of the sample groups' (ibid.: 19, 23).

Population censuses since 1970 have not contained questions about ethnic identity. Nor have there been any other overviews or registers of the Sami or Kven populations in any of the Sápmi lands since the 1970s. Of the three original main categories, 'Lapp', 'Finn' and 'Kven', the latter is the only one to have kept its old meaning. 'Kven' was seldom used during the years between the census of 1930 and the new ethnopolitical movement that began in the 1980s. Today this expression is used along the same lines as that of 'Sami'. Sami are today defined as the indigenious peoples of Norway, while Kven are one of Norway's national minority groups.

The Category 'Finn' and Statistics

What consequences have the evaluations carried out above had on reckoning the size of the non-Norwegian population in northern Nordland, and more precisely on the number of 'Finns' registered?

The number of 'Finns' registered varies considerably between the censuses of 1865, 1875 and 1900 from 600 to 10 to 160. The instruction in 1865 to

Table 9.2 Overview of the Non-Norwegian Population in Northern Nordland

	'lap'	'finn'	'kven'	'mixed'	Notes
1865	1,200	600	60	60	(*finn* + *lap*) = unclear use Total: 1,920
1875	2,010	10	180	600	(*kven* + *finn*) = *kven* Total: 2,820
1900	1,910	160	3	1,780	(*kven* + *finn*) = *finn* Total: 3,853

Sources: data-registered population censuses from, RHD, University of Tromsø.

lump together *finn* and *lap* was followed to varying degrees. Nor was it clear how the groups so lumped together should be designated. In both 1875 and 1900, *kven* and *finn* were defined as synonymous, but designated as *kvener* in 1875 and as *finner* in 1900. Table 9.2 shows the consequences of this from a numerical point of view with regard to registration in northern Nordland.

In 1875 only ten 'Finns' were registered, whereas in 1900 this had increased to 160. The opposite was true of 'Kvens' as a group. Their numbers sank from 180 in 1875 to only 3 in 1900. This was partly due to demographic changes, as well as migration and a rising or falling birthrate, but the main explanation has to be the way in which the categories were defined in the instructions to the census takers, and how this in itself affected the registration. The total number shows an increase of approximately 1,000 people between each of the three census counts.

In conclusion, it has to be said that carrying out research on Norwegian source materials and focusing on the ethnic categories used in the censuses can easily lead the researcher astray unless careful consideration is made as to how the instructions to census takers were read and what definitions were employed in the official statistics. In order to obtain the most reliable results it is also best to make use of the computerized censuses; if these are not available, considerable scepticism is needed when making use of official interpretations of the statistics.

Notes

The chapter was translated by Mary Katherine Jones, History Institute, University of Tromsø.

1. This research formed part of a research project entitled 'Ethnic Relations in Northern Nordland in a Historical Perspective'.
2. The Sea Sami are also known as the 'Sea Finns' in northern Nordland. See, e.g., Qvigstad (1929).

3. Census instructions, 1920.
4. See Norges Offisielle Statistikk (1828–1976).
5. Census instructions, 1865.
6. Census instructions, 1910.

References

Aubert, V. 1978. 'Den samiske befolkningen i Nord-Norge', Artikler fra Statistisk sentralbyrå, No.107. Oslo: Statistisk sentralbyrå.

Berg, G. 1975. *Bygdebok for Skjerstad og Fauske.* Bodø: Bygdeboknemnde, Fauske.

Evjen, B. 1998. *Et Sammensatt Fellesskap: Tysfjord Kommune 1869–1950.* Tysfjord: Tysfjord kommune.

Evjen, B., and L.I. Hansen (eds). 2008. *Nordlands Kulturelle Mangfold: Etniske relasjoner i Nordre Nordlandi et Historisk Perspektiv.* Oslo: Pax forlag.

Hansen, L.I. 1994. 'Samene i Forrige Århundres Folketellinger: Registreringspraksis i Astafjord Prestegjeld 1865–1900', in *Festskrift til Ørnulv Vorren.* Tromsø: Tromsø Museum, pp. 102–129.

Hansen, L.I., and T. Meyer. 1991. 'The Ethnic Classification of the Late Nineteenth-century Censuses: A Case-study from Southern Troms, Norway', *Acta Borealia* 8(2): 13–56.

Imsen, S., and H. Winge. 1999. *Norsk Historisk Leksikon*, 2nd edn. Oslo: Cappelen.

Kiær, A.N. 1882. *Bidrag til en Norsk Befolkningsstatistikk.* Christiania: Det Statistiske Centralbureau.

Kvist, R. 1989. *Rennomadismens Dilemma: Det Rennomadiska Samhällets förändring i Tuorpon och Sirkas 1760–1860*, Umeå: Historiska institutionen.

Lie, E., and H. Roll-Hansen. 2001. *Faktisk Talt: Statistikkens Historie i Norge.* Oslo: Universitetsforlaget.

Norges Offisielle Statistikk. Census 1865, 1875, 1891, 1900, 1910, 1920, 1930, 1950, 1970. 'Folke- og boligtellinger'. Oslo: Statistisk sentralbyrå.

Pedersen, H., and A.R. Nielssen. 1994. *Lødingen, Tjeldsund og Tysfjords historie V: Fra Vidstrakt Prestegjeld til Storkommune.* Bodø: Lødingen, Tysfjord og Tjeldsund kommuner.

Qvigstad, J. 1929. *Sjøfinnene i Nordland.* Oslo: Tromsø museum.

Thorsen, H.C. 1972. 'Registreringen av den Samiske Befolkning i Nord-Norge fra 1845 til 1970', M.A. dissertation. Oslo: University of Oslo.

Thuen, T. 1989. '"Mixed" Descent and Ethnogenesis: Some Comparative Considerations of Contact Situations in the North', *Acta Borealia* 6(1): 52–76

Torp, E. 1986. 'Registrering av Etnisitet i Folketellinger', *Heimen* 23(2): 67–77.

10

TESTING AND CONSTRUCTING ETHNICITY VARIABLES IN LATE NINETEENTH-CENTURY CENSUSES

Gunnar Thorvaldsen

The Norwegian censuses from 1845 to 1930 hold information on ethnicity in the northern part of the country. However, this information is sometimes erroneous and incomplete. A method has been developed to detect inconsistencies in the registration of ethnicity for Sami and Finnish populations. By constructing group-level variables and using complementary sources, a more coherent pattern of the distribution of ethnic groups emerges.

In the northern parts of Norway three different ethnic groups have lived together over the centuries in what has been coined the meeting place of the three 'tribes': Sami, Norwegians and Finns, mentioned in the order they came to settle the region (Schøyen 1918). While this article chiefly aims to discuss ethnic classification in order to employ this as an independent variable in demographic studies, we should be aware of the two-way process: demographic differentials will also affect how ethnic group are composed and defined, especially through migration and inter-marriage. We should remember, therefore, that in this kind of study we are standing on shifting ground while aiming at a moving target.

Definitions of ethnicity in favour today are analogous to a salad bowl, where ethnicity is seen as a dynamic and multifaceted process, resulting from the bringing together of different cultures and gene pools. Through migration, inter-marriage and other forms of social interaction, some ethnic traits are kept, some disappear, while others change uniquely, just as the different components get new flavours in a salad bowl. While this complexity makes ethnicity a most interesting independent variable in demographic studies, it is also crucial to be as precise as possible about how ethnicity is defined in each study. Furthermore, it is usual for independent variables to only explain small or marginal effects in demographic studies. What, for instance, does a difference of a couple of percentage points in infant mortality between ethnic groups signify if ethnicity is murkily defined and perhaps also confounded by other variables such as place of settlement (Jåstad 2003). A further problem concerns how the effect of ethnicity is compared in meta-analyses of several projects, if the concept is defined differently in different studies. This chapter attempts to throw some light on these questions with examples from nineteenth-century censuses taken in northern Norway. This material is the only microdata available from north-western Europe which in principle provides ethnic markers for the whole population.

Norwegian regional and national archives hold nominative sources covering the country's population for a period of more than three centuries. While the ministerial records provide only scant evidence about the ethnicity of some persons, there is little or no such information in the oldest male or statistical censuses taken from the 1660s until 1855. During the century-long period from 1845, however, administrators aimed to map systematically the ethnic characteristics of each individual, household and larger group. I concentrate on the nominative and computerised censuses from 1865, 1875, 1900 and 1910 since the earlier ones are statistical and the later ones are less readily available for analysis due to privacy restrictions. The encoded 1865, 1875 and 1900 censuses are fully available with constructed variables through the North Atlantic Population Project (NAPP), while the 1910 census is currently being processed.[1] Since the chief goal of any census is more cross-sectional than longitudinal, its variables are defined to make possible comparisons within the sampled population rather than being defined so as to reveal characteristics of population change over time. This is especially true of ethnicity variables, which may be more ephemeral and difficult to define than the content of any other field in census questionnaires. Thus, at least in Norway during the period under review, ethnic categories were constructed more with a view to suiting the needs of the particular census year than to mirroring the development of the nation's ethnic composition.

Several historians and anthropologists have already discussed and researched the ethnic categories employed in late nineteenth-century and other censuses, concentrating on single municipalities or parts of them. For instance, Thuen (1987) has primarily studied how the three specific ethnic categories mentioned above were replaced by mixed categories, and how there was an under-reporting of ethnicity in late nineteenth and especially early twentieth-century censuses. Hansen and Meyer (1991), meanwhile, have compared late nineteenth-century ethnic markers in censuses with those for the same individuals in the ministerial records, finding that in the latter sources many who were denoted 'mixed' in the ancestry-based census were classified by the priest as Sami on cultural or language grounds. Their general conclusion is that the ethnic markers used in the censuses are of better quality than according to the opinion of some colleagues. In addition, Torp, who was more critical in an early work (Torp 1986), argued that the lack of consistency in the reporting of ethnicity

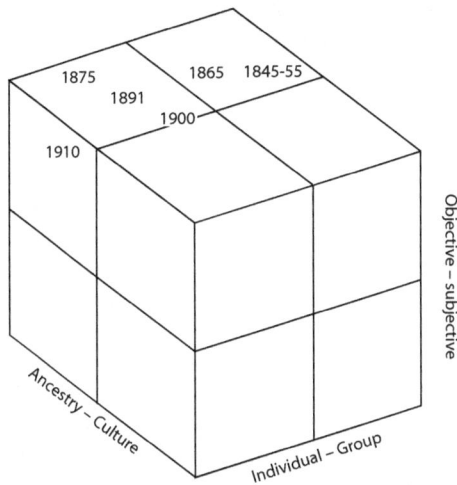

Figure 10.1 Census Ethnicity Dimensions

in different censuses can be explained (Torp 1990). An ethnic 'chameleon' existed in the censuses, people who were recorded as both Sami and Finn in different censuses turned out to be of Finnish stock, but had migrated into Norway with the Sami. Several individuals have been identified in the censuses who were denoted as Sami while living in a Sami community, but were identified with a different ethnic marker after having moved to a predominantly Finnish or Norwegian area.

Ethnicity can be defined both at the individual and group level by subjective versus objective criteria, and on the basis of cultural characteristics as distinguished from an individual's ancestry. As Figure 10.1 shows, this has a direct bearing on the contents of the census manuscripts and aggregates because the methodology recommended in the instructions provided to census takers changed over time.[2] The statistical nature of the pre–1865 material favoured a group-based criterion since no individual information was supposed to be provided. Statistics on ethnicity were created for the first time in the 1845 census. Unlike Gypsies, Sami and Finns were counted as part of Norway's resident population and highlighted especially in the procedural introduction to the census results. Less than 10 per cent of the 14,464 Sami enumerated nationally lived in the southernmost province of Nordland, an obvious undercount. While few Sami lived in southern Norway, nearly one third of the 4,425 Finns counted in the 1845 census were enumerated here, particularly in Hedmark province, where several Finnish settlers had cleared farms in the vast forests not far from the border with Sweden. Next to no Sami were found in Norwegian towns while 378 Finns were enumerated in urban places. In addition, there were colonies of Finns in suburban-like settlements, especially outside Vadsø

(Niemi 1977). As a result of the 1855 census, a table containing the number of Sami and Finns in each town or parish was published. We should note the likely under-enumeration in this table since many Sami were at their winter pastures in Sweden when the censuses were taken.

The ethnic classification of a group might be based on someone significant in the community, usually the male head of household. This applies also to the nominative 1865 census, where ethnicity was reported not in a special column but by splitting households into ethnic groups. It would make things easier for the census taker if an ethnically mixed family was not split up but rather noted together in the manuscript and assigned the ethnicity of the household head. Norwegians should be noted first, followed by Finns, and then settled and nomadic Sami. Supposedly, information about the latter group was easily under-represented. Census takers were instructed to note children's mixed ethnicity, which was easily dropped since this would multiply the number of ethnic groups even further. In the computerised version of the 1865 census, ethnically mixed households were reconstructed manually, and the information about ethnicity was copied from the group headings for each individual. On this basis ethnicity has been encoded in order to be comparable with later nominative censuses.

In addition to ethnicity, census takers were told to note whether people understood the Norwegian language. It is unclear, however, if this applied only to ethnically mixed persons and what level of language skill was required. Since the language comments have been encoded together with the rest of the microdata, we see that the census takers interpreted the instructions verbatim. Nearly all the comments refer to a person's command of Norwegian, saying whether they could speak or understand Norwegian, sometimes in combination with other languages. Three times as many people were noted as having no command of Norwegian than were noted as speaking Sami or Finnish, despite the fact that hose who did not know Norwegian obviously spoke Sami or Finnish, or both. The language competence of the majority of Sami and Finnish was not recorded, and the clear majority of the rest were recorded as understanding Norwegian. It is unclear from manuscripts of the 1865 census whether this means that most of them did not have a command of Norwegian or that the census takers forgot to note their language skills. In the tabulation reports from later censuses, the census authorities commented that the 1865 language variable was never analysed statistically, which is only natural given that it is incompatible with how language was reported in other censuses. In 1875, census takers were instructed to record for 'all Finns and Sami and for persons of mixed ethnicity information about which language they usually spoke' (Statistisk sentralbyrå 1878–91), but this was not analysed either.[3]

Instead they had to rely on the detailed reporting of ancestral ethnicity for both parents in 1875. The number of people of mixed ethnicity more than doubled after 1875, and much of this increase happened during the last decade of the century. There is little doubt that much of this increase was due to the more detailed manner of noting ethnicity. From 1875 onwards, ethnicity was noted in a special field on the census form, which required census takers to ask about each person's ethnicity in particular. The inclination to do so may have been especially marked in 1891 when one separate form was to be filled out for each individual.

Controlling Information on Ethnicity by Census Tract

In addition to the general problem of translating between Norwegian, Sami and Finnish, a more specific language problem may have distorted the census results because of the way in which ethnic groups were categorised in Norwegian. Sami ethnonyms were rendered as *lapper* or *finner* (*lapons* in the French version of the tables), while Finns were called *kvæner* (*Quaines* or *Finnois* in French). The phonetic similarity between one Norwegian word for Sami – *finn* – and the more international word for Finns may have caused confusion. In 1845, 1855, 1865 and 1885, the census instructions used 'Lapp' and 'Finn' as synonyms for Sami. In 1875, 1891, 1900, and 1910, however, the census authorities added to the confusion by using *Finsk* and *Kvænsk* as vernacular synonyms for Finnish in the census instructions and questionnaires. Even worse was the inconsistency in the published aggregates where people from Finland were called *Finner* in 1890 and 1900, while the same word was used for Sami people in 1910 and 1920. The confusion could also affect the recording of the Sami or Finnish language in the census manuscripts. Only in 1930 was a consistent terminology introduced with the modern ethnonyms *Samer* and *Kvener*.

Table 10.1. Ethnonyms and Variable Names in the Census Questionnaires and Published Tables

Census	Field Name	Sami Ethnonym	Finnish Ethnonym	Published Variable	Published Ethnonym
1865	Herkomst	Fin/Lap	Qvæn	Nationalitet	Lappisk
1875	Nationalitet	Lapper	Kvæner/Finner	Nationalitet	Kvænsk
1885	Nationalitet	Lap/Finn	Kvæn	Nationalitet	
1890	Nationalitet	Lappisk	Finsk (kvænsk)	Nationalitet	Finner <> lapper
1900	Nationalitet	Lappisk	Finsk (kvænsk)	Nationalitet	Finner <> lapper
1910	Nationalitet	Lappisk	Finsk (kvænsk)	Nationalitet	Finner = lapper
1920	Nationalitet	Lapper	Kvener (finner)	Nationalitet	Finner = lapper
1930	Avstamning /Rase	Samer (finner)	Kvener	Rase	Samer = finner = lapper

Source: Census instructions (NOS).

A test has been devised to check for this potential inconsistency by cross-tabulating the original ethnicity markers by census tract. In the resulting table two types of problems can be spotted. First, whether each census taker was consistent or whether they used both the *fin*, *lap* and *kven* markers in the same census. It is also possible to spot tracts where the marker *fin* was used in contradiction with the census instruction. For instance, in 1900 *fin* should mean Finnish. If in the table we can spot cells for the same tract with several persons noted as *fin*, no one noted as *lap* and several noted as *kven*, it indicates that the census taker in question used *fin* to mark Sami people, even though instructed otherwise. The test will not work for census tracts in the self-enumerated towns, since these were done by house owners, and so the test would be undermined by disagreement between them. Most Sami and Finnish persons lived in rural places where each census tract was covered by one enumerator. A bigger problem concerns the large variety of markers in the 1865 census, where it is often noted how long a person has lived in Norway, which makes it more difficult to spot inconsistencies.

The test has been run for the three provinces of northern Norway in 1875, 1900 and 1910, for the rural municipalities Tana, Polmak and Nesseby in 1885, and for Hattfjelldal, Vardø town and Båtsfjord in 1891. As expected, some inconsistencies were found in the urban tracts, where *lap*, *fin* and *kven* have all been used in the same tract. Spot checks indicate that this is because different house owners used *fin* to mean Sami while others meant Finnish within the same tract and census. Any notation of ethnicity in towns should, therefore, be analysed with special care. In the rural tracts, however, there were few inconsistencies. The census takers employed here were as a rule educated people, often teachers. The results indicate that they were well aware of the problem with the word *fin*, and possibly smiled when they noticed how the Norwegian Statistical Bureau changed their definition from census to census. When they used the word *fin*, it is often followed by *lap* or *kven* in parenthesis. In a few rural census tracts *fin* is used together with both *lap* and *kven*, but then only a handful of persons were actually called *fin*. I have not been able to spot any census tract with the second kind of problem identified above; that is, using the word *fin* consistently in contradiction with the census instruction.

While this may indicate that the *fin* problem mostly caused confusion in urban places with small minority populations, the test revealed a third and more serious type of problem: census takers might have problems distinguishing between Sami and Finnish people. In a census tract for Skjervøy municipality in 1875, ethnicity was changed at the time from Finnish to Sami for 197 persons out of 663. This often pertained to all the persons in a family, sometimes only some persons in a household. While the error was corrected in this tract, it should alert us to similar errors being made in other tracts, where they might not have been discovered and corrected. This third problem cannot be detected with my statistical test unless spotted by the census taker or his administrators at the time of the census. Future work with the sources at the local level, comparing several censuses and other source materials for the same localities and persons, will be necessary in order to get a fuller picture of the degree to which ethnicity was marked erroneously (see also Evjen, this volume).

Constructed Ethnicity Variables

The next aim of this chapter is to suggest a set of constructed ethnicity variables which will in turn make ethnicity more consistent over time and space as an independent factor in demographic studies. Until recently the encoding of ethnicity followed a rather straightforward one-dimensional scheme, such as the one used by the aforementioned NAPP. Ethnic groups in Canada, the U.S.A. and Norway were listed, but little was said about the ancestral, cultural, individual or group-level basis of the classification. One important task is to construct group-level variables for each individual giving the predominant local or regional ethnicity. Several such variables can be constructed denoting dominant ethnicity at the municipality, ward and farm or place level. A question for the future is whether or not to copy ethnicity markers in regions with heterogeneous ethnicity on the basis of older source material in cases where newer sources lack ethnicity markers for the whole or parts of the population. While in many places ethnicity seems to be quite stable over the decades or even centuries, the situation can be very dynamic – as can be seen along the U.S. western frontier in the nineteenth century or when Norwegians took over rich fishing locales in Sami fjords. Thus, such 'ahistoric' construction must be performed by researchers with relevant knowledge of a community's history.

A further dynamic aspect of ethnicity to be handled more adequately by the constructed variables is the mixing of ethnic groups due to intermarriage and migration, particularly in northern Norway. Background information was lost when individuals were called 'mixed' regardless of which ethnic groups were represented in a given locality. This could be solved with one or more ratio-scale variables indicating the proportion of people in a given place in terms of membership of the dominant ethnic group(s) of that place. A variable giving the proportion of individuals with mixed ethnicity would be useful since it can be used to weight the ethnicity factor in statistical analysis. A further issue concerns to what extent any constructed variable should distinguish between cultural and ancestral factors. A partial answer to this dilemma might be to construct group-level language variables in cases where such information is available. It goes without saying that constructed variables about ethnicity need to be documented thoroughly for each nation and province.[4]

The multilevel coding of ethnicity for this chapter is based on the 1875 census since this source contains the most detailed ethnic markers, with information about both maternal and paternal origins. First, I have attempted to construct a group-level variable in the four municipalities of the northern part of Troms province which are multiethnic and have been singled out for special treatment in several instances: Lyngen, Karlsøy, Skjervøy and Kvænangen. The variable could be constructed algorithmically by counting the number of different ethnic markers found in each household. This would not identify what specific ethnicities were present in each household, but would rather mirror to what degree households were ethnically heterogeneous. The variable is not without its problems, however. To the extent that persons were reported as mixed, the variable under-reports that different ethnic groups may be the underlying cause – for instance, people with Sami-Finnish and Norwegian-Sami parents were denoted in this way, and cannot be distinguished unless the parents were present. On the other hand, some ethnic variation may be over-reported for children with parents of different ethnic stock – for example, the children of a Sami and Norwegian couple would be marked as mixed, thus appearing to different from their parents, and three different ethnic groups would counted while in reality only two were involved. Still, the variable can indicate the extent of ethnic mixture, and can also be used to single out the most multiethnic households for further study.

Since three different ethnic groups were present in the area specified, it comes as no surprise that few households consisted of more than this number of ethnic groups. About 60 per cent of the households were ethnically homogeneous, while 15 per cent had two different markers and 23 per cent had three different markers. On average there were 1.6 different ethnic groups in the households in northern Troms, indicating that even if homogeneous households were the most common, mixed ones were nearly as usual. The differences between the four municipalities were not dramatic, except that Karlsøy on the coast had more homogeneous households (73 per cent), while Skjervøy had fewer in relative terms (50 per

Table 10.2. Number of Households with Different Ethnic Groups and Average Number of Ethnic Groups in Four Municipalities in Troms Province According to the 1875 Census

N ethnicities	Total	Karlsøy	Lyngen	Skjervøy	Kvænangen
1	1209	279	481	270	179
2	308	42	116	108	42
3	465	63	183	151	68
4	18	1	6	9	2
5	1			1	
Sum	2001	385	786	539	291
Average	1,6	1,4	1,6	1,8	1,6

Source: Computerized and encoded version, Norwegian Historical Data Centre.

cent). The differences get much smaller, however, when the number of persons rather than the number of households is counted, so the reason may simply be that there were many small households in Karlsøy which are more likely to contain just one ethnic group.

The rest of the constructed variables apply to all the three northernmost provinces in Norway. The levels coded are the province (sometimes called county), municipality (often corresponding to parish), census tract (usually corresponding to school district) and census form (corresponding to farm or domicile, containing one or a few households). The idea is to provide the ethnic-group context in a wider or narrower sense.

While Norwegians dominated the two southernmost provinces, they made up less than half of the population in the northernmost province of Finnmark according to Table 10.3. Even if the biggest ethnic group, they made up less than half of the population and were in a situation more like

Table 10.3. Ethnic Groups in the Provinces by Father's and Mother's Ethnicity According to the 1875 Census. Missing and Odd Ethnicity Not Reported

Province	Norwegian	Sami	Mixed	Finnish	Total
Father's ethnicity					
Nordland	31443	2348	661	175	104073
Troms	26113	7556	2667	3482	54868
Finnmark	9484	7696	1337	5331	24566
Mother's ethnicity					
Nordland	30007	2449	636	164	104073
Troms	25292	7618	2961	3324	54868
Finnmark	8330	8052	1466	5495	24566

Source: Computerized and encoded version, Norwegian Historical Data Centre.

Table 10.4. Ethnic Groups in Three Towns and Three Rural Municipalities According to the 1875 Census. Mother's and Father's Ethnicity Combined

MUNICIPALITY	Sum	Norwegian	Sami	Mixed	Finnish
Hammerfest town	4354	2793	20	127	816
Vardø town	2706	1817	2	28	237
Vadsø town	3462	1082	20	16	2154
Loppa	1604	12	1480	49	61
Alta	4842	1949	473	431	1859
Talvik	4390	1441	1751	540	613

Source: Computerized and encoded version, Norwegian Historical Data Centre.

Table 10.5. Farm or Domicile Lists with from One to Ten Persons Whose Father's Ethnicity was Sami or Finnish in the 1875 Census for Northern Norway. Absolute Numbers and Cumulative Percentages

# co-ethnic	Sami Lists	Persons	Cumulative	Finnish Lists	Persons	Cumulative
1	1107	1107	27,5 %	1160	1160	42,1 %
2	427	1534	38,1 %	447	1607	58,4 %
3	374	1908	47,4 %	246	1853	67,3 %
4	357	2265	56,3 %	178	2031	73,7 %
5	373	2638	65,5 %	207	2238	81,3 %
6	386	3024	75,1 %	152	2390	86,8 %
7	307	3331	82,7 %	105	2495	90,6 %
8	271	3602	89,5 %	82	2577	93,6 %
9	151	3753	93,2 %	52	2629	95,5 %
10	100	3853	95,7 %	34	2663	96,7 %

Source: Computerized and encoded version, Norwegian Historical Data Centre.

that of a minority, even if they had access to the support of the official authorities during conflicts. Thus the ethnic context for everyone was very different between the northernmost and southernmost parts of this region.

Table 10.4 is an excerpt from a much larger summary of paternal and maternal ethnicity in all the municipalities of the three northernmost provinces of Norway according to the 1875 census. It is clear that variation with respect to ethnicity was huge, not only between the regions but also from parish to parish. Even if we correct for a certain degree of under-enumeration, it is clear that few Sami were living in the three urban settlements in the northernmost province of Finnmark, but that they could dominate rural municipalities. The Finnish, however, were a significant population element especially in the towns. And since many had come to Alta and Talvik in the west of Finnmark to work in the copper mines, here too they lived in more congested, urban-like settlements. A corresponding list (not reproduced here) which tabulates ethnic groups by census tracts, shows that ethnicity is a contextual variable which it is useful to control at several levels of aggregation.

Table 10.5 summarises results from treating paternal ethnicity as a contextual variable at the level of the census list or questionnaire. This will usually comprise the persons and households living on the same farm or in the same domicile at the end of 1875. Having arrived later in northern Norway, and being a smaller group, the Finnish more often lived as single individuals in households dominated by others. More than two-thirds of them lived in households with less than four co-ethnic persons, while this was the case for less than half of the Sami.

Conclusion

The chapter first looked at ethnicity at the intersection of three dimensions: group versus individual criteria, ancestral versus cultural/language criteria, and subjective versus objective criteria. Over time the Norwegian censuses moved in the direction of using more cultural criteria to solve the mixed-group problem, but kept significant ancestral elements. Group-level criteria were less important than the individual assignment of ethnicity from 1875 onwards, and only in the towns would household heads fill in the ethnicity column themselves (subjectively) from 1865 onwards. A test of the consistency of noting ethnicity in each census tract showed that few census takers were confused by the changing definition of the ethnic marker *fin*, which can mean both Sami and Finnish. This test does not work in the towns, but there are too few Sami in urban areas for this to be a significant problem. On the basis of the 1875 census, the ethnicity variables were aggregated onto several group levels. In the southern half of northern Norway, Norwegians constituted a clear majority, but in the northern part of Troms and in Finnmark province there was more variation. Although there were exceptions in the urban parishes dominated by the Finnish, the general picture is that Sami ethnicity is a more influential contextual variable at all aggregation levels.

Notes

1. The results of the NAPP can be found at www.nappdata.org. See also Roberts et al. (2003).
2. See http://www.rhd.uit.no/nhdc/census.html.
3. See the documentation for the 1875 census: Statistisk sentralbyrå (1878–1881).
4. The international project 'Home Hearth and Household' focuses on the ethnic categories in the late nineteenth-century censuses.

References

Hansen, L.I. 1994. 'Samene i Forrige Århundres Folketellinger: Registreringspraksis i Astafjord Prestegjeld 1865–1900', in Storm, D. et al (eds.) *Festskrift til Ørnulf Vorren*. Tromsø: Tromsø Museum, pp.102–29.

Hansen, L.I., and T. Meyer. 1991. 'Ethnic Classification in Late Nineteenth-century Censuses: A Case Study from Southern Troms, Norway', *Acta Borealia* 8(2): 13–56.

Isaksen, K. 1988. 'Folketellinger 1815–1980', *Arkivmagasinet* 2: 21–29.

Jåstad, H.L. 2003. *Spedbarnsdødeligheten i Tana i Perioden 1840–1914*. Tromsø: Universitetet i Tromsø.

Kiær, N. 1882: *Bidrag til en Norsk Befolkningsstatistik*. Christiania: Det Statistiske Centralbureau.

Lie, E., and H. Roll-Hansen. 2001. *Faktisk talt: statistikkens historie i Norge*. Oslo: Universitetsforlaget.

McCaa, R., and S. Ruggles. 2001. 'The Census in Global Perspective and the Coming Microdata Revolution', in J. Carling (ed.), *The 14th Nordic Demography Symposium, Tjøme (Norway)*. Oslo: Nordic Demographic Society, pp.7–30.

Niemi, E. 1977. *Oppbrudd og Tilpassing*. Vadsø: Vadsø kommune.

Roberts, E. et al. 2003. 'The North Atlantic Population Project: An Overview', *Historical Methods* 36(2): 80–88.

Schøyen, C. 1918. *Tre Stammers Møte*. Christiania: Gyldendal.

Statistischen Institut. 1887. 'Thema: Die Verhandlungen und Beschlüsse des Internationalen Statistischen Instituts in Betreff einer einheitlichen Aufarbeitung der Volkszählungen'. Vienna: Internationalen Statistischen Institut.

Statistisk sentralbyrå. 1868/9. 'Resultaterne af Folketællingen i Norge i Januar 1866'. Christiania: Departementet for det Indre.

———— 1878–1881. 'Resultaterne af Folketællingen i Norge i Januar 1876'. Christiania: Det Statistiske Centralbureau.

———— 1894–1898. 'Folketællingen i Kongeriget Norge 1891'. Christiania: Aschehoug and Co.

———— 1906. 'Folketællingen i Kongeriget Norge 3 December 1900: Hovedoversigt'. Christiania: Aschehoug and Co.

———— 1916. 'Folketællingen i Norge 1 december 1910: Hovedoversigt'. Christiania: Aschehoug and Co.

Thorvaldsen, G. 1995. *Migrasjon i Troms i Annen Halvdel av 1800-tallet: En Kvantitativ Analyse av Folketellingene 1865, 1875 og 1900*. Tromsø: Registreringssentral for historiske data, Universitetet i Tromsø.

———— 1997. 'Om Grenser og Områder i Lokalhistorisk Forskning', in J. E.Myhre and K. Kjeldstadli (eds), *Festskrift til Sivert Langholm*. Oslo: Den norske historiske forening, pp.188–211.

———— 2006. 'Away on Census Day: Enumerating the Temporarily Present or Absent', *Historical Methods* 39(2): 82–96.

———— 2007. 'An International Perspective on Scandinavia's Historical Censuses', *Scandinavian Journal of History* 32(3): 237–57.

Thuen, T. 1987. 'One Community, One People? Ethnicity and Demography in a North Norwegian Community 1865–1930', *Acta Borealia* 4(1): 65–83.

Torp, E. 1986. 'Registrering av Etnisitet i Folketellinger', *Heimen* 23(2): 67–77.

———— 1990. 'Information About Information: Relating Different Historical Sources to One Another', *Acta Borealia* 7(2): 81–85.

11

OUT OF THE BACKWATER?
PROSPECTS FOR CONTEMPORARY SAMI
DEMOGRAPHY IN NORWAY

Torunn Pettersen

Introduction

The indigenous Sami people's traditional settlement area is in the north-west of the European mainland. This continuous geographical area, which is divided by the four countries of Norway, Sweden, Finland and Russia, is called Sápmi in the Sami language.

Since 1985 football matches have been organised from time to time between a Sápmi team and other teams enrolled in an international football association for regions and countries that cannot be members of the International Football Federation (FIFA). From the very first match of this kind, Sami have discussed who is entitled to play football with the Sami flag on their chest. That is: Who is entitled to represent the Sami people? These discussions have partly focused on the overall principles involved in team selection and partly on the selection of specific players. In 2006 the Sami Football Association therefore decided to adopt ethnic guidelines for the selection of players. I will return to these guidelines at the end of this chapter, but their relevance here is that discussion of Sami representation in sports relates to frequently asked questions about exactly which individuals constitute the Sami people as such.

Questions about Sami affiliation are asked among both Sami and non-Sami groups. One reason for this unclear situation is the lack of demographic sources regarding data on Sami ethnicity in the countries which have Sami populations. Since the early 1990s, however, increasing attention has been given to various issues relating both to this lack of basic Sami demographic data and to the shortage of Sami statistical data in general. This awareness caused the Nordic Sami Institute (NSI) in Norway to undertake research in order to facilitate the development and operation of technological and organisational solutions for overall and permanent access to various kinds of numerical data regarding contemporary Sami social conditions – first and foremost in Norway.[1]

This chapter is based on the NSI research project. The purpose is partly to give an overview of the current situation of Sami demography, mainly in Norway; and partly to point to some issues that need to be addressed to bring about positive change, given that deficient Sami demographic data is a negative situation. The chapter begins with some comments on the complex global situation regarding official recording of ethno-cultural data. It continues with a description of the status of contemporary Sami demography, followed by some notes on why the insufficiency of Sami demographic data has gained attention recently. In the final section of the chapter a number of requirements for change are pointed out.

The Complex Field of Ethno-Cultural Data and Official Statistics

Official statistics are usually the most important source of demographic data in general and of data on specific population sub-groups in particular. The authorities' need for population statistics is a classic reason – if not the main reason – why practically every country in the world has some sort of national and/or regional unit(s) that provides official statistics to various end-users. However, the official recording of ethno-cultural data on citizens' ethnicity, nationality, language use or religion is a controversial and complex field in which scientific, political, legal and ethical aspects are interwoven.[2]

One general aspect of this field is that practices vary. They vary between countries and they vary over time within countries. Local and historical contexts are thereby significant in terms of the particular practices which are chosen. For instance, since the Second World War it has been a widespread norm in western European countries not to include ethnic categories in official population statistics (Courbage 1998; Haug 1998). This contrasts with other developed countries which are built on traditionally indigenous land – such as New Zealand, Australia, Canada and the U.S.A. – which all have long and continuous traditions of compiling specific official statistics about, among others, the indigenous peoples in those territories. However, in these countries the field of ethno-cultural data is also characterised by recurring variations, conflicts and changes (see, e.g., Cook 2005; Simon 2005).

A more specific aspect of the complexity of this field is the various opinions held about how and even whether data on ethnicity should be officially recorded at all. Differences of opinion are found among and between individuals and institutions, and among the representatives of minority groups as well as among those of majorities. The complexity and dilemmas regarding ethno-cultural categories in official statistics are classic, but for various reasons such issues are also gaining more attention in many countries and regions around the world. Some reasons for this are increased migration, changes in the understanding of ethnic affiliation as a phenomenon, and increased recognition of indigenous peoples and their rights (see Simon 2005).

Sami Demography Today

The Sami are the only indigenous people present in the Sápmi area.[3] Today there are, of course, many Sami individuals who are resident outside Sápmi – as well as many non-Sami persons who are resident within this area. But no one knows exactly how many there are in either of these groups. Nor does anyone know in detail how the present Sami settlements within Sápmi are distributed. At root, it is not possible to provide precise answers to any questions about the number, distribution or composition of the Sami people, either totally or in smaller areas. And why is this so? The simple answer is that at the present time no institution is responsible for collecting Sami demographic data or for producing official Sami statistics in a systematic and regular manner – and therefore almost no basic contemporary Sami data are available.

But it has not always been like this. Previously, and especially before the Second World War, Sami affiliation was – in varying degrees and using different criteria – recorded by census takers in selected areas in the northern reaches of the respective nation-states with Sami settlements.[4] The history of these countries' various census policies cannot be reviewed here, but the last time that census data on Sami affiliation was recorded was in 1970 in Norway, in 1972 in Sweden, and in 1962 in Finland. At the time, this was done at the urgent request of Sami organizations who themselves wanted such information as a basis for documenting Sami presence in the countries in general and Sami living conditions in particular (Aubert 1978; Justisdepartementet 1984: 18). Hence, it was not the national authorities which initiated the last recording of Sami ethnic data, even if the responsibility for completing the censuses was vested in the national statistics agencies.

Current estimates quoted for the size of the Sami population are based on figures extracted from the previous, rather outdated censuses. These estimates can be quite rough: estimates for the total number of Sami tend to vary between 50,000 and 100,000. It is, however, always pointed out that most Sami live on the Norwegian side of Sápmi – specific figures often show the distribution of Sami as 40,000 to 50,000 in Norway, 17,000 to 20,000 in Sweden, about 7,000 to 8,000 in Finland, and around 2,000 in Russia.[5]

These estimates are of course of interest, but we do know that they suffer from grave deficiencies. One example concerns the numbers from the 1970 census in Norway. In the first place, the Sami-related questions were asked in limited geographical areas within Sápmi and excluded the big towns. In the second place, we know that many of those actually asked about their ethnic affiliation and/or language use did not want to answer, or for various reasons chose to answer the ethnicity question in the negative when they could have answered in the affirmative (see Aubert 1978). Also, no registration has ever been conducted of the Sami who live outside the traditional Sápmi region.

What reasons might a person have for not wanting to give information about their Sami identity? The answers to this question vary, but many of them are undoubtedly related to the fact that, from the end of the nineteenth century until as recently as the 1970s and 1980s, the Sami language and other features of Sami culture were under heavy pressure from the respective national authorities. It was, for example, forbidden to speak Sami at school, and many parents therefore chose not to speak Sami actively with their children. The idea was that not teaching them Sami would make it easier for them to integrate into the wider society. In addition, there were other reasons why many people wanted to lay aside their Sami identity and their Sami cultural practices and why they had strategies for doing so. One such reason, at least in some communities, was the social stigmatisation that came from displaying any form of Sami affiliation (Eidheim 1971). For others, knowledge or experience of the Second World War may have caused uncertainty as to whether, in a worst-case scenario, Sami 'ethnic registers' would be abused (Justisdepartementet 1984: 18; Justis- og politidepartementet 1986/7). On the other hand, there could also be more principled reasons for not wanting one's Sami affiliation publicly recorded.

To summarise: the assimilation policy of previous periods vis-à-vis the Sami has for some time been set aside on principle. But the policy of the past still raises unsolved questions regarding Sami affiliation and/or identity in the present. In addition, the Scandinavian countries have – for various reasons – developed a general principle of not recording any kind of ethnic-affiliation data in census or administrative registers.

Analytically the present status of contemporary Sami demography can be described in terms of three partially inter-connected circumstances: lack of criteria, lack of procedures and lack of responsibility. Regarding criteria, there is no simple way to define the number of persons who today make up the Sami demos – or ethnos if one prefers – either geographically or at an individual level. Procedurally, since the Second World War it has been a widespread norm in the Nordic countries – as in the rest of western Europe – not to include ethnic categories in official population statistics. Neither has there been any other kind of systematic official recording of Sami affiliation. As for responsibility, there is for the time being no permanent institutionalised responsibility for dealing with issues regarding contemporary Sami statistics.

Why Focus on Contemporary Sami Demography?

For demographers and others who are dealing with demographic issues in their professional lives, the significance of demographic knowledge goes without saying. But why has the present situation of contemporary Sami demographic data reached the more general agenda? The answer to this is closely related to changes regarding the Sami political position. Recent decades have seen the Sami, as an indigenous people, achieve an increase in political influence and some onsets of self-determination. To pursue such rights, various kinds of data and knowledge are necessary. For instance, demographic data are needed both for overall social planning and as a basis for political decisions. This is especially the case with regard to the Sami representative elected bodies – Sámediggi – that were established in Norway in 1989, in Sweden in 1994, and in Finland in 1996.

A related reason for an increased interest in demographic issue is that both the Sami and the nation-states in which they reside need relevant data in order to describe and document the Sami situation. In the first place, all peoples seem to have a common need for knowing and being able to describe themselves as a people, past and present – for internal purposes as well as externally. In the second place, the documentation of Sami life and population numbers is necessary with respect to the obligations of the respective countries towards the Sami people. Documentation is needed both at a national level with regard to national laws and guidelines, and at an international level regarding the demands of various conventions for documentation.[6]

Further, the lack of Sami demographic data has also gained attention because such data is important for potential Sami contributions to international statistics on, and for, the world's indigenous peoples. The United Nations' Permanent Forum on Indigenous Issues in particular plays a central role in ongoing efforts in that respect (see PFII 2004).

Last but not least, the above mentioned more-or-less political need for relevant Sami demographic data goes hand in hand with the need for this data in the building of a knowledge base regarding Sami and Sami social conditions. Demands for and interest in Sami-related research and development projects are growing and contemporary demographic knowledge can often have serve as a necessary starting point and/or a resource for such projects. But when demographic data are insufficient, this limits the scope of research as well as the methodological repertoire for Sami-related knowledge-building projects.

Having stated all this, it is important to be aware that one kind of 'official' definition and registration of Sami individuals does exist, namely the national laws that regulate who is entitled to participate in the Sámediggi elections in Norway, Sweden and Finland. What the laws have in common is that regulations for inclusion in the electoral registers combine a subjective criterion – a person must claim Sami identity – with a more objective criterion – a person must speak, or one of their ancestors must have spoken, Sami as their first language. Both historical research and local knowledge, however, indicate that many persons who fulfill the criterion of language use have not enrolled themselves in the respective Sami electoral registers. The reasons for this have not been systematically studied, but in any case the situation demonstrates that there is no automatic link between having Sami ancestry and claiming a Sami identity for oneself. The Sami electoral registers are of course of interest from a demographic perspective, but they have by nature been established for the purpose of Sámediggi elections and cannot be treated as (a basis for) complete Sami population registers.

Propositions for the Expansion of Sami Demographic Knowledge

While demographically related questions regarding the Sami people have for several decades been answered by estimates, these estimates seem to be remarkably stable over time. This stability is probably due to the fact that the basic figures mostly draw on the same sources, namely the historical and geographically limited registrations of Sami affiliation that were conducted in earlier times. And since these are the only sources one can adhere to, the unchanging nature of Sami demographic knowledge is hardly surprising. These stable but inaccurate estimates of Sami demographic numbers, combined with deficient systems for providing new data, seem to me to be 'sloshing' around their own axes like eddies in a backwater. Meanwhile fresh water – in the form of social change and new knowledge – passes this backwater by, with no or few consequences for demographic estimates. The estimates based on old sources keep on sloshing around in the backwater. The question is: Does it have to be like this, or can the backwater be opened up?

I would argue that if Sami demographic estimates are ever to get out of this backwater there are certain requirements that must be fulfilled. Some requirements primarily concern procedures and responsibility, while others concern potential sources.[7] One must, however, be aware that it has been decided that all censuses in Norway after 2001 will be register-based. To simply introduce the recording of Sami affiliation on census forms is therefore not an option. Actually, for the time being it seems quite unlikely that any single source in the future will meet all the needs for basic Sami demographic data. Here, I would like to list and briefly comment on what I consider to be seven important and feasible propositions which would help to open up the backwater of Sami demographic knowledge.

First, demand for changes must come from the Sami. Opinions on whether and how data on Sami affiliation should be officially recorded vary among Sami individuals. However, it is the function of the Sámediggi to be an arena both for internal Sami political controversies and for reaching representative decisions that express the Sami people's will. In its plenary session in March 2006, the Sámediggi in Norway discussed the issue of Sami statistics. Its resolution says, among other things, that access to individually based Sami statistics is necessary and therefore the question of how this can be realised should be further explored.

Second, the widespread norm against the registration of ethnic affiliation must be modified, at least for the Sami as an indigenous people. In order to develop and maintain demographic sources on Sami affiliation, basic data on this issue must be recorded. Resistance to the recording of ethnic data seems to be quite strong among relevant stakeholders at an institutional level, including Statistics Norway (see Statistisk sentralbyrå 2003). Hence, this resistance must consider the need to find acceptable ways of dealing with data about and for the Sami as an indigenous people.

Third, the State must be willing to focus on and to spend resources on the issue. The Sami political and administrative system is limited in both resources and power. National agencies and institutions established by the state in order to deal with various aspects of population statistics should therefore also be formally responsible for dealing with Sami demographic data. This includes the funding of all necessary activities in that regard.

Fourth, the Sami right to participation and influence in the wider society must be respected and ensured. This is both an equality and empowerment issue and an instrumental issue, related to the fact that knowledge and understanding of Sami issues, culture and language is often rather weak among representatives and employees of non-Sami institutions. It is in accordance with a general principle of the full participation of indigenous peoples as equal partners in all stages of data collection (planning, implementation, analysis and dissemination, access and return) – a principle specifically pointed out in the recommendations of the Permanent Forum on Indigenous Issues (PFII 2004).

Fifth, Sami demographic sources must cover the whole country. None of the earlier censuses, which to some extent included data on Sami ethnicity, covered the whole country, or even the whole Sápmi area. Whatever the nature of future Sami demographic sources, they must contain information about Sami who are settled both inside and outside traditional Sami communities. This aspect is particularly important at a time when centralisation and urbanisation are increasing.

Sixth, at least one source must be dynamic; that means: open to changes. Data on Sami ethnicity are from time to time collected for use in research projects and/or surveys. These data are most often limited in terms of period, theme and/or geography. Such data have from time to time been combined with other data sources in order to extend the number of persons who might belong to a Sami demos.[8] This kind of 'static' data set collected or constructed for time-specific and thematically limited projects, can of course be interesting and valuable, but overall, future sources of basic Sami demographic data must include elements that are regular and dynamic.

Finally, ethnic self-identification must be the basic principle. It is well known from demographic and ethnicity studies that the ethnic identity of individuals – and/or the public reporting of this – can vary due to circumstances both in people's own lives and in their surroundings.[9] However, in the end it only individuals themselves who can specify their identity (or identities) at any given time. Hence, future sources of Sami demographic data must deal with both the right to self-identification and with how to record possible changes in an individual's reported identity (or identities).

Closing Remarks

I want to end this chapter by emphasising the point that future Sami demographic sources should be developed in ways that make it possible to distinguish between Sami ancestry and Sami identity. In some settings – such as some epidemiological research – it might not always be relevant to differentiate between self-identified Sami and Sami descendants. In other settings this difference is important. For instance, this differentiation does exist in the laws of the three Scandinavian countries in which Sami reside that regulate who is entitled to participate in Sámediggi elections and thereby to be included in the Sami electoral registers: being a Sami descendant is not a sufficient qualification of enrolment for one must also consider oneself to be Sami, to have Sami identity.

And exactly the same limitation has become the case in the rather different domain of Sami international football. Because of recurring discussions over who is entitled to play matches with the Sami flag on their chest, the Sami Football Association decided in June 2006 that all players must meet both of the criteria used for enrolment in the Sami electoral registers. However, players themselves do not have to be actually enrolled. The football team example thereby also illustrates how definitions in one domain of society can leak out and become adopted in other domains.

But having the right to ethnic self-identification does not imply that this is necessarily a simple task. For what is 'Sami identity', and who decides whether someone has it or not? These questions have been issues for both private and academic investigation for some time. It is hardly an exaggeration to say that Sami identity discourses have been a central theme – often the main theme – in a great deal of personal discussion and scholarly analysis regarding Sami social conditions.[10] In real life, identity questions have to be clarified both in terms of affiliation at the individual level and as a category at the system level before data on Sami ancestry and identity can be recorded at all, and hence later found in demographic sources, given that systems for this exist.

The NSI-initiated projects on Sami statistics in general and on Sami demography in particular have brought some processes and principals into play. We hope these will mark a start in opening up the backwater of Sami demography. But the challenges are indeed manifold, perhaps maybe even too many. On the other hand, it is often said that the perfect is the enemy of the good. In our context this saying tells us that it is better to try to work out *some* kind of solution to the Sami demographic data challenge than to do nothing because an optimal soltion may not be reached.

Notes

1. Some of the findings of this project are presented in Pettersen and Høydahl (2005). Updated project information can be found at www.Sami-statistics.info and www.ssb.no/samer/.
2. For a brief introduction to the field, see Pettersen (2006). For relevant background, see, e.g., Haug (1998, 2003), Mirga (2000), Skerry (2000), Allan (2001), Kertzer and Arel (2002), Niemi (2002), Blum (2003), Negrin (2003), Cook (2005), Morning and Sabbagh (2005) and Simon (2005). For an instructive presentation of current variations in census questions on ethno-cultural data, see the online database compiled by the United Nations Statistical Division at: http://unstats.un.org/unsd/demographic/sconcerns/popchar/popcharMeta.aspx.
3. Some people regard the Kvens in Norway as also being an indigenous people, but their official status is, however, currently that of a national minority (see Kommunal- og regionaldepartementet 2000/1). For readers who are not familiar with the Sami, it should be noted that there are no unambiguous visual differences between ethnic Sami and ethnic Scandinavians or Russians, even though Sami are often stereotyped as having certain physical features, such as high cheekbones, dark hair and brown eyes.
4. For Norway, see Torp (1986).
5. The population of the respective in January 2004 was: Norway, 4.6 million; Sweden, 9 million; Finland, 5.2 million; and Russia, 147.8 million in total – or 0.9 million in Murmansk Oblast, i.e. the traditional Sami settlement region of Russia.
6. The Sami legal position varies between the four countries in which they are found, but some examples of relevant conventions are: the United Nations' International Convention on the Elimination of all Forms of Racial Discrimination (CERD), the Council of Europe's European Commission against Racism and Intolerance (ECRI), and its Framework Convention for the Protection of National Minorities (FCNM).
7. While Sami conditions in Norway, Sweden and Finland are largely similar, the following remarks refer to conditions in Norway.
8. The most extensive example is the construction of a database on the health and living conditions of the Swedish Sami population (Hassler, Sjölander and Ericcson 2004).
9. Issues regarding ethnic self-identification are more complex than can be outlined here. For instance, one aspect is the possible conflict between, on the one hand, ethnic self-identification as a right that citizens have in accordance with international recommendations and conventions, and, on the other hand, local practices that more or less require 'group-based recognition' from other members of the ethnic group in question.
10. For some recent examples, see, e.g., Hegg (2000), Andersen (2003), Paine (2003), Thuen (2003a, 2003b), Kramvig (2005) and Dankertsen (2006).

References

Allan, J. 2001. *Review of the Measurement of Ethnicity: International Concepts and Classifications*. Wellington: Statistics New Zealand.

Andersen, S. 2003. 'Samisk tilhørighet i kyst- og fjordområder', in B. Bjerkli and P. Selle (eds), *Samer, makt og demokrati: Sametinget og den nye samiske offentligheten*. Oslo: Gyldendal Akademisk, pp. 246–64.

Aubert, V. 1978. *Den samiske befolkning i Nord-Norge*. Oslo: Statistisk sentralbyrå.

Blum, A. 2003. 'Resistance to Identity Categorization in France', in D. Kertzner and D. Arel (eds), *Census and Identity: The Politics of Race, Ethnicity, and Language in National Censuses*. Cambridge: Cambridge University Press, pp. 121–47.

Cook, L. 2005. 'Political and Methodological Issues in Country Experiences of Measuring Ethnic Communities, Small and Indigenous Populations', unpubished paper presented at the International Association for Official Statistics meeting 'Measuring Small and Indigenous Populations', Wellington, New Zealand, 14–15 April 2005. Retrieved 15 August 2005 from: www.stats.govt.nz/NR/rdonlyres/82B000E5-E314-4-C9D-A63B-AB5B4D733352/0/PAPERPLEN1.pdf.

Courbage, Y. 1998. 'Survey of the Statistical Sources on Religion, Language(s), National and Ethnic Groups in Europe', in W. Haug, Y. Courbage and P.Compton (eds), *The Demographic Characteristics of National Minorities in Certain European States, Vol.1*. Strasbourg: Council of Europe, pp. 23–74.

Dankertsen, A. 2006. '"Men Du Kan jo Snakke Frognersamisk!" Tradisjon og Kulturell Innovasjon blant Samer i Oslo', M.A. dissertation. Oslo: Institute of Social Anthropology, University of Oslo.

Eidheim, H. 1971. *Aspects of the Lappish Minority Situation*. Oslo: Universitetsforlaget.

Hassler, S., P. Sjölander and A. Ericsson. 2004. 'Construction of a Database on Health and Living Conditions of the Swedish Sami Population', in P. Lantto and P. Sköld (eds), *Befolkning och Bosättning i Norr: Etnicitet, Identitet och Gränser i Historiens Sken*. Umeå: Umeå Universitet, pp. 107–26.

Haug, W. 1998. 'Introduction: Statistics on Minorities between Science and Politics', in W. Haug, Y. Courbage and P. Compton (eds), *The Demographic Characteristics of National Minorities in Certain European States, Vol.1*. Strasbourg: Council of Europe, pp. 9–22.

――― 2003. 'Ethnic, Religious and Language Groups: Towards a Set of Rules for Data Collection and Statistical Analysis', *Eumap.org Online Journal*. Retrieved 23 August 2005 from www.eumap.org/journal/features/2003/april.

Hegg, L.S. 2000. *Norsk eller Samisk? I Spenningsfeltet mellom Eksistens og Vitenskap*. Tromsø: Universitetet i Tromsø, Institutt for pedagogikk.

Justisdepartementet. 1984. 'Om Samenes Rettstilling'. NOU No.18. Oslo: Justisdepartementet.

Justis- og politidepartementet. 1986/7. 'Om Lov om Sametinget og andre Samiske Rettsforhold (Sameloven)', Odelstingsproposisjon No.33. Oslo, Justis- og politidepartementet.

Kertzer, D., and D. Arel. 2002. 'Census, Identity Formation, and the Struggle for Political Power', in D. Kertzner and D. Arel (eds), *Census and Identity: The Politics of Race, Ethnicity, and Language in National Censuses*. Cambridge: Cambridge University Press, pp. 1–42.

Kommunal- og regionaldepartementet. 2000/1. 'Nasjonale Minoritetar i Norge: Om Statleg Politikk overfor Jødar, Kvener, Rom, Romanifolket og Skogfinnar', Stortingsmelding No.15. Oslo: Kommunal- og regionaldepartementet.

Kramvig, B. 2005. 'Fleksible Kategorier, Fleksible Liv', *Norsk Antropologisk Tidsskrift* 16(2–3): 97–108.

Mirga, A. 2000. 'Roma and Statistics'. Retrieved 09 September 2005 from: www.per-usa.org/reports/PERStrasbourg.pdf.

Morning, A., and D. Sabbagh. 2005. 'From Sword to Plowshare: Using Race for Discrimination and Anti Discrimination in the United States', *International Journal of Social Science* 57(183): 57–73.

Negrin, K. 2003. 'Collecting Ethnic Data: An Old Dilemma, the New Challenges'. *Eumap.org Online Journal*. Retrieved 23 August 2005 from: www.eumap.org/journal/features/2003/april.

Niemi, E. 2002. 'Kategoriens Etikk og Minoritetene i Nord: Et Historisk Perspektiv', in Den nasjonale forskningsetiske komité for samfunnsvitenskap og humaniora (NESH) (ed), *Samisk Forskning og Forskningsetikk*. Oslo: De nasjonale forskningsetiske komitéer, pp. 22–44.

Paine, R. 2003. 'Identitetsfloke: Same – Same. Om Komplekse Identitetsprosesser i Samiske Samfun', in B. Bjerkli and P. Selle (eds), *Samer, Makt og Demokrati: Sametinget og den Nye SamiskeOoffentligheten*. Oslo: Gyldendal Akademisk, pp. 291–317.

Pettersen, T. 2006.'Etnisk Identitet i Offisiell Statistikk: Noen Variasjoner og Utfordringer Generelt og i en Samisk Kontekst Spesielt', in V. Stordahl (ed.), *Samisk Identitet: Kontinuitet og Endring*. Guovdageaidnu: Sami Instituhtta/Nordisk Samisk Institutt, pp. 53–84.

Pettersen, T., and E. Høydahl. 2005. 'Developing Sami Statistics in Norway: Challenges and Possibilities', unpublished paper presented at International Association for Official Statistics meeting 'Measuring Small and Indigenous Populations', Wellington, New Zealand, 14–15 April 2005. Retrieved 15.08.2005 from: www.stats.govt.nz/NR/rdonlyres/8F762EEB-D437–4448–8C69-BAE573B69CB2/0/PAPER212.pdf.

PFFI. 2004. 'Report of the Workshop on Data Collection and Disaggregation for Indigenous Peoples, New York, 19–21 January 2004'. Retrieved 1 September 2004 from: www.un.org/esa/socdev/unpfii/news/news_workshop_doc.htm.

Simon, P. 2005. 'The Measurement of Racial Discrimination: The Policy use of Statistics', *International Journal of Social Science* 57(183): 9–25.

Skerry, P. 2000. *Counting on the Census: Race, Group Identity, and the Evasion of Politics*. Washington: Brookings Institution Press.

Statistisk sentralbyrå. 2003. 'Høringsuttalelse til NOU 2002: 12 Rettslig Vern mot Etnisk Diskriminering'. Retrieved 15 August 2006 from: http://www.ssb.no/omssb/horing/.

——— 2006. 'Samisk Statistikk 2006 / Sami Statistihkka 2006'. Oslo: Statistisk sentralbyrå.

Thuen, T. 2003a. 'Lokale Diskurser om det Samiske', in B. Bjerkli and P. Selle (eds), *Samer, Makt og Demokrati: Sametinget og den Nye Samiske Offentligheten*. Oslo: Gyldendal Akademisk, pp. 265–90.

——— 2003b. 'Samiske Studier: En Oversikt og noen Problemstillinger', in M. Rugkåsa and K.T. Thorsen (eds), *Nære Steder, Nye Rom: Utfordringer i Antropologiske Studier i Norge*. Oslo: Gyldendal Akademisk, pp. 107–62.

Torp, E. 1986. 'Registrering av Etnisitet i Folketellinger', *Heimen* 23(2): 67–77.

12

THE MYSTERY OF THE MAGNATE REINDEER HERDERS: HOUSEHOLD STRUCTURE AND ECONOMY AMONG LAKE ESSEI IAKUTS, 1926/7

David G. Anderson

In the spring, the rich ones (*baiil*) brought their herds out onto the ice. The surface of the ice turned black – there were so many animals. Then all of a sudden there was a mighty crash. The ice broke. The weight of so many animals broke the ice. It was an amazing sight. The old days were not like now. Some people had many deer. They say that the rich ones had 10,000 head. They would travel and help people with their deer.

Nikolai Savel'evich Utokogir
Khatantaiskoe Ozero

Introduction: Reindeer Herding, Power and Identity

The region of the Putoran plateau in central Siberia is a place of dramatic flat-topped mountains and remote, pristine tundra. It is a place that has attracted Evenki, Iakut and Dolgan reindeer herders for centuries, since the unique alteration of alpine and high arctic ecosystems makes it a perfect place to elaborate the complex strategies needed for large-scale reindeer husbandry. Here, unlike in southern Evenkiia, the forests are thin, making it easy to find a large herd. Additionally, the windswept peaks of the mountains provide a haven from insects in the summer, making a long trip to the Arctic coast unnecessary. Today, reindeer husbandry is still practised in a few communities along the perimeter of this alpine system. The difficult transition to an unsubsidised economy has taken a severe toll on local traditions. In the Soviet era it was a popular pastime to count numbers of reindeer. State-farm directors would boast about their farm having 6,000 head as opposed to the 5,000 head of the neighbouring farm. Today, local herds are measured in groups of 50 to 100. The entire region probably today supports no more than what would have been the herd of a single state farm.

There are many reasons for the collapse of large scale reindeer husbandry under postsocialist conditions, but what remains a constant today is the game of numbers. Elders living in these northern communities today still speak with pride of the majestic herds of the past. A round number – 10,000 head – is commonly cited as the one of the greatest achievements of large scale Iakut reindeer husbandry in the region. Scholars, and young people, often scoff at this figure. Indeed, for anyone with experience of reindeer herding, the level of effort implied by this round number is staggering. It is difficult to manage a herd of 1,000 head with a complement of five or six people; a herd of 10,000 would indeed be a community undertaking on an epic scale.

The size of this round number is also something of a paradox in the historic literature. Early Soviet literature, taking is cue from the analysis of wealth in Russian peasant households, castigated large-scale herders as exploitative elements in society. Indeed this accusation led to arrests and state-sponsored murders in the late 1930s, not to mention a 'rebellion' of native herders in Taimyr in 1934. Despite this controversial history, the grandchildren of these reindeer magnates still speak proudly of their achievements both in high-Soviet times and in the post-Soviet present. The social achievement represented by this history no doubt resonated in their minds with the imperative to large numbers that was peculiar to the Soviet period. The round number was no doubt cited as an example of what was possible in this rich landscape. I suspect that this ideological angle to the story also evoked scepticism about whether or not it was 'really' true.

Anthropologists have a professional ailment for taking old people at their word, and I have always believed these old stories. The elders with whom I spoke were never given to exaggeration in other aspects of their lives; indeed, their daily activities demonstrated that they were experts in their craft. However, I have often wondered about the mechanics and details of how such a large enterprise was organised, and have been surprised that often the details had been lacking in their stories. I reconciled this lack of detail with the deep importance of the endeavour.

The early Soviet period was a tumultuous time in what was then called the Ilimpei tundra. A radical new government had just taken control of the region in 1924 after a drawn-out civil war in eastern Siberia. Earnest young Russians were travelling the region asking detailed questions about reindeer numbers – and I expect asking for a level of detail that people never bothered to achieve themselves. The exact conversations and the exact strategies at this time remain opaque in the historical record, but their transformative results are quite well-known and well-documented. Between the coming of Soviet power in 1924 and the beginning of mass collectivisation of 1934, the people of the tundra of this region had reorganised themselves territorially, economically and in terms of their identity. If during the 1926 census one found Iakuts and Tunguses living in the area around Lake Essei, by 1934 one found the same brothers and cousins spread out over a huge territory from the highlands to the interior of the plateau. By 1960, these territorially dispersed, extended families were given new nationalities, were divided by geographical boundaries, and began to speak different languages. The power that large-scale reindeer ownership evoked in these intense political conditions was of immense importance when trying to understand the history of national identities in the region. As such, no one observer, I suspect, had an overview of these movements. This may be why this exact history is today a matter of myth rather than a matter of narrative.

In this chapter, I wish to apply a recently discovered archive of early statistical data in order to try to shed some light on the 'mystery of the reindeer magnates'.[1] The chapter is framed methodologically. Indeed, my direct intention is to examine how units of analysis form meaningful frames in statistical overviews. Here I will try to rework the concepts of household and community and try to adapt them to this particular region. However, the broader intention of the chapter is to try to understand the social dynamics of reindeer husbandry in the region. In my opinion, this archive sheds some light on social relations between herders, their families, and how their herding activities were related to other materials of life – such as the procurement of trade goods. The chapter tries to link the household structure of people to the herd structure of the animals that supported these households. In so doing it is hoped that there is a broader ecological aspect to what would be otherwise a narrow exercise in historical demography.

The 1926/7 Turukhansk Polar Census Expedition

The main source of data for this chapter comes from the primary records of the Turukhansk Polar Census expedition of 1926/7. This unique archive was digitised in collaboration with the State Archive of Krasnoiarsk Territory (GAKK), the National Archive of the Sakha Republic (NARS), and the Krasnoiarsk Regional Studies Museum (AKKKM).[2] The 'census' was not so much a registering of individuals as a unique exercise in the study of the rural economy whereby every local Russian and indigenous family and their settled or semi-settled communities was described over the course of one year. The scale and detail of the undertaking has more in common with eighteenth-century expeditions of discovery than the narrower undertaking that we associate with national censuses. The primary documents, which by happenstance were preserved in a number of regional archives, provide a unique overview of the region before territorial formation and collectivisation. I have described the expedition in detail in other places (Anderson 2005, 2006).

The bulk of the data for this chapter come from the household cards which give very detailed information on demography, trade and household prices. These data were supplemented by the very detailed community diaries for the region which give a long-hand description of the geography and history of the place. Finally, the enumerator for the region left a handwritten diary of his travels which also provides important details of the region.[3]

The household 'card' in use in this region is also a misnomer. This primary document, printed on a large A2 sheet of paper, consists of over 400 columns and a half-dozen rows, potentially recording approximately 2,000 data points. The interaction between the complexity of this instrument and its accuracy is a separate issue which I have discussed elsewhere (Anderson 2006). However, what is intriguing for the present purposes is the level of detail of the key points of the social world of Siberia and the Russian North at this date. Aside from collecting rather detailed information on the age, occupation and income of every individual in every household, the form also contained what is today one of the most detailed set of questions on the structure of local reindeer 'families'. Broken up into eight age classes (often labelled with indigenous terminology) and four functional types, the cards give an intimate portrait not just of bald numbers but of herd structure. When combined with other highly contextualised information on the card, such as that on the yearly round, it is a small step to inferring herding strategy. In addition, the section on herd structure had cells for two interrelated sub-totals (which were a great help in cleaning the digitised database), and separate sections for herd dynamics (births and acquisitions calculated against twelve categories of loss) and for the long-term loan of reindeer. To some degree, the data on reindeer is more detailed than that on people.

Second to the data on reindeer are the curious indicators of identity contained in the header of each card. Although enumerators were asked to collect information on the mysterious entity of 'nationality' introduced by demographers fluent in the latest techniques from Central Europe, most enumerators instead reported 'tribe', 'clan', 'nickname' and 'tribute unit'. These older identifiers give valuable information on how seemingly separate households link together using an algebra that is not European in origin.

A final important and additional aspect to this interpretation is fieldwork. My familiarity with this case stems from fieldwork in the Lake Essei region between 1998 and 2002. The stories of elders, and exposure to life on the land today, gives an important context to interpreting the marks on these cards, marks which would otherwise have seem fragmented.

Understanding Lake Essei and Its Hinterland

Lake Essei is a large freshwater lake lying on the Kotoi watershed in the extreme north-eastern corner of the Evenki Autonomous District. The lake lies in the foothills of the Putoran plateau and has served as a regional centre for almost 400 years. The first written records of the lake come from the seventeenth century when Russian Cossacks collected tribute at the site. The lake thereafter became a central crossroads for overland travel from Mangazei to Iakutsk. An Orthodox chapel – the first in the region – was built on the southern shore of the lake in 1820. The lake's convenient position make it an ideal site for reindeer husbandry since there is easy access to the alpine meadows that the reindeer need in summer and the lake provides a ready source of fish all year round. The lake itself serves as a centre point for a diverse region made up of other small alpine lakes and large rivers which provide the home for the Iakuts who are the subject of this chapter.[4]

Lake Essei Iakuts in 1926, as today, are a relatively large and self-conscious population of Iakut-speaking hunters and reindeer herders. They are proud of their identity, which in turn is linked to a strong respect for the lake and the landscape around it. They speak a dialect of Sakha which differs from central, literary Sakha. While living within a district of Krasnoiarsk Territory predominantly populated by Russians and Evenkis, there are very few instances of out-marriage in this community today, as in 1926. They have a strong commitment to traditional skills and today still manage to keep reindeer in the difficult conditions created by postsocialism.

The primary data for this chapter come from a set of household cards labelled the 'region around Lake Essei'. This is a data-set of 125 families (135 families if we include documents excluded from the published results for various technical errors), an overall population of 731 individuals. The population in 1926 breaks down as follows: 498 Iakut individuals and 233 Tungus (Evenki) individuals. Among these, there are only nine mixed Evenki–Iakut marriages, and these are at the primarily Evenki settlement

Figure 12.1 The Botulu Family and Their Reindeer 2006. (Photograph by Tatiana Argounova-Low)

at Lake Murukta. It is important to mention that the data-set refers to a region that is approximately 900 square kilometres in size. With the exception of the very destitute, the population was highly nomadic and regularly visited a series of rivers and lakes over the course of the year, with periodic returns to Lake Essei which provided the focal point for their nomadic cycle. The dataset is primarily made up of archived household registers labelled 'Lake Essei', 'Lake Diupkun' and 'Lake Murukta'.[5] This

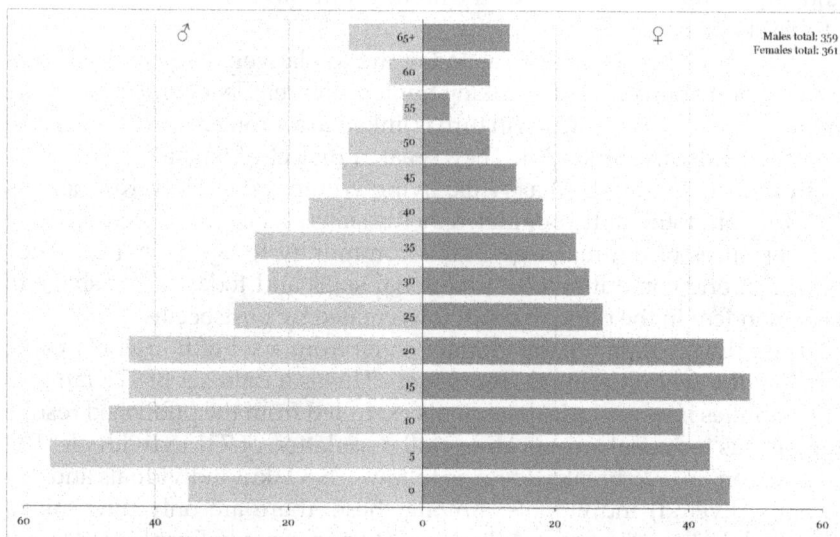

Figure 12.2 Age-Sex Pyramid for Lake Yessei 1926

Figure 12.3 The Chapel at Lake Essei. (Drawing by A.P. Lekarenko, AKKKM 7626-66-579)

region was surveyed primarily by Andrei Lekarenko, an artist by training but who provided sharp observant notes on the region (as well as a wonderful series of paintings and sketches). An age–sex distribution pyramid for the Lake Essei region can be seen below (Figure 12.2), as well as a sketch of the church at Lake Essei by Lekarenko (Figure 12.3).

In addition to this data-set, I have also identified a second group of records which we can call the Lake Essei diaspora. This refers to a set of communities in the heart of the Putoran plateau which served as a second home to many Lake Essei Iakuts. This region today corresponds to the south-western corner of Khatanga District of Krasnoiarsk Territory (formerly the Taimyr Autonomous District). These communities were identified primarily by the individual-level data on the cards, where the identifier 'Essei Iakut' was used. Often these were entire families from Lake Essei who would spend up to ten years living away from the lake in the highlands before returning. In other cases, these references were to spouses married into Iakut or Dolgan families further north. The population of this larger data-set is 1,542 individuals grouped in 283 families, including the Lake Essei sample. In addition to the communities around Lake Essei, this sample contains families representing the communities labelled 'Kamen', 'Nizhnaia Kheta', 'Uriadnik' and 'Paimura', as well as a number of other communities with only one or two families.[6]

The general technique that I have used here is to carefully study the observations made by Lekarenko at Lake Essei proper, and then to extend these observations to the wider region. This represents an attempt to turn qualitative observations into statistical indicators – an attempt that I will show is not entirely successful. In its place I will argue for the need to use a locally generated kinship model to understand the dynamics recorded by in this complex set of census data.

Stratification

One of the primary goals of the early Soviet state in Siberia was the elimination of poverty linked to unfair terms of trade and what was seen to be the concentration of wealth in the hands of a few entrepreneurs. The goals are clearly seen in this early census, which asked enumerators to count various types of capital ranging from traps and tools to reindeer stocks and buildings. Data on capital ownership later came to be interpreted as a source of social power, and parts of this statistical record were used to expropriate and execute wealthy reindeer entrepreneurs in the 1930s. However, it is important not to read these later tragedies into this particular exercise. It would be best to say that in 1926/7 the enumerators had an intense curiosity about how the life of local people was reflected in material objects. To this end they collected a wide range of data on goods and commodities. The Turukhansk expedition distinguished itself for its data on prices for goods, which were often scribbled in the margins beside or above data on the quantities of goods. The price data became part of a vigorous debate on whether or not stratification in rural areas was best measured by monetary values or by the quantities of goods in hand (see Anderson 2006). In many cases, enumerators also began sketching-out trade networks by recording in marginal notes whom people traded with and to whom they lent out reindeer or other provisions. For our purposes, it is these marginal notes which allow us to build up a complex picture of how people were linked to animals and to objects going beyond the labels which were later attached to people.

Bediak, Sredniak, Sostoiatel'nyi

As is well known, the early Soviet state divided people living in precapitalist social formations into three gradations: poor (*bediak*), middle (*sredniak*) and wealthy (*sostoiatel'nyi* or *bogatyi*). At this date, and in this region, the word *kulak* was not used. As the dual programmes of territorial formation and collectivisation got underway, certain guidelines were issued which linked socio-economic status to the number of reindeer held by a household (Suslov 1930). However, at the date of the expedition's survey these measures were not yet firmly formed and the census records give a good example of the thinking that went into these categories.

Lekarenko made an effort to place many households into one of the three categories in the parts of the household cards which left room for notes. From the short paragraphs written here, and some of his observations in his diary, it would seem that he discussed his observations with the people in the communities. It is possible that some of these labels were social distinctions that he reported rather than judgements that he applied mechanically.

Of the 127 households in the Lake Essei region proper, 33 households (26 per cent) were described as being 'poor', 11 (9 per cent) being 'middle', and 10 (8 per cent) as being 'wealthy'. Only 46 per cent of the households were specifically labelled. The remaining half do not show any particular pattern and could be assigned to one or the other category. It is interesting to read Lekarenko's comments which are associated with these labels. In all but three cases, being poor was associated with receiving material aid from relatives and neighbours – a special form of mutual assistance called *posobka* which will be discussed in detail in the next section. In the majority of these cases, material aid was directly related to receiving reindeer and in documenting whether these reindeer were used for food or for harnessing, and what other obligations the recipient might face. Only seven cases of poverty made reference to the lack of material objects or property and in the majority of those cases Lekarenko made reference to the fact that people were homeless. Many of the descriptions are quite touching:

> This is a family of orphans who are extremely destitute [*kraine malomoshchnaia*]. Many [neighbours] help them out. Kapit[on] Ioldagyr' (wealthy) almost feeds them by themselves. Other Tunguses also help them. For this [help]

they send the mother out to work as a porter on the transport caravans (*iamshchit*). Last year she travelled for Kapit[on] Ioldagir' to Agata [about 800km] for 50 roubles.[7])

This family is very poor. They live extremely poorly. They need almost everything.[8].

This family lives roughly (*skverno*). They need everything. They survive only on fish. Sometimes the rich give them a little flour or tea. They are not asked to pay for anything – they have no furs [to pay with].[9]

For our purposes, what is interesting is that poverty at this time was not linked to the number of reindeer or the number of objects that people held. It was almost purely linked to whether or not people received material assistance from their neighbours in the form of reindeer, food or a type of long-term mutual aid which begins to look like a form of adoption.

The next category, that of the 'middle' status, is in most cases marked by the absence of material assistance. Although the number of individuals marked as being 'middle' are small, five of the nine are explicitly described as not receiving material assistance from relatives or neighbours. From this small sample of cases, it would seem that their material conditions of life are similar to those of the poor. The main indicators are repeated here – diet, ability to purchase consumer goods, stationary (versus mobile) dwellings:

Figure 12.4 A Golomo in the Lake Essei Diaspora Region. (Glass plate photograph by N. Naumov, AKKKM 7630-1/90-02).

'Middle status' – eats fish all the time.[10]

'Middle status – does not receive *posobka*. Presently has enough to eat. He bought goods from the rich [herders] in exchange for fur.[11]

Lives in a *balagan* [a stationary, half-buried hut]. Assigned to the 'middle' ones.[12]

To complete this picture, it is not surprising that the 'wealthy' are also evaluated in terms of their relationship to social networks – only in their case they are givers of social assistance. In one case diet and the choice to live a stationary life are also markers of wealth:

He is the son of the wealthy herder Savva Egorov. He lives independently. Every year he gives reindeer for *posobka*.[13]

He is a wealthy reindeer herder who each year gives *posobka* in reindeer, ten reindeer at a time. In the winter lives all the time in one place. His reindeer are taken to pasture far away [by others]. He does not fish much. [14]

The one aspect on the cards that does jump out in terms of the rich are the numbers of reindeer they hold. Those families labelled as wealthy (with one exception) hold between 200 and 700 head of reindeer. All of them manage a variety of dwellings including stationary dwellings such as cabins or *balagans* – or in some cases both. They are the only families who are recorded as having tents, which are presumably sewn from purchased canvas. All of the families also have mobile, conical skin tents as well. Although I have here left out a full analysis of diet and trade goods, information on trade goods for all cases includes notes for every conceivable commodity – and in some cases quite large amounts – suggesting that some of these families were also involved in trade.

Defining Posobka

One of the most interesting aspects of this set of census cards are the number of references to *posobka* – the local Putoran-region social institution of mutual aid. There is very little known about this institution. In the early Soviet period it was condemned as type of proto-feudalism wherein rich reindeer herders indentured starving families over long periods of time in exchange for food or the bare minimum of supplies to keep them alive (Dolgikh 1929; Tarasenkov 1930). The hearsay accounts that I collected in Khantaika, Ust'-Avam and Essei from late twentieth-century Evenkis, Dolgans and Iakuts still describe the practice as 'what relatives do to help each other', and this is interpreted as a form of sharing. The ethnographic data, as well as the census data from the Kamen' plateau gathered by Boris Dolgikh, are today two of the richest accounts of a practice that seemed central to life in the region, and without a doubt continues in a muted or concealed form today.

The household card as such did not contain a cell for *posobka*. Lekarenko wrote the following notes on the practice:

> [This household head is] poor. Last year he received ten reindeer as *posobka* and ate them all. He has been taking *posobka* for three years.[15]

> He is poor. He has been taking *posobka* for 2 years. He takes 8 reindeer. He eats 4 and uses 4 for transport. Before he took *posobka* they had 30 reindeer [of their own]. They got lost and wolves destroyed them.[16]

> This is a rich reindeer herder who gives *posobka* every year as reindeer in groups of ten to fifteen head. He has been providing *posobka* for 6–7 years.[17]

> [He is] well-off (he hid half of his reindeer [from me]). He has been giving *posobka* for three years in groups 3–4 reindeer.[18]

> [There are no lending organisations.] [H]owever, rich reindeer herders sometimes give reindeer completely free of charge and sometimes only for a [short] time. They give them to the poor families, but not to all – only to those that want it and to those [who the owner] was able to guess … needed them. Rent was paid with powdered, dried fish [*porsoi*] or with [rendered] fish oil.[19]

Of 125 households around Lake Essei, 39 are directly listed as either giving or receiving *posobka*, of which 15 are listed as providing *posobka*. According to the textual descriptions, the practice often involved the following aspects:

- the lending of between four and twelve reindeer for a period of one year, often for between two and ten years in a row
- some reindeer would be given without expectation of a return since they were marked for consumption; a common pattern is four for riding and four for consumption
- sometimes *posobka* involved being invited to share housing and food (often described as sharing *kharchi*)
- sometimes the person receiving *posobka* is described as working for the richer partner (but unfortunately these tasks are not described well on the household cards)
- statements describing *posobka* are often accompanied with the explanation that a few years previously the recipient had many reindeer of their own but lost them to misfortune; the implication is that *posobka* is a short to medium term measure to tide families over

The interesting aspect of this practice is that it is difficult to distinguish from kinship obligations in themselves. For example, among the ten families recorded as being wealthy (107 individuals), nine children are described as being adopted and seven adults are recorded as being 'work-ers' (but listed as part of the family). In another part of the form, eleven families are listed as hiring labour to help with reindeer husbandry (some of these being the same families). The implication is that the category of 'worker' blurred with the category of 'family member'.

Further, it seems that if a family received reindeer as *posobka*, these were recorded on the household card as being their own holdings (with a men-tion in the notes that they had received *posobka*). If the family did not men-tion that they had received *posobka* the fact of the transaction would go under-reported. It is quite possible that the practice was more widespread and blended with a general practice of mutual aid.

The information on *posobka* suggests that an analysis of how reindeer estates are related to kinship patterns might be a better way of under-standing the relation between people and animals. As we will see below, this will involve blurring the distinction between a household and a kin-ship group.

Formal Criteria

I tried to extend Lekarenko's comments on stratification to see how the en-tire community would be classified had his observations been formalised into a statistical system. (It is important to emphasise that at this date the data were not organised in this manner.) Using Lekarenko's classificatory notes on a small group of Essei Iakut households, I tried to formalise his criteria of wealth numerically and then apply them first to the entire group of Essei Iakut households and then to the wider region. We can summarise his categories in the following manner by linking them to data held on the household cards for the households that he labelled (see Table 12.1).

From this table it should be clear that the marker that divides mid-dle and poor households is whether or not a household received material aid. The clearest marker dividing the rich from the middle is whether or not material aid is provided. Data on important trade goods such as tea and success in the fur trade also seem to be important qualifiers, although they are difficult ones to use. The quantity and type of reindeer held does distinguish the rich from the others, but this data is also difficult to use. The reason why both trade goods and the quantity of reindeer used are tricky indicators is the fact that the enumerators would record numbers of reindeer present, or bricks of tea, whether or not they were in fact gifts from more wealthy relatives. The key indicator is thus the giving or tak-ing of mutual aid – a quality that can only be ascertained by reading the household cards critically.

Formalising Lekarenko's criteria yielded the following model of re-gional stratification (Table 12.2).

When these criteria were coded first onto the rest of the Essei com-munity, then to the diaspora Essei region, it yielded the following picture (Table 12.3)

Table 12.1. The Stratification of Essei Reindeer Herders Using the Criteria Implicit in A.P. Lekarenko's Fieldnotes

Quality	'Poor'	'Middle'	'Rich'
Total number of reindeer	0 to 26 (average 7)	6–46 (average 22)	200 and more (average 330)
% of herd used for transport	40–100% (average 76%)	46–86% (average 70%)	18–72% (average 39%)
% of herd held as calves	0–60% (24%)	14–54% (average 30%)	30–45% (average 39%)
Receive posobka	yes	no	no
Provide posobka	no	no	yes
Tea (loose and brick)	Average 7 *funt*	Average 12 *funt*	Average 22 *funt*
Flour	Average 4 *pud*	Average 5 *pud*	Average 5 *pud*
Total Fish Caught	Average 188 *pud*	Average 165 *pud*	Average 142 *pud*
No of squirrel caught	Average 0,4	Average 0,9	Average 5
No of Arctic fox caught	Average 17	Average 23	Average 41

A *funt* represents 4 kg. A *pud* represents 16kg.

Table 12.2. A Formal Model of Regional Stratification Using A.P. Lekarenko's Fieldnotes

Quality	'Poor'	'Middle'	'Rich'
Total number of reindeer	0 to 20	21–50	51 and more
posobka	receives	neither gives nor receives	provides
Tea (loose and brick)	8 *funt* and less	9–15 *funt*	15 *funt* and more

This experiment in trying to formalise Lekarenko's qualitative judgements proves, to my mind, three things. First, the model works best for the immediate region that he was describing. The further afield his qualitative categories are applied, the looser the indicators become, generating a very different picture of stratification. Second, it seems that the criteria that he used – numbers of reindeer, the presence of *posobka*, and a study of diet – are much better at labelling the very wealthy households than at distinguishing between poor and middle households. Third, it would

Table 12.3. The Quantification of A.P. Lekarenko's Criteria of Stratification for Lake Essei and Diaspora Regions

Region	'Poor'	'Middle'	'Rich'
Lake Essei Subset as described by A.L. [54 households]	33 [61%]	11 [20%]	10 [19%]
Same subset using the formal model [54 households]	31 [58%]	15 [28%]	7 [13%]
The model applied to the Essei Community [125 households]	73 [58%]	42 [34%]	10 [8%]
The model applied to the Lake Essei Diaspora [262 households]	112 [43%]	111 [42%]	39 [15%]

seem that Lekarenko put more effort into recording the details of wealthy households than other types of households since the number of households reported stays pretty much constant.

Much as the census workers themselves discovered in 1926, I found it very difficult to reduce the richness of observations held in the cards to very simple categories of poor, middle and rich. As I have reported elsewhere (Anderson 2006), this was one reason why the data were never analysed in their own day. Although there seems to be a rough fit to the data, there are still some problems. Lekarenko labelled one family as being rich when they had a very small complement of reindeer (only nine head). Similarly, many of the rich families held exactly the same amounts of consumption goods as the poor or middling families. Outliers such of these are probably not uncommon in statistical analysis, but they confirm to my mind that there may be some problem with the way that households are divided up, as we will see below. If a qualitative household analysis were applied, then the data can lead to some interesting insights into the structure and dynamics of households which would take us far away from questions of power and stratification and closer to understanding the way this pastoral society worked.

Households, Communities, and Kinship Networks

The problem with moving from a numerical portrait of a region to a statistical portrait lies in determining the appropriate unit over which to calculate averages and relationships. The standard units for the 1926/7 census were those of 'household' (*khoziaistvo*) and 'community' (*poselennye*) – both of which were considerably different from the way that both terms are understood today in Europe.

The model for the 'household' was the ideal of a self-functioning economic unit consisting at the very least of a married couple, but in many cases a larger extended family which might hold three to four generations. Connected to the household were the objects and animals over which they exercised their mastery ('masterhood' forming the root of the Russian word *khoziaistvo*). The specific census cards designed for the Turukhansk Polar Census expedition were altered to include extra information that many scholars thought was important, such as clan affiliation, native language knowledge, and specific types of equipment that one could only find in an aboriginal and northern context.

The model for a 'community' was a compact grouping of built structures which were ideally united by a specific name and divided by rather large expanses of forest and tundra. In many of the regions where the Polar Census was undertaken, Lake Essei being one of them, the model of community was stretched to encompass entire watersheds, becoming defined as the entire region over which a single supply point could distribute trade goods. Nevertheless, these huge areas tended to be bounded by national identifiers and by discrete names which would identify one region as a single unit.

Both elements – the idea of a household being an economic unit touched by an idea of a clan, and the idea of a community being a discrete trading zone – have a long history in the Russian colonial situation. For several hundred years, relationships between the state and the regions were regulated by the notion of an administrative clan – a large kinship unit which would hold certain responsibilities before the Russian state (Dolgikh 1960). Although during the 1926/7 census there was an attempt to introduce European standards to the measure of population, both the documents and the way they were filled out show a strong continuity with

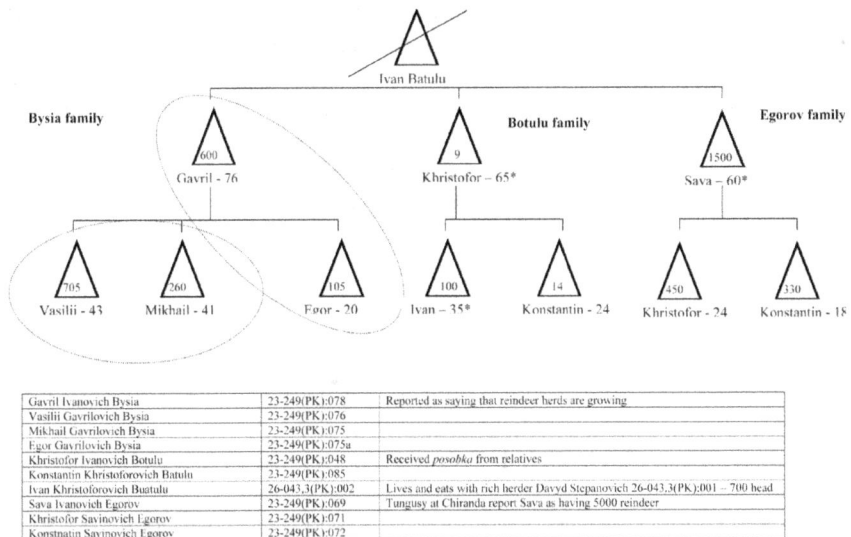

Gavril Ivanovich Bysia	23-249(PK):078	Reported as saying that reindeer herds are growing
Vasilii Gavrilovich Bysia	23-249(PK):076	
Mikhail Gavrilovich Bysia	23-249(PK):075	
Egor Gavrilovich Bysia	23-249(PK):075a	
Khristofor Ivanovich Botulu	23-249(PK):048	Received *posobka* from relatives
Konstantin Khristoforovich Batulu	23-249(PK):085	
Ivan Khristoforovich Buatulu	26-043,3(PK):002	Lives and eats with rich herder Davyd Stepanovich 26-043,3(PK):001 – 700 head
Sava Ivanovich Egorov	23-249(PK):069	Tungusy at Chiranda report Sava as having 5000 reindeer
Khristofor Savinovich Egorov	23-249(PK):071	
Konstatin Savinovich Egorov	23-249(PK):072	

Figure 12.5 The Batulu Lineage at Lake Yessei 1926–27

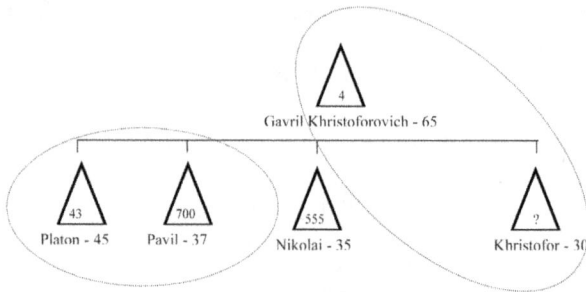

Gavril Khristoforivich Buatulu	26-044(PK):024	Khristofor was reported as not being present during Dolgikh's visit but was hunting with reindeer on a mountain far away.
Nikolai Gavrilovich Buatulu [Katygenskii]	26-043,45-001	
Pavil Gavrilovich Buatulu [Katyginskii]	26-043,1(PK):001	
Platon Gavrilivich Buatulu [Katyginskii]	26-043,1(PK):002	
Afanasii Ivanovich Buatulu [Katyginskii]	26-043,5(PK):002	

Figure 12.6 The Buatulu [Katyginskii] Lineage at Kamen' 1926–27

this older tradition. In my opinion, Lekarenko's and Dolgikh's data can only be interpreted by trying to tease out the element of economic kinship – of clanness – that unites extended families together as economic agents.

In trying to restructure the Lake Essei data into inter-regional household units, I first took the families that Lekarenko labelled as being wealthy and then searched for links between them that were suggested by patrilineal surnames, patronymics, clan affiliation, and extraneous notes on the cards. The wealthy reindeer herders break into three clan groupings: Batulu -Katyginskii, Maimago and Osogostok – essentially the three main clans that still control the community today. For the purposes of this chapter I organised the cards representing the Batulu-Katyginskii clan into two figures: Figure 12.5 represents a kinship grouping at Lake Essei, and Figure 12.6 represents a 'diaspora' group at the nomadic settlement of Kamen' in the Putoran plateau. The index references to the component cards are given at the bottom of each figure.

In both the figures I recorded the name of the household head, the age of the household head, the number of reindeer present, and indicated marginal comments on the cards to the effect that two or more household heads factually lived together (usually ate together). It is important to note that on the cards collected by Boris Dolgikh at the Kamen' escarpment, Dolgikh often mentions that specific household heads bearing the same surname and clan affiliation not only self-identify as Essei Iakuts but possess buildings or other assets at Lake Essei. Thus in this complex picture we have several dimensions that stretch the definition of households:

- Several discrete households (households recorded on separate cards) are recorded as eating and living together. In some cases the enumerators directly write that they should have been recorded as one household.

- It is possible to make an argument that two or three generations of kinsmen tend reindeer together. Factually, it is impossible for one individual to care for a herd that is over 1,000 animals.
- The first table, that of the Lake Essei Batulus, shows a clear picture of wealthy and poor kinsmen living together. Although Lekarenko does not record from whom Khristofor receives *posobka* the chances are that it is from his rich brothers.
- The marginal comments on the cards also point to certain poorer kinsmen being employed by wealthier kinsmen as 'workers', perhaps creating links to other households and families.
- Both tables, and the first one in particular, show a very elastic relation to identity whereby not only locations of kinsmen shift but so do their Russified surnames. As mentioned earlier, eventually nationalities would shift to distinguish different economic units.
- It seems very possible that the wealthy reindeer holders at Kamen and the wealthy reindeer holders at Lake Essei might be jointly tending fragments of a large regional herd.

Using such a model – of uniting households by economically evocative kinship links – it becomes possible to solve some of the problems that we noted with our formal statistical model above.

First and foremost, the model of identifying a regional group of people responsible for tending a complex resource such as reindeer allows us to solve the problem of outliers in the data. Families with few reindeer but a wealthy lifestyle (or those with many reindeer and a poor set of trade goods) might in fact represent fragments a larger, extended family. In short, it seems incorrect to assume that among reindeer herders decisions concerning reindeer management and those concerning consumption are confined to a nuclear family. The cards in this sample show consumption and management flowing between households. Such a conclusion is supported by other ethnographic work that speaks of the importance of the *siida* (a kinship based unit of mutual aid) in Sami reindeer management (Bjørklund 1990), and the role of lineages across Siberian pastoral peoples (Humphrey 1979). In Kenya, Dombrowskii (1993) writes of the importance of identifying a 'megaherd' amongst cattle pastoralists in order to understand how a regional herd is created through a series of gifts during marriage.

Second, the model displays the very dynamic way in which identity is cannily managed in this pastoral society. In communities where valuable estates are managed, it is not uncommon to find instances of kinship groups splitting and forging new identities. The first table shows a very radical drift in surnames which proved to be very effective in spreading reindeer wealth. In some of the Soviet-era literature this was interpreted as a way of 'concealing' wealth in animals. It is not clear to me from reading this archival material that surnames were deliberately altered as part of a plan to divide wealth. It seems more likely that different forms of lo-

214 David G. Anderson

cal solidarity also served to back up these divisions. However, the model does show how direct responsibility for one resource can sit at the level of a nuclear family on one level, but flow across households when it comes to matters of consumption. The instances of *posobka* that seem to flow across the Batulu clan nicely illustrate this point.

What does this model offer our opening question about whether or not Essei Iakut reindeer magnates roamed the tundra of the Putoran plateau in the late 1920s and early 1930s? This complex model of kinship solidarity to my mind confirms the stories of the old people at Lake Essei today, even if in no one case can we find a smug herder sitting with 10,000 head of reindeer around his tent.

First, this kinship-informed model shows how easy it is to allocate reindeer capital among a network of people. The model has only included patrilineal kin (the Russian enumerators only recorded aspects of patrilineal identity). My own fieldwork has shown that Lake Essei Iakuts also have strong matrilineal ties in their society today. Therefore, it is possible that some parts of this regional herd might have been allocated to uncles and cousins, and not just blood brother and sons.

Second, the marginal notes made by Boris Dolgikh and Andrei Lekarenko point to the fact that some estimates of the number of reindeer present might have been modestly reduced, if not cut in half. It is important to note though that in this region the concealment of numbers is not as common as it often is in Sami society or among other reindeer herders.

Third, even if numbers of reindeer were accurately represented, a foundation of roughly 5,000 head of reindeer in a regional herd is more than enough to result in a huge reindeer herd in three or four year's time. Marginal notes on the household cards by Lekarenko report elders observing that reindeer stocks were increasing in spring 1927. Given good ecological conditions, reindeer herds can double or triple in size over the period of two years. To quote a retired veterinarian in Tura, Anatolii Amelkin, 'reindeer herds are like wind, they shift in size and direction, and then blow away'.

Rather than deciding whether the memories of elders at Lake Essei regarding the size of past reindeer herds are true or not, this study underscores the importance of adjusting the meaning of significant units – such as households – to the way that they are activated in everyday life. In this case the important social issue that interests both elders and researchers today is the historical management of reindeer estates and how this links to consumption patterns. This study shows that we need to consider different units if we want to link both aspects together. The study also reveals the important way that a historical demographic study can lead to broader reflections on social solidarity and mutual aid – such as the study of the *posobka* relationship in this particular region.

Conclusion

Community surveys and censuses represent valuable 'snapshots' of human activity at a certain place in time. It is easy for anthropologists and historians to criticise the frames that organise the data recorded in these for not representing the complexity of social relationships as they were locally experienced at these times. However, and in spite of themselves, even the most rigid state-authored matrices often point to the social relationships which bind people together. Just as historical demographers try to establish longitudinal studies threading together the nominal records of particular individuals, it is also possible to weave together separate 'household cards' to show a local network of kin all engaged in common consumption and a common endeavor. Here I have suggested that a more evocative way to read this archive is to read household records as the nominal indicators of larger extended families (or 'clans'). By reaching out to imagine the lateral linkages beyond the household it is possible to get a fuller picture of the solidarities that structured human activity. This strategy is not only relevant to the history of people at Lake Essei, but I suspect it is also one way to build a historical demography of indigenous peoples in the circumpolar North. Essei Iakuts are not the only people in the North who organise themselves into units beyond the confines of the nuclear family. One often hears that population records in the North are too small to be statistically significant. One wonders if this 'smallness' is not a symptom of the units being used. Extensive household records may further reduce the quantity of the relevant units of analysis, but they bring about a different analytic dimension that makes for a nuanced analysis of communities.

Notes

1. Fieldwork in the Lake Essei and research into the 1926/7 Polar Census was initially sponsored by a grant from the Social Sciences and Humanities Research Council of Canada (MCRI–2000–1000). Research on the history of Lake Essei continued with the support of the U.K. Arts and Humanities Research Council under the project 'Archival and Living Transcripts' Grant APN16283. The digitisation of the archive of the Polar Census was conducted with the support of a standard research grant from the Research Council of Norway NFR 167040.
2. The collection of household cards on the Lake Essei region produced by the Turukhansk Polar Census expedition on which this chapter draws is primarily held at GAKK in fond P769, opis 1, dela 405 and 406. However, scattered cards are located in other folders .The collection is supplemented by a duplicate set of cards held by NARS in fond P70, opis 1, dela 1004. The set of household cards is supplemented by a detailed community diary held at GAKK (fond P769, opis 1, dela 354, pp.050–068), with a duplicate at NARS (fond P70, opis 1, dela 789, pp.497–512). The Lake Essei core region was documented by Andrei Lekarenko and the diaspora region by Boris Dolgikh – both of whom became quite famous

figures in the 1960s. Their work in the polar census signalled the beginning of productive careers as an artist and ethnographer respectively. The fact that both had a fine eye for the human condition contributes to the fine detail of the archival collections. Both the sets of household cards and the long many-paged community diaries consisted of detailed notes, often compressed to fit within the arbitrarily-sized boxes given by census administrators. In many cases the notes flow over onto separate sheets. Of all the collections of the Polar Census, these are some of the most detailed, and given the later careers of both enumerators, read as accurate accounts. An edited version of the database is available on the internet at www.abdn.ac.uk/polarcensusdata, with a short introduction to the history and structure of the data. In the notes to this chapter I have provided the classmarks used in the database to index specific communities, as well as the original classmarks for the paper versions of the documents.

3. AKKKM fond 7626 ed.khr.110, Dnevnik A.P. Lekarenko ot 9 sentiabria 1926 po 8 sentiabria 1927 gg.

4. Background literature on the region can be found in Suslov (1884), Vasil'ev (1908), Vasilevich (1951), Voronkin (1984) and Anderson (2009).

5. The registers are indexed on the electronic database as follows: 'Lake Essei' (23–249), 'Lake Diupkun' (23–247) and 'Lake Murukta' (23–248).

6. The latter set of communities is indexed on the database as follows: 'Kamen' (26–043), 'Nizhnaia Kheta' (26–044), 'Uriadnik'(26–025) and 'Paimura' (26–033).

7. GAKK fond P769, opis 1, delo 405, folios.071–072, Pokhozaistvennaia kartochka, ozero Mumurinda, Gurgugyr' Dariia Petrovna. Hereafter, the classmarks of 'fond', 'opis', and 'delo' are separated by a hyphen and the folios prefaced by a colon.

8. GAKK P769–1–406:039–040, Pokhozaistvennaia kartochka, ozero Essei, Bety Evdokiia Basil'evna.

9. GAKK P769–1–405:009–010, Pokhozaistvennaia kartochka, ozero Essei, Espekh Ul'iana Stepanovna.

10. GAKK P769–1–406:023–024, Pokhozaistvennaia kartochka, ozero Diupkun, Petrov Anofrii Pavlovich.

11. GAKK P769–1–406:129–130, Pokhozaistvennaia kartochka, ozero Essei, Nikolaev Egor Afanas'evich.

12. GAKK P769–1–406:089–090, Pokhozaistvennaia kartochka, ozero Essei, Nikolaev Khristofor Prokop'evich.

13. GAKK P769–1–406:091–092, Pokhozaistvennaia kartochka, ozero Essei, Egorov Khristofor Savvinovich.

14. GAKK P769–1–406:121–122, Po khozaistvennaia kartochka, ozero Essei, Matveev Nikolai Matveevich.

15. GAKK P769–1–405:003–004, Pokhozaistvennaia kartochka, ozero Essei, Espekh Nikolai Semenovich..

16. GAKK P769–1–405:005–006, Pokhozaistvennaia kartochka, ozero Essei, Espekh Nikolai Petrovich.

17. GAKK P769–1–405:029–030, Pokhozaistvennaia kartochka, ozero Essei, Maimaga Konstantin Nikolaevich..

18. GAKK P769–1–406:103–104, Pokhozaistvennaia kartochka, ozero Essei, Kipriianov Maksim Prokop'evich.

19. NARS Fond 70, opis 1, dela 789, folio.491, Poselennyi Blank, stoibishche v raione ozera Diupkun.

References

Archives

AKKKM Archive of the Krasnoiarsk Regional Museum [Arkhiv Krasnoiarskogo Kraevogo Kraevedcheskogo Muzeia], Krasnoiarsk, Russian Federation.

GAKK – State Archive of Krasnoiarsk Territory [Gosudarstvennyi Arkhiv Krasnoiarskogo Kraia], Krasnoiarsk, Russian Federation.

NARS National Archive of the Sakha Republic [Natsional'nyi Arkhiv Respubliki Sakha (Iakutiia)], Iakutsk, Russian Federation.

Published Sources

Anderson, D.G 2009. 'Faith, Identity, and Ethnogenesis: Memory and Belonging among Lake Yessei Yakuts', *Research and Identity: Non-Russian Peoples in the Russian Empire, 1800–1855*, ed. M. Branch Helsinki: SKS Kirjat.

———— 2006. 'The Turukhansk Polar Census Expedition of 1926/27 at the Crossroads of Two Scientific Traditions', *Sibirica* 5(1): 24–61.

———— (ed.) 2005. *Turukhanskaia Ekspeditsiia Pripoliarnogo Perepisi: Etnografiia i Demografiia Malochislennykh Narodov Severa*. Krasnoiarsk: Krasnoiarskii kraevoi kraevedcheskii muzei.

Bjørklund, I. 1990. 'Sami Reindeer Pastoralism as an Indigenous Resource Management System in Northern Norway', *Development and Change* 21: 75–86.

Dolgikh, B.O. 1929. 'Naselenie poluostrova Taimyra i prelegaiushchego k nemu raiona', *Severnaia Aziia* 2: 49–76.

———— 1960. *Rodovoi i plemennoi sostav narodov Sibiri v XVII veke*. Moscow: Nauka.

Dombrowski, K. 1993.'Some Considerations for the Understanding of Small Herd Dynamics in East African Arid Zones: The Long-term Consequences of Bridewealth Exchange Networks', *Human Ecology* 21(1): 23–50.

Humphrey, C. 1979. 'The Uses of Genealogy: A Historical Study of the Nomadic and Sedentarised Buryat', in Equipe écologie et anthropologie des sociétés pastorales (eds), *Pastoral Production and Society*. Cambridge: Cambridge University Press. pp. 235–60.

Suslov, M.I. 1884. 'Putevoi zhurnal missioner Suslova pri poezdke k ozeru Esse'i', *Eniseiskaia eparikhal'naia vedomosti* 13: 182–85, 14:207–11, 19: 262–69, 20: 275–79, 21: 292–96.

Suslov, I.M. 1930. 'Raschet minimal'nogo kolichestva olenei potrebnykh dlia tuzemenykh khoziaistv', *Sovetskii Sever* 3: 29–35.

Tarasenkov, G.N. 1930. *Turukhanskii Krai*. Krasnoiarsk: [no publisher listed].

Vasil'ev, V.N. 1908. 'Kratkii ocherk inorodtsev Turukhanskogo kraia', *Ezhedgodnik Russkogo Antropologicheskogo Obshchestva*. St Petersburg: Sankt Peterburzhskii universitet, pp. 57–87.

Vasilevich, G.M. 1951. 'Esseisko-chiringdinskie evenki (po kollektsiia V.N. Vasil'eva, MAE No. 1004)', *Sbornik Muzeia antropologiia i etnografiia. vyp.* 13: 154–86.

Voronkin, M.S. 1984. *Severo-Zapadnaia gruppa govorov Iakutskogo iazyka.* Iakutsk: Iakutskoe kn. izd-vo.

13

MICRODEMOGRAPHICS AND INDIGENOUS IDENTITY IN THE CENTRAL TAIMYR LOWLANDS

John P. Ziker

Identity and Microdemographics

Identity systems in indigenous and small-scale societies are known to include kinship and marriage systems, exchange networks and larger solidarities, such as lineages, clans and regional groups (Fox 1984; Stone 2000). Human identities can be hierarchically embedded on multiple layers and associated with language and national citizenship, and anthropologists have documented how various identities can be employed depending on social context. When governments become involved in enumerating people with complex identities, census categories are not necessarily congruent with native views.[1] In other words, ways of recording identity and related demographic and economic descriptions are subject to the biases of those people conducting the enumeration. These anomalies are both appealing to scholars of demography and particularly important for indigenous populations. In any case, demographic sources, if sufficiently detailed, have the potential to illuminate indigenous kinship or other identity connections, add to family oral histories, and document traditional land-tenure patterns. Demographic details can also provide indices of population health through time and inform debates about dynamic relationships between states and indigenous populations.

One thesis investigated in this chapter follows from the argument that identity is a social construction. In other words, the information provided in historical demographic sources tells us just as much about the biases of the census takers as it does of the populations they recorded. Nikolai Sorin-Chaikov (2003) demonstrates this argument about the mutually constituting nature of the Russian state and Evenki identity: as the government extended its reach and implemented development plans, the Evenki were portrayed more and more as if they existed outside civilisation.

Another thesis follows from the theory that explicit standards in demographic or other research techniques are necessary for the successful comparative analysis of human societies (Hern 1995; Moran 1995). If, for example, any empirical information has been recorded in a demographic source, changes in identity categories can be redressed, and a picture of the conditions of life can be generated. To the extent that reliable and repeatable information is collected in the present and future, historical census materials will provide a timeline for comparative analysis. Of course, census taking can be sensitive to native identity issues, such as in the Canadian and New Zealand cases (see Kukutai, Hamilton, this volume). In addition, some topics for comparative analysis – exchange, for example – are arguably better studied with more specific techniques, such as focused observational studies of hunters and distribution events. When coupled with demographic and identity data, studies of the effects of policies and politics in a particular region can be more effective, particularly in the areas of land and resource use and demographic health.

The Turukhansk Polar Census expedition of 1926/7 to Siberia produced much empirical data on the economy of the region which can be used as a baseline from which one can look at economic identities today (Anderson 2005). The Polar Census information includes detailed counts of various types of products purchased in government and non-government stores, as well as the numbers of domestic animals held by households, quantities of fur and fish traded, and other indicators.

After initial analysis of the Polar Census materials for the Taimyr lowlands (Ziker 2005), one can find at least two essentials of the mixed economy of 1920s Siberia that continue into the present among the native population. One continuity is the emphasis on non-market exchange within native communities and native social networks. Non-market exchanges are involved in a variety of transactions, such as transfers of food and reindeer to relatives and the poor or orphaned. Another trend is market-orientated exchanges of meat, fish and furs with representatives of the larger regional economy. Such exchanges reached a high point during the 1970s and 1980s – that is, the last twenty years of the Soviet Union – but had diminished by an order of magnitude by the late 1990s (Ziker 1998). Variation in external exchange, as well as variation among households in terms of wealth and success at hunting and herding, and the reasons behind this variation, are all important for understanding social processes in small-scale societies. Following Chayanov (1986 [1925]) one might argue that family reproductive cycles has a lot to do with a family's wealth and success at any given moment. In non-market economies, such as those in the post-Socialist Taimyr lowlands, informal exchange institutions help to create social bonds between families and to ameliorate the vagaries of production cycles (Ziker 2002). On the other hand, the Leninist argument is that differentiation is caused by the development of capitalist economies and the ownership of the means of production. Critical to the development of capitalist economies in the Taimyr lowlands is the sale and export of consumer goods, such as fur. Those who more successfully engaged with the wider Russian economy may have been in a position to capitalize on their position and to begin the process of accumulation of wealth.

Settlement and land-use patterns documented in the 1926/7 Polar Census may turn out to be important for people pursuing use rights with regard to traditional lands. At the very least, such information is important for reclaiming the history of the indigenous population. Many native community members in Taimyr have a good notion of where their grandparents and great-grandparents migrated with domestic reindeer (*argish*) and set up their encampments, and the Polar Census provides written documentation of this. Along with more recent demographic records, such as community registry books (*pokhoziaistvennaia kniga*), the Polar Census provides diachronic demographic comparisons, and clues to identity formation and economic strategies.

The 1926/7 Polar Census collected a vast array of data on individuals, households and communities, and documents a complex and variable array of identities. The census enumerators documented a great degree of ethnic, language, and other identity-based diversity in Taimyr. A re-examination of the census data can help us to assess some of the developments of current native Siberian identity. This historical information could be useful for the living descendants of those recorded in the census, as well as aiding academic understandings of the development of minority ethnic groups in the Russian North. The historical information can be combined with more recent (but much less detailed) censuses to help us understand the homogenisation of identity and the development of permanent settlements for native people across Siberia (Ssorin-Chaikov 2003; Savolskul and Anderson 2005; Anderson 2006).

This chapter reviews data from the 1926/7 Polar Census for central districts in the Taimyr region of Krasnoiarskii Krai. The areas under consideration for this chapter include Khatanga volost', particularly the Piasina, Dudypta, and Kotoi Khatanga watersheds, as well as Dudinka volost', particularly in the Chasovnia area, near present-day Talnakh, and north along the east bank of the Enesei River. Most of Dudinka volost' in 1927 was a thin strip around the Enesei River, and will be considered in so far as the central Taimyr population has historical connections to the area. The historical demographic and economic outline focuses on the Khatanga volost' data; the review of individual cards below includes Dudinka volost'. Many of the people from Dudinka volost' ended up in the Avam tundra and the Ust'-Avam community, established in 1971 in the central Taimyr lowlands. This is the area where my own ethnographic work has been conducted since 1994.

Some basic demographic and economic information is summarised in the first section. Following the statistical description, five household cards are studied for the ethnographic details they contain on households in the area. Links to present-day land tenure, kinship and exchange are explored. The final section provides some contemporary demographic data on the Dolgan and Nganasan population in the Avam tundra area and community of Ust'-Avam. They have been experiencing a demographic bottleneck and various reasons for this are discussed.

Current demographic sources can also help to point to the pitfalls and concerns of a native population dealing with a rapidly changing economy and polity. An overview of current basic demographic indicators for one village in the Taimyr lowlands, Ust'-Avam, elucidates public health issues and sectors of the population most at risk, as well as migration and return migration patterns.

Historical Demographic and Economic Outline

The 1926/7 Polar Census enumerators developed a research instrument that listed a number of forms of identity including native name, Russian name and nationality (*natsional'nost'*), as well as native language, tribe, society/village, clan soviet/administrative district, and native clan name. In some cases, there are multiple languages and nationalities found within one household, indicating some use of multiple identities in the population, multiethnic households, and/or the fact that Yakut was the lingua franca of the area. Household cards including but not limited to the following nationalities were preliminarily surveyed: Dolgany, Dolgany Zarechnye, Zatundrinskie Krest'iany, Samoiedy, Samoiedy Avamskie, Samoiedy Vadeevskie, Tungusy, and Yakuty. The household records give details on household members, settlement patterns, administrative affiliation, and economic activities. Information on native names and monikers, tribal affiliation, native language, and Russian fluency and literacy is also provided.[2] Many of the cards are apparently missing from the archives coded so far, so a full picture of the Avam tundra data from the 1920s is not yet possible. The area is included in the 1926/7 district of Khatanga volost'.

The population listed for Khatanga volost' in 1926/7 is 462. This figure appears to be a significant underestimate of the actual population at that time, which may be due partly to the absence of some Samoied (Nganasan) and Dolgan household cards, the likelihood being that the enumerators were not actually able to survey all households, and that some cards are not yet fully coded. The population demography of Khatanga volost' for the available records shows: a male to female ratio of 103.5 males per one hundred females. Meanwhile, 47 per cent of the population is under age twenty, 42 per cent is between 20 and 54, and 11 per cent is over the age of 55. This distribution appears to be representative of the larger data set for 1927, and is healthy in comparison to the present day, which has seen a steady decrease in fertility rates since 1993 (see below).

The average size of 93 households represented in the household cards for Khatanga volost' is 5.2, with the most common household containing 6 members. The average size of the 109 households recorded for Dudinskaia volost' is 5.1, with the most common household also containing 6 members. These figures are comparable with present-day Tukhard, a reindeer herding community to the west of the Enesei River, where the average household contains 5 members (Ziker 2002: 157).

The attempt to define the economic power of households based on the quantity of reindeer owned was a priority for the 1926/7 census. These data were recorded in the first section of the household card. The collection of this information had tragic consequences years later. The issue of reindeer ownership came to a head during the 1930s, when party workers implementing collectivisation policies used information about the ownership of reindeer as proof of socio-economic differentiation and as a means to disenfranchise large herd owners from the political process. Eventually, this led to the 1931 rebellion in central Taimyr. Thus, the Polar Census provided a road map for identifying the wealthy (*kulaks*) and the politicisation of indigenous households. The Polar Census enumerators did not collect exact statistical data about the individual ownership of reindeer, only ownership according to the household and its head (*khoziain*). This Russian-language term presupposes some right to make decisions about a resource that may be at variance with native concepts of human–resource relationships. The meanings of *khoziain* listed in Ozhegov include: owner (*vladelets*), empowered giver of orders (*rasporiaditel'*), leader of the productive unit/house, a person who uses hired labour, and the term of address reflecting the above (Ozhegov 1986: 752). With the presence of this concept in the enumerators' notes, it is apparent that the formal observation of reindeer herds as a means of making judgments about the economic status of herders had begun already by 1926.

In the Khatanga volost' data there were approximately 3,500 domestic reindeer distributed among eighty households, giving an average of 44 reindeer per household.[3] There were only 2 households that possessed no reindeer; 17 households had up to 10 reindeer; 33 households had between 11 and 29 reindeer; 15 households had between 30 and 49 reindeer; 8 households had between 50 and 100 reindeer; and 5 households had more than 100 reindeer. These figures show a slightly biased distribution of reindeer among households, with the modal number of households the 11-to–29 reindeer category (while the average was 44). Most families had below-average-size reindeer herds, and a few families had fairly large herds.

A more fine-grained investigation should focus on the relationship between household size, extended household cooperation and herd size in order to determine the relationships that large herd owners had with owners of medium-sized and small herds. It is likely that the owners of larger herds were the named heads of larger extended families, other relatives and apprentices, all of whom received resources from the collective herd. The demographics of reindeer herds and exchange patterns documented in the census attest to these networks beyond the family.

The Polar Census also provides data on reindeer-herd demographics. This is interesting because it roughly reflects local terminology and management concerns about domestic reindeer. In Khatanga volost' it appears that reindeer are largely used for transportation (with 1,888 animals so used). According to data in the category 'reproductive status among male reindeer,' 1,093 were castrates and 94 were reproductive bulls. This high number of castrates also indicates the importance of transportation for this population. Those households involved in trade across the region most likely used more non-reproductive males, docile and strong. There where 1,224 cows. Queries of 'reindeer by reproductive status' and 'reindeer by use' listed 471 reindeer between one and two years of age, and 636 reindeer calves younger than one year, indicating strong fertility rates.

The Polar Census also provides information on fishing in the region. The data show interesting variation according to the type of fish and quantity caught. Households with intermediate quantities of reindeer caught the most fish, and more fish of the most valuable variety (the so-called 'red fish'). In comparison with other districts of the Turukhansk region, few households in the central Taimyr lowlands practised fishing as their sole type of economic activity. Households with few reindeer and households with many reindeer fished the least. Households with no reindeer fished somewhat more than those with one to ten reindeer, however. This might be expected, since there would be no way to procure food other than by foot. Currently, in one reindeer-herding community in Taimyr, when asked what happens to a reindeer herder that loses all his reindeer, informants say he is 'sitting by the river', implying that he is fishing and possibly participating in some trade, as rivers are important routes of transport in both the summer and winter.

The few families who owned more than one hundred reindeer in 1926/7 were largely involved in the distribution of consumer goods across the region, as will be shown below. Many of the larger reindeer herders apparently worked for government organisations and co-ops in transporting goods to people in the tundra and returning with commodities produced by the native population. A cursory overview of the goods purchased and items sold to trading organisations during the 1920s shows strikingly similar patterns to those of contemporary residents in central Taimyr. Many households in Khatanga volost' obtained their goods through government trade organisations, according to the Polar Census. Items commonly purchased during 1926 and 1927 include flour, sugar, tea and tobacco. In addition, furs, fish and meat were supplied to government stores, either directly or through households involved in transportation.

The data reviewed above shows that the Polar Census provides a baseline from which certain demographic comparisons can be made and consumer patterns analysed. Age/sex distributions and household size are good examples of this approach with available Siberian materials, both historical and current. While being incredibly rich in some respects, the

1926/7 data are limiting in some ways in comparison to current data from household registries. For example, the sex of individuals born and deceased was collected in 1926/7, as well as that of individuals migrating in or out of the household over the previous two years, but ages were not recorded. Thus, age-specific mortality rates for 1924/5 can only be estimated using the available rough categories (child versus adult) in the historic materials. This line of analysis is important when considering the second thesis of this chapter, namely that standards facilitate the comparative analysis of human societies.

The 1926/7 Polar Census also provides information that reflects indigenous concerns about, and the language used to describe, reindeer herds. On the other hand, the use of terms such as *khoziain* in the household cards reveals the use of preconceived notions about property imported from the Russian language. Information on amounts and types of goods purchased and sold in government and cooperative stores also reflects the growing concern of the authorities about economic matters. These lines of evidence supports the first thesis about the mutually constitutive nature of indigenous groups and the states within which they live.

Land-use Patterns, Identities and Economic Activities

A small but noteworthy component of the 1926/7 Polar Census materials is the section for supplementary notes on community forms and household cards. These can be read as mini ethnographies. In this section, I want to highlight five household cards in particular, bringing into view general observations about ethnic identity, land use and economic activities. This set of case studies gives a lively representation of life at the time of the census and examples which can be linked to the present. In the future, statistical analysis of Polar Census entries on seasonal encampments of each household could help to identify relationships and structures affecting land and resource use, if coupled with information on household production and trade. For now, these cases illustrate a range of socioeconomic wealth and identity affiliation.

Household 1

This household is headed by Vitalii Aleksandrovich Barkhatov, sixty years old.[4] His native language is Yakut, and his nationality is listed as 'peasant of the Zatundrinskii community'. Occupation: reindeer herder. Encampment locations: Ikon River (winter); Piasina River and Vvendenskii station (spring, summer, and autumn). Barkhatov is living with his daughter, and has five reindeer. The enumerator, N.A. Ostroumov, wrote in his notes: 'The interviewee lives by the generosity of the whole society. He does not trap arctic fox, and he does not fish'.

Ostroumov makes mention of the traditional system of social support but focuses on what Barkhatov did not do. It would be interesting to know who supported Vitalii Barkhatov and his daughter, and how. The ethic of supporting poor community members exists today among the Dolgan and Nganasan populations in central Taimyr (Ziker 2002: 139–40). In the 1930s, however, such documentation of social generosity was turned on its head to emphasise exploitation of the poor by the rich (ibid., 79–80). Despite his poverty, Barkhatov was able to maintain five reindeer and use them to migrate into a more protected highland valley during the winter.

The family name Barkhatov is found among people who are considered Dolgan in central Taimyr today. Ostroumov described the Vitalii as a Zatundrinskii peasant. It would be interesting to know whether Ostroumov's (or Barkhatov's) choice of this term was connected with the old administrative name, Russian ancestry, or the fact that 'peasant' sounded more appropriate for a poor person.

Household 2

This household is headed by Mikhail Isakovich Suslov, twenty-six years old.[5] His native language is listed as Dolgan, and his nationality as Samoied. The Suslov family includes Mikhail's wife, Elena Ivanovna, and two children. Elena is listed as a Tungus by nationality. Suslov was active in fishing, reindeer herding and hunting. They lived at either Tulai-kamen' or on the shore of Lake Piasinao during the spring and summer, on the river Valek (near present-day Talnakh) during the fall, and in the area of Lake Glubokoe during the winter. Suslov's nickname is listed as Monto. Ostroumov recorded his nationality in a peculiar way: Khantaiskii Samoied – today known as Entsy, they traditionally lived to the north of the Piasina area along the Enesei River. The information was recorded at Chasovnia station, where there was a Russian Orthodox outpost and Dolgan community. Monto hunted arctic hare, arctic fox, and wild reindeer, and also sold over 100 'blue' fox pelts to cooperative and state trading posts.[6] He owned twelve reindeer, which is a fairly small number. During the year he purchased many goods, however, including fifty *pudy* (817 kilos) of flour, a shotgun and strychnine (the latter was possibly used to poison furbearers or predators). He did not have any debts recorded. It would be surprising if a family of four could consume 800 kilos of flour before it spoiled. What Monto did with the flour is also a mystery, although he likely supplied other community members in need or in trade for furs.

In 1996, I heard a story about Monto from an elderly woman, Aksinia Maksimovna Bezrukikh (from the Dolgan clan Edian), who grew up at Chasovnia station. She called the story 'My Enets Uncle' (*Hamai Ehem*):

> Monto and his older brother Paikasi lived in the area of Gol'chikha. The brothers became orphaned, and began to live with their father's brother, who did not feed them and threatened to build a *liat'* (burial teepee) for them, as he built for their parents. They ate what they caught and found. The brothers decided to run away: they took eight reindeer and found the

Dolgan, who were pasturing reindeer not far from a Russian merchant. Monto and Paikasi accepted Christianity and Monto married a woman of that community. Later, the wife of Monto died, and he married the aunt of Aksinia Maksimovna who raised her. Monto had two children, who were moved with their families to Levenskie Peski in 1967.

The story helps clarify the complex nature of Dolgan identity. Here we see three processes that continue today: inter-ethnic marriages, settlement and the administrative reclassification of ethnic identity. Aksinia used the term (and language family) *hamai* – the Dolgan word for Nganasan – which parallels the older state classification, Samoied. Enumerator Ostroumov noted Monto's native language was Dolgan and he ascribed Monto to the old tribute unit Khantaiskii Samoied, suggesting membership in a multi-ethnic group. Monto and his Tungus wife had children who were identified as Samoied in the 1926/7 Polar Census. In 1967, Monto and his family and many other families from the upper Piasina River were moved by the government to the community of Levenskie Peski (across the Enesei River from Dudinka) known today as a Dolgan community. Some people from the upper Piasinao River moved northeast to Ust'-Avam. Similarly, today many people in the Avam tundra trace their ancestry to both Dolgan, Enets and Nganasan.

Household 3

Petr Tuglakov, sixty years old, heads this household.[7] His nationality was left blank, but tribe and language were recorded as Samoied. He was a reindeer herder and considered among the Samoieds to be middle class, according to N.A. Ostroumov's notes. Petr's native name, Avra, was recorded. They also belonged to the Khantaiskii tribute administrative unit. The household was reported to own 163 reindeer, winter and summer *chumy* (teepees), freight and riding sleighs, harnesses, six herding dogs, and six fishing nets. It was reported that he had lent out ten reindeer to 'various' people. According to the record, in 1926 the family camped at Mokhovaia Laida in the spring and Dikson Island and Efremov Kamen' in the summer, returning to Mokhovaia Laida in the fall and the area near Dudinka in the winter. Avra lived with his wife, son, daughter-in-law and grandson. Kurumaku, Avra's grandson, was three years old in 1927. In 2003, Kurumaku Tuglakov, the oldest man living in Ust'-Avam, told me that his parents were Enets, migrating from the area of Voronstovo, a well-known Enets community in the ethnographic literature (see Levin and Potapov 1964). In 1926, the Tuglakovs reported procuring and selling at the trading post: three pelts of arctic hare, four arctic fox, and wild reindeer meat from ten animals, together worth 356 roubles. They purchased goods totalling 487 roubles, including, fifty *pudy* of flour, tea, sugar, tobacco, salt, candles, powder and shot. The household card shows no debt for these purchases, however.

This account of Petr Tuglakov underscores three important processes: seasonal mobility; exchange of trade goods with and between communities;

and reliance on extended family networks. During their yearly transhumant migration, the Tuglakovs covered an enormous amount of territory
along the Enesei River to the Kara Sea, hundreds of kilometres. To cover this
distance, several teams of reindeer were needed. Throughout the year these
and other reindeer would need constant attention, especially during the
summer. This attention would be supplied by other members of the Mokhovaia Laida community. Second, despite the long trip, subsistence and herding requirements, as well as surplus production, Tuglakov obtained enough
fur and meat to sell. The surplus was used to buy goods imported to the
region. Either he was a phenomenal hunter and herder or had the assistance
of relatives and friends in the tundra. Third, despite the fact that this case
was presented as a separate household, there was a big clan of Tuglakovs
at Mokhovaia Laida described on many household cards. Amongst these
households were many complex kinship relations and economic relationships that the individual household cards do not elaborate on. These may
help to explain the large quantity of flour purchased and the apparently
negative balance sheet for the Tuglakov household that year. In any case,
the fact that no debts accrued implies a more complex relationship between
traders and middlemen with the remainder of the native population than
the later collectivist propaganda would portray.

Household 4

This household was headed by Kapiton Mikhailovich Ioldagyr', fifty-
three years old.[8] His native language is listed as Tungus, as is his nationality. His native name is Motok. In 1926 Kapiton's household pastured
their reindeer in the Kotoi River and Ilimpeiskii volost'. In Ust'-Avam and
central Taimyr there are now descendants of a Kapiton Elogir', according to whom Kapiton's nickname was *hetta karmannak*, or 'eight pockets',
because he was prosperous. The details do not quite match, but it is possible that Kapiton Elogir' and Kapiton Mikhailovich Ioldagyr' are the same
person, since Kapiton ('eight pockets') is known to have come from the
Putoran mountains – the northern part of the old tribute unit of Ilimpeiskii
volost'. In 1926 Kapiton Mikhailovich Ioldagyr' lived with his wife, son,
three daughters and a sister. Kapiton's household also contained two
young men who were herding apprentices. They also were considered
Tungus, one also an Ioldagyr', likely making them relatives of some kind.
According to the household card, Kapiton owned 460 reindeer at the time
of the census.

In his notes, enumerator N.P. Naumov shows his negative judgment of
Kapiton's economic activities:

> The number of reindeer was indicated by the owner. According to testimony
> of neighbours, the amount of reindeer (with fawns) reaches 600. This is the
> more exact figure. It shows the turnover of the herd, where the outflow of
> reindeer (which is easier to count exactly) exceeds the yield. According to

the owner and neighbours, the herd, in fact, grows every year. All winter the owner is busy with transporting flour to lakes Chirindu and Ekondu: this year he brought twenty-two sleighs to Ekondu and thirty sleighs to Chirindu, from November through April. He is forced to hire workers whom he pays very poorly. Their grub costs him about eighty to ninety roubles per year (less than shown on the community form). He pays them with old clothes and second-rate reindeer.

However, contradicting the tenor of the first note there is another on the card that says that Kapiton gave ten reindeer to poor Tungus families. In a year, the household of Kapiton Ioldagyr' sold to cooperative stores 1,300 squirrel pelts, 40 ermine pelts, and 8 arctic fox pelts. Kapiton bought many goods (in the winter of 1926/7 he spent 1,000 roubles), including three sacks (*kul'*, a dry measure approximately equal to between 82 and 147 kilos) of rye flour, four *kul'* of wheat flour, five *pudy* of toast, one *pudy* of sugar, as well as tea, tobacco, salt, cotton cloth and wool felt cloth. Also, he bought two thousand caps for percussion muskets, one shotgun, a copper kettle, and a copper teapot. Why he did not purchase any shot is open to interpretation. It could be that they were smelting their own locally.

This case clearly shows the negative nature of the relationship between Naumov and a well-off reindeer herder and trader. The fact that Kapiton sold 1,300 squirrel pelts (although he caught only twenty according to the household card) could be an indicator of exploitation. However, it is equally as likely that he was a well-respected and important local natural leader as he collected pelts from relatives and friends and brought them in exchange for indispensable supplies that he brought back to his relations. It is apparent that Kapiton was an enterprising person who also helped various families.

Household 5

Finally, the household of Aleksei Ivanovich Bezrukikh, sixty years old.[9] His native language and nationality is listed as Tungus, and his native name is Koinonga. Koinonga is a widower, and he alone is listed on the household card. Ostroumov noted that earlier he lived in the Third Letniaia Tungusskaia Uprava, but had joined the Dolgan of the Zarechnoi Uprava. His wife died during 1924/5. The household card notes that the indigenous name of his clan is Yaksat. This clan name is also listed by Dolgikh (1963: 139), but elder Bezrukikh informants in Ust'-Avam did not recognise this name during my 1997 fieldwork. Koinonga owned fourteen reindeer, and pastured them during the spring, summer and autumn near the Sarikha River, which is located to the east of the Enesei gulf. He also trapped and fished, selling arctic fox pelts worth 296 roubles. The Bezrukikh's winter camping area was left blank, but it was most likely somewhere in the Zarechnoi Uprava (east of the Piasina River) – the community in which he had registered. Ostroumov wrote that Koinonga was the father-in-law of Nikolai Sokolo, who helped him. It is possible that Koinonga was the brother of Grigorii Ivanovich Bezrukikh, whose two sons had big families with many living descendants in the communities of Ust'-Avam and Volochanka, and who are considered Dolgan.

It is interesting that there is no information about Grigorii Ivanovich Bezrukikh in the existing household cards. He reportedly had many reindeer, and lived until arrested in 1937. His contemporary descendants say he came to central Taimyr from another district to the west. Aleksei Bezrukikh's card is likely to be a shred from the larger history of the Bezrukikh family. The card confirms that the family came from another area to the north-west, even though they were considered earlier to be members of the Third Letniaia Tunguskaia Uprava (to the south from the central Taimyr lowlands). This also correlates with family history. The document also hints at the economic support that members of the extended family showed one another. The household card underscores the dynamic use of large territories, some of which could have been a response to the changing political climate. In this context, the tsarist-era administrative-ethnic identities began to lose their relevance as people were migrating vast distances and affiliating with social units with whom they could cooperate.

In these five cases, demographic information coupled with socio-economic information for households provides a complex picture of land and resource use, social organisation, and identity for the central Taimyr lowlands in the mid 1920s. Generosity is mentioned for all five cases. The Barkhatovs, Suslovs and Bezrukikhs were recipients of generosity from other community members, and the Tuglakovs and Ioldagyrs were sources of generosity for other, poorer community members. These scant remarks barely scratch the surface of the indigenous social economy of the 1920s. Indigenous institutions encouraging non-monetary transfers of food and reindeer to the poor, orphaned and relatives continue today (see also Anderson, this volume).

The 1926/7 Polar Census provides documentation of market-oriented exchanges of meat, fish and fur for consumer products, generally carbohydrate-rich foodstuffs, and hunting and fishing implements from representatives of the larger regional economy. While this relationship was intensified and formally institutionalised during the Soviet Union in the form of *kolkhozy, sovkhozy* and a *gospromkhoz* in Taimyr, more casual exchange relationships have again developed since the 1991 transformation of the Soviet planned economy.

Transhumant pastoralism was important in all cases. The number of reindeer required for mobility is surprisingly low. The Barkhatovs, a family with five reindeer, was able to migrate. With twelve reindeer, the Suslovs migrated three times a year and were a possible source of food for other households through sharing or trade. Alexei Bezrukikh had fourteen reindeer and migrated from the Putoran plateau in the south to the high tundra in the north of Dudinskaia volost'.

The sharing of locally hunted, fished and gathered foods is highly significant in the lives of the Dolgan and Nganasan. Foraging has sustained these people and their ancestors from prehistoric times to the postsocialist present, but the social relations surrounding subsistence and mobility allow for a variety of success stories. Ironically, recent economic transformations geared towards free-market capitalism, privatisation and the disbanding of state enterprises (*sovkhozy*), and influxes of consumer goods and services from abroad and within the Commonwealth of Independent States (CIS), have only increased the importance of subsistence among these indigenous peoples. Native people living at some distance from urban sources of consumer goods, such as the central Taimyr, spend considerable effort securing a local food supply. Many families depend on relatives and friends who are good producers, as they receive meat and fish through personal sharing networks (Ziker 2002: 47–53). In addition, families and extended relatives are known to pool their money to obtain items of use for the wider family, such as a rifles and snowmobiles.

Demographics and Health

The native communities of central Taimyr, along with those in many areas of the Russian North, have experienced many difficulties resulting from the economic and political turmoil of 1990s (Gray 2003; Ventsel 2005; Crate 2006). This comes after sixty years of Soviet rule and the development of industrial-scale rural enterprises. By the late 1970s, Soviet development had resulted in the complete disappearance of reindeer herding in central Taimyr. My informants view this loss of traditional livelihood, identity and independence as tragic. In the 1970s new housing and job opportunities in the hunting enterprises were attractive to local residents, and the system was supported with technological advances and budget subsidies from government ministries. After the fall of the USSR, residents did not have either Soviet-era economies of scale or traditional means of transportation.

Having lost all domesticated reindeer, villages in central Taimyr became highly dependent on imported equipment goods, and jobs provided by the state. Traditional hunting practices, which relied largely on animal and human-driven power, were less productive in the eyes of the state than industrial-scale hunting, but much more self-sufficient. With the collapse of the Soviet Union in the early 1990s, most men in the study community were laid off from their jobs as hunters and fishermen with the disbanding of state enterprises by President Boris Yeltsin (Van Atta 1993). At the same time, mortalities due to accidents, poisoning, murder and suicide became an increasing problem. Community members blamed uncontrolled sales of alcohol and binge drinking for many of the deaths (Ziker 2002).

The purpose of this review of the census data is to examine the demographic health of one community of 600 or 700 indigenous people in the central Taimyr lowlands, focusing on fertility and mortality rates, and causes of mortality. Since Soviet times, communities throughout rural areas have maintained community registry books (*pokhoziaistvennaia kniga*) enumerating the individuals and families registered to live there. This demographic source book was the community record of those registered to reside (*propiska*) and provides a standardised starting point. In the present case, the community made available the registry book, and now computer list, for this research. Another source of information was the records of the community doctor on causes of death, and the village administration record of those for whom death certificates were issued. Censuses were also made available to me for the years of 1997, 2001 and 2002, and causes of death were available back to 1986 in Ust'-Avam.[10]

Causes of death are categorised as natural and non-natural. 'Non-natural' causes of death include accidents, poisoning, trauma, homicide and suicide , while a 'natural' death is classified as a fatality due to infectious or internal maladies (Vishnevskii 1999: 83). Many non-natural deaths, as well as some natural deaths, in Ust'-Avam are known to have occurred as a result of alcohol consumption. Alcohol-use patterns are known to contribute to non-natural deaths in a variety of indigenous communities (Saggers and Gray 1998). The effect of alcohol on mortality rates in Russia is corroborated by a recent study in Udmurtia (Shkolnikov et al. 2004).

In the central Taimyr settlement of Ust'-Avam, between 1998 and 2002, 34 of 48 deaths (over 70 per cent) were due to non-natural causes. Overall, the five-year average annual mortality rate was 2.3 per cent. There is no significant difference in the causes of death between Dolgan and Nganasan ethnic sub-groups within the community. These data reflect little improvement in community mortality rates compared to the period between 1991 and 1997, during which 60 per cent of deaths were violent (Ziker 2002: 97) and the overall mortality rate was 0.026. The only independent variable that showed any significant relationship to cause of death was age of the deceased (R squared = 0.373, p <0.001). Non-natural death is concentrated in the younger age groups, especially for males. Natural causes of death are concentrated in the elder age groups. An independent samples T-test confirmed that the likelihood of non-natural death is significantly greater for individuals under the age of 50 (T = 8.287, p < 0.001). Multiple regression of independent variables onto the cause of death showed no other relationships. The independent variables tested include: the number of household members employed, the relative involvement of the family in hunting and access to hunting territory, previous violent death in the family, as well as sex, age, ethnicity, and the level of education of the deceased.

The Ust'-Avam census materials also allowed an analysis of community fertility trends. From the late 1980s through the 1990s and into the early 2000s, fertility rates decreased: the average effective fertility rate (EFR) in Ust'-Avam between 1987 and 1993 was 0.73, and between 1994 and 1997 was 0.57 (Ziker 2002: 92–93). The EFR decreased to 0.33 in 2002.[11]

The number of births during the period between 1991 and 1997 (n =

115) was compared with those for the period 1998 to 2003 (n = 40) considering ethnic identity listed in the village registration book. Nganasan women had significantly fewer births in the more recent period (T = 2.266, p < 0.05). There was no significant difference for Dolgan women.

Finally, in comparing fertility and mortality, one can see the depth of the problem for the community. The average five-year birth rate for Ust'-Avam was 10.8 per 1,000 people, while the average five-year mortality rate was 15.2 per 1,000 people.

During the 1990s and early 2000s, the native population of the central Taimyr lowlands – particularly the Nganasan – appeared to be going through a demographic bottleneck. Unnatural death has been a serious problem among indigenous Siberians since settlement in villages during the 1960s, when childhood illness was a greater health threat (Bogoyavlenskii 1997; Krupnik 1997). From 1998 to 2002, rates of non-natural mortality have increased over that for 1993 to 1997, as have fertility rates.

With the collapse of the planned economy in the 1990s, greater periods of inactivity led to binge drinking, occurring on days people received government payments or salaries. In Ust'-Avam, spending money on alcohol has further impoverished a poor population bringing on a demoralised atmosphere. Hunting lands that were regularly accessible with domesticated reindeer until the 1970s are now inaccessible to a population consolidated into larger communities and reliant upon the snowmobile. With the loss of state support for mechanised travel in the 1990s, and the earlier loss of traditional economic institutions, such as those that existed in Siberian native communities during the Soviet era, demographic and identity changes have been heightened. This has led some to assert that the Nganasan are disappearing into a mixed Dolgan and Nganasan population that speaks Russian (e.g., Krivonogov 1990).

Regional government programmes introduced in 2006 and 2007 have improved the situation by providing payments to men and women involved in hunting, fishing and trapping in the tundra, and by hiring unemployed people during the summer for village clean-ups. At the local level, some people have tried hypnosis and have been successful in quitting drinking. In some villages, the word is that hypnosis has worked for many people and that binge drinking is not as common.

Conclusions

Current demographic sources, such as community registry books, in central Taimyr, when used as snapshots over time, can highlight the health issues of a native population dealing with a rapidly changing economic and political structure. These changes can affect identity. Today, village-level identity is becoming predominant in everyday conversation across the region, and people speak of 'Ust'-Avamskie', people from Ust'-Avam, and 'Krestovskie', people from Kresty. There is much evidence for the first thesis of this chapter that enumeration of native peoples goes hand in hand with development and changes in identity.

When comparing current demographic sources with historical ones, such as the 1926/7 Polar Census, some problems stem from the lack of resolution of some categories in the historical source. On the other hand, the Polar Census provides a wealth of ethnographic, economic and demographic data and information on settlement patterns. Current targeted techniques may better describe some of these rubrics, such as economic cooperation, but the historical Polar Census data does provide a link to the past for researchers and native people themselves. Importantly, fine-grained census data helps scholars to understand variation among households, and the reasons behind this variation, in order to better describe social processes in small-scale societies. The historical demographic and socio-economic outline, and the mini ethnographies discussing land use, identity and economic activities, both derived from the Polar Census data, as well as the modern demographic and health data reviewed here, support the idea that empirical standards in ethnographic research are beneficial for cross-cultural research. On the other hand, it is clear from the historical data that the information provided in the 1926/7 Polar Census is skewed by the terminology and categories that the census takers employed. Such skewing can be identified and corrected in order to make use of the valuable information the census contains and which can help us understand social, economic and political processes occurring in human populations. Modern censuses, making use of specific standards of data collection, can be of use to compare populations over time or across geographic areas. These demographic comparisons can be useful for finding threats to the health of native peoples and other effects of large-scale economic change, providing evidence for the second line of argument in this chapter.

Notes

The material discussed in this chapter is based upon work supported by a National Science Foundation-funded project 'Home, Hearth, and Household in Siberia and Northern Canada' (grant no. 0631970), which forms part of a European Science Foundation Eurocores BOREAS collaborative research project entitled 'Home, Hearth and Household in the Circumpolar North'. Parts of this chapter first appeared in Ziker (2005). The demographic and health data were presented at the workshop on Indigenous Identity and Demographic Sources, Centre for Population Studies, Umeå University, in September 2006. I thank Will Palmer for his comments on the manuscript and David Anderson for making available an electronic version of the Turukhansk household cards.

1.   'Identity' is defined as sameness of character across instances, sameness in the reality of a thing, or the distinguishing characteristic of an individual or group (*Merriam Webster's* 1997: s.v.). Social categories, such as 'ethnic group', and the

concept of ethnicity describe a quality of, or affiliation with, a person's people (Brown 1988).

2. The information described below is for household cards coded into a database built with funding through the Baikal Archaeology Project. Electronic images of household cards for what is today Taimyr have been examined. These are hard to read on the computer screen, and thus, most of this preliminary discussion is based on the searchable ACCESS database (www.baikal.arts.ualberta.ca/polarcensus).

3. The total number of reindeer (3,438) for Khatanga volost' given in column 92c of the household cards is slightly different than the total calculated from the constituent data on the number of reindeer by reproductive status (3,518) and the number of reindeer by use (3,504). Nevertheless, these three sources give a consistent picture of the importance of reindeer herding in the population at that time, overall characteristics of reindeer herds, and the relationship of families to reindeer numbers

4. See fond P769, opis 1, dela 415, pp. 025–026, TPC/GAKK. Hereafter, materials from this collection will be listed by fond–opis–dela reference, followed by page numbers.

5. See P769–1–414, pp. 003–004, TPC/GAKK.

6. 'Blue' fox were raised in captivity during the period of the Soviet Union for their pelts, but they also occur in the wild in small quantities.

7. See P769–1–422, pp. 029–030, TPC/GAKK.

8. See P769–1–416, pp. 103–104, TPC/GAKK

9. See P769–1–412, pp. 103–104, TPC/GAKK.

10. Data for the period between 1970 and 1985 is courtesy of Dmitrii Bogoyavlenskii, from an earlier registration book.

11. Effective fertility rate is calculated by counting the number of children under the age of 5 and dividing by the number of women between the ages of 15 and 49.

References

Archives

TPC/GAKK – Turukhansk Polar Census Documents, State Archive, Krasnoiarsk, Krasnoiarsk Territory.

Published Sources

Anderson, D.G. 2006. 'The Turukhansk Polar Census Expedition of 1926–27 at the Crossroads of Two Scientific Traditions,' *Sibirica* 5(1): 24–61.

———— (ed.) 2005. *Turukhanskaia Ekspeditsia Pripoliarnoi Perepisi: Etnografiia i Demografia Malochislennykh Narodov Severe*. Krasnoiarsk: Krasnoiarsk Regional Studies Museum.

Bogoyavlenskii, D.D. and Michael Volshonsk. 1997. 'Native Peoples of Kamchatka: Epidemiological Transition and Violent Death', *Arctic Anthropology* 34(1): 57–67.

Brown, D.E. 1988. *Hierarchy, History, and Human Nature: The Social Origins of Historical Consciousness*. Tucson: University of Arizona Press.

Chayanov, A.V. 1986[1925]. *The Theory of Peasant Economy*. Madison, WI: University of Wisconsin Press.

Crate, S. 2006. *Cows, Kin, and Globalization: An Ethnography of Globalization*. Lanham, MD: AltaMira Press.

Dolgikh, B.O. 1963. 'Proiskhozhdenie Dolgan', in B.O. Dolgikh (ed.), *Sibirskii Etnograficheskii Sbornik V, Trudy Instituta Etnografii im. N.N. Miklukho-Maklaia*. Moscow: Izdatel'stvo Akademii Nauk SSSR, pp. 92–141.

Fox, R. 1984. *Kinship and Marriage: An Anthropological Perspective*. Cambridge: Cambridge University Press.

Gray, P. 2003. *The Predicament of Chukotka's Indigenous Movement: Post-Soviet Activism in the Russian Far North*. Cambridge: Cambridge University Press.

Hern, W.M. 1995. 'Micro-ethnodemographic Techniques for Field Workers Studying Small Groups', in E.F. Moran (ed.), *The Comparative Analysis of Human Societies: Toward Common Standards for Data Collection and Reporting*. Boulder, CO: Rienner, pp. 129–48.

Krivonogov, N.V. 1990. 'Contemporary Ethno Cultural Processes of Nganasan', *Ethnos and Culture* 1: 67–78.

Krupnik, I.I. 1987. 'Demograficheskoe Razvitie Aziatskikh Eskimosov v 1970-e Gody (Osnovnye Tendentsii i Etnosotsial'nye Uslovia),' in V.V. Prokhorov (ed.), *Regional'nye Problemy Sotsial'no-Demograficheskogo Razvitia*. Moscow: Institut Sotsiologicheskogo Issledovaniia, AH CCCP, pp. 85–110.

Levin M.G., and L.P. Potapov. 1964. *The Peoples of Siberia*. Chicago: University of Chicago Press.

Moran, E.F. (ed.) 1995. *The Comparative Analysis of Human Societies: Toward Common Standards for Data Collection and Reporting*. Boulder, CO: Rienner.

Ozhegov, S.I. 1986. *Slovar' Russkogo Iazyka*. Moskva: Russkii Iazyk.

Saggers, S., and D. Gray. 1998. *Dealing with Alcohol: Indigenous Usage in Australia, New Zealand, and Canada*. Cambridge: Cambridge University Press.

Savolskul, S., and D. Anderson. 2005. 'An Ethnographer's Early Years: Boris Dolgikh as Enumerator for the 1926–27 Polar Census', *Polar Record* 41: 235–51.

Shkolnikov, V., V.V. Chervyakov, M. McKee and D.A. Leon. 2004. 'Russian Mortality Beyond Vital Statistics,' *Demographic Research, Special Collection 2, Article 4*. Rostock, Germany: Max Planck Institute for Demographic Research.

Ssorin-Chaikov, N. 2003. *The Social Life of the State in Subarctic Siberia*. Stanford, CA: Stanford University Press.

Stone, L. 2000. *Kinship and Gender: An Introduction*. Boulder, CO: Westview Press.

Van Atta, D. 1993. 'Yeltsin Decree Finally Ends "Second Serfdom" in Russia,' *RFE/RL Research Report* 2(46): 33–39.

Ventsel, A. 2005. *Reindeer, Rodina, and Reciprocity: Kinship and Property Relations in a Siberian Village.* Berlin: Lit Verlag.

Vishnevskii, A.G. (ed.).1999. *Naselenie Russiia 1998.* Moscow: Institut Narodnokhoziaistvennogo Prognozirovaniia RAN Tsentr Demograhpii i Ekologii Cheloveka.

Ziker, J. 1998. 'Kinship and Exchange among the Dolgan and Nganasan of Northern Siberia', *Research in Economic Anthropology* 19: 191–238.

―――― 2002. *Peoples of the Tundra: Native Siberians in the Post Communist Transition.* Prospect Heights, IL: Waveland.

―――― 2005. 'Tsentral'naia Taimyrskaia Nizmennost' v 1926–27 gg.: Samosoznanie i Sezonnyi Tsikl Peredvizheniia Korennykh Narodov,' in D. Anderson (ed.), *Turukhanskaia Ekspeditsia Pripoliarnoi Perepisi: Etnografiia i Demografia Malochislennykh Narodov Severe.* Krasnoiarsk: Krasnoiarsk Regional Studies Museum, pp. 79–87.

14

RUSSIAN LEGAL CONCEPTS AND THE DEMOGRAPHY OF INDIGENOUS PEOPLES

Sergey V. Sokolovskiy

The purpose of this chapter is to trace the conceptual construction of the Russian category of 'small-numbered indigenous peoples' and the influences of their legal status on identity politics, which in turn causes significant fluctuations in demographic dynamics.

In Russian political discourse, 'indigeneity' is not only a qualitative characteristic of a particular category of ethnic communities and individual persons.[1] It also has a quantitative dimension, and is sometimes represented as possessing multiple levels and gradations in intensity. Political discourse and the categorisation of population groups overlap to a significant extent with legal discourse because political categorisation tends to be institutionalised in legal concepts.

One of the examples that immediately comes to mind in this respect is the position of Nogai within the indigenous peoples group of Dagestan. According to the federal law 'On guarantees of the rights of indigenous numerically small peoples of the Russian Federation' (1999),[2] the right to form a list of indigenous minority peoples in Dagestan, due to the complexity of the ethnic composition of its population, 'belongs to the State Council of the republic with subsequent inclusion of this list into the Unified list of the indigenous small-numbered peoples of the Russian Federation'.[3] The Dagestan State Council's list of the indigenous peoples of Dagestan includes all the major ethnic categories of the republic's population: Avars, Azeri, Darghins, Nogai and Russians among them, each numbering hundreds of thousands.[4] The inclusion of Nogai in the list has been debated, not on the grounds that their number exceeds the legally established threshold of 50, 000, but because they arrived to the region 'only at the end of the fifteenth century', which was considered by some of their opponents insufficient to obtain the status of an autochthonous people.[5] Another example from the end of the 1980s concerns the Sakha (Yakut) of the Sakha Republic, whose indigenous status was contested on the grounds of their presumably 'late arrival' in the region.

Thus, the question of who is the most autochthonous among various inhabitants of a certain region has relevance and political salience and often serves as a battleground for competing claimants. Internationally known examples from the former Soviet Union include the regions of Karabakh (contested by Armenians and Azeris), South Ossetia (contested by Georgians and Ossetians), Galskiy district in Abkhazia (contested by Georgians and Abkhazians), the Prigorodnyi district in North Ossetia (contested by Ossetians and Ingush) and literally hundreds of less familiar cases from the Caucasus, Central Asia, Volga-Urals, Southern Siberia and the Far East. These conflicts are fired by mutual territorial claims of neighbouring ethnic groups, supported by discourses of indigeneity, which in turn lead to heated debates about who came first to a region and who came later.[6]

In terms of historical succession ('original inhabitants' versus groups that arrived later), the quantitative character of indigeneity in some regions becomes linked to the genealogical depth of competing resident groups. Less evident is the factor of the scope of contested territory. One might argue that we are all indigenous to this planet; many may legitimately claim that they are indigenous to the continents they still inhabit. Most Europeans, Asians and Africans could be successfully tested to verify such a claim, though this would be difficult for many groups in North and South America and Australia.[7] It seems that the smaller the region, the less historically likely are claims by contemporaries to be descended from the earliest occupants of a place, unless we want to restrict the concept of indigeneity to more recent generations and substantiate it by using the often-biased sources of written history.[8] The aforementioned case of Sakha is complicated by the fact that over 60 per cent of the republic's native population were not born in the district in which they live (Fedorova 1999: 84), and thus technically are not indigenous to the administrative territories they inhabit.[9] The indigenous peoples of the Sakha Republic – Evenki, Even, Chukchi, Yukagir – have historically moved to the territories they now inhabit from more southern and western locations, pushed by Turkic-speaking Sakha, who arrived from the south-west.[10]

The definition of the peculiar Russian legal category *korennye malochislennye narody* (variously translated as 'native minority peoples', 'small-numbered indigenous peoples', 'numerically small aboriginal peoples' and 'indigenous minorities'), and clarification of its content, require comparison with the relevant international concept of 'indigenous peoples', which is often used as a template for understanding various national traditions of population categorisation. In international law, the concept of 'indigenous people' is usually contrasted with those of 'people' and 'minority'. The intellectual history of these three concepts is admittedly different, but all three are currently used in many countries for the categorisation of diverse population groups with concomitant sets of political, cultural and linguistic rights.

The issue of minorities came to the fore of the political agenda during the periods following the two World Wars, its significance lying in the identification of populations of European origin – initially those of Central, Eastern and Northern Europe – who were perceived to reside outside the borders of the states that were considered their 'homelands'; for example, Hungarians in Romania and Slovakia, Germans in Denmark and Poland, Swedes in Finland, and so on. Later the concept of 'minority' was broadened to include the so called 'non-state peoples' and 'immigrants from former colonies'. The intellectual origin of the concept 'minority' has been traced to the initial models of parliamentary democracy (e.g., Petersen 1965: 235).

The reasons that contributed to the emergence of the remaining two legal categories of 'people' and 'indigenous peoples' within international law were quite different. Western social evolutionism and an associated hierarchical taxonomy of human groups and their cultures have influenced the legal construction of the concepts of 'peoples' vs. 'aboriginals'. Anthropology has contributed to this conceptual opposition. As a discipline in terms of both its subject matter and method it had been formed literally on the leftovers from sociology and history, focussing on the study of illiterate 'savages' or 'peoples without history'. The anthropological object – non-European populations of the world, prehistoric and preliterate 'natural peoples' – formed what Trouillot (1991) dubbed the 'savage slot' (see also Carucci and Dominy 2005). Savage slot in its turn had been a factor, during the period of decolonisation, of the legal construction of the 'indigenous slot' in international law (Karlsson 2003). Unlike the concept of 'people' in the body of international law,[11] the concept of 'indigenous people' is restricted in respect of the right to self-determination, as in Article 1.3 of ILO Convention 169 (1989).[12] While the integrationist ideology of the earlier ILO Convention 107 (1957) assigned to governments the primary responsibility 'for developing coordinated and systematic action for the protection of the populations concerned and their progressive integration into the life of their respective countries', an approach that reflected the political attitude of the time, in which the assimilation of 'backward' societies was seen as the first step for the liberation of their individual members, Convention 169 underlined respect for indigenous and tribal peoples' way of life and their refusal to integrate into the mainstream economies of the countries in which they lived.

In Russia, indigeneity is not only a qualitative characteristic of particular categories of ethnic communities and individual persons. It also has a quantitative aspect and thus is often thought of as possessing intensity gradations and multiple levels. The recent addition to official lists of small-scale indigenous peoples of such economically well-integrated peasant societies as that of the Abaza and Shapsug of the North Caucasus, Izhora and Veps of the Russian North-west (Leningrad oblast'), Bessermians (Udmurt Republic) and Nagaibak (Cheliabinsk oblast') of the Urals, has contributed to the erosion of the status of indigenous people as a group of societies which maintain traditional extensive or subsistence economies based on reindeer herding, hunting, foraging, sea-mammal hunting and fishing. On the other hand, many individuals and families from the legal category of 'small-numbered indigenous peoples' of the North are employed in 'urban' professions or live in cities, often far from their native lands and regions of birth.

Russian uncertainty and indeterminacy over the concept 'indigenous' – regarding which, the disputable threshold of 50,000 is only a demographic indicator, and one which does not distinguish between a minority group and an indigenous people – is mirrored at the international level. Some documents adopted by the Committee on Culture and Education of the Parliamentary Assembly of the Council of Europe (PACE) demonstrate that there is an emerging conflation of the notion of 'indigenous peoples' in the sense of ILO Convention 169 and different autochthonous ethnic groups that are neither tribal nor practise a subsistence economy (see PACE 1998, 2004, 2005). Meanwhile, the question of exactly who is indigenous, besides being of crucial importance for the keeping of statistics on indigenous peoples (where blurred boundaries of the concept contribute to errors in measurement), is crucially relevant to persons with legal entitlements associated with the status.

A system of statistical assessment and registration of indigenous populations in the USSR began in the 1920s. In 1925 the Soviet government decided to list the so-called 'small peoples of the North'. According to a Marxist version of salvage anthropology popular at the time, the groups listed were to receive 'socialist development' to bring them up to the level of social advancement of other population categories of the country. The main rationale behind this special treatment was the idea that state protection of the scarce native northern population was needed because of the perceived 'violent exploitation' by 'colonial merchants'. Economic aid for northern native communities was planned and endorsed. Apart from the national All-Union Census of 1926, a special Polar Census of 1926/7 was conducted. The state enumerators registered all households of aboriginal reindeer herders and hunters (see Anderson, Ziker, this volume).

Now the means and methods of counting multiplied, although many uncertainties in the legal framework of indigenous status and the fluid character of identity politics make statistical assessments an especially challenging task. The main sources of population dynamics data are the continuous registration statistics and the census. They are both managed by the Russian Federal Statistical Service (formerly Goskomstat, now Rosstat). Besides these two sources there are surveys and research data collected by the federal Ministries of Education and Health, and selective statistical surveys of private household budgets undertaken by the Ministry of Economic Development, as well as household registration books, migration and vital-events statistics, and passport statistics from local registry offices and passport departments of the Ministry for Internal Affairs. There are additional sources of information, often more reliable, coming from NGOs – such as the Russian Association for the Indigenous Peoples of the North (RAIPON) – and research institutes of the Russian Academy of Sciences and universities. However, all these potentially rich and diverse statistical sources are mostly based on a rigid idea of primordial ethnicity and bounded and unchangeable cultural units. Identity politics, as well as rapid changes in the legal status of indigenous peoples, demand new methods in statistical assessments of fluctuating numbers of individuals who are officially registered as indigenous.

The comparison of Soviet and post-Soviet census data demonstrates a high degree of fluctuation in numbers of certain groups that cannot be accounted for by birth and death rates, or migration. These cases often reflect changes in state policy and the legal status of the group in question, the identity politics employed by group members in adapting to such changes, and sometimes changes in official linguistic and cultural classifications. To give some examples: Dolgans were not officially recognised as a separate people and were counted among Sakha and Evenki until 1959, the year when their census count soared from 650 to almost 4,000. Though the changes in the numbers of Abaza, a Circassian people from the Caucasus and close relatives of Abkhaz, are not so spectacular, in the 1930s linguists decided that their language could be viewed as quite separate from that of the Abkhaz, and their count in the next census reflected this official recognition. Similar stories might be told about Enets, Chuvan, Uil'ta, Kerek, Kamchadal and Aliutor. All such cases demonstrate that state statistics on indigenous peoples reflect, besides demographic processes, changes in state policy and individual identity strategies that are used by people in adapting to changing political, economic and social situations.

The contemporary legal framework for the protection of indigenous peoples' rights has been formed during the post-Soviet period. The law 'On state guarantees and compensation for persons who work and reside in the districts of the Far North and equivalent areas' (1993)[13] has no list of either ethnic categories or territories of residence. It stipulates the general norm, according to which preferences in retirement go to 'citizens, belonging to the small-numbered peoples of the North', as well as 'reindeer herders, fishermen and hunters permanently resident in the districts of the Far North and equivalent areas'.[14] It was the 1994 law regarding the regulation of pensions for those residing in districts of the Far North that led to the enumeration of those due retirement privileges.[15] The enumeration mentions for the first time three new groups – Shor, Teleut and Kumanda – who were added to the previous standard Soviet list of twenty-six peoples. All three new groups were highly urbanised (at a level of between 50 and 70 per cent), and more integrated into mainstream urban culture than the rest (with the exception of the Oroks and Uil'ta of Sakhalin and Nanai of the Far East, who by that time also had very high urbanisation levels). In the governmental decree 'On the uniform registration of indigenous small-numbered peoples of the Russian Federation' (2000),[16] more catego-

Table 14.1. Indigenous Population Groups, % Urban, (Census 2002, Vol. 13, All Ages and Regions)

Indigenous group	Total number	Urban	% urban	Indigenous group	Total number	Urban	% urban
Shor	13975	9939	71.1	Nanai	12160	3702	30.4
Uil'ta/Orok	346	201	58.1	Negidal	567	164	28.9
Kamchadal	2293	1297	56.6	Ket	1494	406	27.2
Veps	8240	4624	56.1	Udege	1657	425	25.7
Kumanda	3114	1704	54.7	Shapsug	3231	810	25.1
Izhor	327	177	54.1	Bessermian	3122	766	24.5
Mansi	11432	5919	51.8	Evenk	35527	8576	24.1
Kerek	8	4	50.0	Chukchi	15767	3402	21.6
Oroch	686	338	49.3	Enets	237	51	21.5
Nivkh	5162	2483	48.1	Nganasan	834	165	19.8
Yukagir	1509	685	45.4	Nagaibak	9600	1889	19.7
Teleut	2650	1142	43.1	Ulchi	2913	564	19.4
Abaza	37942	16283	42.9	Nenets	41302	7844	19.0
Sami	1991	853	42.8	Sel'kup	4249	786	18.5
Taz	276	110	39.9	Dolgan	7261	1334	18.4
Itelmen	3180	1194	37.6	Tofa	837	138	16.5
Khant	28678	9924	34.6	Chelkan	855	135	15.8
Chuvan	1087	366	33.7	Tuba	1565	150	09.6
Even	19071	6116	32.1	Soyot	2769	252	09.1
Aleut	540	172	31.9	Chulym	656	54	08.2
Eskimo/Yupik	1750	557	31.8	Telengit	2399	115	04.8
Koryak	8743	2765	31.6	Todja	4442	7	0.2

ries were added to the list, and the number of officially recognised 'small-numbered indigenous peoples of Russia' reached forty-five. The list of the 'territories of predominant settlement' established by government decree in 1993 was later supplemented by the enumeration of the territories of the Shor, Kumanda, Nagaibak, Teleut and several other peoples.

Data from the 2002 Russian national census demonstrates that approximately one third of the respective populations of half of the peoples classified as 'indigenous' are urban dwellers, and among ten groups the level of urbanisation is near or higher than 50 per cent (see Table 14.1). Only among six groups – Dolgan, Nenents, Oroch, Chukchi, Enets and Nganasan – do we find the level of those involved in a traditional subsistence economy reaching 20 per cent (among Dolgans the figure is almost 30 per cent). Overall, out of the approximately 125,000 indigenous people of working age (15 to 64 years) residing in traditional areas of settlement, 16,280 work in education and health facilities, 5,010 work in finance, administration, social services, real estate business and security, 2,843 work

Table 14.2. Modernisation Scales of Indigenous Groups in Areas of Principal Residence (North, Siberia, and the Far East), Russian Population Census 2002

Ethnic catagory	% urban	Rank	% 'urban' professionals	Rank	% educated (> 10 years)	Rank	Σ of ranks
Tofa	05.8	2	19.6	4	32.8	2	8
Aleut	21.5	13	20.4	5	2.8	1	19
Nenets	17.0	11	24.4	6	33.7	3	20
Selqup	15.9	7	29.0	10	38.1	5	22
Oroch	35.2	24	17.9	2	37.9	4	30
Todja-Tyva	00.0	1	28.7	9	50.1	22	32
Chukchi	16.5	8	29.6	11	45.7	14	33
Enets	12.2	4	34.2	18	45.0	13	35
Sami	38.4	25	19.2	3	43.5	9	37
Ulchi	15.2	6	25.8	7	50.3	24	37
Neghidal	22.8	15	37.4	24	39.5	6	45
Evenk	22.8	16	17.1	1	56.1	28	45
Nivkh	46.7	28	29.6	12	40.4	7	47
Ket	16.7	9	38.7	27	44.5	11	47
Dolgan	16.9	10	31.2	14	51.9	26	50
Chelkan	18.1	12	37.1	23	47.2	17	52
Nganasan	13.6	5	33.6	17	59.2	31	53
Uilta	56.7	31	32.0	16	43.1	8	55
Shor	71.2	32	31.1	13	43.6	10	55
Yupik	25.7	17	34.9	19	49.0	20	56
Tuba	07.8	3	48.8	30	50.2	23	56
Nanai	28.3	18	38.8	28	44.7	12	58
Khant	33.2	22	35.1	20	46.8	16	58
Kumanda	52.7	30	31.5	15	46.3	15	60
Chuvan	29.8	20	37.4	25	48.1	19	64
Koriak	28.6	19	39.8	29	47.7	18	66
Yukaghir	42.0	27	27.8	8	66.7	32	67
Udeghe	22.0	14	58.9	32	50.7	25	71
Even	31.3	21	35.2	22	56.1	29	72
Mansi	50.7	29	35.1	21	53.3	27	77
Teleut	41.2	26	50.0	31	49.8	21	78
Itelmen	34.4	23	38.3	26	58.1	30	79

Source: The Table's entries are counted on the basis of the Census 2002 results (Vol. 13, tables 11 and 12). Column four is counted for the age cohort 15–64; column six is the sum of percentages of those with secondary and higher education.

in construction, transport and communication industries, and only 17,400 derive their income and subsistence from the 'traditional economy sector' (agriculture, forestry, fishing, hunting and so on). However, these estimates concern only those individuals of working age who have been registered either as hired in various enterprises or as deriving their income from property and hired labour in these branches of the economy. Out of 32 indigenous groups listed in the economic tables of the census, only 8 have economic-involvement rates over 50 per cent of the entire working-age population; among the other 24 groups economic inactivity and unemployment are very high. Whether these figures are an artefact of the techniques used during the census – whereby students and the retired were recorded as economically inactive – remains to be seen.

The 'territories of principal residence' of groups that had only recently been added to the official list of indigenous groups were not legally demarcated by the time of the census, with the consequence that the Federal Statistical Service published data only on indigenous populations with legally acknowledged 'territories of principal residence'. Since many of

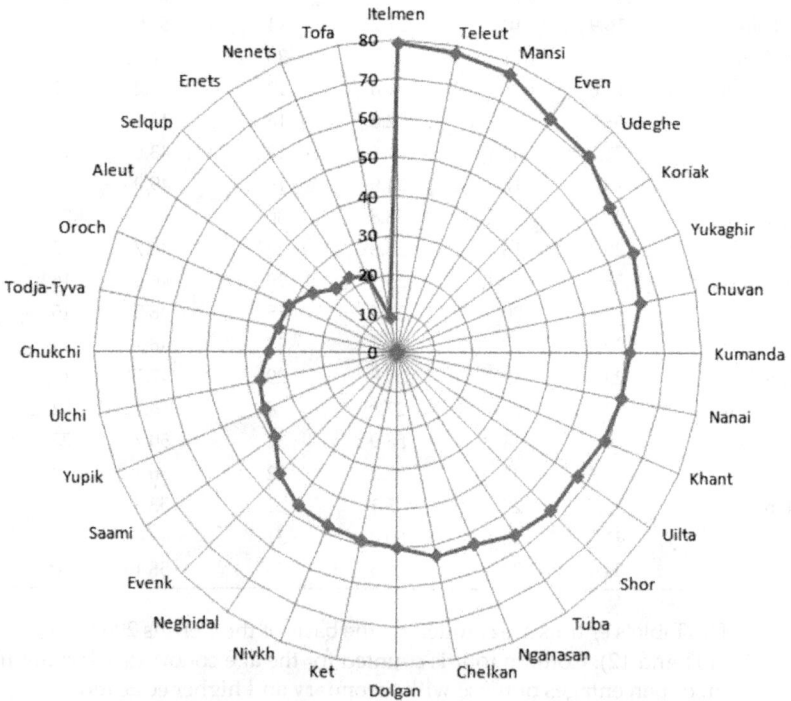

Figure 14.1 Indigenous Groups Ranked by Per Cent Urban, Share of Secondary and Higher Education and Proportion of the 'Non-Traditional' Employment in the 'Territories of Principal Residence'. (Based on Russian Population Census 2002, vol. 14)

the groups that were not recorded as such in the census are in fact more urbanised than those that were, the analysis of the degree of modernisation of the recorded thirty-two groups provides in this respect a reliable estimate of the overall situation.

If we rank each ethnic group in terms of the percentage rate of urbanisation, education (percentage of persons with higher and secondary education), share of 'urban' professionals (percentage of employed in 'nontraditional' economy), and add the three ranks together, we obtain a measure of the degree of modernisation, ranging from 3 points (rank number 1 in all of the three scales) to 96 (rank number 32 in all of the scales). In fact, the groups thus ranked were distributed between scale points 8 and 80. The result of this procedure is shown in Figure 14.1.

The highest level of combined urbanisation and modernisation rates occurs among the Itelmen (Iten'mi): 34 per cent are urban dwellers, 58 per cent have secondary and higher education, and more than one-third of their rural population have 'urban' professions, whereas less than 5 per cent work in the traditional economy.

At present, most members of indigenous communities, often stereotyped in Russia as being involved in reindeer, hunting or fishing economies, have urban professions. Even those who study the indigenous populations do not acknowledge the fact that out of approximately 125,000 persons of working age only 13 per cent are officially employed in some form of activity that is classified as agricultural, including hunting, fishing, forestry and agriculture.

Thus the conceptual difference between 'urban natives' and ethnic minorities, – whose linguistic, cultural and human rights are guaranteed by a different set of special international and national laws – becomes blurred, and the rationale for the application of two different sets of legal measures for these populations turns out to be questionable. In south-western Siberia, where Shor, Khakass, Chelkans and Altai live side by side in the same settlements and are involved in the same economy, the classification of one as 'indigenous' and the others as minorities creates social injustice as indigenes are eligible for a certain set of privileges (earlier retirement, natural resource quotas, exemption from army service, quotas for university enrolment and so on). The same situation is characteristic of Dolgans and northern Sakha in eastern Siberia, or Russian old settlers throughout Siberia.

Post-Soviet policy towards indigenous peoples has effectively continued the Soviet one by endorsing the traditional economy. As this economy depended on state subsidies, its rise and fall followed the ebbs and flows of the country's economy at large. The economic crisis of the early and mid 1990s severely curtailed state subsidies with the result that most of the state farms disintegrated and people either became unemployed or tried to live on those resources that still were handy. This period has been labelled by some researchers as one of 'neotraditionalism' (Pika and Prokhorov 1994). The movement to the land in the 1990s, however, was not a unique trait of indigenous groups; people throughout the country started to develop small plots in neighbouring fields and forests to grow potatoes and vegetables, and even lawns on the periphery of Moscow were used as vegetable gardens. What looked like a return to tradition by groups that had been tribal centuries ago was in fact part of a broader survival strategy employed by many in a time of economic hardship. With the slow recovery of the economy, suburban garden plots were no longer cultivated for food, and the movement to 'traditional subsistence territories' declined to previous levels; people who had left urban settlements came back, and by the time of the census 2002 the structure of employment and sources of income resembled those of pre-crisis times. This is not to say that the social and economic situation in small urban settlements had significantly improved, but rather that government salaries and pensions returned to a subsistence level. The social situation in small urban settlements (*posiolki*) remains depressed, with high levels of alcoholism and unemployment. This is, again, not specific to indigenous settlements: it is true of most small towns throughout Siberia and European Russia. It seems that specific programs for the support of indigenous groups do not work when the economy and social situation have not made sufficient progress to guarantee employment and a decent way of life to the majority of the country's population.

Data from the last census demonstrate that the level of indigenous groups' integration into the mainstream economy achieved during the years of Soviet assimilationist policy is by now so deep that there are no groups left which rely to a substantial degree on the traditional subsistence economy. On the other hand, there are families and groups of families, both among the legal category of 'numerically small people of the North' and among more numerous groups (such as Buriats, Altai, Khakass, Komi and Sakha), who still rely on extensive economy. The cultural survival and land rights of the latter remain uncertain, as they are not protected by current Russian legislation with its essentialised notion of cultures and peoples and its categorisation of groups into 'small' and 'large', the former thought of as endangered and the latter thought of as integrated and thus economically viable.

Notes

I would like to express my gratitude to the organisers of the workshop on 'Indigenous Identities in Demographical Sources', held at Umeå University in 2006, and to those participants whose discussion of this chapter made it possible for me to clarify and amend certain statements made in a previous draft. The usual caveat applies.

1. The term 'indigeneity' functions here as a gloss of such Russian terms as *korennye narody* ('indigenous peoples'), *korennaia natsia* ('indigenous nation'), *korennoe naselenie* ('indigenous population'), *korennoi etnos* ('indigenous

ethnie'), *korenisatia* ('indigenisation'), and so on. There is no noun derived from a Russian root that denotes indigeneity (*korennoi/-aia/-oe* is an adjective), except the obsolete *tuzemets* ('native'). Two Russian nouns for indigeneity (both rarely used) come from Latin and Greek roots: *aborigennost'* (from Latin *ab origine*, 'from the beginning') and *avtokhtonnost'* (from ancient Greek αυτος – 'auto', own, and χθωνος – 'land'. The Russian derivation *tuzemnost'* is considered obsolete as a noun; however, semantically it seems to be the most close correlate of the English 'indigeneity'. A learned borrowing *indigennost'* is also possible, but is scarcely ever used. Another Russian term *pervobytnost'* denotes the first epoch in the early history of mankind, though the expression *pervobytnye narody* is best rendered in English as 'primitive peoples' (from Latin *primus*, 'first'), 'aboriginal peoples', or 'first peoples'. For an analysis of the historical evolution of Russian terms for 'indigeneity', see Sokolovskiy (2000; 2001: 41–82, 207–34).

2. *O garantiyakh prav korennykh malochislennykh narodov Rossiskoi Federatsii* (1999) ['On Guarantees of the Rights of Indigenous Numerically Small Peoples of the Russian Federation'].

3. Quoted from Article 1.1 of the law.

4. See *O korennykh malochislennykh narodakh Respubliki Daghestan* ['On the small-numbered indigenous peoples of Dagestan'], Dagestan State Council decree, 18 October 2000. According to Article 2 of *O edinom perechne korennykh malochislennykh narodov Rossiiskoi Federatsii* ['On the unified list of small-numbered indigenous peoples of the Russian Federation'] (24 March 2000, with changes of 30 September 2000): 'The government of the Republic of Dagestan is to prepare and submit to the State Council of the Republic of Dagestan a proposal on the small-numbered indigenous peoples residing on the territory of the Republic for subsequent inclusion of them in the unified list'.

5. Nogai were not invited to join the Confederation of Mountain Peoples back in the early 1990s on the same grounds.

6. For an analysis of similar competing claims in the Caucasus, see Shnirelman (2001).

7. This haphazard classification of continents implies that Old World cases of indigeneity construction are in general more complex and more often contested, whereas the relevant New World cases seem to be more clear-cut and are challenged less often. They are also contested on different grounds, which have to do mostly with 'blood' or genealogy (in the New World case), but not with 'soil' or historically constructed 'homelands' (as in the case of the Old World). This situation reflects the assumption that in Old World countries, most ethnic groups are more or less 'indigenous' or that the difference between colonists and the 'original inhabitants' of various regions of the New World seems clear-cut.

8. There are ways of documenting the presence of a particular group in a territory other than historical accounts, using bio-anthropological, linguistic and archeological data, for example. Though they are of undeniable value in the construction of the factual account of regional population succession and genealogy with its the assumption that a group has preserved its identity under successive waves of conquest and immigration – they have the drawback that no one can conclusively document the fluid nature of the identity of past generations of groups. These sources are often instrumentally used by competing claimants to a particular territory.

9. The territory of the Sakha Republic (over 3,100 thousand square kilometres) is comparable in size to Western Europe, so migration within the republic can in some cases be legitimately viewed as long-ranged.
10. Precise dating here, using archaeological and historical evidence, is difficult. For details, see Okladnikov (1945) and Levin and Potapov (1956).
11. For uses of the concept of 'people' in international law, see, e.g., the Montevideo Convention on the Rights and Duties of States (1933), the UN Charter (1945); International Covenant on Civil and Political Rights (1966), and the International Covenant on Economic, Social and Cultural Rights (1966).
12. However, see the Preamble and Article 3 of the recently adopted UN Declaration on the Rights of Indigenous Peoples (2007).
13. *O gosudarstvennykh garantiiakh i kompensatsiiakh dlia lits, rabotaiushchikh i prozhivaiushchikh v raionakh Krainego Severa i priravnennykh k nim mestnostiakh* (1993).
14. Quoted from Article 26.
15. Article 4 of the decree *O naznachenii pensii litsam, rabotaiushchim i prozhivaiushchim v raionakh Krainego Severa* ['On retirement payments for persons who work and reside in the regions of the Far North'], Ministry for Social Protection Decree No. 657 (4 August 1994). This stipulates that 'the designated peoples include Nenets, Evenk, Khant, Even, Chukchi, Nanai, Koryak, Mansi, Dolgan, Nivkh, Sel'kup, Ulcha, Itelmen, Udege, Sami, Eskimo, Chuvan, Nganasan, Yukagir, Ket, Oroch, Tofa, Aleut, Negidal, Enets, Orok, Shor, Teleut, Kumanda'.
16. *O edinom perechne korennykh malochislennykh narodov Rossiskoi Federatsii* (2000) ['On the Uniform Registration of the Indigenous Small-Numbered Peoples of the Russian Federation'].

References

Carucci, L.M., and M.D. Dominy. 2005. 'Anthropology in the "Savage Slot": Reflections on the Epistemology of Knowledge', *Anthropological Forum* 15(3): 223–33.

Fedorova, E.N. 1999. *Naselenie Yakutii. Proshloe i Nastoiashchee*. Novosibirsk: Nauka.

Karlsson, B.G. 2003 'Anthropology and the "Indigenous Slot": Claims to Debates about Indigenous Peoples' Status in India', *Critique of Anthropology* 23(4): 403–24.

Levin, M.G., and L.P. Potapov (eds.) 1956. *Narody Sibiri*. Moscow: Academy of Sciences of the USSR Publ. (English translation: *The Peoples of Siberia*. M.G. Levin and L.P. Potapov (Eds.) Translated by Scripta Technica, Inc., edited by S. Dunn. Chicago and London: University of Chicago Press, 1964. viii, 948 pp., bibliography).

Okladnikov, A.P. 1945. *Lenskie drevnosti*. Vypusk 1. Yakutsk.

PACE. 1998. 'Endangered Uralic Minority Cultures', Document 8126. Strasbourg: Committee on Culture and Education, Parliamentary Assembly of the Council of Europe.

——— 2004. 'The Situation of Fenno-Ugric and Samoyed Peoples', Document 10314. Strasbourg: Committee on Culture and Education, Parliamentary Assembly of the Council of Europe.

———— 2005. 'The Situation of the Mari Minority in the Russian Federation', Document 10548. Strasbourg: Committee on Culture and Education, Parliamentary Assembly of the Council of Europe.

Petersen, W. 1965. *The Politics of Population*. New York: Anchor.

Pika, A., and B. Prokhorov (eds). 1994. *Neotraditsionalism na Rossiiskom Severe i Gosudarstvennaia Regional'naia Politika*. Moscow: MNEPU [International Independent University of Ecology and Politics].

Shnirelman, V.A. 2001. *The Value of the Past: Myths, Identity and Politics in Transcaucasia*. Osaka: National Museum of Ethnology.

Sokolovskiy, S.V. 2000. 'The Construction of "Indigenousness" in Russian Science, Politics and Law', *Journal of Legal Pluralism* 45: 91–113.

———— 2001. *Obrazy Drugikh v Rossiiskoi Nauke, Politike i Prave*. Moscow: Put'.

Trouillot, M-R. 1991. Anthropology and the savage slot: the poetics and politics of otherness. In: R. *Fox* (ed.), *Recapturing Anthropology*, pp. 17–44. Santa Fe, NM: School of American Research.

15
Indigenous Populations, Ethnicity and Demography in the Eastern Baltic Littoral in the Nineteenth and Twentieth Centuries

Andrejs Plakans

Two Contrasting Narratives

Few would disagree with the proposition that historical demographic sources, particularly censuses and census-like enumerations, are fated to be somewhat out of step with the societies whose characteristics they seek to portray (Anderson 1988). Censuses classify at a moment in time and produce seemingly precise numbers, whereas the societies they enumerate are always in the process of changing. Census categories require clear-cut decisions about personal and group identities, while identities tend to be protean and may shift for large numbers of people even as a census fixes them in time and place (Eley and Suny 1996). Censuses used by themselves push narrative description toward permanence and essentiality, while narratives rooted in non-census information produce results emphasising process, movement and change. Even when a sequence of censuses is used for analysis, the resulting description suggests that social change takes the form of leaps from one steady state to the next. Thus a census, however 'scientific' it may appear because of its quantitative character and the care with which it is undertaken, and however much 'hard' demographic information it contains about a society, is at the same time always something of a flawed record and must be evaluated by reference to other sources available about that society. Fortunately, in the modern era of the societies where censuses became a normal part of government activities, many other sources have existed in reference to which census information can be evaluated.

The imperfect fit between official population enumerations and the societies being surveyed has a long history in the eastern Baltic littoral, and in the following account I will be using the territory of Latvia as my case study. Because their recent histories are similar, many of the observations made here for Latvia also hold true for Estonia and Lithuania – lying north and south of Latvia, respectively (see Map 15.1). In the centuries before they gained independence during the First World War, Latvians and Estonians, both being predominantly peasant peoples, had the same governing elites – Baltic Germans since the thirteenth century, and both Baltic Germans and Russians since the late eighteenth. All population enumerations before 1920 were prepared by functionaries of these elites and their work reflected, in the main, the concerns of the elites. By contrast, Lithuanians, also a primarily peasant people from the sixteenth century onward, not only had had their own state in the centuries straddling the late medieval to the early modern periods, but since 1569 had been part of a large political entity – the Polish-Lithuanian Commonwealth. When Russia absorbed the eastern part of this Commonwealth in the late eighteenth century, it was Polish-speak-

Map 15.1 The Regions of Latvia c. 1920. Reprinted from the book *The Latvians: A Short History*, p. 114, with permission from the publisher, Hoover Institution Press. © 1995 by the board of Trustees of Leland Stanford Jr. University.

ing magnates who remained as the local elites in Lithuania, joined now by a cadre of Russian administrators. This history also accounts for the fact that virtually all Estonians and most Latvians were Lutherans, whereas virtually all Lithuanians were Roman Catholics.

By the time they achieved independence in 1918, none of the populations of the three Baltic countries was very large. Estonia was the smallest (about 1.06 million in 1920) and Lithuania the largest (about 2.04 million in 1920), while Latvia stood somewhere in the middle (see Table 15.1).

The aggregate numbers for all three before the twentieth century must necessarily be estimates, because their political borders during the Russian imperial period did not correspond to those of the post–1918 era. As subjects of the Russian tsar, the Baltic peoples resided in a cluster of adjacent provinces (*guberniias*), with provincial boundaries having been set primarily for administrative convenience and without any attention to the ethnicity or languages of the general population. The population totals for Latvia in 1881 and 1897 in Table 15.1 are therefore composite figures from three different provinces where Latvians resided: Livonia (Livland in German, Vidzeme in Latvian), Courland (Kurland in German, Kurzeme in Latvian), and the westernmost districts of the province of Vitebsk (these districts being referred to in sources as Inflanty or Lettgallen in German and Latgale in Latvian).

Table 15.2 lists the enumerations made of the population of the territory of Latvia from the late nineteenth century onward. It can be seen that over the past two centuries the Latvian population has enjoyed neither a stable political framework nor a stable society, making a long period of consistent enumeration impossible. The succession of government officials who prepared the census questions and tabulated the final results were 'colonial' in a double sense – Baltic German at the provincial level, and Russian at the imperial level – with neither having an interest in creating census categories beyond those they understood to be included in international practice or those required by the imperial government. They had, in fact, 'larger' concerns. By the second half of the nineteenth century, the Baltic Germans, for many centuries the political and economic elite of Latvian territory, were defending the 'special privileges' that had been granted to

Table 15.1. Total Population of the Territory of Latvia 1881–2000

Year	Population	Year	Population	Year	Population
1881	c. 1,616,000	1935	1,905,936	2000	2,377,383
1897	c. 1,929,000	1959	2,079,948	2006	2,294,590
1920	1,596,131	1970	2,351,903		
1925	1,844,805	1979	2,502,816		
1930	1,900,045	1989	2,666,567		

Source: Pārvalde 2002: 30; for 2006 Latvia Central Statistical Bureau website.

Table 15.2. Population Enumerations in the Territory of Latvia and Selected Variables of Collective Identity: 19th and 20th Centuries

Year	Coverage	Authorizing government	Language of census forms	Language of published results	Variable: Religion	Variable: Nationality/ Ethnicity	Variable: Language	Variable: Social Estate[1]
Pre–1881[2]	Varied	Imperial and provincial	German and Russian	Results not generally disseminated, except for aggregated totals for use by officials	Varied Use	No	No	Yes
1881	Estland, Livland, Kurland[3]	Provincial	German	German; results tabulated differently for each province	Yes	Yes	Yes	Yes
1897	Russian Empire	Imperial	Russian	Russian; results published in 1905	Yes	No	Yes	No
1920	Republic of Latvia	Latvian	Latvian	Latvian and French	Yes	Yes	Yes	No
1925	Republic of Latvia	Latvian	Latvian	Latvian and French	Yes	Yes	Yes	No
1930	Republic of Latvia	Latvian	Latvian	Latvian and French	Yes	Yes	Yes	No
1935	Republic of Latvia	Latvian	Latvian	Latvian and French	Yes	Yes	Yes	No
1943	Latvian district (*Bezirk*) of *Ostland*[4]	German occupation government	German	German; restricted publication	No	No[5]	No	No
1959	Latvian SSR	USSR	Russian	Russian and Latvian	No	Yes	Yes	No
1970	Latvian SSR	USSR	Russian	Russian and Latvian	No	Yes	Yes	No
1989	Latvian SSR	USSR	Russian	Russian and Latvian	No	Yes	Yes	No
2000	Republic of Latvia	Latvian	Latvian	Latvian and English	No	Yes	Yes	No

Source: Clem 1986; Pervaya 1905; Plakans and Wetherell 2004; Pārvalde 2002; Roth 1991; Skujenieks 1938; Statistische Berichte; Zvidriņš and Vanovska 1992.

Table Notes:

1. 'Social estate' (Ger. *Stand*, Russ. *soslovie*; Latv. *kārta*) refers to such classification terms as 'noble', 'burgher', 'peasant', and 'stranger', each of which placed the person classified into a socio-economic grouping that had a unique set of rights, privileges, and responsibilities.

2. The principal pre–1881 enumerations in the Baltic area were the Russian Imperial fiscal censuses called 'revisions of souls'. Initiated by Peter the Great in the eighteenth century, they were supposed to take place every fifteen years, but because of the late entry of the Baltic area into the Empire, the dates of the Baltic revisions do not always correspond to the Imperial schedule.

3. The 1881 census was initiated by the governing bodies of the 'Baltic Provinces' proper. That meant that the Latvian-speaking population of the adjoining eastern province of Vitebsk (Latgale) was excluded from the count. Also, the Illuxt district of Kurland was not counted because the enumerators feared attacks from the local inhabitants. For a description of the 1881 census, see Plakans and Wetherall 2004.

4. Plans for the June 1941 German invasion of the USSR included the merging of Estonia, Latvia, Lithuania, and the Belorussian SSR into a new administrative unit called *Ostland*, with four *Bezirke*. These plans were implemented immediately upon the arrival of the Reich administrators in the region. Population information in the 1943 census (*Volkszählung*) is scanty, and the enumeration seems more interested in economic variables. The results in any event were published only for internal official use (*nur für den Dienstgebrauch*); see *Statistische Berichte* 1943.

5. The absence of the nationality/ethnicity variable in this census did not meant lack of interest by the German administrators. In a table comparing the total 1943 population with the total in 1935, a footnote says that the 1935 figure is being used in a recalculated form 'without Jews' (*ohne Juden*). Already by the spring of 1942, most of the Jews of Latvia – an estimated 80,000 – had been murdered (*Statistische Berichte* 1943, Nr.1/4, 89, Table 86).

---

them by earlier tsars, especially against encroachments during the 'Russification' period starting with the reign of Alexander III in 1881 (Haltzel 1981: 134–49). Precision with respect to ethnic or national identity was not high on their list. Similarly, the tsarist autocracy of imperial Russia had an interest in obscuring possible fissures of any kind in these western borderlands, so that population dynamics in them could be smoothly coordinated with the needs of imperial policies aimed at socio-economic development. At the same time, non-census population descriptions of the western borderlands – often written by the same persons who worked on the censuses, reveal evidence of quite a nuanced understanding of the ethnic, linguistic and national diversity that was characteristic of these small but complex borderland territories.

Markers of Personal and Collective Identity: 1850–1900

In current political discourse in Latvia, one is likely to run across the concept of 'basic nation' (Latv. *pamattauta*), a close relative of the English-language notion of 'indigenous nation'. Since 1991, the idea of 'the basic nation' has been used defensively and with the political intention of distinguishing Latvians from the large Slavic minority population (often loosely referred to as 'migrants') that continued to reside in the country after the 1991 disintegration of the USSR. The idea of the 'basic nation' usually connotes more than numerical preponderance; the phrase is also meant to imply precedence and a generalised primordial right of ownership of the territory of the country. Earlier in the twentieth century and even before 1918, equivalents of this terminology were somewhat different, but the intent, especially in nationalistic conceptualisations of the population, was the same: to underline that 'Latvians' were the 'indigenous nation' and all others – especially German and Slavic speakers were latecomers. The assertion was not about formal citizenship but about which persons and groups could legitimately claim the territory as 'theirs'.

The assertion, when it was made in the nineteenth century, was employed in a socio-cultural context in which markers of individual and personal identity still had deep historical roots but were being hotly contested. The philosophy of 'social estate' or 'social order' (Ger. *Stand*, Russ. *soslovie*, Latv. *kārta*) was still very much alive; of medieval derivation, this classification system was based on the premise that society was made up of sub-populations (corporations), each of which had a unique status and set of functions as well as unique rights and privileges. This notion of society had eroded considerably in Western Europe since the French Revolution, but in tsarist Russia and in the Russian Baltic provinces it had retained its viability. In the Baltic territories that were to become Latvia in the twentieth century, the hierarchically arranged structure of social estates in the mid nineteenth century coincided almost entirely with the structure of language communities. The dominant social estates – the nobility (Ger. *Adelstand*), the urban patriciate (Ger. *Bürgerstand*) and the 'educated professions' (Ger. *Gelhertenstand*) – were primarily German-speaking, while the peasantry (Ger. *Bauernstand*) and urban labourers were primarily Latvian-speaking. These distinctions were widely used in nineteenth-century population enumerations (see Table 15.2), and in fact did not disappear from the published census tabulations and narrative descriptions of the population until the founding of the Republic of Latvia in 1918.

These social-estate designations were frequently used markers of both personal and collective identity, but they also injected into social and political life a heavy dose of ethno-linguistic differentiation, especially among commoners (non-nobles). True, it differentiated between the nobility (mostly landowning) and burghers (urban dwellers), but these two groups, as political history showed, could come together in an assertion of commonality based on language. The great divide lay between these groups and the *Bauernstand*, which, though numerically predominant, stood at the bottom of the hierarchy and, in addition, spoke a different language – namely, Latvian. The older records of the region, having been produced by functionaries of the dominant elites, frequently reinforced the idea that social hierarchy was also a language hierarchy by referring to all persons 'below' the higher estates with the adjective *undeutsch* (non-Germans). This way of thinking was not a function of ignorance; among others, the Lutheran clergy in particular had worked closely with their Latvian-speaking parishioners for many generations, and in fact had been instrumental since the seventeenth century in creating a written language for them. But even among the clergy the opinion was widespread that able and ambitious peasants who aspired to non-agricultural occupations and wanted to seek their fortunes in urban settings could not do so without transforming their identities. They could cease being peasants through hard work but at that moment – so this belief went – they also had to cease being Latvian and become German (Plakans 1995: 84–85).

The view that a personal identity partly based on language needed to give way to the inevitable requirements of socio-economic upward mobility – 'becoming German' – was widespread not only among the upper orders but also among peasants themselves. Memoirs of the period describe the attitude precisely:

> Until the middle of the nineteenth century, a Latvian did not recognise or refer to himself other than as a peasant; he was called that by all who believed themselves higher than he and those who were in fact higher ... If at times the term 'Latvian' was used, it was understood to mean nothing but that, because no one could imagine that the two ideas – peasant and Latvian – could ever be distinguished from each other. Similarly, no one could understand that the ideas of 'German' and 'lord' could be separated, for all Germans were lords, and all lords Germans. (Kaudzite 1994: 24)

The uncertainty about self-classification, described retrospectively many years later, was made even more problematic by the fact that the 'peasantry' in the Latvian territories produced no records of their own. Literacy among them was not inconsequential statistically by comparison with rural populations of the Russian interior, but writing was an activity for which there was little need in daily life, let alone for such weighty subjects as self-identity. In all probability, the peasantry was very conscious of the language distinction between themselves and the upper orders, even though by the mid nineteenth century such consciousness had not yet transmuted itself into any kind of 'nationality conflict'. Peasants were also more likely to identify themselves, when asked, as residents of the province in which they resided (for example, *kurlanders, livlanders*) or, more parochially, as residents of their natal township (*pagasts*) within a particular province. They might even be prone to thinking of themselves – as descriptions in the 1881 Baltic census show – primarily as Lutherans or Catholics in order to distinguish themselves from the local sub-populations of Russian Orthodox and Jews. The written record for the peasantry on this question suggests that individual and collective identity was not firmly fixed in anyone's mind because neither individual peasants nor groups of them were much called upon to declare an identity publicly.

The entire question of who was who was thrown into turmoil by the rapid changes in the consciousness of collective identity that began after the mid nineteenth century among the upper as well as the lower estates of the Latvian territories. Imperial administrators began to push heavily and repeatedly against Baltic German 'historic privileges', especially after the accession of Alexander III to the throne and the systematic Russification of the western borderlands (Thaden 1984). This was due in part to geopolitical reasons, namely the Polish revolt of 1863 and the birth of a unified German Empire in 1871, which led to fears in Russian government circles of separatism in the border provinces. Russification laws promulgated in St Petersburg produced greater solidarity among the German-speaking upper estates – making them more assertive about their Germanness – in defence of their traditional hegemonic hold over political, social and economic life, with nationality consequently becoming more important than social estate. But the upper orders also began to experience challenges from below with the rise during the late 1850s and the 1860s of Latvian nationalism, which struck out against Baltic German privilege, but for different reasons.

The Latvian nationalist movement was spearheaded by rural schoolteachers, and, when they addressed the peasantry, they insisted that Latvian speakers understand many new things about themselves (Plakans 1995: 89–95). They were expected to discover, to begin with, that they were 'Latvians' and not simply members of a *Bauernstand* or residents of this or that Baltic province. They were expected to discover moreover that they were 'indigenous' to the region, and that the Baltic Germans were immigrants, even if they had arrived centuries earlier. Although the term 'basic nation' was not used by this generation, it is in this period that the underlying understanding of the concept became active. Furthermore, they were expected to discover that some 200,000 of their 'compatriots' lived in the province of Vitebsk, in a region called Latgale, adjoining the official boundaries of Livland and Kurland to the east. They also were expected to discover that, as a distinct nationality, they had suffered 'seven hundred years of oppression' at the hands of the Baltic German upper orders, and that before the thirteenth century their ancestors had lived free in an array of Baltic tribal societies (Livs, Latgalians, Selians, Kurs, Semgallians). In short, the ideology of Latvian nationalism proposed a total transformation in the sources of individual and collective identity. Latvians were urged to look to the past, to think of themselves in some sense as the original 'owners' of the lands they now occupied, and to extend their understanding of themselves to include compatriots living beyond the official borders of the Baltic provinces. It was the claim of being the 'indigenous' population that was most significant; with the deployment of this notion, the traditional upper orders, and to a lesser extent the administrators of the tsarist government, were being reconceptualised as latecomers and interlopers, with no right of possession to the territory they currently controlled. At the individual level, Latvians were instructed that upward socio-economic mobility need not lead to the abandonment of one's native language, and that Latvianness as such was a legitimate source of personal identity. Among them nationality was also becoming more important than estate membership.

Population Enumerations in the Nineteenth Century

It is ironic that the first efforts to hold modern censuses in the Baltic region (in 1881 and 1897; see Table 15.2) took place precisely in the decades when the consciousness of personal and group identity was changing so rapidly. Before the nineteenth century, population descriptions and tax enumerations – which were rare to begin with – had had little incentive for or means of producing exact descriptions of different sectors of the population, whether that of the governing elites or the peasantry. In sources prior to 1881, the categories used were almost all drawn from the vocabulary of the social estate: hereditary and non-hereditary aristocracies, burghers, free peasants, serfs and foreigners (that is, short-term immigrants). The 'revisions of souls' (fiscal censuses linked to the imperial head tax) and cadastral registers (land surveys) were replete with this terminology; and ethnic or nationality terms such as 'Latvian', 'German' or 'Jewish' appeared only as adjectives pertaining to language. Indeed, there is no evidence that these linguistic markers had any direct policy relevance, or that they were meant to point to collective identities. Status mattered, language use was an epiphenomenon, and ethnicity and nationality was of little moment.

What appears to a modern sensibility as a rather lackadaisical approach to human inventories began to change with the dawn of the nineteenth century, as Baltic administrators accepted the rationalist notion that their work should be 'scientific', and as the Russian imperial government itself began to take a deeper (other than purely numerical) interest in the populations under its control. This new administrative precision produced, first of all, a new type of descriptive literature – often containing the term *Beschreibung* in the title – which was a mixture of both narrative and numbers (e.g., Keyserling 1805). It is in these writings that one finds a kind of quasi-official recognition, in the manner populations were described, of the fact that the *undeutsch* population was quite varied in terms of religion, language and ethnicity, and these population characteristics begin to be used as grouping variables. This sharpening administrative sense is evident as well in the later nineteenth-century 'revisions of souls' at the level of localities, some of which display a remarkable level of specificity.

Then, in the second half of the nineteenth century, coinciding with the rise of nationalist thinking in the Baltic and shifts in personal and collective identity, administrators launched the first real (modern) censuses – urban censuses in the 1860s, a census of all three Baltic provinces (Estland, Livland, Kurland) in 1881 (Plakans and Wetherell 2004), and finally the first (and only) imperial census of 1897. The provincial administrators created permanent 'statistical committees' to implement this new interest. These carried out trial counts (*Probezählungen*) before the 1881 census, studied international practices of census taking, and hired large numbers of enumerators for the count (Stieda 1881). Yet the counts that were produced reveal these decades to be a transition period during which the sharpened sense of what a population count should yield coexisted with premodern, and increasingly irrelevant, classifications based on the social-estate principle. This was so even as a host of *Beschreibungen*, often written by the same persons who laboured on the censuses, clearly testified to the existence of a complex population mix in the Baltic area. The *Beschreibungen* invariably portrayed Baltic provinces that were rich in ethnic and linguistic sub-groups, whereas, by contrast, in the published censuses, especially those of 1881 and 1897, the populations emerged as far less diverse, with linguistic, national and ethnic markers kept to a bare minimum. The university-educated enumerators must have recognised this mismatch, but evidently made the decision not to go beyond the language of official classifications: social standing (*Stände*), occupations and religious affiliation. Classification by nationality or ethnicity was marginalised and really referred mostly to language use. One obvious sign that nationality and ethnicity continued to be thought of as specific to a locality or province, and a somewhat minor characteristic of populations, was the way in which the results of the 1881 census were published. While Latvian nationalists argued that Latvian speakers in Kurland and Livland (and Latgale) were in fact a single nation, the 1881 results were published in separate volumes for each province, with tables highlighting different variables in each volume and with no mention made of the Latvian speakers in Latgale (Vitebsk province). The province remained the geographic framework of this effort. Precise demographic facts – total population size, births, deaths, marriages, disabilities – evidently were one thing, but population characteristics that could lead to precise aggregate figures for the entire Baltic provincial territory quite another.

The census categories of the 1897 imperial census originated in St Petersburg, and did not reveal any sharp departure from the old sense of what a population consisted of.

Estate (*soslovie*) designators, religion and geographic location again had pride of place in these voluminous tables, and, although language was a variable, the published materials do not suggest that this was thought of by the enumerators as an exceptionally important characteristic (Roth 1991). To be sure, the 1897 imperial census (the results of which were not published until 1905) was meant to be a scientific inventory of the Empire's human capital in general, but there was no way that its users – administrators or general educated population – could have surmised from the tabulations that the populations 'on the ground' in the western borderlands were in the process of being converted to a different definition of themselves that transcended provincial boundaries (see Anon. 1905). Narrative descriptions unrelated to these censuses, however, did recognise the importance of nationality-based diversity, and important Baltic German publications carried numerous articles about the problems of the so-called *Nationalfrage* (Dribins 1997: 42–56).

Nationality and Ethnicity in the Interwar Period

The creation in 1918 of three Baltic republics – Estonia, Latvia and Lithuania – after the collapse of the Russia Empire transformed census taking completely. The new national governments and their census bureaux were now controlled by the previously subordinated peoples who continued to portray themselves as the 'indigenous' population of their respective countries. The modern censuses carried out during the interwar period in Latvia – in 1920, 1925, 1930 and 1935 (see Table 15.2) – were now handled by the Ministry of Interior, staffed mostly by Latvians who carefully adapted to international practices and made certain that the published results were accessible to an international readership by using Latvian and French in the table headings and entries within tables. Such practices were the most helpful in providing models for cross-tabulating purely demographic variables, such as age by sex by marital status. They were not as instructive, however, in how socio-cultural-grouping variables should be dealt with, and in these matters the Latvians devised their own procedures.

Table 15.3. Estimated Proportions of Select Nationalities in the Territory of Latvia 1881–2004

	Latvians	Germans	Russians	Jews	Others
1881	77.0	11.3	4.0	5.5	2.2
1897	76.9	8.4	4.4	4.9	4.5
1920	72.7	3.6	7.8	4.9	11.5
1925	73.4	3.8	10.8	5.2	6.8
1930	73.4	3.6	10.6	4.9	7.5
1935	75.5	3.2	10.6	4.8	5.9
1959	62.0	n.a.	n.a.	n.a.	38.0
1970	56.8	n.a.	n.a.	n.a.	43.2
1979	53.7	.1	32.8	1.1	12.3
1989	52.0	.1	34.0	.1	13.8
2000	57.7	.1	29.6	.4	12.2
2004	58.6	n.a.	28.8	n.a.	12.6

Sources: Zvidriņš and Vanovska 1992; Skujeneeks 1922; Skujenieks 1938; Pārvalde 2002; Misiunas and Taagepera 1993: 353; Zvidriņš 2003: 113; Human Development 2005/06: 33.

If nineteenth-century enumerations were unsurprisingly shallow in capturing the ethnic and national diversity of the counted population, one might expect that a heightened consciousness of nationality and ethnicity among postwar enumerators would mean they were more attentive to nuances. Numerous Latvian publications surveying the population of the new country in the 1920s attested to a thorough familiarity with national and ethnic diversity (e.g., Skujeneeks 1922: 222–60). Moreover, the interwar enumerations had to cope with some facts that made post–1918 governments uncomfortable, such as the fact that only about three-quarters of the population of the country during the interwar period were Latvians (see Table 15.3). Moreover, using the 'historic regions' of Latvian-language residence – Kurzeme, Zemgale, Vidzeme and Latgale – for aggregating population statistics brought into focus the question of how to deal with the easternmost region, Latgale, which until 1918 had not been part of the 'Baltic provinces' proper and still seemed to many 'western' Latvians somewhat alien territory (see Figure 15.1).

The different history of the region, the language spoken there which some claimed was a distinct language while others said it was a dialect of Latvian, the low literacy rates, and the widespread influence of the Catholic Church – all these made Latgale unlike the rest of Latvia even while it was now a constituent part of the new country (Zeile 2006).

By and large, the interwar censuses dealt with these challenges well, though the published results highlighted the fact that Latvians were in charge of the country (Skujenieks 1938). Nationality remained one of the principal grouping variables, as did religion. The fact that the 1922 Constitution, the basic law of the country in the interwar period, spoke in some clauses of 'the nation of Latvia', and thus put into play the concept of the 'political nation', this was normally excluded from the presentation of the data (ibid.). The ethnic sense of the concept of 'nation' dominated, and this usage was not discouraged by the preoccupation of the League of Nations and other international bodies with the rights of 'minority nationalities'. If there were 'minority nationalities', there had to be a dominant nationality. Latvian enumerators conscientiously stayed with the basic ethnic designators – Latvians, Russians, Germans, Estonians, Lithuanians, Poles, Jews, Belorussian and 'Others' – that had been used in the pre–1918 period. The country's Jewish population was also understood to be a 'nationality' and was enumerated as such. A puzzling question concerned the tiny subpopulation of Livs (Livonians), who continued to nurture a non-Baltic Finnish second language, even though by the interwar period most of the Livs had become assimilated within the Latvian population; they were included in the 'Others' category. The Latgalians were more problematic, insofar as Latgalian speakers in the region were classified as 'Latvians', in spite of pleas by some of the Latgalian representatives in Parliament (*Saeima*) that, at the very least, spoken Latgalian and the unique history of the region entitled it to substantial autonomy in language use and administration. Moreover,

Table 15.4. Proportion of Latvians in the Historic Regions of Latvia

	Vidzeme	Zemgale	Kurzeme	Latgale
1920	81.9	78.3	83.0	72.7
1935	93.8	82.8	86.5	61.3
2002	83.2	69.9	73.1	43.4
2004	84.4	67.7	73.3	46.6

Sources: Skujeneeks 1922: .9; Skujenieks 1938; Gadagrāmata 2002:48; Human Development 2006: 33.

Latgale was the least 'Latvian' of the four regions: its population in 1935 was less than three-quarters 'Latvian', the rest being comprised of Jews, Russians, Poles, Byelorussians, Ukrainians and Lithuanians (see Table 15.4).

Clearly, the interwar government feared that awarding Latgale and the Latgalian language a unique standing in the censuses would not only encourage the separatist tendencies evident among some Latgalian intellectuals, but would also somehow empower the non-Latvian populations living there (see Bojtár 1999). After all, the Russians, Lithuanians and Poles in Latgale all had larger 'ethnic homelands' close by, and by the 1930s the problem of irredentism was clearly visible in other areas of Eastern Europe.

Thus, just as in the nineteenth century, the interwar census terminology tended to present too simple a picture of the ethnic diversity of the population in the territory of the new state. The use of the categories 'language' and 'nationality' permitted identification of non-Latvians in the country just as international norms required, to be sure, but the question of who was or was not 'indigenous' was assumed to have been settled by the political events brought about by the outcome of the struggles of the First World War period. The 'indigenous' Latvians were now in charge of the state. Meanwhile, the two former dominant elites – the Baltic Germans and Russians – had become 'minority nationalities', as had all the other 'non-Latvian' subpopulations, in spite of the fact that Germans, Russians, Jews and Poles had been a presence in the country for hundreds of years. The claims by some Liv and Latgalian activists that their 'national' groups were 'more indigenous' than other Latvians were not taken seriously. The central Latvian government followed a very liberal policy toward its 'minority nationalities', funding their schools and cultural initiatives, and endorsing elementary education in minority languages. The government also remained generally satisfied that such efforts promoted social integration as much as could reasonably be expected (Dribins 1998). Ethnolinguistic differences within the 'Latvian' population were documented but were also suspected of having the potential to produce fissures in the unity of the new state. The governmental stance toward the nationality question became less patient under the dictatorship of President Karlis Ulmanis, who came to power in May 1934, and his declared policy of making Latvians full masters of 'their' country. The 'minority nationalities' (especially Germans and Jews) began to lose their position in the economy, and the censorship of the Ulmanis period, mild though it was, promoted the idea that Latvian was or soon would be a well-integrated state under the leadership of one nation (*tauta*). The Livs and Latgalians continued to be mentioned in ethnographic descriptions of the country, but they were portrayed as being linguistically assimilated by Latvians.

The Population Censuses of the Soviet Era

The end of the Second World War in 1945, as well as the last decade of Stalinism in the Soviet Union, brought immense changes to the political status and population composition of the three Baltic states. The three countries were incorporated into the Soviet Union in 1940, experienced German occupation from 1941 to 1945, and reoccupation by the Soviets in 1945. During this period (specifically, from 1939 to 1942), virtually all of the Baltic German population emigrated to Germany in response to Hitler's call for the *Volksdeutsche* or 'German nation' to 'return' to the Reich. At the same time, the Jewish population was almost entirely decimated by the Holocaust; and around 250,000 Balts fled westward ahead of the returning Soviet army in 1944/5, remaining in occupied Germany after 1945 as 'displaced persons'. Wartime deaths (executions, mass murders, military losses) amounted to about 90,000 in Estonia, 180,000 in Latvia and about 280,000 in Lithuania. In several waves of deportations (especially in 1941 and 1949) some 150,000 persons from the Baltic area were transported eastward to various places in the USSR as *kulak*s and 'enemies of the proletarian state'; only about a third of them returned during the amnesty period after 1956. As a result, in aggregate terms the population losses of the wartime period were severe: the estimates are about 15 per cent for Lithuania, 25 per cent for Estonia and 30 per cent for Latvia (Misiunas and Taagepera 1993: 354–56).

The population of the Baltic countries – now Soviet Socialist republics – showed up in the postwar period for the first time in the Russian census of 1959, the first postwar Soviet census. They continued to be enumerated in the next three Soviet censuses in 1970, 1979 and 1989. In this series, many of the problems of classification that had shaped the thinking of the interwar period – such as relative 'indigenousness' and 'minority nationalities' –disappeared, deemed to be the by-products of 'bourgeois nationalist' concerns. The new population paradigms and census models were now fashioned in Moscow (see Table 15.2), and were informed by what was termed 'Leninist nationality policy' of the peaceful coexistence of all peoples and their full cooperation in the building of communism.

Had they been acknowledged in the Soviet-era censuses in some way, the question of 'indigenousness' would have been in any case a very explosive one, especially in Estonia and Latvia, in light of Soviet economic planning in the postwar decades and the new migration patterns this planning created. The Baltic Soviet republics were now part of the 'Soviet system', and economic planning was carried out at the all-Soviet level in Moscow without much regard for how such plans might or might not affect the populations of individual republics. Thus, in the Baltic countries, overall plans called for the creation of industrial enterprises that served the entire USSR regardless of the nature and size of the local labour force. An insufficient local labour supply was corrected by the recruitment to the Baltic republics of hundreds of thousands of Soviet citizens from the Slavic republics of the Soviet Union, largely from the Russian, Ukrainian and Belorussian republics. The proportion of titular populations in the three Baltic republics continued to fall with each census – less in Lithuania, somewhat more in Estonia, very rapidly in Latvia – so that by the late 1980s most of the major cities of the Baltic region where large-scale industry was located had a majority non-Baltic population (see Table 15.3 for aggregate proportions in Latvia). Published census materials during the Soviet decades used the 'nationality' variable in their tables very cautiously, particularly so in the Baltic republics. There was concern even among members of the republics' Communist parties – the so-called 'national communists' – over the possible disappearance of the cultures and languages of the Baltic states as a result of the influx of non-Balts into the region, but challenge to the policies that had created these migration patterns was met with swift reprisals against lingering 'bourgeois nationalism'. The ethnographic sectors of the three academies of science in the Baltic area were permitted to research some questions pertaining to the 'ethnogenesis' of the republic's peoples in the very distant past, but such research was considered undesirable for the postwar Soviet period. Such restrictions were less onerous among researchers in Moscow, but, as we now know, until the 1980s information about the national composition of individual regions tended to be treated as something like a state secret. This avoidance was reflected in the published materials that grew out of all of the censuses of the Soviet period. These enumerations retained the expected nomenclature about nationality and language, but cross-tabulations of demographic data by nationality or language were rare, reflecting an effort to downplay or perhaps disguise nationality differences. There were also abortive political efforts to introduce a new 'nationality' category – 'Soviet' nationality. The theory behind this was that the importance of traditional 'national' and 'linguistic' communities would gradually fade as, under the integrating forces of modernisation, personal identity became linked to a new type of transnational community that transcended the old categories. Nationality, in other words, would cease being ethnic and become political – there would only be a Soviet nationality. Religion also disappeared from the Soviet-era censuses, on the grounds that religious identity was an unimportant relic hindering the effective functioning of a 'progressive' state. It did not, however, disappear from Latvian society itself.

As we now know from studies of the Soviet-era censuses of the Baltic republics, these were perhaps the most politicised documents of the entire series presented in Table 15.2 (see Clem 1986). For ideological reasons, the multinational and multiethnic USSR had to present its population as one characterised by increasingly diminishing rifts and fissures – as a population well on its way toward a modernity in which some forms of group consciousness were disappearing to be replaced by others that were considered 'natural' to a higher stage of historical development. In reality, of course, the consciousness of ethnicity and nationality remained very much alive, particularly so in the Baltic republics. The rapidity with which the Baltic populations rallied around the idea of separate nationalities between 1988 and 1990 during Mikhail Gorbachev's reforms, and the self-evident surprise of the Moscow authorities that this should have happened, are clear evidence of how the Soviet-era censuses failed as reliable guides to the stresses and strains that lay just beneath the surface of the three Baltic republics (Senn 1995: 27–30).

The Latvian Post-Soviet Census of 2000

The three Baltic states regained independence in 1991 as a result of the collapse of the Soviet Union, and this political event moved a host of population questions in Latvia to the forefront of popular discussion, where they have remained ever since (Zvidriņš 2002; Zvidriņš and Vanovska 1992). Latvians' profound unhappiness with Soviet rule was rooted in their strong belief that the population policies of the USSR would lead to the eventual disappearance of ethnic Latvians, or, at least, to a Latvian republic in which Latvians would be a much-reduced minority. The results of the 1989 Soviet census – which showed ethnic Latvians to be about 51 per cent of the republic's total population – was perceived as a danger signal. The continued immigration each year of thousands of ethnic Slavs; the assimilation of Latvians to the Russian-speaking population through intermarriage; the increasing dominance of the Russian language in all spheres of life, including professional life; the low fertility rate among Latvians – all these indicators pointed to the same conclusion, namely, that the sources of Latvian collective identity – particularly language – were in danger. Soviet nationality policy, of course, had argued that in so large and sprawling a multicultural society as the USSR there should be a two-tiered collective identity – a 'national' one, based on the language and culture of particular republics; and an 'international' one, expressed primarily in the use of the Russian language in all activities. But this argument was perceived by Latvians as only an updated version of the Russification policy of the pre-First World War period.

Fear that in the modern world the places where Latvian identity could be acquired and maintained were shrinking in number explains the quasi-nationalistic policies adopted by the new Latvian governments in the decade after independence in August 1991. Latvians, as well as Livs (Livonians) were declared to be the 'basic nations' of the Latvian state; Latvian was declared to be the sole language of the state; and citizenship in the new state was granted only to members of the 'basic nations' and to those non-Latvians whose families could demonstrate a history of residence in Latvia prior to the Second World War. Those who could not, which amounted to about 40 per cent of the population at the time, were expected to go through a process of naturalisation to obtain citizenship. Many of these rather stringent laws, adopted in the years immediately before and after 1991, were later modified as a result of pressures from European international institutions of which Latvia desired membership. But there is no doubt that in the first flush of renewed independence the new government, staffed at the ministerial level primarily by ethnic Latvians, meant to render the sources of Latvian identity more secure by underlining the fact that a large segment of the population – that is, those who mainly spoke Russian but which consisted of persons of many different ethnicities, such as Russians, Belorussian, Ukrainians, Jews and so on – were to be distinguished from the 'basic nation'.

In the decade and a half that followed 1991, population counts in Latvia had to adapt in a number of ways which showed up in the census of 2000, the only one taken since 1991. The inclusion of Livs as a second 'basic nation' of the country was a bow toward the idea of cultural diversity: the Livs, who in census of 2000 were self-identified as a tiny minority of 177 persons, were no threat to the larger Latvian population. They were, in any case, widely dispersed throughout the country and moved easily between their 'Liv' and 'Latvian' identities. However much special attention was paid to them, the Livs were not likely to introduce any uncontrollable fissures into the body politic.

The region of Latgale and its inhabitants (about 500,000 in 2004) presented a rather different problem. The proportion of 'Latvians' in Latgale in 2000 was below half; the region's large Russian-speaking population was located adjacent to the Russian Federation; and on most socio-economic measures of development and well-being, when compared to the four regions of Latvia, Latgale stood at the bottom. Moreover, in the new atmosphere of free public discussion, the question of the standing of the Latgalian language, or dialect, reared its head again. For example, there were allegations that in the 2000 census those residents of Latgale who had put down their 'nationality' as 'Latgalian' (rather than 'Latvian') had had that entry changed to 'Latvian'.[1] A certain resentment continues to simmer even among professionals of Latgalian origin about their disparate treatment in education. A linguist commented to a newspaper reporter:

> In my view, Latgalians and Latgalian culture have not been thoroughly integrated in Latvia. No one has worked to bring the Latgalian cultural heritage into the mainstream of Latvian culture. Even in the first grade, no one cares that I have to break myself into half and enter an entirely different cultural tradition, since up to that time I have spoken only Latgalian.[2]

Moreover, the Russian-speaking population of Latgale tended to orient itself toward the East rather than the West. This was the only sub-population, for example, which expressed grave doubts about Latvia's entry into the European Union (EU). Though many persons of Latgalian ancestry have 'mainstreamed' themselves and no longer reside in Latgale, thereby rendering separatism a historic issue only, this region and its languages and dialects has remained a potential source for an alternative collective identity in the Latvian state. There is no doubt that Russian nationality and the Russian language continued throughout the region to be sources of an alternative national identity, as Russian-language newspapers, and demands to have Russian made into a second state language and separate Russian-language schools all indicate.

It is perhaps for these reasons (among others) that, in contrast to publications based on the interwar censuses (e.g., Skujenieks 1938), the published results of the sole postcommunist census of Latvia in 2000 downplayed the cross-tabulation of population characteristics by region (see VSP 2002; CSP 2002). Results are cross-tabulated by the next smallest administrative division – *rajons* – requiring the reader interested in regional characteristics to do substantial recalculations. This is in contrast to the thrust of the United Nation's human development report for Latvia, which deals explicitly with the relative development of Latvia's four regions and reports, among other things, that 'local identity is most explicit in Latgale' (United Nations 2005: 27). The 2000 census also continued the practice of the Soviet-era censuses of not using 'religion' as a variable (see Table 15.2). Were 'religion' used, it would show the overwhelming Roman Catholicism of the Latgalian non-Russian population, thus underlining another feature differentiating the population of Latgale from 'western' Latvians.

The 2000 census, however, reported one feature of the population of Latvia that may be of greater concern for the country than any potential ethno-national fissures. The total population of Latvia has been diminishing each year since 1991, in part because of emigration and in part because of the low fertility levels in all sub-populations, Latvian and Russian speakers alike. Initially, emigration primarily involved Russian speakers moving to Russia or to other former Soviet republics; that migration has diminished in size more recently, but the drain has continued through the westward migration of working-age Latvians in search of jobs, particularly after 2004 when Latvian became a member of the EU. It is estimated that some 86,000 citizens of Latvia are currently working or studying outside the country. Although the ethnic Latvian component of the total population of the country has grown from about 52 per cent in 1989 to about 58 per cent in 2004 (see Table 15.3), there are now fewer ethnic Latvians in total, in Latvia and the diaspora, than ever.

Conclusion

The contrast between what I have here called 'the two narratives' is heightened in the Latvian case by, first, the political discontinuities of the eastern

Baltic littoral for the period when censuses were carried out; and, second, by the very unsettled nature of the national and ethnic identities of important segments of the population. It is almost as if political regimes, the grouping categories of the enumerations they carried out, and the people being counted were in constant flux, with each time period generating a different mix of the same set of questions about both personal and collective identity. The technical specialists who devised census questionnaires, carried out enumerations and tabulated the results studied international precedents and techniques, worked in good faith and sought to make public a credible result. Yet in retrospect it appears clear that each generation of specialists not only remained products of their times but must have often felt direct pressure to de-emphasise in the published census figures aspects of the counted population the government of the time either had no interest in or felt uncomfortable about. Foremost among these aspects was the idea that a given population had in fact a great many identifiable sub-populations in it, or that a population had characteristics the official acknowledgement of which could buttress the self-consciousness of this or that group.

At the same time as decisions were made by enumerators about which group characteristics to use, however, descriptions in less official sociological, linguistic and anthropological studies were making patently clear the protean nature of personal and collective identity in Latvia, which then ensured that any given census was a poor representation of what at a given moment in time the society was really like. The two-narrative problem therefore seems to be a permanent fixture of any numerical attempt at thoroughly understanding any given population; change, being a constant, means that as a population is tallied its composition is changing in large and small ways, and this change will have altered its make-up by the time a census is published in a permanent form.

Notes

1. See the press report in *Laiks*, 26 August–1 September 2006, p. 15.
2. *Laiks*, 26 August–1 September 2006, p. 15.

References

Anderson, M.J. 1988. *The American Census: A Social History.* New Haven, CT: Yale University Press.

Anon. 1905. *Pervaya vseobshchaya perepis naseleniya Rossisckoi imperii, 1897. g. XXI. Liflyandskaya guberniya.* St Petersburg.

Bojtár, E. 1999. *Foreword to the Past: A Cultural History of the Baltic People.* Budapest: Central European University Press.

Clem, R.S. (ed.) 1986. *Research Guide to the Russian and Soviet Censuses.* Ithaca, NY: Cornell University Press.

CSP. 2002. 'Latvijas demogrāfijas gadagrāmata 2002'. Riga: Centrālā statistikas pārvalde.

Dribins, L. 1997. *Nacionālais jautājums Latvijā 1850–1940*. Riga: Latvijas Zinātņu Akadēmijas Filozofijas un ssocioloğijas institūts.

——— (ed.) 1998. *Mazākumtautību vēsture Latvijā*. Riga: Zvaigzne.

Eley, G., and R.G. Suny (eds). 1996. *Becoming National: A Reader*. New York: Oxford University Press.

Haltzel, M. 1981. 'The Baltic Germans', in E. Thaden (ed.), *Russification in the Baltic Provinces and Finland, 1885–1914*. Princeton, NJ: Princeton University Press, pp.111–204.

Kaudzīte, M. 1994[1923]. *Atmiņas no Tautiskā Laikmeta*. Riga: Zvaigzne ABC.

Keyserling, P.E. von. 1805. *Beschreibung der Provinz Kurland*. Mitau: Steffenhagen und Sohn.

Misiunas, R., and R. Taagepera. 1993. *The Baltic States: Years of Dependence*. Berkeley: University of California Press.

Plakans, A. 1995. *The Latvians: A Short History*. Stanford, CA: Hoover Institution Press.

Plakans, A., and C. Wetherell. 2004. 'The 1881 Census in the Russian Baltic Provinces: An Inventory and an Assessment', *History of the Family* 9: 47–61.

RkO. 1943. 'Statistische Berichte für das Ostland', Nos.1–12. Riga: Reichskomissar für das Ostland.

Roth, B. 1991. 'Sprachen', in H. Bauer, A. Kappeler and B. Roth (eds), *Die Nationalitäten des Russsichen Reiches in der Volkszählung von 1897, Vol.2*. Stuttgart: Franz Steiner Verlag, pp.135–284.

Senn, A.E. 1995. *Gorbachev's Failure in Lithuania*. New York: St Martin's Press.

Skujeneeks, M. 1922. *Latvija: Zeme un Iedzīvotāji*. Riga: Valsts statistiskā pārvalde.

Skujenieks, M. 1938. *Latvijas Statistikas Atlass*. Riga: Valsts statistiskā pārvalde.

Stieda, W. 1881. 'Zur Bevorstehenden Volkszählung', *Baltische Monatschrift* 28: 141–58.

Thaden, E. 1984. *The Western Borderlands of Russia, 1710–1870*. Princeton, NJ: Princeton University Press.

United Nations. 2005. 'UN Human Development Report 2004/05: Latvia'. Riga: Advanced Social and Political Research Institute, University of Latvia.

VSP. 2002. 'Latvijas 2000. gada tautas skaitīšanas rezultāti'. Riga: Valsts statistiskā pārvalde.

Zeile, P. 2006. *Latgales Kultūras Vēsture*. Rezekne: Latgales Kulturas Centrs.

Zvidriņš, P. 2002. *Demogrāfija*. Riga: Latvijas Universitāte.

Zvidriņš, P., and I. Vanovska. 1992. *Latvieši: Statistiski Demogrāfisks Portretējums*. Riga: Zinātne.

16
WHO ARE THE BRITISH?

John MacInnes

The 'identity categories' of successive censuses from the late nineteenth century up to the recent present show an extraordinarily rapid, superficially arbitrary, series of changes, in which categories are continuously agglomerated, disaggregated, recombined, intermixed, and reordered (but the politically powerful identity categories always lead the list) … [A]s the colonial period wore on, the census categories became more visibly and exclusively racial.

—Benedict Anderson, *Imagined Communities.*

Introduction:
Identity Categories in Official Censuses and Surveys

Identity categories usually fit poorly into the ordered classification systems of official censuses and surveys since they lack an external, standard referent. People can make claims about their own or others' identity that are not subject to the kind of verification applicable to their sex, place of birth or current occupation. Identity categories are 'fluid', not in the sense that they might change over time, like occupation, but in the sense that being entirely discursively constructed there neither is, nor can there be, any mechanism to endow them with a fixed meaning. Because of this, measuring identity in this way produces results that depend more upon implicit or explicit agreements reached between the state and those claiming to represent the groups thus measured (identity 'entrepreneurs') than upon any supposed characteristics of the population that lie beyond such an agreement.

Identity categories are usually the product of conflicts over power and material or symbolic resources. Because of this, the powerful or affluent often have less need to mobilise these categories in such an overt way. Paradoxically, this may make the fluidity of these categories rather more visible to the sociologist. Therefore this chapter examines the use of ethnic categories in U.K. censuses, focusing on the category that leads the list of these and asking: Who are the British? The U.K. offers a useful case study because although the 'British' are not an 'indigenous people' in the sense that sociologists and anthropologists normally use this term, most people born in Britain, especially if they are white, would probably think of themselves as such, especially in contrast to those they might regard as 'immigrants'. Moreover we find that, especially in the context of discussing immigration or race, social scientists often follow them in using the word 'indigenous' itself.

The U.K. is a good place to look at official attempts to enumerate ethnic or other 'identities' for two other reasons. One is the happy accident that the British census is administered by three different organisations: the Office for National Statistics (ONS) in England and Wales, the General Register Office Scotland (GROS), and the Northern Ireland Statistics and Research Agency (NISRA). Their decisions about questionnaire formulation may be coordinated but are not centrally controlled, presenting opportunities for comparison. Second, the initial difficulties encountered in introducing a suitable ethnicity question in the decennial population census prompted the inclusion of such questions in several large-scale voluntary sample surveys such as the Labour Force Survey (LFS). This not only gives social scientists an invaluable range of other information to correlate with how respondents answer questions about ethnicity, but also facilitates a rare opportunity to examine the impact of different forms of question wording and order. Given the substantial sample sizes – 0.5 per cent of the adult population in the case of the LFS – and frequency of repetition, we can look at very small groups within the general population, especially if successive waves of a survey are combined. The data in this paper comes from combining seventeen successive quarters of the LFS, from spring 2002 to spring 2007 inclusive. This provides just under half a million cases, corresponding to a cross section of the U.K. population across this time period. For ease of presentation, results have been weighted to correspond approximately to the U.K. population of 2005. In addition to the LFS, the British Social Attitudes Survey (BSAS) and Scottish Social Attitudes Survey (SSAS) also ask respondents about Britishness. However, their much smaller sample sizes (around 2,000 respondents) do not let us examine views of minority ethnic groups within the population.

The British as 'Indigenous'

A coherent definition of a people as 'indigenous' has to refer specifically to the wave of imperial expansion associated with the rise of market society in Europe from the fifteenth century onwards. Archaeological and historical evidence suggests that human society has always been highly mobile, so that the term does not usually refer to some 'original' occupation of a territory but rather to the clash between 'native' peoples and colonisers over the extension and nature of state power, usually legitimated by racially inspired theories of 'civilisation'. The putative connection between soil and people can be exploited in two, diametrically opposed, directions. It can be argued that mobility signals superiority, while connexion to the soil marks a people's imprisonment in the poverty of social, historical and cultural development. Alternatively, in the context of migration towards Europe, and given the tight connexion between territory and state there, 'indigenous' can come to signal the putative link between nation and state, and thus privileged access to the protection of the state, higher status and informal or formal economic advantages.

No group of any political significance explicitly claims to be indigenous in the U.K. Gaelic and Welsh speakers in Scotland and Wales demand and receive special treatment of and protection for the use of their languages, but there is no attempt in either case to link language to descent (just the opposite in fact) or to broaden the issue to other dimensions of culture or heritage. However, none of this prevents public discourse and political discussion using the term British as if it referred self-evidently to a group which is at once rooted in a specific territory (the U.K.) and associated with a definite (but unspecified) culture or set of values. Those able to trace their lineage back a few generations might think of themselves as 'indigenous' but would meet none of the other criteria conventionally associated with the concept of indigenous people as marked out in International Labour Organisation (ILO) or United Nations conventions by virtue of the U.K.'s imperial past. On the contrary, most political discourses now use the imagery of successive waves of migration or some other analogous process to claim diversity for the U.K. population and claim a purely civic character to its political union. A good example comes from a speech by the former Prime Minister, Gordon Brown:

> While we have always been a country of different nations and thus of plural identities – a Welshman can be Welsh and British, just as a Cornishman or woman is Cornish, English and British – and may be Muslim, Pakistani or Afro-Caribbean, Cornish, English and British – there is always a risk that, when people are insecure, they retreat into more exclusive identities rooted in nineteenth-century conceptions of blood, race and territory – when instead we the British people should be able to gain great strength from celebrating a British identity which is bigger than the sum of its parts and a union that is strong because of the values we share and because of the way these values are expressed through our history and our institutions ... If we are clear about what underlies our Britishness and if we are clear that shared values – not colour, nor unchanging and unchangeable institutions – define what it means to be British in the modern world, we can be far more ambitious in defining for our time the responsibilities of citizenship ... British patriotism is, in my view, founded not on ethnicity nor race, not just on institutions we share and respect, but on enduring ideals which shape our view of ourselves and our communities ... What has emerged ... from the 2,000 years of successive waves of invasion, immigration, assimilation and trading partnerships ... is a distinctive set of values. (Brown 2006)

However the assumption that most people of white skin colour are almost all descendents of individuals long settled in the U.K. is so general that even social scientists resort to casual use of the term 'indigenous' as, for example, when Booth (1985: 259) distinguishes 'indigenous whites' from more recent migrants from Europe. Neither have all successive waves of migration been seen as equal. Thus Sillitoe and White describe the 'influx of people from other continents' (the West Indies, East Africa and Asia) that began in the 1950s as 'historically unique' because of 'the important fact that, unlike most of their predecessors, these later immigrants were clearly distinguishable from the indigenous population by the colour of their skins' (Sillitoe and White 1992: 141).

One of the few groups to make explicit claims about the indigenous character of the British, in order to portray this last wave of immigration as different from its 'historic' antecedents, is the British National Party (BNP), a neo-Nazi group with a scattering of local councillors. Condor (2006), makes an illuminating comparison between the discourse used by groups like the BNP and the dominant 'multicultural British' discourse, as used by Gordon Brown. The BNP's mission statement declares:

> The British National Party exists to secure a future for the indigenous peoples of these islands in the North Atlantic which have been our homeland for millennia. We use the term indigenous to describe the people whose ancestors were the earliest settlers here after the last great Ice Age and which have been complemented by the historic migrations from mainland Europe. The migrations of the Celts, Anglo-Saxons, Danes, Norse and closely related kindred peoples have been, over the past few thousands years, instrumental in defining the character of our family of nations ... We have lived in these islands near on 40,000 years! We were made by these islands, and these islands are our home. When we in the BNP talk about being British, we talk about the native peoples who have lived in these islands since before the Stone Age, and *the relatively small numbers of peoples of almost identical stock*, such as the Saxons, Vikings and Normans, and the Irish, who have come here and assimilated. (BNP 2006, original emphasis)

Immigration from the West Indies, East Africa, India, Bangladesh and Pakistan became the focus of moral panic in the 1960s. In 1968, Enoch Powell predicted 'rivers of blood' flowing as a result of racial conflict caused by the inexorable rise in the proportion of black immigrants in the U.K. In the course of that decade the issues of immigration and race became intimately related in British politics, with race being defined almost entirely in terms of skin pigmentation. The key issue came to focus on the number of non-white immigrants living in Britain, since those opposed to such immigration argued that too large a number would frustrate their integration, increase unemployment, create new demands on public services and 'threaten' British 'culture'. Thus a year before becoming Prime Minister, Margaret Thatcher declared:

it is not easy to get clear figures from the Home Office about immigration, but there was a committee which looked at it and said that if we went on as we are then by the end of the century there would be four million people of the new Commonwealth or Pakistan here. Now, that is an awful lot and I think it means that people are really rather afraid that this country might be rather swamped by people with a different culture and, you know, the British character has done so much for democracy, for law and done so much throughout the world that if there is any fear that it might be swamped people are going to react and be rather hostile to those coming in.[1]

Note how immigrants (signalled as coloured by the terms 'new Commonwealth' and Pakistan) are associated with 'a different culture' which is contrasted with a civic 'British character' whose potential hostility is legitimated in advance as a defence against being 'swamped'. White immigration was a non-issue, despite being of roughly equal volume. Around

Table 16.1. Resident Population of England, Wales and Scotland by Date of Arrival

Date of arrival in U.K. 'Ethnic group'	Born in U.K.	1940s–70s	1980s–90s	since 2000	All (000s)
White					
British	97.7	1.5	0.6	0.2	50200
Other White	44.5	12.8	17.8	24.9	2757
Mixed					
White and Black Caribbean	95.4	1.9	1.9	0.9	216
White and Black African	70.4	3.7	13.6	12.3	81
White and Asian	84.9	6.8	4.8	3.4	146
Other Mixed	69.5	8.5	12.8	9.2	141
Asian or Asian British					
Indian	44.5	28.1	15.0	12.4	1091
Pakistani	56.5	16.7	17.8	9.0	802
Bangladeshi	50.2	11.4	29.8	8.6	325
Other Asian	24.4	14.6	28.1	32.9	377
Black or Black British					
Black Caribbean	63.3	26.2	6.4	4.1	592
Black African	35.5	5.1	31.9	27.5	670
Other Black	68.4	12.3	10.5	8.8	57
Chinese or other group					
Chinese	26.3	17.4	26.8	29.6	213
Other	23.2	12.2	29.1	35.5	707
All	90.5	3.4	3.2	2.9	58375
Weighted N (000s)	52808	1987	1877	1703	58375

Sources: U.K. Labour Force Survey 2002–2007; author's calculations.

5.5 million people currently living in Britain were not born there, of whom about 2.7 million describe themselves as white. In turn, popular semantics have tended to fuse 'colour', 'ethnicity' and immigration over time so that in much of the popular imagination and in language use (in the tabloid press, for example) all those from beyond Europe and its former imperial settlements are 'coloured', regardless of skin pigmentation, while for those born in these areas but with dark skin pigmentation, the latter overrides their place of birth. For both groups, the term 'immigrant' may be used, even when it is a misnomer. Table 16.1 estimates the population of England, Wales and Scotland in terms of the ethnic categories used in the 2001 census and date of arrival in the U.K. for those not born there. The earliest immigration was from the Caribbean, India, Bangladesh and Pakistan, and although not shown separately, Ireland. The table also shows that around a half of those reported in the non-white and 'other white' ethnic groups have been born in the U.K.

The Census, Migration and Ethnicity

This focus on numbers and race led to an interest in including a question on ethnicity in the 1981 census. Some believed it would substantiate claims about the size of the 'immigrant' community. Conversely, supporters of racial equality saw it as providing vital information about discrimination and unequal treatment. Previous censuses had asked about place of birth, and parents' birthplace, but this had two drawbacks: it failed to distinguish between whites and others born in the same place – for example, children of imperial civil servants – and could not identify grandchildren of immigrants (Booth 1985). In the event, it was a Conservative government led by Margaret Thatcher that abandoned the attempt. Community activists linked the inclusion of an ethnicity question in the census with what they argued were government plans to restrict immigration, restrict the rights of those already settled or even encourage repatriation. The pre-census test was a failure, with many objecting to questions about ethnicity or place of birth, or refusing to complete the census (House of Commons 1983; Bulmer 1986; Sillitoe and White 1992).

This episode had two important consequences: a shift to using sample surveys to explore how to gather information on ethnicity, and an emphasis on consultation with minority ethnic groups on formulating questions aimed at capturing how these groups identified themselves. As well as providing results usable by policy makers, the ONS has emphasised 'the importance of ensuring that any decisions are trusted by the various communities and not seen as part of a constraint on cultural identity. [The chief statistician] considers that ethnic groups themselves need to "own" the labels as well as the identity' (ONS 2001).

In part because of the successful trial of questions in sample surveys in the intervening decade, and in part because of efforts to involve minority ethnic organisations in its formulation, a question on ethnicity was asked with no resistance in the 1991 census and repeated with some small changes in 2001. For brevity's sake I shall concentrate on the details of the 2001 question. The precise form of the evolution of the question has a well-documented history (see Booth 1985; Bulmer 1986, 1996; Sillitoe and White 1992; Ballard 1997; Dale and Holdsworth 1997). Table 16.2 shows the questions from the ONS and GROS census forms and the corresponding proportions of populations identifying themselves with each ethnic category in the census, and in the successive waves of the LFS between 2002 and 2007.

Table 16.2. Ethnicity Question England and Wales 2001 and Scotland 2001 Censuses

England and Wales (ONS)	Census 2001	LFS 2002–7	Scotland (GROS)	Census 2001	LFS 2002–7
A White			**A White**		
British	87.5	85.6	Scottish	88.1	97.7
Irish	1.2	4.4	Other British	7.4	
Any other white background	2.6		Irish	1.0	
			Any other white background	1.5	
B Mixed			**B Mixed**		
White and black Caribbean	0.5	0.4	Any mixed background	0.3	0.4
White and black African	0.2	0.1			
White and Asian	0.4	0.3			
Any other mixed background	0.3	0.3			
C Asian or Asian British			**C Asian or Asian Scottish or Asian British**		
Indian	2.0	2.0	Indian	0.3	0.3
Pakistani	1.4	1.5	Pakistani	0.6	0.7
Bangladeshi	0.5	0.6	Bangladeshi	*	*
Any other Asian background	0.5	0.7	Chinese	0.3	0.2
			Any other Asian background	0.1	0.2
D Black or Black British			**D Black or Black Scottish or Black British**		
Caribbean	1.1	1.1	Caribbean	*	*
African	0.9	1.2	African	0.1	0.2
Another black background	0.2	0.1	Another black background	*	*
E Chinese or Other ethnic group			**E Any other background**		
Chinese	0.4	0.4		0.2	0.3
Other ethnic group	0.4	1.3			

Note: Respondents were asked 'What is your ethnic group? Choose one from section A to E and then tick the appropriate box to indicate your cultural background.' * = less than 0.1 %.
Sources: ONS and GROS census tables and LFS 2002–2007; author's calculations.

The majority of respondents found the question reasonably easy to complete, based as it is on common-sense categories frequent in everyday speech, and supposedly 'owned' by the respondents. The price of respecting common sense, and 'ownership', is a considerable empirical and analytical muddle. Isn't China part of Asia? If British is a subset of 'White', what is 'Black British'? Does Asian British refer to place of birth or skin color? Where are non-whites who think of themselves as British rather than as Asian, Black or African to place themselves? Since when did Bangladesh, India or Pakistan constitute ethnic or cultural communities rather than states? Are 1960s immigrants from what is now Bangladesh Pakistani? If its population comprises only fellow Asian-Indians, why is Kashmir riven by particularly murderous ethnic conflict? Where do non-white 'Europeans' go? What about white South Africans who do not consider that their colour takes precedence over their continental or national origin? The muddle also arises from the difficulty of referring to the indigenous population straightforwardly as 'white', which might expose the racial foundations marking 'ethnic' distinctions and which Sillitoe and White (1992) report was resisted by the government. Because of this, 'Asian' is a euphemism for skin color rather than a geographical category.

Britishness in Northern Ireland, Scotland and Wales

The muddle does not stop there, however. Not all those who reported themselves as 'British' under the ethnicity question in the census necessarily preferred to think of themselves as such in other contexts. Indeed, the meanings which can be read into the term are manifold, referring not only to ethnicity but also to citizenship, national identity (concentric, complementary to or conflicting with other national identities in the U.K.) or various places of birth, but also capable of signalling, in different contexts, a range of different social or political affiliations. This explains the rather different wording of the census in Scotland: here, Scottish appears as the first 'white' category, and the inclusion of the word 'other' before 'British' implies this is to be taken, unlike 'Irish', as a subset of 'British'.[2] Moreover, the place in the U.K. where we find the most strenuous assertions of Britishness and where the dominant political party founds its entire worldview on 'loyalty' to the British Crown – Northern Ireland – is also the only place where 'British' does not appear as an ethnic category and is indeed directly replaced by a racial marker: 'white'. Table 16.3 shows the categories used in Northern Ireland and the corresponding proportion of population. The reason for this yet more piecemeal approach – where do non-white Europeans or North Americans go? are Irish travellers non-whites? – is simply to avoid categories associated with the fierce political conflict between those variously described as Nationalist, Republican, Irish or Catholic and Loyalist, British and Protestant.

Table 16.3. Northern Ireland Census 2001: Ethnicity

White	99.15
Irish Traveller	0.10
Mixed	0.20
Indian	0.09
Pakistani	0.04
Bangladeshi	0.01
Other Asian	0.01
Black Caribbean	0.02
Black African	0.03
Other Black	0.02
Chinese	0.25
Other ethnic group	0.08

Note: Respondents were asked 'To which of these ethnic groups do you consider you belong?'
Source: Northern Ireland Statistics and Research Agency.

One of the key demands of minority ethnic groups within the census consultation exercises prior to both the 1991 and 2001 censuses was the addition of the suffix 'British' to ethnic categories like Asian or Black. Indeed, survey pilots have also registered resistance on the part of many people from minority ethnic communities to be defined as anything other than British. Since 'British' is the first qualifier to the 'white' category in England and Wales, it seems reasonable to suppose that both those asking and those answering the question wished British to be understood as an ethnic category, associated, *inter alia* with their skin colour. Leaving aside the difficulty that the term British thus appears in three out of six categories, interesting results appear when we compare census results for different parts of the U.K., obtained by subtle changes in question wording.

As Table 16.1 shows, respondents in Scotland were invited to describe themselves as Scottish rather than British. The description of the subsequent sub-category as 'other British' could be taken to imply that White Scottish, in this context, was to be seen as composite part of 'White British'. In any event, the overwhelming majority of those born in Scotland chose this option, with those born elsewhere in the U.K. divided between this category and 'other British', so that 88 per cent described themselves as 'white Scottish'.

Scotland and Wales share very similar ethnic mixes – in the specific sense of the proportion of the population describing themselves as white – and broadly similar strengths of national sentiment and proportions of the population born there, in the rest of the U.K. and abroad. We might, therefore, expect the ethnic mix of the population as described by the census to be similar. However, they could hardly be more different. Only 14 per cent of the population in Wales declared themselves to be 'white Welsh'. How could this come about?

For some reason, presumably an oversight, no special category was included for 'Welsh' within the Census for England and Wales in the way in which Scottish was offered as a sub-category of 'white' in the Scottish Census. Thus, although 'white' respondents in Scotland were asked to choose between Scottish, other British and Irish backgrounds, respondents in Wales were given no corresponding option. This drew protests from Welsh nationalist MPs in the House of Commons prior to the census. However, they received a rebuke from Allan Rodgers, Labour MP for Rhondda in south Wales, who, responding to the Welsh nationalist Plaid Cymru MP Simon Thomas, asserted, 'I am sorry that the hon. Gentleman is so unsure of his Welshness that he needs a tick box to affirm it'.[3]

At one level the exchange was part of the ritual of arguing over which identities are more relevant and consistent: Rodgers and later his party colleague Llew Smith implied that 'identification' with Welshness or choosing that as an ethnicity was less relevant than Britishness, as well as racial in its definition. The latter accused Plaid Cymru of using racial definitions of Welshness in the past and rejecting inclusive British identities: 'if someone from England comes to live in Wales and identifies with Wales, he may be regarded as Welsh. If that is your argument, it is against the whole history of your party which has been based on anti-English sentiment'.[4] For his part Thomas turned the tables, asserting that his definition was the civic one, 'Welshness is anyone who lives and works in Wales and wants to be Welsh',[5] while it was the term British that 'designates a mostly white ethnic background'.[6]

Why should a tick box matter? Rodgers's rebuke unwittingly contains a deeper insight. Were Welsh identity, whether ethnic or national, obvious and routine – like place of birth or sex – writing it in on a census form would probably not be a problem. But when such identity either has less salience, or less banal presence, tick boxes or other stimuli, may be of great importance. An audience routinely classified and addressed as Welsh, Ruritarian or whatever may come to regard itself thus, and sustaining a 'national' or ethnic sentiment may be vitally dependent on such address and classification. Insofar as this is the case, census classifications, rather than being empirical exercises of consistent categorisation, become political conflicts over the likely consequences of alternate schema. Were national or ethnic sentiment that which its entrepreneurs portray it to be, tick boxes, either literal or metaphorical, should be of little importance. If identity is so fundamental and obvious that it is simply realised or represented rather than shaped and constructed, surely its bearers, finding it written on their hearts, would write it without hesitation on their census forms.

In the event, conscious of its error, the government proceeded to fund a public information campaign urging people to write 'Welsh' under the 'Other white background' category. The results confirmed that Plaid Cymru was quite right to be concerned about tick boxes. Only 14 per cent of the population wrote in that they were Welsh. This could not have been because the strength of Welsh identity was so much weaker in Wales than Scottish identity was in Scotland. Tick boxes matter. But what might matter even more is whether we treat with sufficient caution the kind of empirical evidence we have about a phenomenon when the mere presence or absence of a tick box transforms our results. It is not a question of variation of a few percentage points but of the greatest possible contrast: 14 per cent versus 88 per cent.

The above suggests that, even when treated explicitly as an ethnic category by census makers, the term 'British' is rather elastic. In spatial terms it can, on the one hand, include not only the 'British Isles' but also the former territories of the British Empire – one reason why immigrants from these countries prefer to think of themselves as British – while on the other hand the term 'British Isles' is something of a misnomer. The Republic of Ireland occupies a significant part of these Isles, but its inhabitants would certainly not think of themselves as British. Moreover, many white people in the 'home nations' of England, Scotland and Wales claim not only to be Scottish, Welsh or English but do so to the exclusion of being British, if prompted in the right way.

Evidence on Britishness from the Labour Force Survey

Sample surveys, such as the LFS, become useful here, since they ask questions not only about ethnicity, but also about national identity, nationality, place of birth and a range of other characteristics. Moreover, changes in question wording and position allows us to make some judgement of their impact. The term 'British' is still considered too politically sensitive for use in surveys in Northern Ireland, so we can only use the LFS to look at England, Wales and Scotland.

The experience of Wales suggests that we must pay close attention to how questions are framed. In the LFS, respondents are first asked: What is your nationality? Because of the legacy of empire, the nature of citizenship and nationality in the U.K. is astonishingly complex (Karatani 2003). To this day its inhabitants may be citizens of Europe but remain subjects of the Crown. English common law distinguished between 'foreigners' and 'subjects' and extended this definition to the Empire, so that regardless of their descent or the circumstances of their birth, those born in the colonies or dominions became subjects of the British Crown. The U.K. state started to regulate movement across its frontiers at the start of the twentieth century in response to moral panics about Jewish immigration from Eastern Europe, and the first attempt to codify citizenship rights was the *Nationality Act 1914*. Decolonisation prompted further legislation in 1949, and since 1962, when governments started to restrict immigration in response to new moral panics about coloured immigration, successive restrictions on rights of entry have gone along with attempts to bring some order to this complexity, but usually in second place to political principle or expediency. Although earlier censuses asked a question about nationality, it was dropped after 1961 as the results were, unsurprisingly, unreliable. Accordingly I do not consider them here, except to note that around 90 per cent of respondents believe themselves to have British nationality. Respondents are then asked their country of birth, and those giving a place of birth outside the U.K. are asked: 'Which year did you arrive in this country?' All are then asked:

> What do you consider your national identity to be? Please choose as many or as few as apply.

> English
> Scottish
> Welsh
> Irish
> British
> Other (specify)

In England, Scotland and Wales the order of the categories is altered so that the national identity corresponding to the particular country comes first. Finally, all are asked:

> To which of these ethnic groups do you consider you belong?

> White
> Mixed
> Asian or Asian British
> Black or Black British
> Chinese
> Other ethnic group

Respondents are then asked to specify which of the ethnic sub-categories of the groups used in the 2001 census they consider themselves to belong. This gives us four different questions where respondents might describe themselves as 'British': in terms of nationality, place of birth, national identity and, finally, ethnicity. Should respondents query what is meant by national identity, interviewers are instructed to reply 'whatever it means to you'. How do people respond?

By using the question about national identity, we can distinguish those within different ethnic groups – such as 'Black or Black British' – who think of themselves as British. Table 16.4 shows the percentage of each ethnic sub-group, in terms of their answers to the ethnicity question, who said that they thought of their identity as British, those who reported a 'home nation' identity – that is, English, Welsh or Scottish – and those who gave any other national identity. As we have already seen, respondents

Table 16.4. Percentage Reporting British National Identity by 'Ethnic' Group LFS 2002–7

| Ethnic group | National Identity | | | |
	British	'Home Nation'	Other	N (000's)
Bangladeshi	72	4	29	212
Pakistani	71	9	27	559
Black Caribbean	69	16	21	472
Other Black	67	19	24	37
Indian	66	7	34	880
White and Asian	55	37	16	71
Other Mixed	50	25	34	83
White and Black Caribbean	50	49	7	96
White and Black African	46	30	33	43
Chinese	42	7	57	187
Other Asian	43	6	56	294
Black African	43	5	57	456
British	37	70	1	41,404
Other	31	4	68	554
Other White	7	35	50	2,434

Note: Ns are weighted to mid 2005 population estimates.
Sources: LFS 2002Q2 – 2007Q2. Excl. Northern Ireland; author's calculations.

could give as many identities as they thought relevant, although in practice few gave more than one.

These results are at first sight surprising, but with a little reflection quite understandable. Given the chance to express their Britishness, Britons from Pakistan, Bangladesh, India and the Caribbean not only do so unequivocally but are almost twice as likely to do so as the white British. Overall, 56 per cent of those in the non-white ethnic groups described themselves as British compared to 36 per cent of whites. Those arriving in the U.K. in the latter half of the twentieth century were rather more likely to describe themselves as British than whites born there. This is partly because the latter are more likely to describe themselves in terms of their home nation. Although non-whites were also more likely to choose the response 'other' than that of either British or a home nation category, this was rarely a matter of claiming the national identity of the place of origin associated with their census ethnic category. A mere 13,000 described themselves as 'Bangladeshi', 53,000 as Indian, 29,000 as Pakistani and less than 20,000 as Caribbean, West Indian or from one of the islands comprising this area. If we examine identity by year of arrival, we can see that it is only the most recent migrants who are less likely to see themselves as British (Table 16.5).

Table 16.5. Percentage Claiming British National Identity by Ethnic Group and Year of Arrival in the U.K., LFS 2002–7

'Ethnic' group	Born in U.K.	40s–70s	80s–90s	since 2000	All
White					
British	37	60	59	42	37
Other White	7	19	9	1	7
Mixed					
White and Black Caribbean	49	75	59	0	50
White and Black African	55	58	38	19	46
White and Asian	56	66	56	5	55
Other Mixed	58	70	33	12	50
Asian or Asian British					
Indian	80	78	57	12	66
Pakistani	81	80	69	15	71
Bangladeshi	86	84	72	24	72
Other Asian	73	78	47	8	43
Black or Black British					
Black Caribbean	72	76	47	20	69
Black African	76	73	49	10	43
Other					
Other Black	77	85	38	4	67
Chinese	71	62	48	6	42
Other	63	62	34	5	31
Total	37	60	41	7	37

Sources: LFS 2002Q2 – 2007Q2. Excl. Northern Ireland; author's calculations.

British Identity in the British and Scottish Social Attitudes Surveys

Since BSAS and SSAS are sample surveys they cannot provide reliable estimates for minority ethnic groups, but can do so for those classifying themselves as whites in terms of their racial origin, and it is these whose responses I consider here.[7] Without referring to either ethnicity or national identity, these surveys ask respondents:

> Please say which, if any, of the words on this card describes the way you think of yourself. Please choose as many or as few as apply.
>
> British
> English
> European
> Irish
> Northern Irish

Scottish
Welsh
Other answer (WRITE IN)
None of these

In both 2003 and 2005, two thirds of white respondents in England, Wales and Scotland chose the response 'British' either on its own or in combination with others. When asked which was the single 'most important' category, only 45 per cent of respondents chose 'British': about half the proportion that had opted for 'White-British' in the census. BSAS and SSAS also pose a question that invites respondents to compare the category British directly with home-nation ones and invites themselves to describe themselves as:

Only British
More British than English/Welsh/Scottish
Equally British and English/Welsh/Scottish
More English/Welsh/Scottish than British
Only English/Welsh/Scottish

This question has the merit of investigating to what extent respondents see 'British' and 'home nation' identities as concentric or contradictory, although with the considerable demerit of simultaneously implying that, although separate, to adopt more of one identity implies recognising less of another. Here very few white respondents indeed think of themselves as 'only British'. In contrast, as Table 16.6 shows, around one quarter of respondents in England (24 per cent) and over one third in Scotland (37 per cent) explicitly reject the term British, despite the fact such respondents had almost all been happy to check the categories 'white British' or 'white Scottish' (as 'other British') in the census. It appears that it is not just in Wales that tick boxes matter.

Table 16.6. Comparison of British and Home Nation Identities, BSAS and SSAS

	England (2003)	Scotland (2005)
Only British	9	5
More British than English /Scottish	13	4
Equally British and English /Scottish	33	22
More English/Scottish than British	21	33
Only English/Scottish	18	33
Other/none	6	4
N	1692	1488

Sources: BSAS 2003, SSAS 2005; author's calculations.

The Meaning of Britishness

BSAS 2003 also asked respondents about 'what it takes to be truly British'. The results were rather ambiguous. Only 15 per cent of respondents thought that it was necessary to be 'white'. However, just under half thought it was very important to have been born in Britain, but only one quarter thought it was about having British parents. Most thought 'true' Britishness depended upon speaking the language, respecting the law and 'feeling' that way. However a YouGov opinion poll conducted in July 2005, in the aftermath of the London terrorist bombings, suggested a thoroughly civic interpretation of Britishness, as Table 16.7. suggests.

However the YouGov poll provides another surprise. As we have seen, in their responses to SSAS, people in Scotland generally prioritise a Scottish over a British identity, and no less than 37 per cent explicitly reject a British identity altogether. The YouGov poll also asked respondents about their pride in Britishness, and as well as the response 'not proud to be British' offered them the option of stating that they were 'not British'. However, only 5 per cent of respondents in Scotland chose this option, while just under 8 out of 10 declared themselves 'very' or 'fairly proud' to be British, a similar proportion to those in the rest of Britain.

Table 16.7. Descriptions of Britishness, Yougov Poll, July 2005

% thinking each of the following phrases as important in defining 'Britishness':	
British people's right to say what they think	91
British people's sense of fairness and fair play	90
The achievements of Britain's scientists and engineers	89
Britain's defiance of Nazi Germany in 1940	87
British justice	86
People's politeness and consideration towards one another	86
Our parliamentary democracy	84
Their tolerance of other people and other people's ideas	81
The Royal Navy	79
The House of Commons	78
The Monarchy	69
The BBC	65
Double-decker buses	50
Red telephone boxes	49
The Church of England	45
Cricket	45
Warm British beer	23

Note: not all options are reproduced in the above table.
Source: Yougov poll archives available at http://www.yougov.com/extranets/yg-archives/content/archivesMain.asp?rID=4. (accessed 23 2 2007).

Defining Discursive Identities

The problem starts when one expects to find 'identity' within the body or mind of the individual. This is to look in the wrong place for the operation of identity … To have a national identity is to have a way of talking about nationhood … [O]nly if people believe that they have national identities, will such homelands, and the world of national homelands, be reproduced … Nor is national identity to be explored by taking a scale from the psychological library of tests and administering it to suitable populations … National identities are forms of social life, rather than internal psychological states; as such, they are ideological creations, caught up in the historical processes of nationhood.

—Michael Billig, *Banal Nationalism*

There are two sets of explanations for the pattern of results presented above, one broadly technical, the other to do with the sociological nature of identity categories. Research has suggested two relevant issues that affect how people answer multiple-choice-type survey questions. The first is that items at the top of a list are more popular than those lower down. The ONS tested this for national identity categories. Currently, the LFS places the 'home nation' responses first and 'Britain' last. Reversing this order increases the percentages choosing 'British', in the case of Scotland quadrupling the number of respondents who report that they are Scottish and British (Haselden and Jenkins 2003).

A second issue is that respondents, particularly in the context of a face-to-face interview (the standard format for first-wave LFS interviews) may be reluctant to repeat the same answer to different questions as it violates norms of conversational practice (Schwartz, Strack and Mai 1991). It may take some conversational stamina to insist on British nationality, Britain as a place of birth, British national identity and ethnicity too. However, it is unlikely that such an effect could explain the pattern of our results, since respondents seemed happy to choose British ethnicities in the final question in the list.

This takes us to the nature of identity categories and how respondents use them. Five conclusions can be drawn from our brief review of attempts to measure or define who the (indigenous) British are. The first is that while social scientists or demographers might wish for census classifications based on scientific principles alone, or what Brubaker and Cooper (2000) have called 'categories of analysis', this would ignore the inescapable fact that the census is a political process, and that as such, 'categories of practice' take precedence. This does not mean that states simply design and implement them in such as way as to get the results they want, although this may occur. It does mean that the origin of census classifications is about the negotiation of conflicting interests. These may well include the views of civil servants who may have purely scientific standards in mind, but will also include pressures from those who have an interest in constructing ethnicity or other identity categories in particular ways, such that potentially liquid identities can be crystallised in terms of one set of classifications rather than in terms of other, competing ones. This process of negotiation, which led to the way Britishness is measured in the U.K. census, has been well recorded, and I have alluded to it in the above account. It remains for a few conclusions to be drawn about the results, anticipated or otherwise, of this process, and their implication for how we think of 'indigenous' peoples.

The second, and perhaps most important conclusion, is that although we might assume ethnicity to be a category that allows us to avoid racialised or even directly racist arguments, in the context of the British census it looks more like a category used to maintain the salience of traditional racial divisions, but under a more acceptable terminology. As Ballard has commented on the census classification, '[n]ot only does it confirm the central importance of skin colour as an identifier as far as members of Britain's indigenous [sic] majority are concerned, but also that from their perspective Britain's racial and ethnic disjunctions appear to be regarded as virtually synonymous' (Ballard 1997: 186). If we accept that races exist only in the imagination – albeit an imagination with powerful, and at times fatal, consequences – we ought not to endow ethnicity with anything more substantial without falling back on arguments reminiscent of their explicitly racist predecessors. To do otherwise is to fall into the kind of discourse that the House of Commons discussion of Welsh identity exhibited so well: my identity group is civic and inclusive while yours is racial and exclusive.

The third is that whites born in Britain appear neither to think of themselves systematically as British, nor treat this consistently as a racial, ethnic or national category. Depending on how they are asked, and the context in which they are asked, they give quite different answers. The simple presence or absence of a tick box has a very substantial effect. One has to ask how important and salient is an identity if its incidence is so dependent on how one asks questions about it. Nor can we conclude that whites in Britain simply take this identity 'for granted' to the extent that they have difficulty reporting it on census forms. Most census respondents take their sex for granted but have no difficulty recalling it if asked. Yet if Britishness is so ephemeral, how is it that about half the population of Britain declare themselves 'very proud' to be so?

The fourth conclusion is, therefore, that, being socially constructed, both ethnicity and the state of being 'indigenous' can change. Moreover, this is not just a question of sequential evolution (although it can include that) but of simultaneously self-identifying in diverse ways in different social contexts. The proportion of those in England, Wales or Scotland identifying themselves as 'British' varies so much not because people lie or have fertile imaginations but because in different contexts they may clearly think of themselves as unambiguously inside or outside the category. Just as they can travel with their feet, so people can roam in their imaginations across these categories, assuming and discarding them as they see fit, including, for example, thinking of themselves as British in some ways and contexts, and as very definitely not British in another. What each respondent means by British is almost infinitely variable.

One can get a good sense of this, ironically, from Gordon Brown's speech. Hardly pausing to draw breath after noting the tremendous 'cultural' and 'national' variety of the U.K., Brown proceeds to assert that Britishness comprises a set of values that all in Britain share. This is, of course, empirically highly unlikely. The horrific events of 7 July 2005 were a powerful reminder that some Britons certainly do not share these values, while one could hardly sensibly define all those in the rest of the world who do happen to share them as 'British'. It is also logically problematic to describe as 'shared values' things that appear to have far more to do with procedural than substantive issues – free speech, democracy, due process of law and so forth. Brown's speech is, of course, a political exercise, neither a sociological analysis nor an attempt at demographic classification. Brown's own imagination of what Britishness is effortlessly mutates from sentence to sentence, not because he is a bad social scientist but because he is a good politician. As not only a 'category of practice' but also the hegemonic one, Britishness needs to be not only banal but also universally inclusive. As Billig (1995) notes, its simplest and most powerful form is the plural 'we'.

Finally, there is a fundamental contradiction within any concept of race, ethnicity, people, nation or their analogues insofar as they have a spatial referent that is rarely acknowledged. Any spatial referent can only have a straightforward meaning in the absence of significant migration. Only if people do not move is it easy to associate place with culture, or state territory and 'people'. On the contrary, however, it is only because people do move that the demand for such referents can arise in the first place. This demand arises, it hardly needs stressing, not from enumerators but as part of conflicts over power and resources, either as the 'indigenous' are colonised, or as migrants are sucked into more affluent societies. In the course of such conflicts, all kinds of races, ethnicities, nations and peoples may come to be imagined, in the sense of the term used by Anderson (1991). And a fundamental prerequisite of such imagination, as Anderson makes clear, is a capacity for selective amnesia about the thoroughly social and fluid origins of categories that must be deployed as if they were fixed in order to do their job.

It is perhaps too easy to regard the categories deployed by nineteenth-century enumerators to classify their populations, especially in a colonial context, as products of a fevered imperial imagination. Terms like 'mulatto' or 'quadroon' leap off the page. We may too readily assume that contemporary scientific, rationalised, reflexive or 'empowering' approaches are different. However, just as ethnic categories come to grief when transplanted across different political contexts, so may our current categories come to appear just as quaint to succeeding generations. No matter how visible this amnesia might be to the social historian a few decades hence, when the meaning of the categories will have moved on, the inevitable price of working with such identity categories as are thrown up by the contemporary state of these conflicts is to succumb to it.

Census makers would therefore do well to reflect upon Billig's observation about national identity but equally applicable to ethnic identity. Identity categories, whether ethnic, national or of many other forms, cannot ever describe an empirical reality that exists at the individual level. Rather, they describe ways of imagining or constructing putative communities that those so constructing them have a political project for. Crucially, it is the latter that determines the former. Thus, for example, many people living in Britain who can routinely expect to be treated as less than full citizens or suffer discrimination on grounds of some socially interpreted characteristic – be it their skin colour, dress, place of birth, language abilities, accent or religion – may choose to insist on their Britishness in order to legitimate their demand for social inclusion, and precisely because some others try to treat them (identify them) as non-British. At the same time, and for the same reason, they may wish to emphasise their difference to other Britons: as a black, or as a Muslim or as a Scot, I am a (potential) object of discrimination, such that I may make common cause with my fellows. Their chosen identities are inevitably about their aspirations for their destinies, or as it has often been put, about routes rather than roots.

Thus the key point to grasp is that it is not only the authors and victims of discrimination who travel in their imaginations in this way. 'We' social researchers or census makers are also inside this particular whale. It is our responsibility to become a little more conscious of the journeys our imaginations make when we employ identity categories. In particular, we have the responsibility of avoiding the unconscious reproduction of identity categories whose roots lie elsewhere.

Notes

1. This quotation is taken from an interview with Thatcher on Granada Television, 'World in Action', 27 January 1978.
2. We might note too that in the Scottish census China rejoins Asia.
3. Hansard, HC (series x), vol. 355, col. 574 (30 October 2000).
4. Ibid., col. 575 (30 October 2000).
5. Ibid., col. 576 (30 October 2000).
6. Ibid., col. 574 (30 October 2000).
7. Material used in this section comes from the British Social Attitudes Surveys, 2003–2005, produced as computer files by the National Centre for Social Research and distributed by the Economic and Social Data Service; and the Scottish Social Attitudes Survey, 2005, available as computer files and distributed by U.K. Data Archive of Colchester (ref. SN 5617).

References

Anderson, B. 1991. *Imagined Communities*. London: Verso.

Ballard, R. 1997. 'The Construction of a Conceptual Vision: "Ethnic Groups" and the 1991 U.K. Census', *Ethnic and Racial Studies* 20(1): 182–94.

Billig, M. 1995. *Banal Nationalism*. London: Sage.

BNP. 2006. 'Mission Statement'. Retrieved 2 May 2008 from: http://www.bnp.org.uk.

Booth, H. 1985. 'Which "Ethnic Question"? The Development of Questions Identifying Ethnic Origin in Official Statistics', *Sociological Review* 33(2): 254–74.

Brown, G. 2006. Speech to the Fabian Society, London, 14 January. Retrieved 7 April 2008 from: http://www.hm-treasury.gov.uk/newsroom_and_speeches/press/2006/press_03_06.cfm.

Brubaker, R., and F. Cooper. 2000. 'Beyond Identity', *Theory and Society* 29(1): 1–47.

Bulmer, M. 1986. 'A Controversial Census Topic: Race and Ethnicity in the British Census', *Journal of Official Statistics* 2(4): 471–80.

——— 1996. 'The Ethnic Group Question in the 1991 Census of Population', in D. Coleman and J. Salt (eds), *Ethnicity in the 1991 Census, Vol. 1: Demographic Characteristics of the Ethnic Minority Populations*. London: HMSO, pp. 33–62.

Clark, H. 1985. 'Language Use and Language Users', in G. Undsay and E. Aronson (eds), *Handbook of Social Psychology, Vol 2*. New York: Random House, pp. 179–232.

Condor, S. 2006. 'Representing, Resisting and Reproducing Ethnic Nationalism: Official U.K. Labour Party Representations of "Multicultural Britain"', unpublished paper presented to the 8th International Conference on Social Representations, Rome, 30 August 2006.

Dale, A., and C. Holdsworth. 1997. 'Issues in the Analysis of Ethnicity in the 1991 British Census', *Ethnic and Racial Studies* 20(1): 160–80.

Haselden, L., and R. Jenkins. 2003. 'The National Identity Question: Methodological Investigations', ONS Survey Methodology Bulletin, 51,18–26.

House of Commons. 1983 'Ethnic and Racial Questions in the Census'. Home Affairs Committee Report. House of Commons Paper HC 33, Parts 1–3. London: HMSO.

Karatani, R. 2003. *Defining British Citizenship: Empire, Commonwealth and Modern Britain*. London: Frank Cass.

ONS. 2001. 'The Classification of Ethnic Groups'. Retrieved 16 Feb 2001 from: http://www.statistics.gov.uk/about/Classifications/ns_ethnic_classification.asp.

Schwartz, N., F. Strack and H.-P. Mai. 1991. 'Assimilation and Contrast Effects in Part-whole Sequences: A Conversational Logic Analysis', *Public Opinion Quarterly* 55: 3–23.

Sillitoe, K., and P.H. White. 1992. 'Ethnic Group and the British Census: The Search for a Question', *Journal of the Royal Statistical Society* 55(1): 141–63.

EPILOGUE: FROM INDIGENOUS DEMOGRAPHICS TO AN INDIGENOUS DEMOGRAPHY

Per Axelsson, Peter Sköld, John P. Ziker and David G. Anderson

There has always been a close association between enumeration, the classification of peoples and state power. Demographers working with indigenous populations find themselves at the intersection of these forces. Demographic arguments have often been marshalled when settler states have an interest in taxation, in 'protecting' rural minorities or enfranchising populations to vote in ethnically stratified parliaments. At the start of the twenty-first century there are now populations on all inhabited continents making claims to indigenous status, and with each of those claims come sociological and demographic representations of their entitlements in each place. The workshop and the dialogue which lead to this volume have aimed at the broader goal of sketching out what might be called an indigenous demography. Although the context of the indigenous situation in each place is important, the contributions here show that there are also commonalities which make it a good time to introduce a new field.

At the heart of indigenous demography is a critical analysis of the categories which define and encapsulate indigenous populations as well as a mastery of the source data produced from those categories. By combining cultural and statistical techniques, historians, anthropologists and demographers point towards general patterns and methods. The outline of an indigenous demography has already been sketched in a number of key works. Taylor and Bell (2004), in their influential volume, identify a 'New World demography' in Australia and North America stemming from the relationship between indigenous peoples and the predominantly British settlers who first dispossessed them of their lands and then developed peculiarly paternalistic policies for measuring their survival. In a similar spirit, health professionals have identified commonalities in the epidemiology and general state of health of indigenous populations, although each of these studies has tended to make comparisons across similar geographic regions. There is already a fine list of work comparing the countries of the circumpolar north (Milan 1980; Pika and Bogoyavlensky 1995; Waldram, Herring and Young 1995; Macmillan et al. 1996; Bjerregaard and Young 2008; Sköld and Axelsson 2008), places under former Iberian rule (Kennedy and Perz 2000; Montenegro and Stephens 2006) and British imperial rule (Trovato 2001). Perhaps the most prolific area of research has been that which is concerned with 'reconstructing' the pre-contact demographics of specific populations which may have suffered severe declines due to pandemic disease, military conquest or deliberate policies of assimilation (Dolgikh 1960; Millar 1976; Newson 1986; Cane 1990; Deneven and Lowell 1992; Shoemaker 1999; Warrick 2008). This retrospective research is itself part of several older, imperial-era traditions concerned with the 'disappearance' of indigenous peoples and therefore underwrote paternalist policies to preserve them (Thornton 1987; Brantlinger 2003; Kovalaschina 2007). Linked to both of these agendas, and greatly invigorating the field of indigenous demography today, has been the discovery of a 'demographic turnaround' among many indigenous peoples (Hudon 1999; Gomes 2000; Norris et al. 2000; McSweeney and Arps 2005). Like the structure of the field itself, the discovery that indigenous populations are now burgeoning is based on a combination of qualitative and quantitative factors, such as increased fertility, nested within increasing the willingness of local people to subscribe to indigenous categories. Although it is imperative that historical and cultural contexts be respected in any research project, as the indigenous category becomes globalised there is now even a greater need for a field that seeks commonalities between indigenous communities worldwide.

This volume can be viewed as only a first step towards an indigenous demography. Represented here are studies predominantly from Australia, Scandinavia and the New World, with significant contributions from Russia, the Baltic and Britain. The tone of analysis is predominantly historical. Although historical and contextual analysis is crucial, an important aspect to a future indigenous demography would be an analysis of trends evident in the present. The case studies in this volume identify a number of themes which can be used to build an indigenous demography. Here we have divided them into two sections: reflections on identity and reflections on method.

Making Populations Visible:
State Policy and the Response of Indigenous Peoples

One of the startling commonalities in most of the case studies presented here is the question of how indigenous populations become visible to the state. The background to this issue is deeply rooted in both the exploitative as well as the activist qualities of postcolonial states. If colonial states were interested in taxing or assimilating local populations, indigenous families would understandably have avoided being counted. However contemporary states with radical liberal programmes often shy away from distinguishing any population on the basis of ethnicity, making difficult affirmative action policies aimed at improving the living conditions of formerly exploited peoples. An indigenous demography is situated in the middle of these difficult conflicting agendas; it supports the idea that scholars and states should have access to the maximum amount of information and data on indigenous peoples while undertaking to use that data in the interests of improving local livelihoods. In any one particular setting it is not clear if both objectives can always be achieved, placing a heavy responsibility on indigenous demographers on selecting the appropriate level of data for the question at hand. These decisions on the appropriateness of data are necessarily linked to an understanding of the complexities behind any attempt to measure or enumerate an indigenous population.

The Practice of Enumeration

The studies in this volume show that enumerators have struggled with similar problems when trying to count indigenous peoples. Although they were often chosen for their familiarity with particular tribes (Hacker and Haines, this volume), in some regions highly mobile and dispersed populations were difficult to find, and if found might be double-registered by neighbouring enumerators (Hamilton and Inwood, this volume; Anderson, this volume). This was even more complicated when national borders divided indigenous homelands (Evjen, this volume; Thorvaldsen, this volume). The results might also be influenced by the professional background of the enumerators. The results returned by hired enumerators might be influenced by norms set in order to receive their pay. Alternately, in some remote areas, the clergy responsible for converting rural peoples might be asked to double as enumerators, creating a different set of conflicts (Axelsson, this volume).

It is important to remember that the enumeration of individuals in many settings is a very recent interest. The enumeration of people was often conducted not with the purpose of identifying a particular population but in order to make lists of people responsible for paying taxes or to serve in armies. Sometimes the enumeration of domestic animals or agricultural resources was considered to be of greater importance than the counting of people themselves. As we remark below, this implies a certain methodological flexibility in applying coefficients and rules of thumb in order to understand the relationship between population numbers and stocks of animals. In many cases, surveys of domestic architecture or livestock might serve as proxies for the enumeration of people (Anderson, this volume; Smith et al., this volume).

State policies have been decisive in the shaping of classification systems, including ethnic or indigenous categories. This agenda has often served the interest of the state (Hansen, this volume). Plakans (this volume) concludes that Soviet-era censuses from the Baltic countries describe homogeneous and not complex populations as a result of politicisation. In the United States, American Indians were encouraged to assimilate into the general population, where they were less likely to be identified as indigenous (Hacker and Haines, this volume). This lack of interest in indigeneity partly stemmed from the fact that administrators assumed that native peoples would soon be extinct (Axelsson, this volume; Kukutai, this volume), but a stronger motive was the appropriation of indigenous peoples' land by making its inhabitants statistically invisible (Hamilton and Inwood, this volume; Smith et al., this volume). In Russia, on the other hand, the addition of relatively well-integrated peasant societies into an official list of small-numbered indigenous peoples has contributed to the erosion of the status of the most rural and sparse populations (Donahoe et al. 2008; Sokolovskiy, this volume).

Indigenous Responses

Although this book is very much concerned with how states have registered, analysed and made use of indigenous population statistics, the response of indigenous peoples to these state actions is of course of equal interest and something that needs attention. Peter Schweitzer states that, the 'tools of identity and nation making have come into global circulation and translation ... [I]ndigenous community members and their political leaders are highly skilled in navigating the challenges and opportunities of national identity politics' (Schweitzer 2008: 1014). While some indigenous societies have accepted, or have been forced to accept, state registration protocol definitions of indigenous persons, other indigenous communities extended their group definition by accepting all persons who were *not* counted by the state (Kukutai, this volume). In the light of ongoing tensions, enumeration has also been viewed with suspicion, and quiet acts of resistance, disinformation and a reluctance to participate in census taking have all been common over time (Hamilton and Inwood, this volume; Kukutai, this volume). In some instances rebellions were explicit responses to census-taking practices (Saether, this volume).

The cultural revitalisation of the 1960s and 1970s removed blood requirements from legal and other bureaucratic definitions. As indigenous identity became less stigmatised, the number of indigenous persons has grown due to changing state policies and a more positive attitude towards registration (Kukutai, this volume; Smith et al., this volume). In Scandinavia, the contemporary debate includes indigenous proposals for enumeration and categorisation, since the indigenous Sami need this in their fight for rights, but it is stressed that changes must come from indigenous initiatives (Pettersen, this volume).

These practical accommodations have arguably created some of the biggest difficulties for an indigenous demography today. If there is any argument against developing an indigenous demography it would be the worry that such a field would only increase the study of difference between people and not accentuate the cultural practices and accommodations that bring people together. This makes it necessary for those who would develop an indigenous demography to understand the ramifications of the categories that they employ.

Indigenous Identity

History shows that most population records are based on rigid ideas of unchangeable cultural units. Prior to the nineteenth century many local peoples relied on very inclusive identity systems based on kinship, while governments increasingly relied on race-based definitions that focused on the individual's blood quanta (Hacker and Haines, this volume). 'Full-bloods', 'half-castes', 'quadroons' and 'octoroons' have all been categories in Australia, New Zealand, the U.S.A., Canada, Sweden and Norway. This of course led to problems with 'boundaries' illustrated, for instance, by Hamilton and Inwood's example where a non-Aboriginal woman who married an Aboriginal man became Indian by law, while an Aboriginal woman marrying a non-Aboriginal man lost her indigenous identity.

State definitions of who to include as a member of a category, or national minority, were often based on certain stereotypes of cultural belonging or behaviour that might have been well removed from the realities of life lived out on the land. These 'pure' categories by necessity also created 'mixed' categories when enumerators discovered cases of 'mixed marriage' or the accommodation of settler ways through the mastery of the language of the incomers or their economic practices. In some cases, 'mixed' cases cause indigeneity itself to disappear (as in cases of assimilation). In other cases, entirely new peoples were created, such as the Canadian Métis or the Metizaje of Latin America (Gould 1998).

Indigenous peoples, despite legal exclusion, defined indigeneity as they always had, as a matter of cultural identification and community recognition (Smith et al., this volume). Nevertheless, they learned that records were kept for varying reasons and that it was sometimes best to have an indigenous identity, but sometimes it was preferable to be included among the majority population (Evjen, this volume; Pettersen, this volume). Others experienced exclusion from an indigenous identity due to state policy and legislation (Axelsson, this volume), and yet others were incorrectly categorised because enumerators could not grasp the complexity of their situation (Thorvaldsen, this volume). The nature of indigenous identities is certainly complex (Ziker, this volume), and the demographic records rarely give a realistic representation of indigenous identity. MacInnes (this volume) argues that identity categories in general fit poorly into the ordered classification systems of official censuses and surveys, since they lack an external standard referent. Thus, valuable exceptions provide an opportunity for understanding household formations and socio-economic relations, and these can give a better representation of indigenous societies (Anderson, this volume).

Indigenous identity, indigenous status and indigenous rights have been debated in many parts of the world over the last few decades (Sokolovskiy, this volume). One might take a critical standpoint and ask how important and salient identity is, if its incidence is so dependent on how we ask about it (MacInnes, this volume)? But the contemporary situation includes hundreds of millions of individuals all over the world with an indigenous identity, and neither generally nor regionally is there a single definition of who is indigenous, or what constitutes indigenous populations (Kukutai, this volume). The dilemma of indigenous identity is an existing fact today, and also a challenge for researchers (Karlsson 2003; Merlan 2009).

Methods for an Indigenous Demography

This volume displays a variety of ways of working with demographic data on indigenous peoples, combing different sources. Mainstream historical demography and current demography have yet to explore how to best make use of demographic records in which indigenous groups are included. The Australian example illustrates how the authors have attempted to reconstitute the Aboriginal population, combining family histories with information contained in the colonial censuses and vital registrations, and in the Board's censuses. Jåstad uses an ethnographic map from 1861 that provides analysts with a great opportunity to evaluate the strength of ethnic registration in the population census of the time using a comparison between previous censuses and the one dating from when the map was done. Thorvaldsen worked out a test of the consistency of noting ethnicity, revealing that few census takers seemed confused with changing definitions of ethnic markers.

Many of the categorisations of populations that demographic researchers, policy makers, health officials and so on make use of today have been constructed decades, even centuries ago under different political and social conditions. And when 'new' ethnicities are formed to fit censuses or demographic investigations they are added to a scheme that has a long and winding history, a history that nation-states take pride in. Nevertheless, as Anderson (1991), Scott (1998) and others point out, the procedure to name, divide and count people is a highly political act. We must therefore strive to uncover the motives that lay behind why there are (or are not) demographic records of indigenous peoples; when, how and by whom they were collected; if these procedures have changed over time; and also if possible how these records have been used. If one wants to make a longitudinal study, the historical context is crucial for understanding how the sources change over time.

The Relation between Registration and Taxation

There is generally a link between population registers and taxation, which unsurprisingly has been an additional complicating factor in the indigenous context. In Scandinavia, the Sami were already included in different tax records in the sixteenth century, where they were individually measured in terms of economic wealth. The ethnic categorisation in these records is surprisingly detailed (Sköld 1992). The Russian Polar Census enumerators were instructed to count various types of capital and possessions (Anderson, this volume), and resistance towards census taking among Aboriginal persons in Canada was sometimes due to rumours that enumerators were really poll tax collectors (Hamilton and Inwood, this volume). Tax records have an important control function (Hansen, this volume), and taxation had important consequences for the way in which indigenous peoples were counted (Saether, this volume). The consequence for indigenous persons of not being included in tax registers was exclusion also from population registers (Hacker and Haines, this volume).

Censuses and Other Demographic Records

There is certainly no guarantee that categories representing ethnicity or indigeneity are included in demographic records past or present. The vast majority of native peoples living in the United States before 1850 were not enumerated by a census, and it was not until the 1940s that all American Indians were registered (Hacker and Haines, this volume). This was also true for many Indian reserves in western Canada (Hamilton and Inwood, this volume). The late nineteenth century witnessed a trend in census taking, with ethnicity being included among numerous categories, a practice which some countries continued during the twentieth century. In the large majority of states with an Iberian colonial past, ethnic or racial categories are absent from the censuses during certain periods of time. This is in marked contrast to all other islands, territories or states under European dominion in the Caribbean (Saether, this volume). Since 1945 it has been usual in West European countries not to include ethnic categories in official population statistics (Pettersen, this volume). In Baltic censuses, on the other hand, ethnicity became the principal grouping category in the twentieth century (Plakans, this volume).

Identity categories and the groups they seek to describe are neither natural nor objective but are historical and political constructions, where decisions about group boundaries have tangible political consequences (Kukutai, this volume). Census numbers were used to justify colonial policies (Hamilton and Inwood, this volume), and an optimal representation of social and cultural complexity was rarely strived for. Demographic records historically supported the patriarchal family structure dominant among enumerators (Hacker and Haines, this volume), and it is generally difficult to visualise the indigenous household structure and complex social relations of the people recorded in censuses (Anderson, this volume). For example, group level criteria – important in an indigenous perspective – were less important than the individual assignment of ethnicity (Thorvaldsen, this volume).

Irrespective of continent, demographic records have changed considerably over time. Ethnic categories have been in a state of flux (Evjen,

302 Per Axelsson, Peter Sköld, John P. Ziker and David G. Anderson

this volume; Saether, this volume), and censuses classify a moment in time and produce seemingly precise numbers, whereas the societies they enumerate are always in the process of changing (Plakans, this volume). Changing definitions of indigeneity over time rendered many people in a statistically invisible position (Smith et al., this volume). The instructions issued to enumerators were important for the results obtained (Evjen, this volume), even if they often were difficult to interpret (Jåstad, this volume). Sometimes only a few variables were included, sometimes a census sheet had 400 columns (Anderson, this volume). There are numerous examples of the delicate problems enumerators experienced when trying to fulfil the instructions and interpret indigeneity (Kukutai, this volume; Thorvaldsen, this volume).

Censuses are often taken only every fifth or tenth year, which creates certain problems. Nevertheless, Hacker and Haines (this volume) conclude that with proper care the American Indian censuses can be used for a great variety of demographic analyses and thereby become a valuable contribution of indigenous demography. It is also obvious that demographic records are not 'only numbers' as a lot of other qualitative information can be derived from the sources as well. Ziker and Anderson (both this volume) show that the Russian Polar Census of 1926/7 contains information on economic activities, identity and land use, although it may be biased by the terminology and identity categories that the census takers employed. Anderson (this volume) links household structure to the structure of animal herds that supported reindeer-herding households, giving his research a broader ecological aspect. He stresses that the problem with moving from a numerical portrait of a region to a statistical portrait lies in determining the appropriate unit over which to calculate averages and relationships.

Nowadays, representations of indigenous identities in demographic records are more flexible and inclusive, but they still are influenced by a complex set of political, social, legal and cultural factors. Ethnic categories not only enable the statistical depiction of collective identities, they also portray a particular vision of social reality that often privileges the discourses of dominant groups (Kukutai, this volume). With proper care, demographic records offer an opportunity to better understand social interaction between ethnic groups (Anderson; Jåstad; Ziker, all this volume).

Standards for Indigenous Demography

Beyond the analysis of historical demographic records, a new world of indigenous demography is opened up when fieldworkers – scholars or indigenous people themselves – take demographic methods into their own hands. This approach allows for a more fine-grained representation of indigenous identity by incorporating the categories that are relevant to the population. Further, when demographic methods are coupled with other field methods one has the ability to address problems related to the demographic health of a population – for example, warfare, disease, alcoholism and non-natural causes of mortality. Such an approach has the dual purpose of engaging with the problems faced by people and addressing theoretical problems or debates in academic fields.

There is a history of the use of demographic methods in some anthropological circles, where the first step in a field research project is a community census. Starting with a census, the researcher can then apply methods of statistical sampling to pick interviewees for more specific sorts of study questions or observations. Without a census, the researcher cannot argue that the materials they are collecting are representative of the community as a whole. In some studies this is not an issue, but in others it may be more important. Further, basic demographic information can be compared and contrasted within a community over time, across communities of a region, or between societies.

At the community level, a census provides information on the age-sex structure that can be used to discuss demographic patterns. Combined with longitudinal ethnographic or ecological data, hypotheses about changes in age–sex structure (indicating changes in fertility, mortality, or migration rates) can be developed. Warren Hern (1995) developed a series of standards for micro-ethnodemographic research following Emilio Moran's challenge to provide information for the comparative analysis of human societies (Moran 1995). Hern's standards are an excellent starting point for a future indigenous demography, although he does not deal with identity directly. Where individual-level data are being collected according to his recommendations, it is not arduous to add information on a variety of identities that the individual may or may not have, as well as genealogical, economic and educational information. These identities can later be coded and used to analyse demographic information to describe variation within and between categories.

The benefit of micro-ethnodemographic research has been proven in previous analyses of population–age structures of indigenous populations across a region. Napoleon Chagnon (1998) discovered significant differences in age–sex distributions in Yanomamö villages according to their proximity to religious missions. Those communities in close proximity to and distant from missions had lower mortality rates than those at an intermediate distance. The reason for this regional pattern was twofold: communities close to missions had exposure to disease brought in from outside along with some level of medical attention; communities distant from missions had less direct contact and less exposure to non-indigenous diseases; but communities of intermediate distance from missions had exposure to outsiders through the missions but little access to medical attention. These results pointed to the development of policies that could aid the indigenous population but unfortunately were seen as anti-missionary.

Indigenous demography can utilise and engage cutting-edge theory and research that is cross-disciplinary. For example, life-history theory addresses how organisms should allocate time and energy in the face of the trade-offs faced throughout a lifetime. Should an individual accumulate resources or reproduce, reproduce now or in the future, have many offspring or fewer, or invest in mating or reproduction? Optimal allocations vary throughout a lifetime, and life-history theory generally asks questions about the forces that shape the timing of life events involved in development, growth, reproduction and ageing. For example, availability of resources and mortality patterns were found to correlate with varying adolescent growth regimes found in a cross-cultural study of twenty-two human societies (Walker et al. 2006). In another life-history study, predictions from two models of male parental investment were tested with demographic data from the Tsimane to address the question of why men marry and why do they stray (Winking et al. 2007). These studies indicate that indigenous demography can be used to address tough theoretical questions that can only be answered with rigorous empirical data.

The analysis of fertility and mortality statistics of indigenous communities through time poignantly shows the effect of recent economic changes on communities. Misuse of alcohol and other drugs is one of the most serious issues facing indigenous populations as constituent minorities in industrial states (Saggers and Gray 1998). This seems to be the case whether the context is colonial, postcolonial or postsocialist (Hawkins and Blume 2002; Coyhis and White 2006). This is another area where micro-ethnodemographic methods could be used to positively benefit indigenous populations (Ziker, this volume).

The Future of Indigenous Demography

The difficulty of defining indigeneity paired with the problems of gathering comprehensive and reliable data, especially in Africa and Asia, constitute obstacles to research (Cordell 2000; Bramley et al. 2005; McSweeny and Arps 2005; Siiskonen, Taskinen and Notkola 2005; Bartlett et al. 2007; Perz, Warren and Kennedy 2008). Moreover, an indigenous demography encourages scholars to work on case studies of smaller populations, since increased sensitivity to categories and definitions have a tendency to make aggregated statistical analysis more difficult (Taylor 2009). Nevertheless, global perspectives are important and few researchers would dispute the notion that the indigenous peoples of the world experience demographic transitions much later than do non-indigenous populations, and over the past few decades a growing body of literature has highlighted the fact that indigenous peoples are the most disadvantaged groups in the world, comprising what is often referred to as 'the fourth world' (Kunitz 1990; Axelsson and Sköld 2006). This statement is backed up by, for instance, health research showing that most indigenous peoples do not benefit at all from the general health improvements in society and that their health situation has long been and continues to be a cause for alarm (Trovato 2001; Stephens et al. 2005; Anderson et al. 2006; Montenegro and Stephens 2006; Ohenjo et al. 2006; Smylie et al. 2006; Stephens et al. 2006; Gracey and King 2009; King, Smith and Gracey

2009). Yet estimating and improving health conditions among indigenous peoples are difficult tasks if these peoples are unrecognised and uncounted. We hope that researchers will continue to respond to the call for more research on indigenous demography and indigenous issues in general. The field is important for all scholars, but the perspective and knowledge of researchers with an indigenous background are particularly crucial. Western understandings and descriptions have frequently been the result of narrow interpretations, where stereotyped categories have obstructed cultural and social understanding. It is no more than a few decades ago that scholars and politicians referred to the subjects of their investigations as 'primitives'. Since then, conventions and scientific publications have formed a vague understanding of the term indigeneity, which constitutes not only a legal category and an analytical concept, but also an expression of identity (Niezen 2002: 1–5). Indigeneity involves both an individual affiliation and a collective representation, and studies based on demographic registers have experienced great difficulties in accounting for consistent use of the term (Kinfu and Taylor 2005).

We believe that the role of indigenous demography is not to work with questioning or judging who is indigenous or not. The field needs to be open to critique from different angles and positions. By doing so we hope that more indigenous and non-indigenous scholars will take part in this emerging discourse and develop, deepen and broaden the field of indigenous demography.

References

Anderson, B. 1991. *Imagined Communities: Reflections on the Origin and Spread of Nationalism*. London: Verso.

Anderson, I., S. Crengle, M. Leialoha Kamaka, T. Chen, N. Palafox and L. Jackson-Pulver. 2006. 'Indigenous Health in Australia, New Zealand, and the Pacific', *Lancet* 367: 1775–85.

Axelsson, P., and P. Sköld. 2006. 'Indigenous Populations and Vulnerability: Characterizing Vulnerability in a Sami Context', *Annales de Demographie Historique* 111(1): 115–32.

Bartlett, J.G., L. Madariaga-Vignudo, J.D. O'Neill and H. Kuhnlein. 2007. 'Identifying Indigenous Peoples for Health Research in a Global Context: A Review of Perspectives and Challenges', *International Journal of Circumpolar Health* 66(4): 287–307.

Bjerregaard, P., and T. Young (eds). 2008. *Health Transitions in Arctic Populations*. Toronto: Toronto University Press.

Bramley, D., P. Hebert, L. Tuzzio and M. Chassin. 2005. 'Disparities in Indigenous Health: A Cross-country Comparison Between New Zealand and the United States', *American Journal of Public Health* 95(5): 844–50.

Brantlinger, P. 2003. *Dark Vanishings: Discourse on the Extinction of Primitive Races, 1800–1930*. Ithaca, NY: Cornell University Press.

Cane, S. 1990. 'Desert Demography: A Case Study of Pre-contact Aboriginal Densities', in B. Meehan and N. White (eds), *Hunter-gatherer Demography: Past and Present*. Sydney: University of Sydney Press, pp. 149–59.

Chagnon, N.A. 1998. *Yanomamö*, 5th edn. Fort Worth, TX: Harcourt Brace.

Cook, D.N. 1981. *Demographic Collapse: Indian Peru, 1520–1620*. Cambridge: Cambridge University Press.

Cordell, D.D. 2000. 'African Historical Demography in the Years since Edinburgh' *History in Africa* 27: 61–89.

Coyhis, D.L., and W.L. White. 2006. *Alcohol Problems in Native America: The Untold Story of Resistance and Recovery – The Truth About the Lie*. Colorado Springs: White Bison.

Denevan, W.M., and W.G. Lovell. 1992. *The Native Population of the Americas in 1492*. Madison: University of Wisconsin Press.

Dolgikh, B.O. 1960. *Rodovoi i plemennoi sostav narodov Sibiri v XVII veke*. Moscow: Nauka.

Donahoe, B., J.O. Habeck, A. Halemba, and I. Sántha. 2008. 'Size and Place in the Construction of Indigeneity in the Russian Federation', *Current Anthropology* 49(6): 993–1020.

Gomes, M.P. 2000. *The Indians and Brazil. Translated by J. W. Moon*. Gainesville, FL: University Press of Florida.

Gould, J.L. 1998. *To Die in This Way: Nicaraguan Indians and the Myth of Mestizaje 1880–1965*. Durham, NC: Duke University Press.

Gracey, M., and M. King. 2009. 'Indigenous Health, Part1: Determinants and Dsease Patterns', *Lancet* 374(9683): 65–74.

Hawkins, H.H., and A.W. Blume. 2002. 'Loss of Sacredness: Historical Context of Health Policies for Indigenous People in the United States', in P.D. Mail, S. Heurtin-Roberts, S.E. Martin and J. Howard (eds), *Alcohol Use Among American Indians and Alaska Natives*. Bethesda, MD: U.S. Department of Health and Human Services..

Hern, W.M. 1995. 'Micro-ethnodemographic Techniques for Field Workers Studying Small Groups', in E.F. Moran (ed.), *The Comparative Analysis of Human Societies: Toward Common Standards for Data Collection and Reporting*. Boulder, CO: Rienner, pp. 129–48.

Hudon, S. 1999. 'Conjoncture démographique des Innus du Québec, 1973–1993', *Cahiers Québecois de Demographie* 28(1–2): 237–69.

Karlsson, B.G. 2003.'Anthropology and the "Indigenous Slot": Claims to and Debates about Indigenous Peoples' Status in India', *Critique of Anthropology* 23(4): 403–23.

Kennedy, D.P., and S.G. Perz. 2000. 'Who Are Brazil's Indígenas? Contributions of Census Data Analysis to Anthropological Demography of Indigenous Populations', *Human Organization* 59(3): 311–24.

Kinfu, Y., and J. Taylor. 2005. 'On the Components of Indigenous Population Change', *Australian Geographer* 36(2): 233–55.

King, M., A. Smith and M. Gracey. 2009. 'Indigenous Health, Part 2: The Underlying Causes of the Health Gap', *Lancet* 374(9683): 76–85.

Kovalaschina, E.P. 2007. 'The Historical and Cultural Ideals of the Siberian Oblastnichestvo'. *Sibirica* 6(2): 87–119.

Kunitz, S.J. 1990. 'Public Policy and Mortality among Indigenous Populations of North America and Australia', *Population and Development Review* 16(4): 647–72.

MacMillan, H.L., A.B. MacMillan, D.R. Offord and J.L. Dingle. 1996. 'Aboriginal Health', *Canadian Medical Association Journal* 155(11): 1569–78.

McSweeny, K., and S. Arps. 2005. 'A "Demographic Turnaround": The Rapid Growth of Indigenous Populations in Lowland Latin America', *Latin American Research Review* 40(1): 3–29.

Merlan, F. 2009. 'Indigenity: Global and Local', *Current Anthropology* 50(3):303–333.

Milan, F.A. 1980. 'The Demography of Selected Circumpolar Populations', in F.A. Milan (ed.), *The Human Biology of Circumpolar Populations*. Cambridge: Cambridge University Press, pp. 13–35.

Millar, V.P. 1976. 'Aboriginal Micmac Population: A Review of the Evidence', *Ethnohistory* 23(2): 117–27.

Montenegro, R.A., and C. Stephens. 2006. 'Indigenous Health in Latin America and the Caribbean', *Lancet* 367(9225): 1859–69.

Moran, E. 1995. *The Comparative Analysis of Human Societies: Toward Common Standards for Data Collection and Reporting*. Boulder: L. Rienner Publ

Morphy, F. 2007. 'Uncontained Subjects: "Population" and "Household" in Remote Aboriginal Australia', *Journal of Population Research* 24(2): 163–84.

Newson, L. 1986. *The Cost of Conquest: Indian Decline in Honduras Under Spanish Rule*. Boulder, CO: Westview Press.

Niezen, R. 2002. *Origins of Indigenism: Human Rights and the Politics of Identity*. Berekeley: University of California Press.

Ohenjo, N., R. Willis, D. Jackson, C. Nettleton, K. Good and B. Mugarura. 2006. 'Health of Indigenous People in Africa', *Lancet* 367: 1937–46.

Perz, S.G., J. Warren and D.P. Kennedy. 2008. 'Contributions of Racial-ethnic Reclassification and Demographic Processes to Indigenous Population Resurgence: The Case of Brazil', *Latin American Research Review* 43(2): 7–33.

Pika, A., and D. Bogoyavlensky. 1995. 'Yamal Peninsula: Oil and Gas Development and Problems of Demography and Health among Indigenous Populations', *Arctic Anthropology* 32(2): 61–74.

Saggers, S., and D. Gray. 1998. *Dealing with Alcohol: Indigenous Usage in Australia, New Zealand, and Canada*. Cambridge: Cambridge University Press.

Scott, J.C. 1998. *Seeing like a state. How Certain Schemes to Improve the Human Conditions Have Failed*. New Haven and London: Yale University Press.

Schweitzer, P. 2008. Comment on Donahoe et al., 'Size and Place in the

Construction of Indigeneity in the Russian Federation', *Current Anthropology* 49(6): 1013–14.

Shoemaker, N. 1999. *American Indian Population Recovery in the Twentieth Century*. Albuquerque, NM: University of New Mexico Press.

Siiskonen, H., A. Taskinen and V. Notkola. 2005. 'Parish Registers: A Challenge for African Historical Demography', *History in Africa* 32: 385–402.

Sköld, P. 1992. *Samisk Bosättning i Gällivare 1550–1750*, Umeå: Center för arktisk kulturforskning, Umeå universitet.

Sköld, P., and P. Axelsson. 2008. 'The Northern Population Development: Colonization and Mortality in Swedish Sápmi 1786–1895', *International Journal of Circumpolar Health* 67(1): 29–44.

Smylie, J., I. Anderson, M. Ratima and M. Anderson. 2006. 'Indigenous Health Performance Measurement Systems in Canada, Australia and New Zealand', *Lancet* 367: 2029–31.

Stephens, C., C. Nettleton, J. Porter, R. Willis and S. Clark. 2005. 'Indigenous Peoples' Health: Why are They Behind Everyone, Everywhere?' *Lancet* 366: 10–13.

Stephens, C., J. Porter, C. Nettleton and R. Willis. 2006. 'Disappearing, Displaced, and Undervalued: A Call to Action for Indigenous Health Worldwide', *Lancet* 367: 2019–28.

Taylor, J. 2009. 'Indigenous Demography and Public Policy in Australia: Population or Peoples?' *Journal of Population Research* 26: 115–30.

Taylor, J., and M. Bell. 2004. 'Continuity and Change in Indigenous Australian Population Mobility', in J. Taylor and M. Bell (eds), *Population Mobility and Indigenous Peoples in Australasia and North America*. London: Routledge, pp. 13–43.

Thornton, R. 1987. *American Indian Holocaust and Survival: A Population History since 1492*. Norman: University of Oklahoma Press.

Trovato, F. 2001. 'Aboriginal Mortality in Canada, the United States and New Zealand', *Journal of Biosocial Science* 33: 67–86.

Waldram, J.B., D.A. Herring and T.K. Young. 1995. *Aboriginal Health in Canada: Historical, Cultural and Epidemiological Perspectives*. Toronto: University of Toronto Press.

Walker, R., M. Gurven, K. Hill, A. Migliano, N. Chagnon, R. De Souza, G. Djurovic, R. Hames, A.M. Hurtado, H.Kaplan, K.Kramer, W.J. Oliver, C. Valeggia, T. Yamauchi. 2006. 'Growth Rates and Life Histories in Twenty-two Small-scale Societies', *American Journal of Human Biology* 18(3): 295–311.

Warrick, G. 2008. *A Population History of the Huron-Petun, AD 500–1650*. New York: Cambridge University Press.

Winking, J., H. Kaplan, M. Gurven and S. Rucas. 2007. 'Why Do Men Marry and Why Do They Stray?' *Proceedings of the Royal Society* 274(1618): 1643–49.

Notes on Contributors

David G. Anderson is Professor of Anthropology at the University of Tromsø, Norway. He is involved in archival and field research in several areas of the circumpolar Arctic including the Kola peninsula, Taimyr, Evenkiia and Zabaikal'e in Russia, the Mackenzie Delta in Canada, and in northern Norway. He is the author of *Identity and Ecology in Arctic Siberia* (2000) and editor of a recent collection *The 1926–27 Polar Census Expeditions* (2011).

Ian Anderson is Professor of Indigenous Health and Director of the Centre for Health and Society, University of Melbourne. Recent publications include the co-authored papers 'Aboriginal Society and Health', *Annual Review of Health Sociology* (2002) and 'Voices Lost: Indigenous Health and Human Rights in Australia', *Lancet* (2004).

Per Axelsson holds a Ph.D. in history and is a researcher at the Centre for Sami Research at Umeå University, Sweden. His research interest and recent publications focus on medical history and historical demography of the Sami and settlers in northern Sweden during the time of colonisation, Sami reindeer herdings' adaptation to climatic and societal change, and also the history of polio during the twentieth century.

Jane Beer was a research assistant, School of Population Health, University of Melbourne.

Joanne Evans is a fellow at the eScholarship Research Centre, University of Melbourne and is lecturer at Monash University.

Bjørg Evjen is Professor of Indigenous Studies and academic coordinator in the master's programme in Indigenous Studies at the Centre for Sami Studies, University of Tromsø, Norway. Her research interests include polar history, industrial history, social history, gender history and Sami history at.

J. David Hacker is Associate Professor of History at the State University of New York, Binghamton. His research focuses on the demographic history of the United States before 1940. He has published articles on mortality trends and determinants, correlates of marriage, the onset of marital fertility decline, the impact of parental religiosity on fertility differentials, and the impact of the American Civil War on southern marriage patterns.

Michael R. Haines is Banfi Vintners Professor of Economics at Colgate University, Hamilton, New York, and a research associate at the National Bureau of Economic Research, Cambridge, Massachusetts. His current areas of research include the historical study of fertility and mortality in the United States and Europe, biological aspects of the standard of living, and historical consumer and housing demand. He is one of the editors in chief of *Historical Statistics of the United States* and is part of the National Historical Geographic Information System project for the United States. He is the author of *Fertility and Occupation: Population Patterns in Industrialization* (1979), co-author of *Fatal Years: Childhood Mortality in Late Nineteenth-Century America* (1991), and co-editor of *A Population History of North America* (2000), and numerous articles.

Michelle A. Hamilton was a Postdoctoral Fellow in Rural History and a member of the 1871 and 1891 census project team, both at the University of Guelph, Canada. She is now an Assistant Professor and Director of Public History at the University of Western Ontario.

Lars Ivar Hansen is Professor of Medieval and Early Modern History at the University of Tromsø, Norway. His primary research focus is social and economic history, with a special focus on Sami history, the history of inter-ethnic relations in northern Scandinavia and legal history. He has published two volumes of a regional history of Astafjord parish in the southern part of Troms county, Norway (2000, 2003), and is co-author of *Samenes historie fram til 1750* (2004).

Kris Inwood is Professor of Economics and History at the University of Guelph, Canada, where he directs a project to create public-use microsamples from the Canadian 1871 and 1891 censuses. He is also interested in early Canadian industrialization and comparative physical well-being across the British Empire. His recent publications include 'The Great Transformation', *Economics and Human Biology* (2007), 'Hecksher-Ohlin in Canada', *Australian Economic History Review* (2007) and 'Social Consequences of Legal Reform', *Continuity and Change* (2004).

Hilde L. Jåstad is a Ph.D. student at the Centre of Sami Studies, University of Tromsø, Norway, researching household structure and fertility in Skjervøy and Kautokeino parishes (1865–1930). Her work considers the relationship between household demography and material conditions.

Tahu Kukutai is Senior Research Fellow at the National Institute of Demographic and Economic Analysis, University of Waikato. A sociologist, she has written on a broad range of Maori and indigenous population issues population. Her current research interests include indigenous transnationalism and comparative models of ethnic classification and counting. Her tribal affiliations are Waikato-Tainui, Ngati, Maniapoto and Te Aupouri.

Janet McCalman is Director of Murrup Barak Institute for Indigenous Development and Director of Research and Innovation at the Lowitja Institute for Aboriginal and Torres Strait Islander Health Research.

Gavan McCarthy is director of the eScholarship Research Centre, University of Melbourne.

John MacInnes is Professor of the Sociology of European Society, University of Edinburgh, fellow of the Centre d'Estudis Demogràfics, Universitat Autònoma de Barcelona, and Strategic Advisor to the U.K.'s Economic and Social Research Council on quantitative methods teaching. His interests include changes in gender relations, the relationship between sociology and demography, and the uses and misuses of the concept of identity in all its dimensions. He has published various books and articles, including *The End of Masculinity* (1998).

Torunn Pettersen is a political scientist and researcher at Sami University College in Kautokeino, Norway. Her main research interest is knowledge building and opinion formation on Sami issues. She is responsible for the research and development project Sami Social Science Database, focusing on how to develop and manage Sami statistics in Norway. Her recent publications include the co-authored paper 'Contemporary Sami Demography: A "Black Hole" in Research and Policy Making', in Elenius and Karlsson (eds), *Cross-cultural Communication and Ethnic Identities* (2007).

Andrejs Plakans is emeritus Professor of History at Iowa State University, Ames, Iowa, and author of *Kinship in the Past: An Historical Anthropology of European Family Life 1500–1900* (1984), *The Latvians: A Short History* (1995), and co-editor of *Family History at the Crossroads: Linking Familial and Historical Change* (1987). He also co-edited the journal *History of the Family* from 1995 to 2002. A foreign member of the Academy of Sciences of Latvia since 1991, he received an honorary doctorate from Umeå University, Sweden, for his contributions to the field of family history in 1999. He is currently writing a general history of the Baltic states of Estonia, Latvia and Lithuania.

Steinar A. Saether is Associate Professor of Latin American Studies and at the University of Oslo. His research mainly focuses on eighteenth- and nineteenth-century Latin American social and political history, with emphases on marriage patterns, ethnic and racial identities and political conflicts.

Peter Sköld is Professor of History at Umeå University, Sweden, and director of the Centre for Sami Research. He has an academic background in historical demography and medical history, and is presently working on two major projects concerning Sami demographic transition and the ageing population. Sköld is also responsible for the research area Northern Studies at Umeå University. His recent publications have focused on health issues and vulnerability among indigenous peoples.

Len Smith Adjunct Associate Professor, The Australian Demographic and Social Research Institute, Australian National University.

Sandra Smith is a research officer in Indigenous Cultures, Museum Victoria.

Sergey V. Sokolovskiy is a senior research fellow of the Institute of Ethnology and Anthropology, Russian Academy of Sciences, Moscow, and editor-in-chief of the Russian anthropological journal *Etnograficheskoe obozrenie*. His main research interests include the history of Russian anthropology, identity politics, indigenous peoples and minority rights. He is the author of numerous publications, including: *Kriashens in the Russian Population Census of 2002* (2004), *Ethno-cultural Policy Perspectives in the Russian Federation* (2004), *Images of Others in Russian Science, Law and History* (2001), *Minority Rights: Anthropological, Sociological, and International Law Perspectives* (1997) and *The Altay Mennonites* (1996).

Gunnar Thorvaldsen is Professor of History at the Norwegian Historical Data Centre, University of Tromsø, Norway. He has published several methodological and empirical books and articles on the social and population history of Scandinavia, including *Databehandling for historikere* (1999), 'Away on Census Day: Enumerating the Temporarily Present or Absent', *Historical Methods* (2006), 'An International Perspective on Scandinavia's Historical Censuses', *Scandinavian Journal of History* (2007) and 'Swedes in Siberian Diaspora', *Sibirica* (2008).

John P. Ziker is Associate Professor of Anthropology at Boise State University, Idaho. He holds a doctorate from University of California at Santa Barbara, and was a fellow at the Max Planck Institute for Social Anthropology in 2001–2003. Beyond demographics, his interests include indigenous land tenure systems and their sustainability, human sociality, the circumpolar north and postsocialist societies. He is also a member of the editorial board of *Sibirica*, an international journal of Siberian studies, and a contributing editor for *Anthropology News*.

Index

Abaza 241, 243, 244
Abkhazia (and the Abkhaz) 240, 243
Aboriginal Act (Australia, 1928) 20
Aboriginal Act (Victoria, 1869) 18
Aborigines 7, 15, 17, 18–19, 19–20, 21–2, 24, 25, 26–7, 28, 95
   Aboriginal Heritage programme in Victoria 24–5
   Aborigines Protection Act (Victoria, 1886) 7, 19
   births, deaths and marriages, registration of 23
   Board of Protection of Aborigines 15
   census counts in Victoria 21, 26–7
   Central Board for the Protection of Aborigines 18–19, 20, 21, 23, 25, 28, 29
   colonial decline of population 16–17, 25
   family, regulation of 20–21
   forced assimilation 24
   fractional identity and citizenship 19–20, 24, 29
   genealogical identity 22
   'invisible Aborigines' 21–2, 25
   emergence of 25, 26–7
   Koori Health Research Database (KHRD) 24–5, 26–7
   legislating aboriginality 19–20
   native administration and 'half-caste problem' 18–19
   race, political arithmetic of 20
   regulation of the family 20–21
   subgroups in Victorian population 23
   Victorian Aborigines Protection Act (1886) 7, 19
Acts
   Aboriginal Act (Australia, 1928) 20
   Act Respecting Indians (US, 1886) 103
   Births and Deaths Registration Act (New Zealand, 1951) 50n10
   Census Act (Canada, 1879) 98
   Census Act (Canada, 1891) 104
   Census Act (New Zealand, 1877) 36

   Chinese Immigrants Act (New Zealand, 1881) 51n15
   General Allotment Act (US, 1887) 75
   Immigration Restriction Act (New Zealand, 1908) 51n15
   Indian Act Amendment (Canada, 1888) 104
   Maori Affairs Amendment Act (New Zealand, 1974) 40
   Maori Land Act (New Zealand, 1909) 50n10
   Maori Representation Act (New Zealand, 1867) 50n10, 51n13
   Maori Social and Economic Advancement Act (New Zealand, 1945) 50n10
   Nationality Act (U.K., 1914) 283
   Native Land Amendment Act (New Zealand, 1912) 37, 50–51n11, 51n17
   Undesirable Immigrants Exclusion Act (New Zealand, 1919) 51n15
   Victorian Aboriginal Act (1869) 18
administration 7, 18–19, 21, 25, 127, 136, 246
   language use and, autonomy in 264
   village administration record 232
affiliation of Sami
   census recording of 187
   questions regarding 185–6
Africa 8, 304
   East Africa 276
   South Africa 8, 38
age 10, 11, 15, 23, 59, 60, 125, 126
   age classes 200
   age models 79, 81, 82, 83, 84, 85, 86, 87
   Age-Sex Pyramid for Lake Yessei (1926) 202, 203
   age-specific mortality data 9, 73–4, 87, 225
   Indian Life Tables 84–5, 87–90
   marriage duration and 79–83
   microdemographics in Central Taimyr Lowlands 222, 224, 232
   misstatement by American Indians 79

structure 45, 46, 303
working age 246–7, 270
Alba, R. and Nee, V. 34
Alberta, Canada 98, 99, 108
alcohol (and alcoholism) 65, 231–3, 248, 302–3, 304
Aleut 244, 245, 250n15
Alexander III 257, 260
Aliutor 243
All-Union Census (Soviet Union, 1926) 242
Allan, J. 42, 193n2
allodial rights 138, 139–40, 141, 142
   Sami allodial properties 139, 140, 141, 142
   Sami allodium 139–40, 141
Altai 247, 248
Alterman, H. 95
Amelkin, Anatolii 214
American Indians 9, 49n3, 51n12, 73–91, 109, 297–8, 301, 302
   age misstatement 79
   Apache 60, 78, 91n5
   assimilation policy for 74
   Blackfoot 78
   Brass method on child mortality 77–9
   Bureau of Indian Affairs 77, 91n1
   censuses (1890, 1900 and 1910) 73–4, 74–7, 91n8
   Cherokee 75, 77, 78
   Cheyenne 78
   Chickasaw 78
   child survivorship, Life Tables from data on 77–87
   Chippewa (Ojibwa) 78, 108, 110n11
   Choctaw 78
   classification scheme for 77, 91n5
   Creek 78
   cultural differences, difficulties of 76
   diversity of population 77
   enumeration of 74–5, 75–6, 76–7, 90–91
   'Indian blood,' census question on 76
   Indian Census Integrated Public Use Microdata Series (IPUMS) 76, 77, 87, 88, 91n4, 91n7, 91n8
   'Indians,' definition of 74–5, 75–6
   intermarriage with white population 90
   Iroquois 78
   Kiowa 78
   life expectancy 73, 86
   Life Tables, construction of 73–91
   marriage duration 79, 81, 82, 83, 91n6
   mortality 73, 81, 86, 91
     following European contacts 73
   Navajo 78
   Osage 78
   Paiute 78

Pima 78
Potawatomie 78
Preston-Bennett Method, application to population (1900-1910) 88–90
Pueblo 78
Puget Sound Salish 78
remarriage, problem of 86
Seminole 78
Shoshone 78
Sioux 77, 78
Tohono O'Odham 78
two-census methods, Life Tables from 87–90, 91n7
ancestral ethnicity 149–50, 151, 154, 155, 176–7
Andean highlands 62
Andersen, S. 193n10
Andersen, T. and Poppel, B. 5
Anderson, Benedict 6, 273, 291, 300
Anderson, David G. 10–11, 197–216, 220, 221, 234, 242, 295–305, 309
Anderson, I. et al. 304
Anderson, Ian 5, 7–8, 15–29, 297, 298, 299, 302, 309
Anderson, M.J. 253
Anderson, Rodney 59
Anderson, W. 20
Andersson, T. 5
animals 197, 199, 204, 208, 211, 213, 220, 227
   domestic animals 220, 297
   see also reindeer
anthropology 3, 198, 215, 219, 241, 271, 303
   salvage anthropology 242
   social anthropology 135
Apache 60, 78, 91n5
Appelbaum, Nancy 66
Aranda Census (1768) 59
archaeology 16, 35, 135, 158, 250n10, 274–5
   Baikal Archaeology Project 235n2
Archer, William Henry 22–3
archives 110n5, 112, 217, 222, 235
   Archivo General de Indias, Seville (AGI) 67n7, 67n8
   Australian archives 25
   Barwick's oral history archive 24, 25
   household registers for Lake Essei 202–3, 215
   National Archive of the Sakha Republic (NARS) 199
   Norwegian National Archives, Oslo 141, 143, 144, 174
   State Archive of Krasnoiarsk Territory (GAKK) 199
   U.K. Data Archive, Colchester 292n7
   Yougov poll archives 288

arctic fox 209, 225, 226, 227, 229
Arel, D. 3, 6, 7, 34, 120, 125, 129, 193n2
Argentina 57
Arosenius, Edvard 127–8
Asia 8, 276, 280, 304
  Central Asia 240
  south-east Asia 35
assimilation 7, 9, 19, 20, 42, 158, 159, 241,
  268, 299
  policies of 24, 26, 27, 37, 74, 88, 90, 108,
    188, 248, 296
Assiniboia 98, 99, 108
Athabasca 98
Aubert, Vilhelm 169–70, 187, 188
Australia 1, 7–8, 186, 299, 300
  archives in 25
  family, regulation of 20–21
  Institute of Aboriginal and Torres Strait
    Islander Studies (AIATSIS) 24
  Research Council (ARC) 24
  see also Aborigines; Victoria, State of
Avam tundra 221, 222, 227
Avars 239
Axelsson, P. and Sköld, P. 130, 304
Axelsson, Per 1–12, 117–31, 169–70, 295–
  305, 309
Azeri 239, 240

Bakewell, P. 67n3
Ballara, A. 36
Ballard, R. 279, 290
Baltic countries 254–7
  Baltic Germans 254, 256, 259, 262, 265,
    266
  Baltic Socialist Republics 26–8
  political discontinuities within 253–9,
    270–71
  tribal societies 260
  see also Latvia
Bangladesh (and Bangladeshis) 276, 277,
  278, 279, 280, 281, 284, 286
Barickman, B.J. 67n2
Barkhatov, Vitalii Aleksandrovich 225–6, 230
Barth, Frederick 34, 44, 47, 119
Bartlett, J.G. et al. 6, 304
Barwick, D. 16, 17, 19, 20, 21, 22, 24–5
  oral history archive 24, 25
basic nation, concept of 257
Baskerville, P. and Sager, E. 110n1
Batulu family lineage 201, 211, 212, 213, 214
Bauernstand (peasantry) in Latvia 258, 260
Beattie, John 110n11
Beckwith, Charles 110n11
bediak (poor grade people) in Soviet Russia
  204–5, 209, 210

Beer, Jane 7–8, 15–29, 297, 298, 299, 302, 309
Belich, J. 35, 37, 51n14
Bell, Martin 6, 295
Bennett, N. G. 73, 87, 88–90, 91n9
Berg, G. 164
Berg, T.F. 127
Bernardi, L. and Hutter, I. 4–5
Beskow, V. 123
Bessermians 241, 244
Bezrukikh, Aksinia Maksimovna 226–7
Bezrukikh, Aleksei Ivanovich 229–30, 231
Billig, Michael 289, 291
Birch, T. 5
births 17, 22–3, 27, 79, 87, 124–5, 200, 233,
  261
Births and Deaths Registration Act (New
  Zealand, 1951) 50n10
Bjerregaard, P. and Young, T. 295–6
Bjørklund, I. 213
Blackfoot 78
blood quantum 8, 35, 39, 42, 48
  extension of (New Zealand) 37–8, 51n12
  terminology in US 51n12, 75–6
  voting rights and 51n13
Blue, A.N. 111n19
Blum, A. 193n2
Board of Protection of Aborigines 15
bogatyi (wealthy people) in Soviet Russia
  204, 206, 209, 210
Bogoyavlinskii, Dmitrii 233, 235n10
Bojtár, E. 265
Bolívar, Simón 64, 65
Bolivia 57, 64, 65, 66
Booth, H. 276, 278, 279
Borah, W. 67n1
borders 90, 241
  administrative 2
  border treaty negotiations (Sweden/
    Norway-Denmark) 136–7
  cross-border reindeer herders 168–9
  national 1, 28, 33, 260, 297
  political 87–8, 254
  US-Canada border crossings, problem
    of 103–4
boundaries 199, 242, 254, 259–60, 262, 299,
  301
  boundary building in official statistics
    34–5
  bureaucratic definition of ethnic
    boundaries in New Zealand 35
  cultural boundaries 119
  electoral boundaries, determination of
    52n19
  ethnic 33–52
  national boundaries 56

racial boundaries 38, 130
registration boundaries 156
statistical boundaries 166
Bourbon Spain 57, 59, 60, 61, 63
Bourdieu, Pierre 119
Bourke, E. A. 7, 11
Bradbury, B. 110n2
Brading, D.A. 67n3, 67n5
Bramley, D. et al. 304
Brantlinger, P. 296
Brass method on child mortality 77–9
British 7, 12, 16, 49–50n5, 49n4, 57, 98,
    273–92, 295
    British civilisation 19
    British Empire 18
    British Isles 36
    British law 50–51n11
    Britishness 280–83, 283–6, 288
British Columbia 96, 97, 98–9, 100–102, 103,
    104–5, 107–8
British National Party (BNP) 12, 276
British Social Attitudes Survey (BSAS) 274,
    286–7, 288, 292n7
Brookes, A.A. 110n2
Brooks, F.J. 67n1
Broome, Richard 16, 18, 19, 20, 21, 25
Broughton, J. 35
Brown, D.E. 234–5n1
Brown, Gordon 275, 276, 291
Brubaker, R. and Cooper, F. 289
Buck, I. et al. 110n2
Buck, Peter 52n18
Bulmer, John 24
Bulmer, M. 278, 279
Burdeu, APA 15
Bureau of Indian Affairs 77, 91n1
Burgmann, V. 21
Buriats 248
Burkholder, M.A. and Johnson, L.L. 62
Buström, B. 5
Butlin, N.G. 16, 17

cadastral records 65, 140, 142, 260
Cahill, D. 62, 65
Callister, P. 45
Callister, P., Didham, R. and Potter, D. 39,
    52n20
Cameron, Indian Agent E.D. 106–7, 111n41
Campbell, J. 16, 17
Campbell, L.G. 62
Canada 1, 9, 95–112, 186, 299, 301
    aboriginal population and 1891 census
        97–101
    Act Respecting Indians (1886) 103
    Agriculture Department 96–7, 98–9,

101–2, 104–6, 108, 109, 112n44
Alberta 98, 99, 108
Assiniboia 98, 99, 108
Athabasca 98
British Columbia 96, 97, 98–9, 100–102,
    103, 104–5, 107–8
Census (1891) 97–101, 108–9
Census Act (1879) 98
challenges of aboriginal enumeration
    101–4
citizenship status 103
colonial policies, 1891 census and 107–8
culture, classification of 102
Department of Indian Affairs (DIA)
    95–6, 99, 100, 103, 105–6, 107, 108,
    111n33
enumeration of aboriginal peoples
    (1851-1891) 96–7, 98–9, 100–101,
    101–4, 105–7, 108–9
Euro-Canadians 97
Hudson's Bay Company 99, 100, 102
Indian Act Amendment (1888) 104
Indian Affairs, Dept of 103, 107
Indians, status of 103
Keewatin 98
linguistic interpretation 102
Manitoba 97, 99, 100, 101, 108
matrilinearity 103
Métis 98, 104, 110n3
migration, monitoring of 99
New Brunswick 97
Northwest Territories 96, 98
Nova Scotia 97
Ontario 97, 101, 105–7
Prince Edward Island 97
property, households and 103
Quebec 97, 101
Queen Charlotte's Islands 101
resistance to and suspicion of
    enumeration 104–7
Saskatchewan 98, 99, 101, 108
US border crossings, problem of 103–4
Cane, S. 296
Caribbean 8, 56, 57, 60, 62–3, 278, 286, 301
    Afro-Caribbean people 275, 277, 279,
        281, 284, 285
Carucci, L.M. and Dominy, M.D. 241
categories 45–7, 63, 66, 99, 110n4, 120–21,
    122, 125–6, 265, 267, 299
    age 79
    of analysis 289–92
    category *indio* in Latin America 61, 62
    category *libres* in Latin America 63, 64
    census 8, 11, 47, 56, 61, 63, 64, 65, 112,
        163–6, 170, 219, 253, 256, 262, 273

colonial 64
common-sense 280
construction of 3, 11–12, 48, 55–6, 95–6, 118, 156, 171, 204–6, 208–10, 260, 271
demographic 3, 4
design of 8, 58
either/or categories 160
ethnic 8, 10, 12, 34, 35, 47, 56–8, 60, 63, 119, 124, 150, 156, 158, 171, 174, 183n4, 186, 188, 239, 243, 273, 278, 279, 280, 281, 283, 285, 286, 291–2, 301, 302
ethno-cultural 186–7
identity 4, 6, 12, 34, 37, 42–7, 220, 273–4, 289–90, 292, 299, 301, 302
indigenous 296, 297–8
legal 241
marriage duration 79
mixed 174, 299
NOS (Norwegian Statistical Office) 168
occupational 121
ordering of 284
'out-group' 136
population 241–2
racial 56, 57, 64, 66, 74, 88, 90, 130, 301
ramifications of, need for understanding of 298–9
of reindeer loss 200
rough categories in historic materials 225, 234
social 59, 64, 234–5n1
statistical 96, 121
validity of 1, 9
categorisation
category 'Finn' and statistics in Norway 170–71
in censuses, scepticism in Latin America on 58
colonial ethnic categorisation 34, 35, 47, 56, 57, 58, 60, 63
demographic 3, 4
ethnic 8, 10, 12, 119, 124, 150, 156, 158, 171, 174, 183n4, 186, 188, 239, 243
indigenous demography and 300, 301–2
juridical 58, 61, 62
moral 4
in Norwegian population surveys 136–7
politics of act of 300
population studies 3, 4
racial 56, 57, 64, 66, 74, 88, 90, 130, 301
resistance towards 7
of Sami (17th and 18th centuries) in Norway 136–7

skin colour 36, 49, 276, 280, 281, 290, 292
source data and categories 295
statistical categorisation 1–2
tick-box 39, 282, 283, 287, 290
U.K. ethnic categorisation 270–80, 273, 278, 281, 283, 286, 291–2
Catholics 60, 68, 100, 255, 259, 264, 270, 280
Caucasus 240, 241, 243, 249n6
censuses
All-Union Census (Soviet Union, 1926) 242
American Indians in (1890, 1900 and 1910) 73–4, 74–7, 91n8
ancestral ethnicity in census statistics 176–7
ancestry criterion in 1865 Norwegian census 149–50, 151, 154, 155
Aranda Census (1768) 59
Baltic Census (1881) 259
Canada, aboriginal population and 1891 census 97–101
categories in Latvia 256, 260, 262, 264, 265, 267, 271
categorisation in, Latin American scepticism on 58
category *indio* in Latin America 61, 62
category *libres* in Latin America 63, 64
census (1981, 2001), migration and ethnicity in U.K. 278–80
census (1855) and Friis's ethnographic map (1861) compared 151–3
Census Act (Canada, 1879) 98
Census Act (Canada, 1891) 104
Census Act (New Zealand, 1877) 36
Census Canada (1891) 97–101, 108–9
census categories 8, 11, 47, 56, 61, 63, 64, 65, 112, 163–6, 170, 219, 253, 256, 262, 273
census counts in Victoria 21, 26–7
census takers 3, 10, 38, 56, 98, 102, 149–50, 154, 155, 156, 157, 160, 161n2, 164–5, 166–7, 168, 171, 175–7, 178, 183, 187, 219, 234, 300, 302
colonial policies in Canada, 1891 census and 107–8
computerised 174, 176
counts of Aborigines in Victoria 21, 26–7
cultural criterion in 1865 Norwegian census 154–5
data for Finnmark, perspectives on ethnicity in 149–61
data in Norway, Sami population in 142–4
definitions of 'Finn' in Norway 167
development in Latin America of 57–8

England and Wales 278–80
ethnic categories in Latin America 56–8
ethnicity, registration on census forms
    in Norway 163–5
ethno-cultural 186–7, 193n2
extraordinary tax 144, 146, 146n5
Finn as category in censuses in Norway
    163–72
fixed data in changing societies 253
Floridablanca Census (1787) 59
Godoy Census (1797) 59
imperial 60, 61, 261, 262
'Indian blood,' census question on 76
Indian Census Integrated Public Use
    Microdata Series (IPUMS) 76, 77,
    87, 88, 91n4, 91n7, 91n8
indigenous demography 301–2, 303
instructions to Norwegian census
    enumerators 150–51, 156, 160
Kven as category in Norway 163–5,
    170, 171
Lapp as category in Norway 163–5
linguistic criteria in census statistics 176
makers 12, 283, 292
male 142, 143, 146n4
Maori census (1926) 37–8, 50n8
Maori population, census and identity
    33–4, 35–40, 40–42
'mixed' as category in censuses in
    Norway 165
modern 8, 40–42, 58, 234, 260–61, 263
new republics in Latin America,
    censuses in 64–6
New Zealand 33, 36, 40–41, 49n3, 52n18
nomenclature in Sweden 127
nominative 127, 176
Northern Ireland 278–80
in Norway (1845-1865), statistics of
    ethnicity from 175–6
Norwegian National Census (1769) 146n6
Polar Census (1926-7) 222–5, 230–31, 234
popular responses to taking of 58
population censuses (1865 and 1875) in
    Finnmark 156–7
population censuses of Soviet era
    Latvia 266–8
population enumeration and societal
    change, imperfect fit between
    253–4
post-Soviet census (2000) in Latvia
    268–70
quality in Latin America 57
register-based 190
reliability of censuses in Spanish
    America 61–2

reports 36, 37, 50n9, 99
republican 63, 64, 65, 66
resistance against
    categorisation 7, 9, 96, 104–7, 191,
        281, 298, 301
    censuses in Spanish America 62
Russian National Census 244
Sami population in 1865 Norwegian
    census 153–4
schedules 36, 52, 76, 77, 95, 96, 98–9,
    100, 109
Scotland 278–80
Sea Sami as category in censuses in
    Norway 164, 165, 166–7, 171n2
social reality and 6
Spanish America, censuses in late
    colonial times 59–63
statistical ambiguities, Lapp, Finn and
    Kven on census returns in Norway
    165–8
Sweden 118–19, 127–9
tabulations 37, 43, 77, 95, 176, 257, 262,
    267, 270
taking in Latin America, modelled on
    Spanish practices 59–60
taxation and censuses in Latin America
    58, 59, 60
tract for, control of ethnicity
    information in 177–9
Turukhansk Polar Census expedition
    (21926-7) 199–200
two-census methods, Life Tables from
    87–90, 91n7
urban 261
US Census Bureau 74, 75–6, 77, 88–90,
    91n2
in Victoria, Australian State of 23, 28
Centeno, M.A. 58
Central Board for the Protection of
    Aborigines 18–19, 20, 21, 23, 25, 28, 29
Centrālā Statistikas Pārvalde (CSP) 270
Chagnon, Napoleon 303
Chayanov, A.V. 220
Cheliabinsk oblast' 241
Chelkans 244, 245, 247
Cherokee 75, 77, 78
Cheyenne 78
Chickasaw 78
children 19, 20, 24, 37–8, 52n18, 73–4, 75,
    76, 79, 81
    child mortality 5, 73, 77–87
    welfare of 18
Chile 57, 60
Chinese Immigrants Act (New Zealand,
    1881) 51n15

Chippewa (Ojibwa) 78, 108, 110n11
Choctaw 78
Christian IV 138
Chukchi 240, 244, 245, 250n15
Chulym 244
Church Law (1894) in Sweden 122–3, 127–8
Church records in Sweden 122–4
Chuvan 243, 244, 245, 250n15
citizenship 90, 168, 219, 257, 268–9, 275, 280, 283
    fractional citizenship 19–20
    status in Canada 103
Civil and Political Rights, International Covenant on (1966) 250n11
civil status, conception of 59–60
clan groupings, Lake Essei Iakuts 212
Clark, I.D. 28
classification 9, 11, 12, 56, 61, 77, 91n5, 112n44, 137, 179, 247, 249n7
    cultural 102, 243
    ethnic classification 10, 62, 130, 173, 176, 227
    in New Zealand 33–4, 34–5, 40–41, 48
    official classification 39, 261
    scheme for American Indians 77, 91n5
    self-classification, Latvian uncertainty on 258–9
clearings 139, 140, 141, 144
Clem, R.S. 256, 267
Clubine-Ito, C. 110n1
Coale, A.J. and Demeny, P. 81, 82, 83
Coates, Ken 6
Coats, Robert Hamilton 99, 110n9
collective identities
    in Latvia, markers of 257–60, 257–61
    in Sweden 120
Colombia 1, 8, 57, 59, 60, 62–3, 64, 65–6
colonialism
    colonial decline of Aborigine population 16–17, 25
    colonial government in Victoria, distinctive features of 18
    colonial identity categories in New Zealand 37
    colonial policies, 1891 census in Canada and 107–8
    ethnic categorisation 34, 35, 47, 56, 57, 58, 60, 63
    knowledge production and 4
    Spanish America, censuses in late colonial times 59–63
colonisation 1, 5–6, 16, 17, 22, 51n16
    decolonisation 6, 241, 283–4
Committee on Culture and Education of the Parliamentary Assembly (PACE) 242

communities 60, 303
    Aboriginal 9, 22, 24–5, 28, 95, 97, 107, 108–9
    coastal (in Canada) 102
    cultural 280
    ethnic 174–5, 188, 191, 197–8, 199, 203, 204, 208–10, 213–14, 221–2, 223–4, 239, 241–2, 281
    indigenous 5–6, 60–61, 119–20, 232, 247, 296, 298, 304
    linguistic 257, 267
    outside and inside traditional communities, need for recording of 191
    political 49n2
    traditional groups 63
Community Lapps 137, 145
conceptualisation
    bureaucratic, of race 35
    bureaucratic, of society 58
    indigenous peoples 6
    nationalistic 257
    new republican, of nation 66
    society 65
Condor, S. 276
Congress of Cúcuta (1821) 64
constructions
    categories 3, 11–12, 48, 55–6, 95–6, 118, 156, 171, 204–6, 208–10, 260, 271
    ethnicity variables 179–82
    ideological 3
    indigeneity 249n7
    legal 241
    Life Tables of Indians 73–91
    political 34, 301
    social 4, 6, 219
    statistical 1, 44, 47
consumer patterns 224–5
contextualisation 3, 5, 10, 182, 183, 200, 296
Cook, L. 186, 193n2
Cook, N.D. 67n1
Cordell, D.D. 304
Cornell, S. and Hartmann, D. 34
costs 19, 25, 45, 50n8, 57
Council of Europe
    European Commission against Racism and Intolerance (ECRI) 193n6
    Parliamentary Assembly (PACE) 242
Courbage, Y. 186
Courland 254
Coyhis, D.L. and White, W.L. 304
Crate, S. 231
Creek Indians 78
Critchett, J. 28
Cuba 57
culture

biculturalism 42
classification in Canada of 102
conservatism 6
cultural complexity 3, 301
cultural criterion in 1865 census in
 Norway 154–5
cultural differences in American Indian
 society, difficulties of 76
identity and 3–4
processes 1
Swedish cultural identities 120
Cummeragunga 24
Curr, E.M. 16
Curtis, B. 95–6, 110n2

D'Aigle, Michel (Chief Dokis) 102, 105–6,
 111n40
Dale, A. and Holdsworth, C. 279
Dalgliesh, Jean 110
Dankertsen, A. 193n10
Darghins 239
Darroch, G. 110n1
Davison, G. 18
death, causes of 232
definitions
 discursive identities 289–92
 ethnic boundaries in New Zealand 33, 35
 ethnicity 173–4, 175–6
 of 'Finn' in Norway 167
 household definition, dimensions of
  212–13
 'Indians,' definition of 74–5, 75–6
 indigenous identity in Sweden 119
 indigenous peoples 5–6
 Maori population, statistical definition
  of 34, 40–41, 47–8, 49
Demographic Database, Uneå University
 118, 131n3
demography 2–3, 11, 119–20, 129, 186,
 192–3, 219, 222
 age-distribution 23, 59–60, 79, 80, 87,
  88, 91n7, 202, 203, 224–5, 303
 behaviour 2, 37
 cause of death 232
 demographic examination of Sami
  peoples 117–18
 development 7, 33–4, 151–2
 dynamic demography, Sami in 191
 historical demography 199, 215, 300
 indigenous 1, 7, 295–305
 in Latin America, difficulties with 55
 modernisation theories and 3
 Sami demography today 187–8
 sex-distribution 23, 59, 60, 77, 78, 125,
  126, 127, 202, 203, 224–5, 303

sources 4, 6–7, 33, 117–31, 149–51,
 233–4, 295
 see also indigenous demography
Deneven, W.N. and Lowell, W.G. 296
Denmark 136, 241
Department of Indian Affairs (DIA),
 Canada 95–6, 99, 100, 103, 105–6, 107,
 108, 111n33
developmental paradigm 2–3
Dharmalingam, A. 3
Díaz Granados, Governor José Ignacio 65
Dillon, L.Y. 110n1
discrimination 8, 20, 38, 118, 121
 UN International Convention on the
  Elimination of all Forms of Racial
  Discrimination (CERD) 193n6
 in United Kingdom 278, 292
discursive identities, definition of 289–92
District Lapps 137, 142, 144, 145
Dolgans 197, 203, 206, 222, 226–7, 229–30,
 231, 232, 233, 243, 244, 245, 247, 250n15
Dolgany Zarechnye 222, 229
Dolgikh, Boris O. 206, 212, 214, 215–16n2, 296
Dombrowskii, K. 213
domicile lists 182
Domschke, E. 56–7, 58
Donahoe, B. et al. 298
Dopico, F. and Rowland, R. 59
Dribins, L. 263, 265
Dunae, P.A. 96, 101, 107, 110n2
Duncan, Eric 101
Durie, M. 34, 43
Dyrvik, S. 135

ecology 16, 199, 214, 302
Economic, Social and Cultural Rights,
 International Covenant on (1966) 250n11
economy 19, 122, 220–21, 265–6
 categories 12
 economic activities in Polar Census
  (1926-7) 222–5, 225–31, 233–4
 economic advantages 275
 economic aid 242
 economic conditions 20–21, 51n17,
  64–6, 222, 248
  of new republics in Latin America
   64–5
 economic description in
  microdemographics 219, 220–21,
  222–5, 225–31
 economic imperatives 50–51n11
 economic kinship 211–13
 economic strategies 221
 planned 11, 233, 266–7
 political 18

resources 28, 129
rural 199
Russian 221
self-functioning 210–11
socio-economic characteristics 11, 34,
    45, 74, 124, 204, 234, 256n1, 258, 269
subsistence 241–2, 244–6
traditional 11, 28, 233, 246, 247
unsubsidised, transition to 197–8
Ecuador 57, 64, 65, 66
education 18, 37, 42, 45, 76, 90, 98, 109, 119,
    232, 242, 244–6, 247, 265, 269, 303
Edvinsson, Sören 122
Eidheim, H. 188
Elder, B. 28
elderly 86, 226–7
    elders' stories 198
Eley, G. and Suny, R.G. 253
elites 8, 65–6, 255, 256, 258, 260, 265
Ellinghaus, K. 20
employment 25, 45, 103, 248
    of indigenous workers in Russia 244–6
    unemployment 46, 246, 248, 276
endogenity, problem of 52n24
Enesei River 221, 223, 226, 227, 228, 229
Enets 227, 243, 244, 245, 250n15
Enlightenment 65
enumeration
    of aboriginal peoples (1851-1891) in Canada
        96–7, 98–9, 100–101, 101–4, 105–7, 108–9
    aggregated 47, 118–19, 183, 304
    of American Indians 74–5, 75–6, 76–7,
        90–91
    data 95–6
    enumerators 9, 27, 36, 39, 50n7, 76–7,
        88, 90, 95–6, 97–8, 99–105, 107, 109,
        110n11, 110n12, 150, 200, 203–4, 208,
        212, 214, 216, 221, 222–3, 242, 256n3,
        261–2, 264, 271, 291, 297, 299, 301, 302
    ethnic enumerations of populations in
        Sweden 120
    Indian agents 99, 100, 101, 102, 103,
        104, 106
    of individuals in Finnmark 149–50,
        157, 160
    instructions to census enumerators
        Finnmark 150–51, 156, 160
    instructions to Norwegian census
        enumerators 150–51, 156, 160
    in New Zealand 33–4, 36, 38, 39–40, 42,
        44, 48, 50n8
    practice of 297–8
    state power and 295
    suspicion of 9, 36, 104–7, 298
epidemics 16–17, 124

Eskimo 244, 245
Essei Iakuts *see* lake Essei Iakuts
Estonia
    peasant peoples of 254
    Second World War in 266
ethnic boundaries in New Zealand
    ambiguity about 49
    definition of 33
    sociological understanding of 34–5
ethnic categories
    classification in New Zealand 33–4,
        34–5, 40–41, 48
    composition of population in Finnmark
        150–51
    ethnicity variables 174–5
    Latin America 60, 62, 63, 65
    in Latin America 56–8
ethnic groups 11, 34, 40, 41, 42, 44–5, 47,
    52n20, 58, 149–50, 157, 179–82, 193n9,
    234–5n1, 240, 242, 247, 249n7
    categorisation in Norway 177
    distribution patterns of 173, 176
    legal status 11, 47, 138–9, 239, 243
    Maori Ethnic Group (MEG) 43
    minority groups in north Russia 221
    by parental ethnicity 181–2
    social interaction between 160, 302
    in United Kingdom 274, 277, 278, 279,
        281, 284, 285, 286
ethnicity
    ancestral 25, 26, 176–7, 179, 183
    collective 44
    definition of 173–4, 175–6
    ethnic affiliation 188, 190, 191, 192, 211,
        212, 222
    ethnic boundaries 33–52
    ethnic identification 43, 45
    ethnic markers 1, 52, 122, 124, 150, 153,
        156–7, 174, 178, 179, 180, 261, 300
    ethnic origin 40, 41, 170
    ethnonyms 177
    in Latvia 262–6
    linguistic criterion 151, 155
    multifaceted process of 173–4
    primordial 3, 11, 243
    registration in Sweden 118
    registration on census forms in Norway
        163–5
    Sami data, recording of 186–7
    semantic confusion in U.K. on 278
ethnicity variables 173–83
    ancestral ethnicity in census statistics
        176–7
    census of 1845, statistics of ethnicity
        from 175

census of 1855, statistics of ethnicity from 176
census of 1865, statistics of ethnicity from 176
census tract, control of ethnicity information in 177–9
constructed ethnicity variables 179–82
definitions of ethnicity 173–4, 175–6
domicile lists 182
dynamics of ethnicity 173–4
ethnic categories 174–5
ethnic groups by parental; ethnicity 181–2
linguistic criteria in census statistics 176
multifaceted process of ethnicity 173–4
North Atlantic Population Project (NAPP) 174, 179, 183n1
northern Norway, ethnic groups in 173
Norwegian regional and national archives 174
population statistics in Norway 174
ethno-cultural data, complexity of 186–7
ethno-linguistic differentiation in Latvia 258
ethnography 3, 11, 39, 206–7, 213, 215–16n2, 221–2, 225, 227, 234, 266, 303
ethnographic maps 149, 150–51, 152, 300
ethnographic sectors 267
ethnonyms 177
Euro-Canadians 97
European Union (EU)
European Commission against Racism and Intolerance (ECRI) 193n6
Latvian accession to 270
Evans, Joanne 7–8, 15–29, 297, 298, 299, 302, 309
Even 240, 244, 245, 250n15
Evenki 197, 201, 206, 219, 226, 240, 243, 244, 245, 250n15
Evenki-Iakut relationships 201–2
Evjen, B. and Hansen, L.I. 136, 137, 163
Evjen, Bjørg 10, 163–72, 179, 297, 299, 301–2, 309
expeditions
canoe expeditions in Canada 101
Turukhansk Polar Cencus Expedition (1926–7) 199–200, 203–4, 211, 215–16n2, 220
exploitation 19, 23, 198, 226, 229, 242
Eyler, J.M. 23

family 2–3, 23, 35, 56, 103–4, 105, 150–51, 155, 166–7, 176, 199, 204–5, 208
extended 211, 213, 228, 230

family histories 7, 22, 24–5, 219
names, heritage and 124
nuclear 214, 215
reconstitutions 28–9
regulation of 20–21
reproductive cycles 220–21
structures 76
Farr, William 22
Fedorova, E.N. 240
Felton, P. 27
Fenton, F.D. 36, 51n16
fertility 6, 79, 87–8, 296, 303, 304
differential fertility 77
fertility rates 222, 224, 232–3, 235n11, 268, 270
statistics of, analysis of 304
Finland 120, 164–8, 169–70, 177, 185, 187, 189, 193n5, 193n7, 241
Finlanders 166, 167–8
Finn as census category in Norway 163–72
Finn leidang 138, 141
Finneodel 139–40
Finnish 123, 126–8, 136, 165, 170, 173, 175, 176, 177–8, 180–83, 264
Finnmark 149–61, 169
ancestry criterion in 1865 census 149–50, 151, 154, 155
census (1855) and Friis's ethnographic map (1861) compared 151–3
census data and perspectives on ethnicity in 149–61
cultural criterion in 1865 census 154–5
enumeration of individuals 149–50, 157, 160
ethnic composition of population 150–51
ethnic identity 149–50, 151, 155, 158, 159, 160
ethnic registration 149, 151, 153, 155
Finns 150, 161n2
instructions to census enumerators 150–51, 156, 160
inter-ethnic relationships 158–9
Kvens 150, 158, 159, 160
Lapps 150
linguistic composition of population 150–51
linguistic criterion in 1865 census 155
mapping linguistic knowledge 151
mixed marriages 149, 150–51, 153–4, 154–5, 157–60
Norwegianisation 158–9, 159–60
population censuses (1865 and 1875) 156–7
registration practice 156, 160

reindeer herders 152
Sami, nomadic and settled 150
Sami households 151, 152, 153, 154, 158
Sami population, registration of (1855-1861) 152-3
Sami population in 1865 census 153-4
source materials 149-51
Finns (or Sea Sami)
    Finnmark 150, 161n2
    Norway 136, 137, 144
    Sami 136, 165, 170, 173, 175, 176, 177-8, 180-83
First World War 254, 265
Fisher, J. 67n3
Fisher, J., Kuethe, A.J. and MacFarlane, A. 67n3, 67n5, 67n6
fishing 121, 125, 145, 179, 224, 226, 227, 230, 233, 242, 246, 247
Floridablanca Census (1787) 59
food 15-16, 107, 204-7, 220, 224, 230, 248
    local food supplies, security of 231
Forbes, J.D. 95
forced assimilation 24
Forest Lapps 137
Fortier, Ashley 100, 102, 110
Foucault, Michel 4
Fox, R. 219
foxes 209, 225, 226, 227, 229, 235n6
France 59
Fricke, T. 2
Friis, Jens Andreas 149, 150-51, 161n3
    ethnographic map (1861) 151-3
full-bloods 7, 19, 24, 36, 39, 48, 128

Gadagrāmata 265
Gaelic and Welsh speakers 275
Gaffield, C. 98, 110n1, 110n2
Gagan, D.P. 96, 110n5
Galois, R.M. 110n2
Galskiy in Abkhazia 240
Gans, H. 34
Gardner, G. and Bourke, E.A. 7, 11
genealogical identity 22
genealogical records 24-5
General Allotment Act (US, 1887) 75
Germanisation of Latvia 258
Germany 266, 288
Godoy Census (1797) 59
Gomes, M.P. 296
Gootenberg, P. 67n2
Gorbachev, Mikhail 268
Gosnell, R.E. 110n10
Gould, J.L. 299
government 16, 18-19, 20, 22, 27, 35-6, 49n4, 61, 122, 253-4, 255, 256

Canadian government 97, 98, 103, 104, 105, 106-7, 108
Conservative government in U.K. 278, 280, 282-3
Dano-Norwegian government 138, 139, 140
federal government (US) 74, 75, 76
government finances 64-5
Latvian government 265, 269, 271
Norwegian government 151
Russian government 233, 244, 248, 259, 260
Soviet government 198-9, 219, 220, 224-5, 227, 231, 242
Swedish government 130
Goyer, D.S. and Domschke, E. 56-7, 58
Gracey, M. and King, M. 304
Granados, Governor José Ignacio Díaz 65
Gray, P. 231
Green, Ronald E. 104-5, 111n29, 111n30
Greenhalgh, S. 3
Greer, Frederick 100-101, 101-2, 105
Guajiro (Wayúu) Indians 60
Guillod, Harry 110n11
Gustavson, Wesley C. 110
Gutiérrez, R. 67n2
Gypsies 121, 175

Hacker, J. David 9, 73-91, 110n1, 297, 298, 299, 301, 302, 309-10
Hacker, J.D. and Haines, M.R. 91n3
Hacking, Ian 4
Haines, Michael R. 9, 73-91, 297, 298, 299, 301, 302, 310
Haines, M.R. and Preston, S.H. 79
'half-caste problem' 18-19
Hall, P.K. 110n1
Hallencreutz, C.F. 131n6
Haltzel, M. 257
Hamilton, Michelle A. 9, 95-112, 220, 297, 298, 299, 301, 310
Hansdatter, Elen 154
Hansen, Lars Ivar 9, 120, 135-46, 150, 151, 152, 163, 197, 301, 310
Hansen, L.I. and Meyer, T. 174
Hansen, L.I. and Niemi, E. 152
Hansen, L.I. and Olsen, B. 158
Härnosand diocese in Sweden 123
Haselden, L. and Jenkins, R. 289
Hassler, S. 130
Hassler, S., Sjölander, P. and Ericcson, A. 193n8
Haug, W. 186, 193n2
Hawaii 35, 51n12
Hawkins, H.H. and Blume, A.W. 304

Hayter, H.H. 23
health 5, 18, 45, 118, 219–20, 222, 246, 295, 300, 304–5
  demographics and 231–3, 234, 302–3
  Koori Health Research Database (KHRD) 24–5, 26–7
  Public Health Services (US), Indian healthcare and 73, 86
  Sami health issues 130, 193n8
  Soviet Ministry of Health 242
Hegg, L.S. 193n10
Hendry, Hamilton 24
Henige, D. 67n1
herding *see* reindeer herding
Hern, Warren M. 220, 303
history
  Historical Data Centre in Norway 180, 181, 182
  historical demographic, Polar Census (1926-7) 222–5, 230–31, 234
  indigenous demographics and historical context in Sweden 119–20
  population studies, historical records in 5
Hochschild, J. and Powell, B.M. 33, 34, 39
Hogarth, William 106, 111n36, 111n37, 111n40
Högström, Pehr 123
Höjer, Henrik 120–21, 129
Hollos, M. 95
Hopper, J. 23
Horden, Bishop John 100, 110n14
House of Commons 278
household
  cards 199–200, 201–2
  definition, dimensions of 212–13
  extensive 215
  head 102, 104, 157, 176
  registers for Lake Essei 202–3, 215
  structure among Lake Essei Iakuts 197–216
Howitt, A.W. 24
Hoxie, F.E. 88
Hoy, Benjamin 110
Hudon, S. 296
Hudson's Bay Company 99, 100, 102
Hull, J. 95
Humphrey, C. 213
Hunn, J.K. 50n10
Hunt, Paul 118, 130
hunting 10, 17, 105, 121, 125–6, 220, 226, 230, 232–3
  traditional practices 231, 241–2, 246, 247

Iberia 57, 58, 59, 296
Icaza, Francisco Pablo 65

identity
  Aboriginal 7, 20, 73–4, 96–7, 109
  categories 273–4, 289–90, 291–2, 299–300, 300, 301–2
  civic 275, 277, 282, 288, 290
  collective 2, 33, 35, 120, 257–60, 257–61, 261, 268, 270, 271, 302
  culture and 3–4
  economic 220
  ethnic 6, 9, 43, 45, 48, 117–18, 120, 149–50, 151, 155, 158, 159, 160, 170, 192, 225, 227, 230, 233, 271, 292
  ethnic identity in Finnmark 149–50, 151, 155, 158, 159, 160
  fractional identity and citizenship 19–20, 24, 29
  genealogical identity 22
  indigenous identity 119, 299–300
  individual 34, 243
  management of, dynamics of 213–14
  Maori 8, 33–52
  microdemographics and 219–22
  mixed 19, 37, 39, 43, 60, 76, 88, 90, 98, 108–9, 150, 163–5, 174, 299
  nationality 2–3, 199, 211, 256, 270, 280, 283, 284, 285, 286, 289, 292
  plurality in U.K. of 275, 290–91
  politics of, fluid character of 242–3
  reconstituted 24–5
  Sami 9, 121, 122, 124, 125, 188, 189, 190, 192
  self- 95, 192, 212, 258, 269, 290
  statistical construction 1, 44, 118
ILO Convention 107 (1957) 241
ILO Convention 169 (1989) 241, 242
immigration 12, 21, 98, 249n8, 268, 274–8, 283
  Immigration Restriction Act (New Zealand, 1908) 51n15
  moral panic in U.K. and 276–7
imperialism 4
Imsen, S. and Winge, H. 164, 166
India 276, 278, 280, 286
Indian Act Amendment (Canada, 1888) 104
Indian Affairs, Canadian Department of 103, 107
Indian Census Integrated Public Use Microdata Series (IPUMS) 76, 77, 87, 88, 91n4, 91n7, 91n8
Indian Life Tables
  age 84–5, 87–90
  child survivorship, from data on 77–87
  from two-census methods 87–90, 91n7
'Indianness' in Latin America 61, 62, 66
Indians *see* American Indians; Canada; Latin America

indígena in Latin America 55, 64, 66
indigeneity 239, 241–2, 248–9n1
indigenous communities in Latin America
  60–61
indigenous demography
  categories, source data and 295
  categorisation 300, 301–2
  censuses 301–2, 303
  cross-disciplinary research, engagement
    with 303–4
  cutting-edge theory, engagement with
    303–4
  demographic records 301–2
  demographic records, changes in 301–2
  enumeration, practice of 297–8
  fertility statistics, analysis of 304
  future of 304–5
  identity categories 299–300, 300, 301–2
  indigenous identity 299–300
  indigenous responses to enumeration
    298–9
  literature on 295–6
  methods for an 300–305
  micro-ethnodemographic research 303
  mortality statistics, analysis of 304
  registration and taxation, relationship
    between 300–301
  retrospective research 296
  standards for 302–4
  state policy and indigenous peoples
    296–300
  visibility 296–300
indigenous groups, territories of principal
  residence and 246–7
indigenous identity 119, 299–300
indigenous in Russia, indeterminacy over
  concept 11, 242
indigenous in U.K., British as 274–8
indigenous peoples
  analysis of 6
  censuses, social reality and 6
  conceptualisation 6
  defining features in New Zealand 49n2
  definition of, issue of 5–6
  enumeration in Latin America of 55
  legal category in Russia 241
  notions concerning 4
  perspectives on 5–7
  sources of data on, construction of 6–7
indigenous responses to enumeration
  298–9
indigenous small-numbered 11, 239, 242,
  243, 249n4, 250n16, 298
indigenous societies 3, 5, 6, 11, 298, 299
  understanding complexities of 5

indigenous status 239, 242, 295, 299
indigenous studies 8, 119–22
indigenousness
  dynamic indigenousness 290–91
  during Soviet era in Latvia 266–7
indio in Latin America 56, 60, 61, 62, 63,
  64, 66
Institute of Aboriginal and Torres Strait
  Islander Studies (AIATSIS) 24
instructions
  to census enumerators in Finnmark
    150–51, 156, 160
  census instructions 10, 88, 90, 95, 96–7,
    99, 126–7, 149, 160, 161n2, 164,
    165–6, 167, 168, 171, 175, 176, 302
integration of indigenous groups in Russia
  248
inter-ethnic relationships in Finnmark
  158–9
intermarriage of American Indians with
  white population 90
International Football Federation (FIFA)
  185
International Labour Organisation (ILO)
  275
interviews 170, 225, 285, 289, 292n1, 303
'invisible Aborigines'
  Aborigines 21–2, 25
  emergence of 25, 26–7
Inwood, K. and James, K. 96
Inwood, K. and Reid, R. 110n1, 110n2
Inwood, Kris 9, 95–112, 297, 298, 299, 301,
  310
Ioldagyr', Kapiton Mikhailovich 228–9, 230
Ireland 278, 283
Iroquois 78
Itelmen 244, 245, 247, 250n15
Izhora 241, 244

Jack, Chelsea 110
Jackomos, Alick 24
Jakobsen, John 155
Jåstad, Hilde L. 10, 149–61, 174, 300, 302,
  310
Jews 121, 123, 133, 256, 259, 262, 264, 265,
  269
Jiménez de Gregorio, F. 59
Jobe, M.M. 74, 95
Johansson, Henning 123, 125
Johansson, S.R. and Preston, S.H. 77
Johnson, George 102, 107–8, 111n16, 111n20,
  111n36, 111n37, 112n42
Jones, D.S. 88, 91n1
Jones, Mary Katherine 171
jural domain 3

Kamchadal 243, 244
Karabakh 240
Karatani, R. 283
Karetu, T. 43
Karlsøy in Norway 180, 181
Karlsson, B.G. 241, 300
Kashmir 280
Kauanui, K. 35
Kaudzite, M. 259
Kaufmann, E. 47
Keewatin 98
Kennedy, D.P. and Perz, S.G. 296
Kerek 243, 244
Kertzer, D.I. 2
Kertzer, D.I. and Arel, D. 3, 6, 7, 34, 120, 125, 129, 193n2
Ket 244, 245, 250n15
Keyserling, P.E. von 261
Khakass 247, 248
Khant 244, 245, 250n15
Khatanga volost' 221–2, 223, 224, 235n3
khoziain (household head) 223, 225
Kiær, A.N. 151, 159–60, 165, 166
Kinfu, Y. and Taylor, J. 119, 305
Kinfu, Yohannes 119
King, M., Smith, A. and Gracey, M. 304–5
kinship 19, 22, 36, 75, 203, 207–8, 219, 222, 228, 299
  networks 35
    Iakut communities and 210–14
Kiowa 78
Kippen, R. 88
Klein, Herbert S. 63, 64, 65
Klein, H.S. and Barbier, J.A. 62
Knight, Nicholas 29
Kock, K. 127
Kolsrud, Knut 139, 140
Komi 248
Koori Health Research Database (KHRD) 24–5, 26–7
Koryak 244, 250n15
Kovalaschina, E.P. 296
Kralt, J. 110n4
Kramvig, B. 193n10
Krasnoiarsk Territory 199, 201, 203, 221
Kreager, Philip 3–4
Krivonogov, N.V. 233
Krupnik, I.I. 233
Kukutai, Tahu 4, 8, 33–52, 220, 298, 300, 301, 302, 311
Kumanda 243, 244, 245, 250n15
Kunitz, S.J. 304
Kuper, A. 49n2
Kurs 260
Kurzeme 254, 264, 265

Kuznesof, E.A. 67n2
Kvaenangen in Norway 180
Kvens
  as category in censuses in Norway 163–5, 170, 171
  in Finnmark 150, 158, 159, 160
Kvist, R. 164

Labour Force Survey (LFS)
  evidence of Britishness in 283–6
  United Kingdom 274, 277, 279, 283, 284, 285, 289
Lake Essei Iakuts 10–11, 197–216
  Batulu family lineage 201, 211, 212, 213, 214
  bediak (poor grade people) 204–5, 209, 210
  bogatyi (wealthy people) 204, 206, 209, 210
  clan groupings 212
  elders' stories 198
  Evenki-Iakut relationships 201–2
  exploitation 198
  household cards on, data contained in 199–200, 201–3
  household definition, dimensions of 212–13
  household structure among 197–216
  identity management, dynamics of 213–14
  interpretation of household cards on, context of 200
  kinship networks, communities and 210–14
  Lake Essei and hinterland 200–203
  Lake Essei diaspora 203
  Lekarenko's notes on 201–3, 204–6, 207–8, 208–10
  mass collectivisation 198–9
  outliers in data, problem of 213
  posobka (mutual aid institution) 206–8
  reindeer herding 197–9
  self-consciousness 201
  size of population 201
  sostoiatel'nyi (wealthy people) 204, 206, 209, 210
  Soviet criteria for stratification 208–10
  Soviet era, counting reindeer during 197
  Soviet era, tumult and change in 198–9
  Soviet gradations, stratification and 204–6
  Soviet literature 198
  sredniak (middle grade people) 204, 205–6, 209, 210
  stratification 203–10

territorial dispersion 198–9
Turukhansk Polar Census expedition (21926-7) 199–200
unsubsidised economy, transition to 197–8
Lake Tyers 24
land 6, 8, 11, 15–16, 19, 25, 49n4, 101, 105, 121, 248–9n1, 299
  access 61, 62, 63
  agricultural, control of 65
  ancestral 44
  clearance of 137
  control of 65, 121, 126
  divisions 28
  grants 104
  indigenous 186, 298
  land-tenure patterns 219, 222
  land-use patterns, identities and 220, 221, 225–31, 234, 302
  landless 63
  Maori Land Act (New Zealand, 1909) 50n10
  owners 140
  property system 139
  registers 140, 141, 260
  reserve-land 37, 107
  rights 21, 248
  speculation 98
  succession 43
  tax 138
  tribal 90
language
  Aboriginal 102, 106
  Church and ethnicity in Sweden 123, 127–9
  English 37, 49n4, 50–51n11, 257
  interpreters 100, 102
  language use 186, 188, 190, 225, 260, 261, 264, 278
  linguistic composition of population in Finnmark 150–51
  linguistic criteria in census statistics 155, 176
  linguistic interpretation in Canada 102
  mapping linguistic knowledge in Finnmark 151
  native 211, 222, 225, 226, 227, 228, 229, 260
  Norwegian 150, 155, 176
  Russian 225, 268, 270
  Sami 117, 130, 170, 185, 188
Lappförsamling 123–4, 125
Lapps
  as category in censuses in Norway 163–5
  Finnmark 150

Norway 136, 137
  population statistics in Sweden on 125–6
  see also Sami
Larson, A. 23
Laslett, Peter 56
Latgale 254, 256, 259, 261, 264, 265, 269, 270
Latgalians 260, 264, 265, 266, 269, 270
Latin America 8, 55–67, 58, 299
  Andean highlands 62
  Aranda Census (1768) 59
  categorisation in censuses, scepticism on 58
  census category *indio* 61, 62
  census category *libres* 63, 64
  census quality 57
  census taking
    development of 57–8
    modelled on Spanish practices 59–60
  civil status, conception of 59–60
  Congress of Cúcuta (1821) 64
  demographics of, difficulties with 55
  economic conditions (and interests) of new republics 64–5
  ethnic categories 60, 62, 63, 65
  ethnic categories in censuses 56–8
  Floridablanca Census (1787) 59
  Godoy Census (1797) 59
  Guajiro (Wayúu) Indians 60
  'Indianness' in 61, 62, 66
  Indians in, categorisation of 63
  indigenous communities 60–61
  indigenous populations, enumeration of 55
  mestizo, declarations of 61
  nation, new republican conceptualisation of 66
  New Grenada 63
  new republics in, censuses in 64–6
  personal contribution (*contribución personal*) 64, 65
  poll tax (*tributo*) 60, 61, 64–5
  quantitative work on indigenous populations, difficulties with 55–6
  racial categories 60, 63
  reliability of censuses in Spanish America 61–2
  resistance against censuses in Spanish America 62
  Santa Marta 62–3, 64, 65
  society, conceptualisation by bureaucrats of 58
  society, liberal ideas of 65–6
  Spanish America, censuses in late colonial times 59–63

Spanish America, demographic studies
of 56
taxation and censuses in 58, 59, 60
Yungas valleys 63, 64
Latvia 1, 11–12
basic nation, concept of 258–9
Bauernstand (peasantry) in 258, 260
census categories 253, 255, 261, 262,
265, 267, 271
Centrālā Statistikas Pārvalde (CSP) 270
collective identity in, markers of 257–61
ethnicity 263–6
ethno-linguistic differentiation 258
Gadagrāmata 265
Germanisation of 259
'indigenousness' during Soviet era
266–7
Kurzeme 255, 264, 265
Latgale 255, 257n3, 260, 262, 264, 265,
269, 270
Leninist nationality policy 266
nationalist movement in 260–61
nationalities (and minorities) in 263,
264, 265, 266
nationality 263–6
peasant peoples of 254
population censuses of Soviet era 266–8
population enumerations (19th century)
261–3
population of 255–7
post-Soviet census (2000) 268–70
Russification of 257, 260, 268
Second World War in 266
self-classification, uncertainty on 259
social estate, philosophy of 257n1,
258–9, 261, 262
socio-economic development 257, 258,
259, 261, 269
trial population counts 262
Valsts Statistikā Pārvalde (VSP) 270
Vidzeme 255, 264, 265
Zemgale 264, 265
Lavrin, A. 67n2
Lekarenko, Andrei 203, 204, 207, 208, 209,
210, 212, 213, 214, 215–16n2, 216n3
notes on Lake Essei Iakuts 201–3,
204–6, 207–8, 208–10
Leningrad oblast' 241
Levin, M.G. and Potapov, L.P. 227, 250n10
Lie, E. and Roll-Hansen, H. 163
life expectancy 9
of American Indians 73, 79, 81, 82, 83,
86, 87, 88, 90
life history 303–4
Life Tables 73–91

Lindbekk, K. 135
literacy 18, 122, 222, 258, 264
Lithuania
Polish-Lithuanian Commonwealth 254
Second World War in 266
living conditions 5, 135, 187, 193n8, 297
Livonia 255
Livs (Livonians) 260, 264, 266, 268, 269
Ljungberg, Carl Edvard 121
Loft, Solomon 110n11
Lomas, W.H. 110n11
Lourandos, H. 16, 17
Lowe, John 106, 111n35, 111n39
Loy, J.M. 67n6
Lundmark, Lennart 121–2, 129, 130
Lutherans 255, 258, 259
Lyngen in Norway 180, 181

Macassa, G. 5
McCaa, Robert 56, 67n1, 67n2
McCalman, Janet 7–8, 15–29, 297, 298, 299,
302, 311
McCarthy, Anne 24
McCarthy, Gavan 7–8, 15–29, 297, 298, 299,
302, 311
MacFarlane, A. 67n3, 67n5, 67n6
MacInnes, John 11–12, 273–92, 299, 300, 311
McInnes, R.M. 110n2
Macintyre, S.F. and Clark, A. 16
McLean, Charles 20
McLean Commission 27
Macmillan, H.L. et al. 295
McSweeney, K. and Arps, S. 296, 304
Mandemaker, K. and Dillon, L.Y. 110n1
Manitoba 97, 99, 100, 101, 108
Manne, R. 16
Mansi 244, 245, 250n15
Maori 8
adaptability of, faith in 37, 50–51n11
cultural revitalisation 39–40
descent 34, 40–41, 42, 43–4, 45, 46, 47,
50n10, 52n19
ethnicity 34, 41, 43–4, 45, 46, 47, 52n20
group boundaries, diverse nature of
45–7
identity categories 42–4
characteristics of 44–7
kinship, centrality of 35–6
Maori Affairs Amendment Act (1974) 40
Maori census (1926) 37–8, 50n8
Maori Ethnic Group (MEG) 43
Maori-European individuals,
documentation of 36, 52n18
Maori incorporation 38, 51n14
Maori *kawanatanga* (governance) 49n4

Maori Land Act (1909) 50n10
Maori Pioneer Battalion 52n18
Maori Representation Act (1867) 50n10,
    51n13
Maori Social and Economic
    Advancement Act (1945) 50n10
population
    census and identity 33–4, 40–42
    statistical definition of 34, 40–41,
        47–8, 49
    responses to identity quantification 39
    tribal affiliation 43–4
    whakapapa 34, 43, 47–8
markers
    cultural 2
    ethnic 1, 10, 52, 117, 150, 151, 153, 154,
        156, 157, 158, 160, 174–5, 179–80,
        183, 261, 300
market-oriented exchanges 230
marriage 7, 10, 20, 22–3
    duration and age 79–83
    inter- 37, 88, 173, 179, 268
    marriage certificates 24, 25
    marriage duration 79, 81, 82, 83, 91n6
    mixed 10, 121, 130, 149, 150–51, 153–4,
        155, 157–60, 299
    mixed marriages in Finnmark 149,
        150–51, 153–4, 154–5, 157–60
    patterns 56, 158, 159
    re-marriage 81, 86, 91
Martin, James 110n11
Martinez-Alier, V. 67n2
Martinez Cobo, José 5–6
Martley, Captain John 101
mass collectivisation 198–9
Massola, Aldo 24
Mathisen, P. 158
Matos Rodríguez, F.V. 67n2
matrilinearity 103, 214
measles 5
Meisel Roca, A. and Aguilera Díaz, M. 67n2
mercantilism 120, 121, 123, 124
Meredith, P. 37, 50–51n11, 51n17
Merlan, F. 300
Merli, M.G. 91n9
mestizo, declarations of 61
Metge, J. 39
methods
    Brass method on child mortality 77–9
    hermeneutic 3
    for indigenous demography 300–305
    population in Norway, alternative
        methods for estimation of 142–4
    Preston-Bennett Method, application to
        population (1900-1910) 88–90

qualitative methods 4–5
quantitative methods 4–5
two-census methods, Life Tables from
    87–90, 91n7
Métis in Canada 98, 104, 110n3
Metizaje 299
Mexico 57, 59, 61–2
Meyer, T. 174
Michaud, J.P Joseph 105–6, 111n32, 111n33,
    111n34, 111n38
micro-ethnodemographic research 303
microdata 76, 77, 87, 174, 176
microdemographics 219–35
    Barkhatov household 225–6
    Bezrukikh household 229–30
    in Central Taimyr lowlands 222, 224,
        232
    current demographic sources 233–4
    death, causes of 232
    economic description 219, 220–21,
        222–5, 225–31
    fertility rates 232–3
    health and demographics 231–3
    historical demographic, Polar Census
        (1926-7) 222–5, 230–31, 234
    identity and 219–22
    Ioldagyr' household 228–9
    land-use patterns, identities and 225–31
    local food supplies, security of 231
    market-orientated exchanges 230
    mortality rates 232, 233
    Polar Census (1926–7) 222–5, 230–31,
        234
    regional government, payments from
        233
    sharing, significance of 231
    social processes in small-scale societies,
        description of 234
    Suslov household 226–7
    traditional hunting practices 231
    transhumant pastoralism 230–31
    Tuglakov household 227–8
migration 6, 10, 62, 74, 87–8, 90, 122, 167,
    171, 173, 179, 187, 228, 242–3, 250n9
    census, migration and ethnicity 278–80
    monitoring in Canada of 99
    patterns of 222, 266–7, 270, 275
Milan, F.A. 295
Millar, V.P. 296
Miller, G.M. 67n2, 67n3, 67n5
Mills, George B. 105–6, 111n31
Minchom, Martin 61
ministerial records 174
Minnesota Population Center 77, 118,
    131n3

minorities 38, 48, 304
  ethnic 247
  indigenous 240
  issue in Russia of 240–41
  minority languages 265
  National Minorities, Framework
    Convention for the Protection of
    (FCNM) 193n6
  native minority peoples *(korennye
    malochislennye narody)* in Russia 240
  rural 295
  urban natives and ethnic minorities,
    conceptual differences between 247
Mirga, A. 193n2
miscegenation 37–8, 39
Misiunas, R. and Taagepera, R. 263, 266
missionaries 99, 100, 101, 108, 123, 131, 136,
  137
Mitchell, J. 5
mobility 6, 36, 61, 62, 228, 230, 231, 258,
  260, 275
modernisation 245, 247, 267
  theories 3
Montenegro, R.A. and Stephens, C. 296, 304
Montevideo Convention on the Rights and
  Duties of States (1933) 250n11
Moran, Emilio F. 220, 303
Moreno Yáñez, S. 62
Morgan, Mary Angeline 17
Mörkenstam, Ulf 121, 129
Morning, A. and Sabbagh, D. 34, 39, 51n12,
  193n2
mortality 6, 17, 124
  age patterns of 90
  age-specific 9
  of American Indians 73, 77, 81, 86, 87, 91
    following European contacts 73
  child 5, 73, 77, 79, 81, 82, 83, 87, 91n3,
    173–4
  female 87
  male 87
  maternal 88
  microdemographics and rates of 232, 233
  in Norway 144
  sex-differentials 88, 91n3
  statistics of, analysis of 304
Mortensen, Elias 155
Moscow 248, 266, 267, 268
Mountain Finns 169
Mountain Lapps 137
Mulvaney, D.J. 16

Nagaibak 241, 244
Nagel, J. 34–5
Nanai 243, 244, 245, 250n15

nation, new republican conceptualisation
  of 66
National Archive of the Sakha Republic
  (NARS) 199
National Archives in Norway 141–2, 143,
  144, 146n4, 146n5
National Census (1769) in Norway 146n6
National Minorities, Framework
  Convention for the Protection of
  (FCNM) 193n6
national policies 7, 12, 59, 65, 104, 130, 220,
  297–8
National Statistics in Sweden 117, 118, 120,
  122, 123, 124–6, 127
National Union of the Swedish Sami (SSR)
  130
nationalism in Latvia 259–60
nationality 12, 49–50n5, 126–7, 150, 159–60,
  165, 169, 186
  British 283–4, 285, 289
  in Central Taimyr lowlands 222, 225,
    226, 227, 228, 229
  introduction of entity of 200
  in Latvia 255–6, 259, 260, 261–2, 262–8,
    269, 270
  Nationality Act (U.K., 1914) 283
Native Land Amendment Act (New
  Zealand, 1912) 37, 50–51n11, 51n17
native minority peoples *(korennye
  malochislennye narody)* in Russia 240
Naughton, Kate 29
Naumov, N.P. 228–9
Navajo 78
Negidal 244, 250n15
Negrin, K. 193n2
Nelson, Marie Clark 121, 125–6
Nenets 244, 245, 250n15
networks 35, 43, 68, 204, 206, 210, 214, 215,
  223, 231
  exchange networks 219
  family networks 228
  social networks 220
  tribal networks 47–8
New Brunswick, Canada 97
New Grenada 63
New Zealand 1, 8, 33–52, 186, 299
  Births and Deaths Registration Act
    (1951) 50n10
  blood quantum, extension of 37–8,
    51n12
  blood quantum, voting rights and
    51n13
  boundary building in official statistics
    34–5
  bureaucratic definition of ethnic

boundaries 35
census 33, 36, 40–41, 49n3, 52n18
census, Maori population in 35–40,
	40–41
Census Act (1877) 36
Census and Statistics Office 38–9, 50n8,
	52n18
Chinese Immigrants Act (1881) 51n15
colonial identity categories 37
demographic sources 33
endogenity, problem of 52n24
enumeration 33–4, 36, 38, 39–40, 42, 44,
	48, 50n8
ethnic boundaries, definition of 33
ethnic boundaries, sociological
	understanding of 34–5
ethnic classification 33–4, 34–5, 40–41,
	48
European settler population 35, 37,
	49–50n5
Immigration Restriction Act (1908)
	51n15
indigenous peoples, defining features
	of 49n2
Maori adaptability, faith in 37, 50–
	51n11
Maori Affairs Amendment Act (1974)
	40
Maori census (1926) 37–8, 50n8
Maori cultural revitalisation 39–40
Maori descent 34, 40–41, 42, 43–4, 45,
	46, 47, 50n10, 52n19
Maori Ethnic Group (MEG) 43
Maori ethnicity 34, 41, 43–4, 45, 46, 47,
	52n20
Maori-European individuals,
	documentation of 36, 52n18
Maori group boundaries, diverse nature
	of 45–7
Maori identity categories 42–4
Maori identity categories,
	characteristics of 44–7
Maori incorporation 38, 51n14
Maori *kawanatanga* (governance) 49n4
Maori kinship, centrality of 35–6
Maori Land Act (1909) 50n10
Maori Pioneer Battalion 52n18
Maori population, census and identity
	33–4, 40–42
Maori population, statistical definition
	of 34, 40–41, 47–8, 49
Maori Representation Act (1867) 50n10,
	51n13
Maori responses to identity
	quantification 39

Maori Social and Economic
	Advancement Act (1945) 50n10
Maori tribal affiliation 43–4
Maori *whakapapa* 34, 43, 47–8
miscegenation 37–8, 39
Native Land Amendment Act (1912)
	37, 50–51n11, 51n17
phenotypical distinctions 36–7
political change and social movements
	in 42
'race alien' designation in 8, 38–9
racial boundaries, manipulation of 38–9
racial taxonomies, influences on 39
Registrar General 36, 37, 50n7
Undesirable Immigrants Exclusion Act
	(1919) 51n15
Waitangi, Treaty of (1840) 35
Waitangi Tribunal 42–3, 49n4
Newbold, Bruce 119
Newman, A.K. 37
Newson, L. 296
Nganasan 222, 226, 227, 231, 232, 233, 244,
	245, 250n15
Nielssen, Alf Ragnar 135, 140
Nielssen, A.R. and Pedersen, H. 140
Niemi, E. 176, 193n2
Niezen, R. 305
Nilsen, Arne 155
Nivkh 244, 245, 250n15
Nobles, Melissa 4, 34, 88
Nogai of Dagestan 239
nomadism 96–7, 99, 102, 107, 121, 124, 126,
	128–9, 164, 165, 202, 212
	Sami nomads 127, 136, 137, 145, 150,
		151–3, 161n3, 169, 176
nominative data 127, 163, 174, 176
Nordic Sami Conference, Enare (1959) 169–70
Nordic Sami Institute (NSI) 185–6, 192–3
Nordland 135–46, 164–5, 167–9, 170–71,
	175, 181
	population in 136, 138–9
	population statistics for north of 164,
		165, 167, 168, 169, 170, 171
North America *see* Canada; United States
North Atlantic Population Project (NAPP)
	174, 179, 183n1
North Ossetia 240
Northern Ireland
	Britishness in 280–83
	Statistics and Research Agency 281
Northwest Territories 96, 98
Norway 1, 9, 10, 299
	cadastral records 140, 142
	categorisation in population surveys
		136–7

categorisation of Sami (17th and 18th centuries) 136–7
category 'Finn' and statistics 170–71
census data, Sami population in 142–4
census definitions of 'Finn' 167
Community Lapps 137, 144
cross-border reindeer herders 168–9
District Lapps 137, 142, 144, 145
ethnicity, registration on census forms 163–5
Finlanders 166, 167–8
Finn as category in censuses in 163–72
Finn leidang 138, 141
Finneodel 139–40
Finns 136, 137, 144
Forest Lapps 137
Historical Data Centre 180, 181, 182
Justice, Department of 187, 188
Karlsøy 180, 181
Kvaenangen 180
Kven as category in censuses in 163–5, 170, 171
Lapp as category in censuses in 163–5
Lapps 136, 137
Lyngen 180, 181
'mixed' as category in censuses in 165
mortality 144
mountain Finns 169
National Archives 141–2, 143, 144, 146n4, 146n5
National Census (1769) 146n6
Nordland, population in 136, 138–9
northern Nordland, population statistics for 164, 165, 167, 168, 169, 170, 171
Norwegian National Archives, Oslo 141, 143, 144, 174
Ofoten 140, 145, 167
old tax system in 137–8
Parish Lapps 137
population census (1769) 163
population surveys in 135
postwar (Second War) censuses 169–70
regional and national archives 174
Sami allodium 139–40, 145
Sami allodium, pressure against 140
Sami conscription 138, 142
Sami demography in, contemporary prospects 185–93
Sami dialect designations 136
Sami nomads 136
Sami population, alternative methods for estimation of 142–4
Sami tax 138–9, 141–2, 146
Sea Finns 136, 137

Sea Sami 136, 142, 143, 145
Sea Sami as category in censuses in 164, 165, 166–7, 171n2
settled Sami 136, 144–5
Skjervøy 178, 180
statistical ambiguities, Lapp, Finn and Kven on census returns 165–8
Statistical Bureau (NOS) 168, 176, 177, 183n3
Statistics Norway 159–60, 161n2, 191
tax registers, Sami population and 135, 138–9, 143, 144, 145–6
taxation principles 140–42
terminology for population surveys 136–7
Troms 138, 150, 164, 180, 181, 183
Tysfjord 140, 141, 143, 145, 164, 166, 167
under-registration in 166, 170
see also ethnicity variables; Finnmark
Norwegianisation 158–9, 159–60, 166
nosology, uniformity in 22–3
Nova Scotia 97
nutrition 5

occupations 10, 59, 60, 61, 90, 100, 103, 121, 124–5, 126, 127, 129, 200, 225, 258, 261, 273
Office of National Statistics (ONS), U.K. 274, 278, 279, 289
Ofoten, Norway 140, 145, 167
Ohenjo, N. et al. 304
Okladnikov, A.P. 250n10
old tax system in Norway 137–8
Olsen, Bjørnar 120
Ontario 97, 101, 105–7
opinion polls 288
Oroch 244, 245, 250n15
Oroks 243, 244, 250n15
Osage 78
Ostroumov, N.A. 225–6, 227, 229–30
outliers in data, problem of 210, 213
Ouweneel, Arij 61, 62
Ozhegov, S.I. 223

Paine, R. 193n10
Paiute 78
Pakistan 275, 276, 277–8, 279, 280, 281, 284, 285, 286
Palmer, Will 234
Paraguay 57
Parish Lapps 137
parish records 56, 58, 64, 129
parish registers 122–4, 125, 127, 129–30, 138
Parkinson, A. 5
Pass, Forrest 110

pastures
  reindeer pasture 136–7, 161n3, 168–9,
    176, 206, 228, 229–30
  summer pasture 136, 161
  winter pasture 136, 168, 169, 176
Pearce, A.J. 59
peasant societies 62, 65, 139, 298
  in Latvia 254, 256n1, 257, 258–9, 260
  in Russia 198, 225–6, 241–2
Pedersen, H. and Nielssen, A.R. 164, 166
people, Russian legal category of 241
Pepper, P. and De Araugo, T. 17
personal contribution *(contribución personal)*
    64, 65
Peru 59, 63, 64–5, 66
Perz, S.G., Warren, J. and Kennedy, D.P. 304
Peter the Great 256n2
Petersen, W. 241
Pettersen, T. and Høydahl, E. 193n1
Pettersen, Torunn 10, 185–93, 298, 299, 301,
    311
Phelan, J.L. 67n6
phenotypical distinctions 36–7
Phillip, Governor Arthur 16
Piasina River 221, 225, 226, 227, 229
Pika, A. and Bogoyavlensky, D. 295
Pika, A. and Prokhorov, B. 248
Pima American Indians 78
Piteå diocese in Sweden 123
Plaid Cymru in Wales 282
Plakans, A. and Wetherell, C. 256, 257n3,
    262
Plakans, Andrejs 11–12, 197, 253–71, 301,
    302, 311
Platt, Tristan 65
Poland 241
Polar Census (1926-7) 242, 301, 302
  microdemographics 222–5, 230–31, 234
policies 1, 59, 267, 304
  affirmative action 296–7
  assimilation 24, 26, 27, 37, 74, 88, 90,
    108, 188, 248, 296
  census 187
  collectivisation 223
  colonial 37, 107, 301
  imperial 256–7
  of incorporation 51n14
  integration 42
  national (state or government) 7, 12, 59,
    65, 104, 130, 220, 297–8
  nationalistic 268–9
  paternalistic 295, 296
  political 1, 11, 95
  population 268
  public 4

racist 51n15
reserve-land 37
poll tax *(tributo)* in Latin America 60, 61,
    64–5
Polo Acuña, J. 60
Pool, I. 34
population
  categorisation 164–5, 240, 242
  census (1769) in Norway 163
  censuses (1865 and 1875) in Finnmark
    156–7
  censuses of Soviet era in Latvia 266–8
  current Aboriginal population, descent
    of 25, 28–9
  decline 7, 16–17, 23, 35, 108, 296
  enumerations (19th century) in Latvia
    260–62
  estimates 99, 137, 284
  growth 87
  of Latvia 255–7
  majority 10, 299
  population form (1805) in Sweden
    125–6, 128
  reconstruction 27–8
  settled 9, 126, 133, 142, 144, 164
  statistics 21, 264, 298, 301
    in Norway 174, 186, 188, 191
    in Sweden 117, 118 119–22, 125, 129
  subpopulations 257, 264, 265
population studies
  categorisation 3, 4
  colonialism, knowledge production and 4
  contextualisation 3, 5
  culture, identity and 3–4
  demographic sources 4
  demography, modernisation theories
    and 3
  developmental paradigm 2–3
  historical records 5
  identity and culture 3–4
  imperialism, knowledge production
    and 4
  indigenous societies, understanding
    complexities of 5
  national identities in 2–3
  new approaches to 2–5
  qualitative methods in research 4–5
  quantitative methods in research 4–5
  research methods 4–5
population surveys
  in Norway 135
  terminology for 136–7
Portugal 56
posobka (mutual aid institution) in Soviet
    Russia 206–8

Potawatomie American Indians 78
Powell, B. M. 33, 34, 39
Powell, Enoch 276
power 199, 223, 273–4, 274–5, 291
    stratification and 203–10
Preston, S.H. and Bennett, N.G. 73, 87,
    88–90, 91n9
    Preston-Bennett Method, application to
        population (1900–1910) 88–90
Preston, S.H. and Haines, M.R. 79, 81, 82,
    83
Preston, S.H., Heuveline, P. and Guillot,
    M. 77–9
Prevost, Reverend Father 100, 111n15
Prigorodnyi in North Ossetia 240
primitives 248–9n1, 305
Prince Edward Island 97
property, households and 103
Public Health Services in US 73
Pueblo American Indians 78
Puget Sound Salish 78
Puranen, B. 88

Quebec 97, 101
Queen Charlotte's Islands 101
questionnaires 10, 151, 174, 177, 182m 271,
    274
Qvigstad, J. 171n2

race 4, 22, 39–40, 49–50n5, 49n1, 51n17, 56,
    74, 109, 126, 169
    blood and, nomenclature of 42, 75, 275
    bureaucratic conceptualisations of 35,
        76, 96–7, 128–9, 165, 291
    immigration and, in British politics
        276–7, 278
    mixed-race individuals 19, 90, 98
    policy in Victoria on 27
    political arithmetic of 20, 99
    prevailing logics of 34, 48
    'race alien' designation in New Zealand
        8, 38–9
    racial boundaries in New Zealand,
        manipulation of 38–9
    racial categories in Latin America 60, 63
    racial divisions in U.K. 290
    racial taxonomies in New Zealand 39
    spatial dimensions of 66
    statistical determinations of 37–8, 40–41
racism 21, 38, 51, 130, 193, 290
Radcliffe-Brown, A.R. 16
Rallu, J., Piché, V. and Simon, P. 34
Rata, E. 42
registration 22–3, 117, 233, 242, 243–4, 298
    act of 160

of births, deaths and marriages in
    Victoria 22–4
data 73, 77, 87
ethnic registration 118, 149, 151, 153,
    173, 300
ethnic registration in Finnmark 149,
    151, 153, 155
national population registers in
    Sweden, establishment of 120–21
practice in Finnmark 155, 156, 160
of Sami 173, 188, 189, 190–91
and taxation, relationship between
    300–301
under-registration 166
reindeer
    categories of reindeer loss 200
    cross-border reindeer herders 168–9
    herding 10, 117–18, 121, 125–6, 129–30,
        136, 145, 152, 164–5, 166, 223–5, 226,
        227, 229, 231, 235n3, 242, 302
    pasture 136–7, 161n3, 168–9, 176, 206,
        228, 229–30
    Sami reindeer herding law (1928) in
        Sweden 129
    Soviet era, counting reindeer during 197
reindeer herders
    Finnmark 152
    Lake Essei Iakuts 197–9, 201, 206, 207,
        212, 213, 214
    Sami 117–18, 121, 125–6, 129–30, 136, 170
religion
    Catholics 60, 68, 100, 254, 259, 264, 270,
        280
    Lutherans 254, 258, 259
remarriage, problem of 81, 86, 91n6
research
    cross-disciplinary research, engagement
        with 303–4
    indigenous studies, previous research
        in Sweden on 119–22
    Koori Health Research Database
        (KHRD) 24–5, 26–7
    micro-ethnodemographic research 303
    Northern Ireland Statistics and
        Research Agency 281
    qualitative methods 4–5
    quantitative methods 4–5
    quantitative work on indigenous
        populations in Latin America,
        difficulties with 55–6
    Research Council of Australia (ARC) 24
    retrospective research 296
residence 18, 36, 43, 61, 76, 97–8, 166, 169
    resident population by arrival date in
        U.K. 277

territories of 243, 246–7, 264
resistance
  acts of 298
  against censuses in Spanish America 62
  to enumeration in Canada 104–7
rights
  allodial rights 138, 139–40, 141, 142
  blood quantum, voting rights and
    51n13
  Civil and Political Rights, International
    Covenant on (1966) 250n11
  Economic, Social and Cultural Rights,
    International Covenant on (1966)
    250n11
  land rights 21, 248
  Montevideo Convention on the Rights
    and Duties of States (1933) 250n11
  of participation for Sami, need for
    respect for 191
  UN Declaration on the Rights of
    Indigenous Peoples (2007) 49n2,
    250n12
Rípodas Ardanaz, D. 67n3
Roberts, E. et al. 183n1
Robinson, George Augustus 18, 23
Rodgers, Allan, M.P. 282
Rogers, J. and Nelson, M.C. 121, 125–6
Rogers, John 121, 125–6
Romania 241
Roth, B. 256, 262
Rowland, R. 59
Royal Academy of Science in Sweden 124
Ruggles, S. and Menard, R.R. 110n1
Ruggles, S. et al. 77, 78, 82, 83, 84, 85
Ruggles, S., Sobek, M. and Gardner, T.
  110n1
Rumar, L. 124
Ruppert, E.S. 96
Russia (and Soviet Union) 1, 10–11, 298
  Abaza 241, 243, 244
  Aleut 244, 245, 250n15
  All-Union Census (1926) 242
  Baltic Socialist Republics 26–8
  Bessermians 241, 244
  Caucasus 240, 241, 243, 249n6
  Cheliabinsk oblast' 241
  Chelkan 244, 245, 247
  Chukchi 240, 244, 245, 250n15
  Chulym 244
  Chuvan 243, 244, 245, 250n15
  Dolgans 197, 203, 206, 222, 226–7,
    229–30, 231, 232, 233, 243, 244, 245,
    247, 250n15
  employment of indigenous workers
    244–6

Enets 227, 243, 244, 245, 250n15
Eskimo 244, 245
Even 240, 244, 245, 250n15
Evenki 197, 201, 206, 219, 226, 240, 243,
  244, 245, 250n15
Federal Statistical Service (formerly
  Goskomstat) 242
Galskiy in Abkhazia 240
historical succession 240
identity politics, fluid character of
  242–3
indigeneity 239, 241–2, 248–9n1
'indigenous,' concept in 11
indigenous, indeterminacy over
  concept of 242
indigenous groups, territories of
  principal residence 246–7
indigenous peoples, legal category of
  241
integration of indigenous groups 248
Itelmen 244, 245, 247, 250n15
Izhora 241, 244
Kamchadal 243, 244
Karabakh 240
Kerek 243, 244
Ket 244, 245, 250n15
Khant 244, 245, 250n15
Koryak 244, 250n15
Kumanda 243, 244, 245, 250n15
legal concepts and demography of
  indigenous peoples 239–50
Leningrad oblast' 241
Mansi 244, 245, 250n15
minorities, issue of 240–41
modernisation 247
Nagaibak 241, 244
Nanai 243, 244, 245, 250n15
native minority peoples (korennye
  malochislennye narody) 240
Negidal 244, 250n15
Nenets 244, 245, 250n15
Nganasan 222, 226, 227, 231, 232, 233,
  244, 245, 250n15
Nivkh 244, 245, 250n15
Nogai of Dagestan 239
North Ossetia 240
Oroch 244, 245, 250n15
Oroks 243, 244, 250n15
peasant societies 241–2
people, legal category of 241
Polar Census (1926-7) 242
Prigorodnyi in North Ossetia 240
Russian Association for the Indigenous
  Peoples of the North (RAIPON) 243
Saami 244, 245

Sakha Republic 239, 240
Sel'kup 244, 250n15
Shapsug 241, 244
Shor 243, 244, 245, 247, 250n15
Siberia 11, 197–8, 200, 203, 213, 220–21,
     224, 233, 240, 245, 247, 248
small-numbered indigenous peoples
     11, 239–40, 242, 243–4, 249n4,
     250n16
South Ossetia 240
Soviet and post-Soviet census data,
     comparison of 243
Soviet and post-Soviet policy towards
     indigenous peoples 247–8
Soyot 244
statistical assessment of peoples in 242
stereotyping of indigenous peoples 247
Taz 244
Telengit 244
Teleut 243, 244, 245, 250n15
Todja 244, 245
Tofa 244, 245, 250n15
Tuba 244, 245
Udege 244, 250n15
Udmust Republic 241
Uil'ta 243, 244
Ulchi 244, 245
Urals 241
urban natives and ethnic minorities,
     conceptual differences between 247
urbanisation 244, 247
Veps 241, 244
Volga-Urals 240
Yakut of Sakha Republic 239
Yukagir 240, 244, 250n15
Yupik 244, 245
Russian Federation
  small-numbered peoples 11, 239–40,
     242, 243–4, 249n4, 250n16
  Statistical Service 242
  see also Russia (and Soviet Union)
Russification 257, 260, 268

Saami 244, 245
Saether, Steinar A. 8, 55–67, 298, 301, 302,
     311–12
Safford, Frank 64, 65
Sager, E.W. 110n1
Saggers, S. and Gray, D. 232, 304
Sakha 201, 240, 243, 247, 248
Sakha Republic 199, 217, 239, 240, 250n9
Sami 9–10
  affiliation of
     census recording of 187
     questions regarding 185–6

assimilation policy 188
clearings 139, 140, 141
conscription tax in Norway 138, 142
conversion to Christianity 123
demographic examination of 117–18
demography in Norway, contemporary
     prospects 185–93
demography today 187–8
dialect designations 136
discrimination against 121
District Lapps 137, 142, 144, 145
dynamic demography 191
ethnicity data, recording of 186–7
ethno-cultural data, complexity of
     186–7
Finns 123, 127–8, 136–7, 138, 144, 145,
     150, 161n2, 164–5, 166–8, 169, 170–
     71, 173, 175–6, 177
focus on contemporary Sami
     demography 189–90
Forest Lapps 137
funding for gathering population
     statistics 191
households in Finnmark 151, 152, 153,
     154, 158
identification of, need for 125
Lapps 123, 125–6, 128, 129, 133, 136–7,
     142, 144, 145, 150, 164, 166, 169
markasamer 137
Mountain Lapps 137
nomadic and settled in Finnmark 150
nomads in Norway 136
Nordic Sami Conference, Enare (1959)
     169–70
Nordic Sami Institute (NSI) 185–6,
     192–3
official statistics and ethno-cultural
     data, complexity of 186–7
outside and inside traditional
     communities, need for recording
     of 191
Parliament in Sweden 130
population in Finnmark
     census of 1865 of 153–4
     registration of (1855-1861) 152–3
population in Norway, alternative
     methods for estimation of 142–4
pressures in Sami culture 188
reindeer herding law (1928) in Sweden
     129
rights of participation, need for respect
     for 191
Sami demographic knowledge,
     proposals for expansion of 190–92
Sami Football Association 185, 192

Sami identity, resistance to recording ethnic data 188, 191
Sami tax in Norway 138–9, 141–2, 146
Sea Sami 136, 139, 142, 143, 144, 164–5, 166–7, 171n2
self-identification 192, 193n9
settled Sami 9, 136, 137, 139, 144, 145, 146n3
siida system 124, 139, 213
size of population, current estimates of 187–8
statistical determinations in Sweden for 125–6
in statistical sources in Sweden 117–31
Swedish policy towards 121–2
traditional settlement area 185
Sami allodium 139–40, 145
pressure against 140
Samoieds 222, 226, 227
Samoiedy Avamskie 222
Samoiedy Vadeevskie 222
Santa Marta 62–3, 64, 65, 67n7
Sápmi Population Database 118
Sargison, George 98–9, 103, 110n8, 110n12, 111n23
Saskatchewan 98, 99, 101, 108
Savolskul, S. and Anderson, D. 221
Scandinavia *see* Denmark; Finland; Norway; Sweden
Schnitler, Major Peter 136, 142–3
Schøyen, C. 173
Schwartz, N., Strack, F. and Mai, H.-P. 289
Schweitzer, Peter 298
Scotland
  Britishness in 280–83
  General Register Office (GROS) 274, 279
  Scottish Social Attitudes Survey (SSAS) 274, 286–7, 288, 292n7
Scott, J.C. 3, 300
Scott, S. and Duncan, C.J. 5
Sea Finns 136, 137
Sea Sami
  as category in censuses in Norway 164, 165, 166–7, 171n2
  in Norway 136, 142, 143, 145
Second World War
  effects in Sweden 122, 129–30
  in Latvia 266
Seed, P. 59, 67n2
self-classification 258–9
self-consciousness 201
self-determination 21, 33, 189, 241
self-identification 192, 193n9
Selians 260

Sel'kup 244, 250n15
Semgallians 260
Seminole 78
Senn, A.E. 268
Serle, G. 18
settlement 16, 21, 29, 35, 49n4, 98, 212, 221, 222, 227, 232–3, 234, 244, 246, 247–8, 278
  settled Sami 9, 136, 137, 139, 144, 145, 146n3
  traditional Sami settlement area 185, 187–8
settlers 18–19, 27–8, 35, 49, 104, 118, 140, 164, 165–6, 175, 247, 276, 295
sexual exploitation 23
sexuality 56
Shapsug 241, 244
sharing, significance of 231
Shkolnikov, V. et al. 232
Shnirelman, V.A. 249n6
Shoemaker, N. 73, 76, 77, 79, 88, 95, 111n22, 296
Sholkamy, Hania 3
Shor 243, 244, 245, 247, 250n15
Shoshone 78
Siberia 11, 197–8, 200, 203, 213, 220–21, 224, 233, 240, 245, 247, 248
siida system 124, 139, 213
Siiskonen, H., Taskinen, A. and Notkola, V. 304
Sillitoe, K. and White, P.H. 276, 278, 279, 280
Simon, P. 186–7, 193n2
Sinclair, R. 111n34
Sioux 77, 78
Skerry, P. 193n2
skin colour, categorisation by 36, 49, 276, 280, 281, 290, 292
Skjervøy, Norway 178, 180
Sköld, P. and Axelsson, P. 124, 296
Sköld, Peter 1–12, 117, 120, 123, 124–5, 127, 295–305, 312
Skujeneeks, M. 263, 264
Skujenieks, M. 256, 263, 264, 265, 270
Small, H.B. 100, 110n14, 111n15
small-numbered indigenous peoples 11, 239–40, 242, 243–4, 249n4, 250n16
Smith, Chief A.G. 107
Smith, Len 7–8, 15–29, 297, 298, 299, 302, 312
Smith, Llew 282
Smith, Sandra 7–8, 15–29, 297, 298, 299, 302, 312
Smylie, J. et al. 304
Smyth, R.B. 16
Snipp, C.M. 6, 35, 73

social anthropology 135
social attitudes surveys, British identity in 286–7
social class 59–60, 64, 204–6, 234–5n1
social constructions 4, 6, 219
social estate, philosophy of 257–8
social processes in small-scale societies 234
social relations 96, 199, 215, 231, 301
society
    conceptualisation by bureaucrats of 58
    liberal ideas of 65–6
socio-economic development in Latvia 256–7, 258, 260, 269
sociology 241
Söderlind, Nils 123, 131n5, 131n6, 131n7
Sokolovskiy, Sergey V. 11, 239–50, 298, 299–300, 312
Solander, Dean Carl 123, 125
Sørensdatter, Sophie 155
Sorrenson, M.P.K. 37
sostoiatel'nyi (wealthy people) in Soviet Russia 204, 206, 209, 210
sources
    current microdemographic sources 233–4
    of data on indigenous peoples, construction of 6–7
    historical 5, 25, 108, 149, 234
    source materials in Finnmark 149–51
    vital registration 22, 73, 77, 87, 300
South Africa 8, 38, 280
South Ossetia 240
Soviet Union
    All-Union Census (1926) 242
    counting reindeer 197
    criteria for stratification of Lake Essei Iakuts 208–10
    gradations, stratification and 204–6
    literature on Lake Essei Iakuts 198
    population censuses of Soviet era Latvia 266–8
    Soviet and post-Soviet census data, comparison of 243
    Soviet and post-Soviet policy towards indigenous peoples 247–8
    tumult and change 198–9
    see also Russia (and Soviet Union)
Soyot 244
Spain 56, 57, 59–60, 62, 64
Bourbon Spain 57, 59, 60, 61, 63
Spanish America
    censuses in late colonial times 59–63
    demographic studies of 56
Spruhan, P. 75
sredniak (middle grade people) in Soviet Russia 204, 205–6, 209, 210

Ssorin-Chaikov, Nilolai 219, 221
St Petersburg 259, 261
standards for indigenous demography 302–4
Stark, D.M. 67n2
State Archive of Krasnoiarsk Territory (GAKK) 199
State Institute for Racial Biology, Sweden 129
Statens Offentliga Utredningar (SOU) 117, 130
states 1, 3, 4, 21–2
    Baltic 266, 267, 268
    collective identities in 120
    colonial 296–7
    Commonwealth of Independent States (CIS) 231
    European 58
    fiscal needs of 65
    homeland states 241
    indigenous populations and 219, 225, 298
    industrial 304
    inner strength of 59
    Kolsrud 139
    Montevideo Convention on the Rights and Duties of States (1933) 250n11
    multicultural 42
    multiethnic 33
    nation states 121, 187, 189, 300
    postcolonial 57, 296, 301
    state policy and indigenous peoples 296–300
    white-settler 33–4, 295
statistics 2, 7, 21, 24, 26, 39
    ethnic statistics 34
    indicators 5, 45, 138, 200, 203, 205, 208, 209, 215, 220, 222, 268
    official statistics 1, 34–5, 42, 47, 49–50n5, 119, 146n6, 151, 165, 171, 186–7
    statistical ambiguities, Lapp, Finn and Kven on Norwegian census returns 165–8
    statistical assessment of peoples in Russia 242
    Statistical Bureau (NOS) in Norway 168, 176, 177, 183n3
    statistical categorisation in Sweden 121
    statistical sources in Sweden, note on 118–19
    Statistics New Zealand 37, 39, 40–41, 43, 49–50n5
    Statistics Norway 159–60, 161n2, 191
    Statistische Berichte 256
Stavig, W. 67n2
Stephens, C. et al. 304

stereotyping of indigenous peoples 247
Stern, S. 67n6
Stieda, W. 262
Stone, L. 219
Storm, D. 136
stratification 203–10
suicide 231–2
Suslov, I.M. 204
Suslov, Mikhail Isakovich 226–7, 230–31
Sweden 1, 9, 299
    Agriculture Ministry 130
    census nomenclature 127
    censuses 118–19, 127–9
    Church Law (1894) 122–3, 127–8
    Church records 122–4
    collective identities 120
    cultural identities 120
    Demographic Database, Uneå
        University 118, 131n3
    ethnic enumerations of populations
        in 120
    ethnicity, registration of 118
    geographical information, availability
        of 124
    Härnosand diocese 123
    historical context, indigenous
        demographics and 119–20
    indigenous identity, definition of 119
    indigenous studies, previous research
        119–22
    language, Church and ethnicity in 123,
        127–9
    Lappförsamling 123–4, 125
    Lapps, population ststistics on 125–6
    national population registers in,
        establishment of 120–21
    National Statistics 117, 118, 120, 122,
        123, 124–6, 127
    National Union of the Swedish Sami
        (SSR) 130
    parish registers 122–4, 129–30
    Piteå diocese 123
    population form (1805) 125–6, 128
    population statistics in 117, 119–22
    Royal Academy of Science 124
    Sami, conversion to Christianity 123
    Sami, discrimination against 121
    Sami, identification of, need for 125
    Sami, policy towards 121–2
    Sami, statistical determinations for
        125–6
    Sami in statistical sources 117–31
    Sami Parliament in 130
    Sami reindeer herding law (1928) 129
    Sápmi Population Database 118

Second World War, effects of 122,
    129–30
State Institute for Racial Biology 129
Statens Offentliga Utredningar (SOU)
    117, 130
    statistical categorisation in 121
    statistical sources in, note on 118–19
    Tabellverket 117, 118, 120, 122, 123,
        124–6, 127
    Table Commission 124, 126, 127
    tribe and race in statistical
        nomenclature 127–8, 129
    underpopulation in, fear of 124
synodal acts 123, 125, 131n7
Szreter, S., Sholkamy, H. and
    Dharmalingam, A. 3
Szreter, Simon 3

Tabellverket in Sweden 117, 118, 120, 122,
    123, 124–6, 127
Table Commission in Sweden 124, 126, 127
Taché, Joseph-Charles 99
Taimyr lowlands, Siberia 11, 198, 203,
    219–33, 233–4, 235n2
    see also microdemographics
Tarasenkov, G.N. 206
Tasmania 21
taxation
    censuses in Latin America and 58, 59, 60
    contribution tax 138, 141
    extraordinary *(ekstraskatten)* 143, 144,
        146, 146n5
    poll tax 51, 60, 62, 63, 64, 104, 301
    principles in Norway 140–42
    Sami conscription tax 138, 142
    Sami tax 138, 141, 142, 146, 146n2,
        146n3
    systems of 59, 63, 64, 65, 66, 137–9
    tax registers, Sami population and 135,
        138–9, 143, 144, 145–6
Taylor, J. and Bell, M. 6, 295
Taylor, John 5, 304
Taz 244
Te Puri Kokiri 45
Telengit 244
Teleut 243, 244, 245, 250n15
TePaske, J.J. 59
terra nullius 16
territorial dispersion 198–9
Thaden, E. 260
Thatcher, Margaret 276–7, 278, 292n1
Thomas, Simon, M.P. 282
Thomasson, L. 124
Thornton, Arland 2
Thornton, R. 73, 296

Thorsen, H.C. 163, 169
Thorvaldsen, Gunnar 10, 173–83, 297, 299, 302, 312
Thuen, T. 158, 163, 174, 193n10
Tindale, Norman 24
Todja 244, 245
Tofa 244, 245, 250n15
Tohono O'Odham 78
Torp, E. 163, 174–5, 193n4
Torres Strait Islands 24
trade and traders 35, 64, 102, 138, 140, 145, 158, 220, 224, 225, 226, 229, 231
    goods 199, 206, 208, 211, 213, 228
    middlemen and traders, relationship between 128
    terms of trade, unfairness in 203–4
transhumant pastoralism 230–31
treaties 33, 74, 98–100
    Aboriginal treaty areas 103
    border treaty negotiations (Sweden/ Norway-Denmark) 136–7
    treaty and non-treaty Indians 100, 103, 104, 109, 110n13
    Treaty of Waitangi (1840) 35, 49n4
    treaty payments 103, 104, 107
trial population counts 261
tribes 16–17, 18, 23, 122–3, 173, 200, 222, 227, 297
    American and Canadian Indians 77, 78, 79, 109
    civilized and uncivilized tribes 74
    Finnish and Lappish tribes 127–8
    Maori of New Zealand 34, 35, 36, 41, 42, 49n4
    membership of 74–6
    and race in statistical nomenclature (Sweden) 127–8, 129
    tribal affiliation 43
    tribal registers 48, 66
Troms, Norway 138, 150, 164, 180, 181, 183
Trouillot, M.-R. 241
Trovato, F. 296, 304
Tuba 244, 245
tuberculosis 17, 88
Tuglakov, Petr 227–8, 230
Tuhiwai Smith, Linda 4
tundra 197, 198, 211, 214, 221, 224, 228, 231, 233
    Avam tundra 221, 222, 227
Tunguses 198–9, 201, 204–5, 222, 226, 227, 228, 229
Turukhansk Polar Census expedition (1926–7) 199–200
Twinam, A. 67n2
Tysfjord, Norway 140, 141, 143, 145, 164, 166, 167

Udege 244, 250n15
Udmust Republic 241
Uil'ta 243, 244
Ulchi 244, 245
Ulmanis, Karlis 265–6
under-registration 166, 170
underpopulation, fear of 124
Undesirable Immigrants Exclusion Act (New Zealand, 1919) 51n15
unemployment 46, 246, 248, 276
United Kingdom 1, 12
    British National Party (BNP) 12, 276
    British Social Attitudes Survey (BSAS) 274, 286–7, 288, 292n7
    census (1981, 2001), migration and ethnicity 278–80
    Data Archive, Colchester 292n7
    discrimination 278, 292
    discursive identities, definition of 289–92
    dynamic indigenousness 290–91
    House of Commons 278
    identity
        categories of 273–4, 289–90, 291–2
        plurality of 275, 290–91
    immigration, moral panic and 276–7
    'indigenous,' British as 274–8
    International Labour Organisation (ILO) 275
    Labour Force Survey (LFS) 274, 277, 279, 283, 284, 285, 289
        evidence of Britishness in 283–6
    meaning of Britishness 288
    Northern Ireland, Britishness in 280–83
    Office of National Statistics (ONS) 274, 278, 279, 289
    racial divisions 290
    resident population by arrival date 277
    Scotland, Britishness in 280–83
    semantic confusion on ethnicity 278
    social attitudes surveys, British identity in 286–7
    spatial referent in concept of race or ethnicity 291
    Wales, Britishness in 280–83
United Nations (UN) 77, 275
    Charter of the 250n11
    Declaration on the Rights of Indigenous Peoples (2007) 49n2, 250n12
    General Assembly 49n2
    Human Development Report (2004/5) 262, 265, 270
    International Convention on the Elimination of all Forms of Racial Discrimination (CERD) 193n6

Permanent Forum on Indigenous Issues (PFII) 189, 191
Statistical Division 193n2
United States 1, 9, 186, 299, 301
  blood quantum terminology in 51n12
  border crossings with Canada, problem of 103–4
  Census Bureau 74, 75–6, 77, 88–90, 91n2
  General Allotment Act (1887) 75
  Public Health Services 73
  see also American Indians
unsubsidised economy, Iakut transition to 197–8
Urals 241
urban areas 183
  natives and ethnic minorities in, cenceptual differences between 247
urbanisation 43, 48, 191, 243, 244, 247
Urla, J. 6

Valsts Statisttikā Pārvalde (VSP) 270
value system 6
Van Aken, M. 64, 65
Van Atta, D. 231
Van Young, E. 67n6
Vankoughnet, Lawrence 106, 111n35, 111n38, 111n39, 111n41
variables 57, 59, 173–83, 232, 255–6, 261, 263, 264, 302
  constructed 179–82
  cultural 3
  ethnicity variables 174, 179–82
Vasil'ev, V.N. 216n4
Vasilevich, G.M. 216n4
Venezuela 64
Ventsel, A. 231
Veps 241, 244
Victoria, State of 7–8
  Aboriginal Act (1869) 18
  Aboriginal births, deaths and marriages, registration of 23
  Aboriginal Heritage programme 24–5
  Aborigines Protection Act (1886) 7, 19
  assimilation, policy of force in 24
  censuses in 23, 28
  Central Board for the Protection of Aborigines 18–19, 20, 21, 23, 25, 28, 29
  current Aboriginal population, descent of 25, 28–9
  distinctive features of colonial government in 18
  genealogical records 24–5
  native administration and 'half-caste problem' 18–19
  nosology, uniformity in 22–3

race policy, effect of 27
registration of births, deaths and marriages 22–4
Vidzeme 254, 264, 265
Vishnevskii, A.G. 232
visibility
  indigenous demography and 296–300
  invisibility and 8, 29
Vitebsk 254, 256, 259, 261
Volga-Urals 240
Voronkin, M.S. 216n4

Wahlund, S. 129
Waitangi
  Treaty of (1840) 35
  Waitangi Tribunal 42–3, 49n4
Waldram, J.B., Herring, D.A. and Young, T.K. 295
Wales
  Britishness in 280–83
  Plaid Cymru in 282
Walker, F.A. 91n2
Walker, R. et al. 304
Wannerdt, Arvid 122
Ward, A. 37, 51n14
Warrick, G. 296
Waters, M. 42
Watts, R. 95
Wawanosh, William 110n11
Webb, S. 17
West, Alan 24
West Indies 276
White, P.H. 276, 278, 279, 280
White, P.M., Badets, J. and Renaud, V. 110n4
Wimmera in Australia 28
Windschuttle, K. 16
Winking, J. et al. 304
Wright, Robin 3

Yakut of Sakha Republic 239
  see also Lake Essei Iakuts
Yanomamö 303, 306
Yeltsin, Boris 231
Yougov Poll (2005) 288
Yukagir 240, 244, 250n15
Yungas valleys 63, 64
Yupik 244, 245

Zatundrinskie Krest'iany 222
Zeile, P. 264
Zemgale 264, 265
Ziker, John P. 11, 219–35, 242, 295–305, 312
Zvidriņš, P. 262, 268
Zvidriņš, P. and Vanovska, I. 256, 263, 268

www.ingramcontent.com/pod-product-compliance
Lightning Source LLC
Chambersburg PA
CBHW060024030426

42334CB00019B/2164